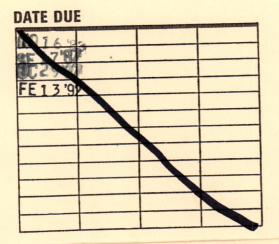

HUMAN COMPETENCE
Engineering Worthy Performance

THOMAS F. GILBERT

McGraw-Hill Book Company

New York St. Louis San Francisco Auckland Bogotá
Düsseldorf Johannesburg London Madrid Mexico
Montreal New Delhi Panama Paris São Paulo
Singapore Sydney Tokyo Toronto

For Marilyn

Library of Congress Cataloging in Publication Data

Gilbert, Thomas F.
  Human competence.

  Includes index.
  1. Performance. 2. Motivation. 3. Learning,
Psychology of. I. Title.
LB1062.6.G54   158'.1   77-26700
ISBN 0-07-023217-2

1234567890   KPKP   78654321098

The editors for this book were Robert A. Rosenbaum and
Lynne Lackenbach, the designer was Elliot Epstein, and the
production supervisor was Teresa F. Leaden. It was set in
Caledonia by University Graphics, Inc.

Printed and bound by The Kingsport Press.

Contents

iii

Preface

Human competence fascinates us, and countless books have been written about one aspect of it or another. But the general subject matter has never been treated in a comprehensive and systematic way—at least, not as I define it. This book attempts to correct the deficiency.

It is a book of theory; but practical-minded readers need not turn away. Some years ago I established several practical criteria that I would have to meet before I could write such a book:

- First, I would have to be able to define human competence in a precise and unambiguous way that would be reasonable to those seriously interested in the subject.

- Next, I must have a method for measuring competence with considerable precision.

- Third, I would need a model for engineering human competence—for finding out why it is lacking and what to do to get more of it.

- Finally, I must be able to translate the theoretical principles that met these criteria into step-by-step procedures thoroughly proven in a great variety of applications, and especially in those two places where competence is so important: at work and in school.

I believe that this book meets these criteria of rigorous definition, measurement, and procedure. Moreover, numerous examples and some two dozen case histories, all taken from life, illustrate how the theory has been made to work in a variety of settings, both in the world of work and in the world of schools. More of the examples are from the world of work. But this is simply because this world provides such a great variety of situations in which theories can be put to the test. It also baffles me why so many social scientists and philosophers, like most literary people, either ignore this world or regard it with distaste, as if it were somehow a disreputable and an unnatural appendage to the real flow of life. But I am convinced that any theory of human competence that does not apply to both the world of work and the world of schools has not done its job regardless of its academic popularity. A really

general theory of human competence must have considerable scope. The one I present here illustrates matters as diverse as how to teach kids the multiplication tables and how to manage a factory; as different as how to design a school curriculum and how to make economic decisions about industrial training.

And it describes how to do these things well; it is not a diatribe on how poorly they are usually done. This is *not* a book about human incompetence. There are plenty of those around. My focus is constructive. I have not been content to talk about what is wrong with the world. Rather, my intent is to say how to make things better—how to make the institutions of work and school more productive, happier places. Not in a general, speculative way; but through specific steps, supported by sensible concepts that give these steps meaning.

Of course, new and useful theories must resolve a certain number of old controversies; and when they do this, they often lead us to unexpected conclusions. Here is a small sample of the conclusions that I believe serious readers will come to accept as obvious good sense after they have finished the book:

- The more incompetent people are, the easier it is to improve their performance.
- Human competence is inversely related to knowledge, hard work, and motivation.
- The most incompetent person in the world might be the most efficient.
- Human competence cannot be found in human behavior.

The attempt to create a theory that is comprehensive and also can be put to so many uses has posed the problem of who my audience is, because, after all, everyone has a stake in the subject matter of human competence. For this reason I have struggled mightily, and with generous help from my wife, to present the subject so that the general reader can follow the presentation easily. Struggle was indeed necessary, since I grew up learning to write in those turgid sentences that pass for style among so many academics.

By its very nature, however, much of the content of the book is technical and written to be immediately useful to individuals who make human competence their business. There are four major groups of such people: managers in the world of work; educators and teachers; psychologists and certain other social scientists; and an assortment of people in personnel-related professions, ranging from training directors to industrial engineers.

The structure of the book follows the theory. As I have said, a good theory must be able to show us how to identify, measure, and create human competence. Part I does these three things and lays down the basic rules of the system. Chapter 1 presents a definition of competence that most readers will find novel and contrary to the way we usually think. But I am confident that they will find its good sense compelling. Chapter 2 describes a way of measuring human competence with surprising precision. The basic unit of measurement reveals not only how much competence exists but also how much more can be created. The system of measurement does not employ intelligence tests, or anything like them, because these things have little to do with human competence. Chapter 3 presents a model for discerning important components of human competence; it is a tool that makes it much easier to diagnose the cause of incompetence and to determine what must be done to realize human potential.

Part II (Chapters 4 and 5) introduces a system of performance analysis—a guide for helping people make orderly decisions when they try to set up a competent performance system or find out how to improve one that already exists. It includes several troubleshooting sequences that I have found useful in conducting what I call a performance audit.

Part III (Chapters 6 through 10) discusses various aspects and techniques of engineering competent performance, ranging from education to motivation. Although those who read my original manuscript judged it to be the most interesting part of the book, I had to place it near the end because the basic groundwork must be covered before readers fully appreciate this part.

Part IV (Chapter 11) summarizes by explaining the abstracted and logical characteristics of the system and comparing it with other disciplines.

Finally, the Appendix is a detailed case study of performance engineering.

Acknowledgments

Marilyn Gilbert, my wife, has contributed so much to this book that she could well demand to be its co-author.

For the realities that support this material, I owe nearly everything to my dear friend and partner, Geary Rummler, and to the devoted staff of the Praxis Corporation. It is their work my words are all about.

I must give special thanks to Warren Searls, Carl and Gerry Vogelsberg, and Kenneth Junkins for the many critical hours they gave to the manuscript and for their great moral support. I also received invaluable help from these readers of the early manuscript: Kjell Austad, Mike Barber, Carol Bocchino, Al Corbet, Jim Evans, George Geis, Sarah Gilbert, Dan Leahy, Dave Miller, and John R. Murphy.

This work would not have been possible without my clients, and I am grateful to all of them. But I must give recognition to the special support I have received from Ron Hawkins and his staff at the Uniroyal Corporation, from Harry Shoemaker and Paul Ross of American Telephone and Telegraph, and from Kenneth Sperling of Warner Lambert.

The people who have most shaped my thought, both personally and professionally, have been the late Lee Brown, Ted Cureton, Joe Hammock, Fred Keller, Bill ("Prof") McCall, John McKee, Byron Menides, David Sage, Paul Siegel, the late James R. Simmons, Fred Skinner, Kershaw Walsh, and Jerry Whitlock. I, like everyone who works in this field, am in debt to George Odiorne both for his substantive work and for his "spiritual" leadership.

Finally, I wish to acknowledge my own greatest accomplishments in life: Kathy, Micah, Sarah, Adam, Jessie, Robby, and Eve.

Part One
THE LEISURELY THEOREMS

*Only those who take leisurely what the people
of the world are busy about can be busy about
what the people of the world take leisurely.*

TAOIST MAXIM

This book describes the general principles of engineering human competence, an undertaking that may seem audacious. Some will think that anyone who writes such a book must consider himself very competent indeed, but nothing could be farther from the truth. Investigators need not share the qualities of the things they investigate, or botanists would have to be flowers and physicians diseased. The system I describe here has been 20 years in the making, which alone should attest to my inefficiency. But my own incompetency has served me well, because in my years of refining and testing the system in the real world, I have learned even more from my many failures than I have from my few successes. Fortunately, I have had competent colleagues, students, and clients, and it is because of their increasing success in applying these principles that I have finally decided the system is sufficiently coherent to make a useful book.

But what manner of subject matter is human competence? psychology? economics? education? sociology? It is no one of these things, although it relates to all of them and to others as well. The best way I

know to introduce it to you is through an analogy from quite another area.

In the early 1960s many people became interested in something engineers call "total energy systems." To understand what "total energy" (TE) is, first imagine building an apartment house with engines in the basement to generate all the electricity the building requires. In the typical setup, these engines are fueled by the burning of natural gas. Part of the heat runs the generator, but most of it simply goes up the stack as waste heat. A TE system captures this waste heat and uses it for other things, such as heating, air conditioning, and hot water. If the system is designed carefully, much of this energy can be saved.

In 1960 a small firm—we'll call it Starbright and Wise—was hired to develop a training course to teach energy experts about TE engineering. This firm very quickly discovered that there really was no TE technology—only a lot of other technologies that had more or less application to TE. Engine specialists, for example, knew a great deal about generators, but virtually nothing about the considerable sociology of energy use or the heat loss of a building. Heating engineers knew a lot about computing heat loss, but next to nothing about electrical generation, generator controls, or the financing of such equipment. Energy financial specialists knew little about heat engineering or electrical generation. Put all together, these experts could not design the most efficient TE system. The parts of the elephant were well understood; but the assortment of experts, when asked to make one, usually had the trunk where the tail should be, or legs too small to support the beast.

The Starbright and Wise team was temporarily baffled. Still, a few people had designed excellent TE systems, although they insisted that their achievements were the result of an "art"—one they believed others could not be trained to copy. Undismayed, Starbright and Wise pursued these "artists" anyway and asked them to describe how they had designed their energy systems. Our team was not surprised to find that the descriptions of the artists did not at all match what had been done.

Starbright and Wise reasoned that if they were to teach TE technology they first had to "invent" it. They did such things as create worksheets to plot the "sociological" patterns of energy uses, optimal generating systems, and financial feasibility analysis. And the system they eventually developed became the standard for the industry. Not only could they teach ordinary people to design quite acceptable TE systems, but even some of the already successful "artists" acknowledged that their systems would have been substantially improved if they had followed the procedures of Starbright and Wise. In fact, the new system

so simplified things that much of the work that once required experts to perform could now be done by laypersons with very little training. One sure sign that a technology has been created is when technicians appear.

We can easily sort out what Starbright and Wise did and did not do. They certainly did not discover new facts about the principles of energy. They did not create new methodologies for designing engines or buildings or for financing and fueling them—although they did greatly simplify many procedures of analysis. What they did do was put into a single system some very diverse ways of looking at a complex subject. Their contribution could be judged by three standards: (1) by how broad and complex a range of problems it could help people solve—that is, by its usefulness; (2) by the simplicity of the system itself—the simpler they could make it without sacrificing its usefulness, the better; (3) and, finally, by its coherence—by how well it had put all those many vantage points together so that the new theory would have a certain elegant "unity." In short, we judge their theory of total energy by the age-old criteria that the philosophers of science have applied: utility, parsimony (simplicity), and elegance (coherence).

What Starbright and Wise did for total energy, I have tried to do for the subject of human competence. I have tried to create a useful, simple, and coherent system for engineering more worthy performance in individuals and especially in groups of people. In doing this, I have not discovered any new or startling facts about human conduct. I have simply put together some of the vast knowledge and many methods we already have that are relevant to competent human performance.

My method is a method of engineering and is, in many ways, just the opposite of the method of science. Once, when I was a young behavioral scientist working in the laboratory, I was (quite properly) impressed with how little we know about human conduct. Scientists approach their fields of study with humility, seeing themselves as small spots of intelligence "surrounded by a vast sea of ignorance," to quote Isaac Newton from memory. Gradually, I discovered that I did not have the temperament for science, because I was increasingly impressed by how much we know about human performance that we have never applied very well. I saw myself, unlike Newton, as a tiny spot of ignorance surrounded by a vast sea of intelligence. This is the proper attitude for the engineer. The scientist approaches nature as a little child does, to discover what it is like. The engineer approaches nature with a swagger, determined to change it into something it never has been and never would be if left to itself. The scientist has a well-developed methodology and follows it wherever it may lead; the engineer knows precisely where to go, and will use any available methodology to get there. I have summarized just some of their contrasting views:

Scientist	Engineer
Approaches nature with humility, for there is so much we do not know—we are surrounded by a vast sea of ignorance.	Approaches nature with assuredness, because there is so much we know that we have not applied—we are surrounded by a vast sea of intelligence.
Is content to find out what the world is like as it is.	Is intent on remaking the world.
Has a well-developed methodology, and will go wherever it leads.	Knows precisely where to go, and will use any methodology to get there.
Makes no value judgments of nature—it is what it is.	Begins with value judgments of nature—and seeks to create changes that people will value.
Sees knowledge as an end, valuable for its own sake; and worth great expenditures to gain it.	Sees knowledge as a costly means that should be applied efficiently if the costs are not to detract from the valuable ends.

Surely both points of view, as well as many others, are legitimate and useful, depending on our purpose. And some people must pursue each of them. In one sense, science lags behind engineering, because the engineer must use whatever knowledge is available. We did not wait for the knowledge required to develop the internal combustion engine before we designed the wheel and the cart. Yet engineering lags science, because it often requires a large amount of new knowledge before it can be put together to create new uses. We did not wait for someone to invent the automobile before we performed experiments on the heat engine.

But engineering is never really new; primitive people have designed really excellent energy systems for their times and purposes. Engineering can only get better—by applying new knowledge that science creates and by arranging existing knowledge into simpler and more powerful systems. People have also been engineering performance since the Year One. What I have to offer is a new way of looking at how we can do this.

In creating this method of engineering, however, I have used neither the method of science nor of engineering, but the method of philosophy. For some 16 years, since I left the laboratories and classrooms of the academy, I have experimented with the system I describe in this book, both in the world of work and the world of schools. These experiments have constituted a sort of "philosophical laboratory" for me; and although I have done the things I describe here, I have been

more interested in developing and testing the theory than in actually engineering human performance myself.

And what is philosophy? Its subject matter is, I believe, the vantage points that people can stand in. The true philosophers, from Adam to Zuckerman, have always sought ways of rearranging our points of view into more orderly, simpler systems for understanding and coping with the world. Unfortunately, we tend to see theories of philosophy and science as absolute truths or falsities rather than maturing human vantage points. Long ago the late James R. Simmons* taught me that it is not useful to see the history of philosophy and science as the history of error. Einstein did not prove Newton wrong, nor did Hume disprove Berkley. The history of science and philosophy (and, I might add, engineering) is the history of successive approximations to the "truth"—the gradual improvement in the ways we organize our vantage points.

So, what I offer here is not so audacious after all; it is simply another attempt to improve on the principles we have been applying in our long history of engineering human competence.

Those who hold to the "history-is-error" point of view could easily read this book as an attack on behaviorism. Nothing could be farther from the truth. I owe much of what I have learned to B. F. Skinner; as a *scientist* he has few peers. But I have found the methods of Skinner as an *engineer* wanting, and I believe I have ordered some principles that represent a decidedly superior approximation to where we want to go when we seek to create more competent cultures and institutions. Of course, the test of my claim to a superior approximation should be found in the greater usefulness, simplicity, and coherence of my system.

I am at least a behaviorist, and I have employed some of the methods of behaviorism as well as those of other subsidiary technologies. But even though I have borrowed freely where I have felt the need, the system I propose is no eclectic assortment of points of view; it emerges with a character all its own. Although eclectic systems may sometimes be useful, they seldom have the simplicity and never the elegance that I have held as criteria of success. It is not that eclectic systems are wrong; it is just that they have not resolved the apparent contradictions in the ideas they assemble. But eclectics do have one sensible quality that all who offer ideas might envy: They know there is more than one way to look at the world.

The "history-is-error" people not only tend to see systems as either all right or all wrong, but are also inclined to view the world as having only one truth. They are likely to take their "truths" home from work

---

*Jim Simmons was a Class D baseball player and a philosophy professor.

and insinuate their cyclopean viewpoint in every situation. There are psychotherapists who see their families as patients floating in a mass of unresolved motives. Even worse, in my own personal experience, are those behaviorists who see their homes as extensions of the animal laboratory, and treat their families accordingly.

In spite of all that I owe to the behaviorists—and chiefly to B. F. Skinner—the primary reason that the system I describe here is not behaviorism is that behavior is not my focal subject matter. This may sound surprising, because when I ask people if human competence is a function of human behavior, I always get a "yes" answer. I also get a "yes" when I ask this question: "If I want to know if people are competent, I have to observe how they behave, don't I?"

My answer to such questions is a firm "No!" I have had to reject behavior as my focus for a simple, practical reason: I was not making any real progress in developing a system of performance engineering.

Fortunately, there is some precedent for abandoning common-sense "imperatives." Advances in science and technology are often made when people turn cherished and seemingly undebatable "truths" upside down. Astronomy leaped light years ahead when we reversed the view that the earth was the center of the universe; and physics made comparable progress by moving the forces of motion from the inside of particles to the outside. Indeed, whenever technology seems locked in place or slow to move, it might be a good idea simply to scrap our fundamental assumptions and begin anew with their opposites. There are an incredible number of schools of thought about improving human competence, and some of them have seemed to have a hold on some edge of truth. But what has been missing is a "grand plan" that converts the many ideas we have about ourselves into a methodology for engineering our conduct—a methodology both systematic *and* acceptable.

Thus we can ask: "For all their differences, what is the common assumption of these many theories of human conduct—theories as diverse as behaviorism and transcendental meditation; as different as psychoanalysis and biofeedback?" If we can isolate that single common assumption, perhaps *it* will prove to be the barrier to progress; and by upending it, we may be able to go forth much more rapidly.

I began this book with an attempt to do just this—to invert the most unquestioned and seemingly unquestionable assumption about the nature of human competence. We should examine it again, because it seems so obviously true: Human competence, almost all of us agree, is found in human behavior. If you want to see whether people are competent, look at their behavior. There are, of course, a multitude of different viewpoints about *what* behavior to look at or *how* to look at it. But the fundamental assumption is nevertheless there: Begin by looking at people.

This viewpoint, for all its commanding plausibility, creates a disturbing and as yet unresolved dilemma. If human competence resides in behavior, then to set about to engineer human competence means that we must manipulate human behavior, since engineering is always a system of manipulating things. For some people, this conclusion alone is sufficient to disclaim any interest in engineering other people's performance. Whoever felt comfortable being known as a manipulator of people's minds? Not many of us.

More important, for all its plausibility, our basic assumption has not really gotten us very far toward a genuine system of engineering human performance—one that would be complete with basic theorems, agreeable and precise methods of measurement, and handbooks of procedure. Suppose we scrap it, then, and begin anew. We have little to lose except 3 million years of very little technical progress in this direction. First, however, we should investigate the nature of what I call the "great cult of behavior"—the egocentric view that competence somehow dwells within us—because I hope to convince you that it really has been the crippling assumption.

THE GREAT CULT OF BEHAVIOR

In the great cult of behavior* the appeal is to control or affect behavior in some way. There is little or no technology of ends and purposes. Indeed, behavior itself is viewed as an end rather than as a means to an end.

The great cult is rather neatly divided into three major subcults. The first is the subcult of *work,* which values the expenditure of human energy in the form of hard work, sacrifice, and self-denial. The second is the subcult of *knowledge,* which pays homage to those who possess great stores of information, theories, and skills. The third is the subcult of *motivation,* which esteems eagerness and the display of positive and amicable attitudes.

The behavior cult, of course, sees its enemy as people, because it puts great store on how people behave, their fashions, and their style of doing things, regardless of what they actually accomplish. Hard work and self-denial are virtues because they make great demands on behavior, which is the standard—the autonomous end of human competence. To be able to shape behavior and control the mind is considered the highest virtue.

I confess that I too was once devoted to classifying people by how they behave and making assumptions about their limited potential for behavior—through IQ tests and blinding "insights" into their urges.

*George Odiorne calls it the "activity trap." I have elevated his "trap" to the higher status of a cult. (See his *Management and the Activity Trap,* New York: Harper & Row, 1973.)

But as a reformed member of the behavior cult, I must now insist that the enemy is not people. Rather, it is a point of view, and one that attacks all of us, like an invisible germ, and distorts our outlook. It must be exorcised absolutely and completely, leaving no trace to multiply and reinfect us.

The Subcult of Work

One of the most powerful agents of the behavior cult is the subcult of work, which focuses on the amount of energy people expend. Not so long ago, the disease virulently attacked the White House—beginning, I think, with the Kennedy administration, where to be patriotic and do one's part a person had to work 6 days a week and 14 hours a day, and run 50 miles on Sunday. Those of us who lazed in the sun were made to feel like drones. The subcult of work rose to its pinnacle in the Nixon administration, when Sunday work was instituted, the swimming pool was converted to a press room, and even the 50-mile runs were considered self-indulgent escapes from labor. I believe it is no coincidence that what came out of the White House was a series of disastrous policies, from unnecessary war to crime in high places. After Nixon, the Ford administration wanted to make hard work and sacrifice the national policy. And President Carter seems equally devoted.

But the subcult of work was not invented by the Kennedy clan. I have a large collection of incidents in which people have been fired because they did not "work hard enough," although no one had ever assessed their accomplishments. And I have also compiled numerous instances in which people were promoted and rewarded because of the energy and time they gave to their jobs, regardless of what they accomplished. Unless you come to work on time and look busy, you are not interested—or so the work ethic says. This attitude can convert a perfectly legitimate business into an unpleasant "busyness." And, as I shall show, the subcult of work breeds sloth, wastefulness, inefficiency, inflation, and incompetence.

Labor unions are other victims of the work ethic. In these institutions, all value is placed on labor; and people's worth is equated to the energy they have for sale, not the accomplishments they can make. The unions work hand in hand with business to promote the work ethic, and they seek shorter work hours only as a means of increasing the value placed on labor—particularly through overtime pay. But the work ethic is, in the long run, the worst enemy of working people; and I shall show how they can actually work less and get paid more.

It is only recently that I have broken the habits demanded by the work cult. I was long pleased to imagine myself a "workaholic," doing grave damage not only to the English language but to good sense. What

a relief—and what a pleasant surprise—it was for me to learn that there is no special virtue in hard work.

The Subcult of Knowledge

In the great cult of behavior, knowledge is given the place of honor—knowledge for its own sake. Even to suggest a union of knowledge with accomplishment is to promote a marriage beneath its station. Instead, we place knowledge in museums, called universities; we enoble it with medals; and we house these museums with guards who are charged with making it difficult for common folk to touch it. We place such great value on knowledge for its own sake that, as if it were the Hope diamond, we lock it away in vaults and instead display counterfeit substitutes: complex rituals of speech, learned societies, academic robes and processions, arcane publications, and high-sounding titles. And the unwary traveler seeking knowledge in this land of Oz will, like the Scarecrow, be given a diploma instead.

It is easy to discover that human competence is not one of the qualities that the knowledge industry cares greatly about. Open your encyclopedia to *H* for "human competence," or to *C* for "competence." There are no entries. Search the file cards in the libraries, and pickings will be lean.* Or look under *A* for "accomplishment"; your eye will go unrewarded until it comes to rest on "accredited colleges."

Indeed, it is difficult to discover just how *quality* is determined in the behavior cult, until you remember how sly and insidious the cult really is. The person who is most knowledgeable, we then discover, is the one who knows the most. Quality is great heaps of unused knowledge stored in the endless, unreachable tiers of the libraries. And so important is quantity as a measure of quality that the vendors of knowledge, like the pushers of heroin, carefully dilute it when they place it up for sale.

The Subcult of Motivation

The subcult of motivation is perhaps the most pernicious of the enemy's agents. If people's behavior departs sufficiently from the fashionable standards of the behavior cult, we say that they are "sick" or "mentally ill"; the usual explanation is that their motivations are diseased and corrupted. But this is a dangerous explanation, and it has more dangerous consequences than being arrested for a crime. More people are locked behind bars without due process in so-called mental

*As this goes to press, a flurry of books on teachers' "competencies" are being produced. You will soon realize that my concept of competence differs sharply from that used by many educators.

hospitals than there are duly processed inmates in our prison system. Indeed, the subcult of motivation is the most subtle branch of the behavior cult, as well as the most dangerous.

Now, there is no denying that people have "problems of living," as Thomas Szasz* calls it; but we have only the word of certain professionals that the causes of these problems are "motivation." But these professionals have a vested interest: because of the "deep mysteries" our motivations hold, only the same people who diagnose the problems of living can get paid to "treat" them. There is, of course, no evidence that these professionals have been in the least successful in solving such problems. But that doesn't matter; the standards of their profession are behavioral and have nothing to do with accomplishments. What psychiatrists were ever defrocked because they were not successful in helping their patients? And how would anybody ever know? Yet if they placed notices in the newspapers to advertise the results of independent studies proving that they helped their patients, they *would* be defrocked. Such advertising is "unethical" (meaning "unfashionable")—it violates the canons of the subcult of motivation.

The leisurely reader will of course see through the guise of the subcult of motivation, and look to other explanations of incompetence: explanations such as not knowing what accomplishments are expected of us, or whether we are performing well or not; or not knowing how to perform; or being punished for performing well; or not having the leisure or the tools to perform well; or being judged by *how* we did something, not *how well*. Only when managers and teachers (and psychiatrists) have examined these possibilities does it make much sense to look to motivation. And then, they probably should not look at motives but at incentives.

COMPETENCE AND THE LEISURE ETHIC

These, then, are the big guns of the enemy, manned by mental sloth and ignorance, to force us into the servitude of devotion to hard work and of homage to knowledge and motivation. Gradually and painfully, I have come to a radically different point of view, and I call the system I have derived from it *teleonomics*, which combines the Greek words for the "laws" (*nomos*) of "ends" (*teleos*). Teleonomics is a particular system for studying, measuring, and engineering human competence. It begins by focusing on the results, or products, of behavior (and other events); and it views behavior as only one of the inputs or "causal" variables.

---

*See Thomas Szasz, *The Manufacture of Madness* (New York: Harper & Row, 1970). This is one of the great classics of social science.

Teleonomics, the system of performance engineering I describe, should itself begin with a purpose. What, we can ask, is the aim of performance engineering? I have said that all engineering systems have a fundamentally economic purpose; but that does not mean that the purpose of performance engineering is simply to "make money." Money is often a convenient measure of engineering success, and usually a required means. But the economic ends of engineering are not to be confused with money as a means and convenient measure. To confuse them is to fail to understand the fundamentals of engineering.

There is a word that once described the most desirable and valuable aim of any attempt to improve human competence: that word is *leisure*. In a world that puts great store by the display of activity, especially in the form of hard work, this once delightful word has lost much of its earlier meaning. Gradually, it has taken on the disreputable connotations of laziness and frivolity.

Leisure comes from an old French word that means "permission." When we are permitted a break from arduous labor, we have the opportunity to accomplish other things. The *Oxford English Dictionary* calls it "an opportunity afforded by freedom from occupations," and, again, "time allowed before it is too late." I especially like the second definition. We can reason from it that if we learn to get more leisure, and better use what leisure we have, it will not be too late so soon.

Alas, the notion of opportunity has slipped away from our use of *leisure*. Most of us now, when we hear the word, think only of the time component—a lot of time with no special opportunities at all. But the concept "the duration of opportunity"* remains a marvelous one, because what could people value more than both time and opportunity?

If (old-style) *leisure* is the product of time and opportunity, it is, indeed, the worthy aim of a system of performance engineering, and the one I consider to be its true purpose. But because the idle connotations of *leisure* have become so great, we need another term to express our meaning. In keeping with the economic properties of any system of engineering, I have chosen the more ponderous term *human capital* to do the duty for which *leisure*† would once have been adequate.

In summary, the purpose of performance engineering is to increase human capital, which can be defined as the product of time and opportunity. Opportunities without time to pursue them mean nothing. And time, dead on our hands, affording no opportunities, has even less

*Oxford English Dictionary.

†I have not chosen to abandon this word completely; but wherever I use it, I do so only in the old and complete meaning.

value. The beginning point of performance engineering is therefore human potential; its end point is the increase of human capital. We can best convert human potential into human capital by proceeding in an orderly and sensible manner. All we mean by any technology is an orderly and sensible set of procedures for converting potential into capital.

These, admittedly, are great abstractions. The challenge I try to meet in this book is to give them precise and useful definitions and procedures. Only the reader can judge if I have met the criteria of simplicity, coherence, and usefulness.

Chapter One

A Leisurely Look at Worthy Performance

VANTAGE POINTS

The eye can travel to a star
So fast that Science cannot measure;
How vast a scope the eye can grasp—
Infinitudes of pounding pleasure.

And Science can little comprehend
What tiny things the eye can see:
Imaginary rebuffs of love—
Infinitesimal misery.

T.F.G.

The Summer of '49

The Capitol Grill slumped in an ill-smelling corner of Columbia, halfway between the elegance of the Old Campus and the grand old Capitol building, which still proudly bears the scars of Sherman's shells. The Grill served up the finest fried oysters in the Sandhills, plump and ever so lightly battered, and 50 cents the dozen. But only during "R" months, and this was July—no mistaking it. Few of the 50 T-shirted students had food in mind as they slouched around the front of the Grill in the mortal lock of the morning sun. They had gathered there to await the truck that would carry them out Two Notch Road, and then along the Dentsville back road into the piney woods, where they would begin a new job—for many of them, their first.

There among the longleaf and loblolly, they would dig for spent bullets, the refuse of soldier training on a Fort Jackson firing range, loosely dug into the bark and earth. At 75 cents an hour, this labor would buy a lot of food and beer back at the Capitol. In 9 years a million GIs had enfiladed these beach-white sands, leaving, we can imagine, a half-billion pieces of lead in their harmless targets.

Barton Hogg had achieved a dream he thought might be worthy of Midas. The contract to mine this easily accessible lode was the culmination of a frustrating apprenticeship in the politics of military contracts. He might have reflected, as he stood with his beefy red hands and neck sticking from his khaki boss-man's shirt, that all his failures were a reasonable investment toward this moment. There must be $100,000 lying there for him, just for the sifting. That would be a lot of pewter for Hogg, who had found the sudden riches of the 1940s eluding him.

But he was worried. The 60 laborers he had found by scraping the countryside weren't getting the lead out fast enough. He had hoped to have all that money in the bank before the dog days had passed. But he would have to admit that his overalled regiment looked busy enough, bent over their shovels and sieves in a long line, just as he had deployed them. He had them working in cadence: a shovel of bleached sand into the hardware-cloth box, a sifting of the box, and then the thudding dump into the milk pails he had bought from army salvage. He had worked out the cadence himself, and was quite pleased with it. Now, if the 50 college students he had had the inspiration to hire could work as well, perhaps he could escape this awful sun a rich man.

The truck arrived annoyingly late, and the platoon poured off in shouting disarray. Hogg's heart sank as he watched this undisciplined crew, hands too soft for labor, form into a scraggly group. My God! A few of them even carried portable radios, and some had newspapers under their arms; not a pair of overalls among them. Suddenly, Hogg had to identify himself with his laborers, who had paused in their cadence to watch. He had not been to college, and he resented people who had. Well, he would give that crew an education all right. He would teach them how to dig for lead.

They listened to Hogg's instructions with the same blank inattention they had learned to give their professors—and they followed his instructions just as poorly. Straggling off into groups (the radios seemed to form the social nucleus), they proceeded to work completely out of cadence. Most were soon on their haunches and shouting blasphemies, radios blaring, with no hint of order. Soon the shovels were discarded, and they were scraping the sieves directly into the sand. Jokes and ribaldry poured out faster than the lead. Hogg ran from one student to another, shouting each to his feet and inserting the shovel back into his hands. This went on all morning, and to no avail. Shaping these guys up was like sculpting in mercury. Derisive hoots chased him into retreat.

Come lunch, he slunk into the woods to devise a new strategy for appealing to these thieves. He would appeal to their honor—to their sense of capitalism. He gathered the throng for his lecture. Hadn't he fed them well? two large sandwiches of good barbecued pork with tomatoes and plenty of iced tea? Didn't they, like their affluent families, believe in an honest day's work? the dreams of capitalism?

Then Hogg played his ace. He appealed to the opinion of "Joe." Joe was a football hero from the 1930s, and the proprietor of the Capitol Grill. It was

Joe, plastering ads and passing the word, who had recruited them. "What would Joe think?" Hogg pleaded with this larcenous gang. And a burly GI-biller retorted "Who the hell is Joe?" to establish a refrain taken up by 50. pairs of lungs. "Who the hell is Joe?"

Defeated, Hogg spent the rest of the afternoon in the shade of a truck, visions of Midas shattered. That evening he called them together once more; and in anger and tears, he fired them, every last one of them, with a bitter diatribe on the lack of morals of a lost generation.

The next morning, beneath the unrelenting sun, he decided he would make a point to his friend Joe. Buckets of lead, left at odd angles in the sand, attested to the rout of the incompetent students. He would count the lead they had mined and report it to Joe. For whatever that was worth. *But the unruly gang had sifted out three times as much lead per labor-hour as the cadenced crew!*

Back at the Capitol Grill he tried again to recruit the students, but the word was out. Bart Hogg was boycotted, even by his friend Joe. He lost money on his contract, and spent the next 25 years working in an assembly plant near Hartsville. The Grill has since been replaced by a high-rise, and you have to go all the way to Charleston to get really good fried oysters.

The story of Barton Hogg is true and only slightly embellished. His lesson was too late for him, but it can be instructive for us because his fundamental error is not uncommon: When we make judgments about the competence of human conduct, we often look at performance from the wrong vantage point. We often confuse behavior with performance. And that is the main problem of investigating human competence. Many vantage points are available to us, and we must learn to decide which ones to use. We can measure performance in so many ways that we shall talk at cross purposes unless we make explicit just how we are measuring it. In order to know what we are doing and to avoid Hogg's error, we need to define performance quite carefully.

The system this book describes is based on three theorems summarizing my major assumptions about the nature of human competence. I call them Leisurely Theorems, using *leisure* as a synonym for *human capital,* which is the product of time and opportunity. This chapter presents the First Leisurely Theorem, defining *human competence* and *worthy performance;* it also demonstrates the importance of distinguishing between behavior and accomplishment.

WORTHY PERFORMANCE

Behavior is a necessary and integral part of performance, but we must not confuse the two. Unfortunately, we often do. To equate behavior and performance is like confusing a sale with the seller. Naturally, we

cannot have one without the other. But the sale is a unitary transaction, with properties all of its own; and we can know a great deal about it even though we know little—perhaps nothing at all—about the seller.

Suppose we focus on some particular behavior for a moment—say, the behavior of a young man who fancies himself a hunter. We watch him lift his gun to his shoulder, take sight, and pull the trigger. We are observing the more overt aspects of some rather complex behavior. Now we can observe the same pattern again; but this time we shall measure it: the speed with which the gun is lifted, the width of the hunter's stance, the pressure on the trigger, and (with electrodes) the pulse and brain waves of the rifleman. And so on. We can even interview the hunter in depth to get an account of his feelings as he fired the gun. But no matter how often or how exhaustively we measure this behavior, we cannot tell what kind of performance it is. Is it murder, food gathering, or target practice? Is it legal, ethical, effective, valuable?

To answer these questions, we must first look away from the behavior, to see what effect it has upon the world. Did the hunter kill a person or shoot a rabbit; hit a target; or fail to hit anything at all? When we observe the whole transaction, including both the hunter's behavior and what he accomplished by it, we are observing performance. And the performance of hitting the bullseye of a target is quite different from the performance of killing a person, even if the behaviors in both cases were identical. In contrast, the identical performance of killing a person can be produced by enormous varieties of behavior. Our young hunter could shoot a person with a pistol held between his legs, or a blunderbus held above his head, without markedly changing his performance. Performance (P), then, is a transaction involving both behavior (B) and its consequence (C). Or, in shorthand,

$$P = B \rightarrow C$$

In performance, behavior is a means, and its consequence is the end. And we seldom have any reason to try to modify other people's behavior in complete isolation of consequences. About the only reason would be to study it. By viewing behavior in convenient isolation we can learn many things about it, ranging from measures of visual acuity to useful information about the perseveration of habits. But those things *by themselves* tell us very little about performance.

Nor do we have much reason to modify people's performance in isolation from its context. Is the performance of killing legal and moral—or is it a heinous crime? We cannot tell this merely by observing the whole performance transaction. We can measure the frequency or accuracy of striking the target; we can measure how many

bullets were used. We can even correlate these measures with our measures of behavior. But none of these measures will tell us whether the performance is valuable, legal, or moral.

No sensible person tries to modify other people's behavior just because it is there, or their performance just because it can be done. When we set about to engineer performance, we should view it in a context of value. We should not train someone to do something differently unless we place a value on the consequence—unless we see that consequence as a valuable *accomplishment* (A).[1] So, the kind of performance we want to engineer is *valuable performance*, which can be expressed in shorthand as

$$P = B \rightarrow A$$

Now we have limited our definition of performance to valuable performance. If, for example, we can change the way our hunter handles his gun so that he can hit the rabbits we value, we have engineered valuable performance.

But is the performance worth it? Suppose that we really do value the rabbits we have taught the hunter to kill. But our hunter requires an expensive rifle, charges us heavily for his services, and uses a lot of ammunition. Although we may value his accomplishment, we will not find the performance worthy because his behavior costs us too much. Our engineering, then, is a failure. So, what we really want to engineer is not just valuable performance, but *worthy performance*—in which the value of the accomplishment exceeds the cost of the behavior.

All engineering begins with the simple economic purpose of creating valuable results at a cost that makes those results worth it. Worth, then, is the net we have when we subtract the costs from the values: $W = V - C$. Or, we can express worth in another way: as the ratio of value to cost:

$$\text{Worth} = \frac{\text{Value}}{\text{Cost}}$$

Which says only that worth gets greater as value increases and cost decreases.

When we set out to engineer human performance, it is axiomatic that we place value on accomplishments but that the behavior costs us something. We may value the rabbit; but we must pay for the hunter's work, knowledge, and incentives, as well as for his gun and ammunition. We value the crop but pay for the plow and the plowman.

Roughly speaking, *competent* people are those who can create valuable results without using excessively costly behavior.

THE FIRST LEISURELY THEOREM

I define human competence, then, as a function of worthy performance. This is the First Leisurely Theorem:

> **Human competence is a function of worthy performance (W), which is a function of the ratio of valuable accomplishments (A) to costly behavior (B).**

A shorthand way of expressing the theorem[2] is

$$W = \frac{A}{B}$$

Since the remaining leisurely[3] theorems are derived from this one, and since it is the key to a system of engineering human competence, it is important to understand what it tells us:

1. It tells us that the way to achieve human competence is to increase the value of our accomplishments while reducing the energy we put into the effort. The true value of competence is derived from accomplishment, not from behavior.

2. It tells us that great quantities of work, knowledge, and motivation, in the absence of at least equal accomplishment, are unworthy performance. And this says, in turn, that knowledge, motivation, and work, when used competently, are to be husbanded and spent wisely.

3. It tells us that great accomplishments are not worthy if the cost in human behavior is also very great. In my opinion, the Egyptian pyramids stand as silent monuments to worthless achievement, although the subcult of knowledge would have us honor them. A really worthy, though less honored, achievement of the early Arabs was the alphabet, a labor-saving device of incalculable worth.

4. Money, energy, or time invested in reducing the behavior required of performance can pay off splendidly. Later, we shall see that these efforts can simultaneously increase the numerator (accomplishment) as they decrease the denominator (behavior), so that we are doubly rewarded. On the other hand, we shall also see that an increase in behavior requirements often decreases the unit value of

accomplishments, so that we are doubly duped. (See Chapter 9 and the "Law of Training.")

5. A system that rewards people for their behavior (work, motivation, or knowledge) encourages incompetence. And a system that rewards people only for their accomplishments, and not for the net worth of their performance, is an incomplete system that fails to appreciate human competence. When such a system is used by managers in the world of work, and teachers in the world of schools, it invites them to squander other people's energies.

6. Human capital can be best achieved through worthy performance only if we measure and respond directly to human competence. And human competence is found in overt performance, not in hidden behavior.

The First Leisurely Theorem identifies the subject matter of human competence, then, and it warns us against confusing the plow (behavior) with the crop (accomplishment).

DISTINGUISHING BEHAVIOR AND ACCOMPLISHMENT

Nothing better illustrates the importance of distinguishing behavior and accomplishment than a study of the ways in which we can measure performance. When we think of measuring performance, we usually think of tests. And psychologists have certainly provided us with enough of those. By the traditional view, the way to assess performance is to administer tests of apparent job or school relevance (e.g., mathematics, spatial relations, mechanical aptitude), and then to establish a cut-off score for the selection of employees or the advancement of students.

This traditional view is mistaken in two ways. First, traditional tests, at their best, are only crude statistical instruments, usually poorly correlated with the economic realities of performance. For example, personality tests for salespeople have been correlated with such supervisory ratings as "interpersonal effectiveness" and "ability to conduct an interview," but never, to my knowledge, with the quality of sales prospecting. Very often those things so easily assumed to be correlatives of actual performance simply are not. As a matter of fact, the best salesperson (by dollar volume) I have ever seen never smiled and had a fish-like handshake; and a leading medical photographer I once knew is color-blind, one-eyed, and severely astigmatic in the one "good" eye.

Second, tests are unfair in that the people who score poorly on them

have far more potential for successful job and school performance than we have been able to tap. A test score rates people low on the *assumed* correlatives of the job or school requirements; but it does not identify precisely what must be developed in them for us to make good their potential. Tests are usually too indirect; we need to go more directly to performance. And that is what psychological testing has helped prevent us from doing. That is also why psychological test batteries have been so half-heartedly accepted in industry. They have been better accepted in the schools, but only because the schools have been so little concerned with the worldly use of human performance.

Assessment of human performance has teetered on a dilemma. Here are its horns:

1. We all know that there are great individual differences among people (the statistical "science" of psychological testing is grounded in this assumption).

2. But we know equally well that people are pretty much alike (or there could be no science of humans beings, biological or psychological).

Now, I believe both of these propositions, and so does everyone else I have ever talked to about them. But their contradiction is clear and surely needs a resolution. The system of performance analysis described here has emerged from a resolution of this dilemma—from realizing how both of these commanding, yet seemingly contradictory, beliefs about differences in human performance can be true but not contradictory.

Let me summarize here a bit of the theory that has led me away from the statistical view of human performance assessment and to a satisfactory resolution. Table 1-1 summarizes the performance measures of two hypothetical people, Mr. Quik and Mr. Sloe, on several tasks. Two different kinds of performance measures, which I shall call measure *A* and measure *B*, are given for each task. Even before we take the measurements, we confirm that Mr. Quik is supposed to be an expert at all four tasks, whereas Mr. Sloe is known as a complete novice at each. Both measures *A* and *B* confirm Quik's expertise, but only measure *A* discloses Sloe's total ineptness. Although both are direct, valid, and useful measures of performance, the *B* measures tend to substantiate our belief that people are pretty much alike, whereas the *A* measures reflect great differences among individuals. Then why the discrepancy? To answer that, we must know what is common to the *B* measures, what is common to the *A* measures, and how these measures differ.

It is really quite simple. In *all* of the *B* measures, we get a score by looking directly at the *B*ehavior of the person performing the task. In

TABLE 1-1   COMPARISON OF TWO DIFFERENT KINDS OF PERFORMANCE MEASURES

			Scores			*Scores*	
	Tasks	*Measure A*	*Quik*	*Sloe*	*Measure B*	*Quik*	*Sloe*
I.	Rifle marksmanship	Target scores	100	0	Checklist of rifle-handling behaviors	100%	98%
II.	Long division	Number of correct answers in 100 problems	100	0	Percentage of long-division operations performed correctly	100%	98%
III.	Insurance sales	Percentage of sales volume quota sold	100%	0	Ratings of sales techniques, scale 1–10	10	7
IV.	Speaking Spanish	Percentage of instructions that a Spaniard can follow	100%	0	Percentage of language elements in repertory	94%	70%

the *A* measures, we never need to look at the behavior of the performer, but at something else: the product of this behavior, or the effect that this behavior has on the world—the Accomplishment. But why do the *B* measures seem to deceive us about Sloe's capability? First, they need not deceive us at all; rather, they can sometimes reveal the causes of a poor showing on the *A* measures. Suppose we look at the *B* measures more closely, watching Mr. Sloe go through each bit of behavior on a checklist. Say Mr. Sloe performed beautifully with the rifle: He put the stock to his shoulder, the barrel out, index finger on the trigger; he closed his left eye, pointed the rifle in the direction of the target, sighted along the gun-sights, and squeezed the trigger. Only in this last bit of behavior do we see something amiss: He failed to hold the rifle steady as he squeezed the trigger. As a result, he never hit the target at all.

We also watch Mr. Sloe perform each behavior (*B* measure) required in doing long division. Mr. Sloe set up the problem according to the conventional algorithm, estimated various quotients accurately, multiplied well enough to convince us he knows the multiplication table, correctly subtracted all manner of number combinations, borrowed, carried, properly indicated the remainder, correctly positioned the integers, and precisely identified the decimal point. Only in setting up

the problem initially did he make a tiny mistake: He confused the dividend and the divisor. When he saw $23 \div 12$, he set it up like this: $23\sqrt{12}$. Obviously, he never got the right answer—and this accounts for his score of 0 in long division by the A measure.

Similarly, in selling insurance, as we follow Sloe around, we are impressed with his B measures—his poise, his arguments, and his persistence. He seemed to have only one major weakness to warrant a 7 rather than a 10: He failed to get the information needed to qualify the people he called on as serious sales prospects. Now we know why he failed to sell any insurance.

Or take Spanish. Mr. Sloe says he knows nothing of Spanish. But when we compared his language repertory with that of a Spaniard, as in the B measure, we concluded differently. He does know how to pronounce the "difficult" Spanish r; and he does this every time he utters the *tt's* in the word *butter*. Because English syntax and grammar are more like Spanish than they are unlike it, his grammatical knowledge of Spanish was considerable even before he began to master the language. And common linguistic roots put him far beyond zero in his mastery of Spanish vocabulary. Yet the relatively little he does not know is so essential to communication that he cannot have the desired effect on a listener: Spaniards do not understand him. As a result, his A scores are zero.

So we can say that Mr. Sloe *knows* a great deal (B scores), but has *accomplished* nothing (A scores). The B scores are direct measures of the Behavior that goes into the task, and the A scores are measures of the product—the effects on the world—Accomplished by the task.

If we generalize from these examples, we find the resolution to our dilemma: People are very much alike in their behavior repertories (B measures), but there are great individual differences in what they accomplish (A measures).

COROLLARIES OF THE FIRST LEISURELY THEOREM

By seeing that performance has at least two aspects, behavior and accomplishment, we not only resolve the dilemma of individual differences, but we also arrive at some useful corollaries of the First Leisurely Theorem to help us measure performance meaningfully.

One important corollary of the distinction between measures of accomplishment and measures of behavior is that *if we know what we are doing, education must be highly economical.* Only one of the two measures reflects value to those who propose to improve performance; the A measures alone can be translated into a dollar return. In other words, we do not care how people hold the gun if they hit the target;

nor do we care how they behave while selling so long as they get sales and satisfied customers. Accomplishments alone have direct value to us. And because we must make an investment in order to get those accomplishments, behavior changes are simply things that cost us money.

But if small changes in behavior can produce great changes in accomplishment, then small investments in cost can generally produce great returns in value. If we view any program to mold performance as an economic issue, we can see that to decide whether it is worthwhile to launch the program is a function of the ratio of expected value return to the expected cost. If this ratio is greater than 1, we can expect a return on our investment. Because *V*alue is a function of the *A* measures, and *C*ost is a function of the *B* measures, worth is essentially a reflection of the ratio of expected changes in *A*ccomplishment (*A*) to the needed changes in *B*ehavior (*B*):

$$W = \frac{A}{B} = \frac{V}{C}$$

This brings us to a second corollary of the distinction between behavior and accomplishment: *We have no need to measure behavior until we have measured accomplishment.* Even then, we may never need to measure behavior. Accordingly, there can be no purpose in identifying deficiencies in rifle handling until we have established that there are deficiencies in hitting the target. And we have no reason to measure a person's repertory of Spanish until we have determined that this person has a problem in communicating to other Spanish-speaking people. Or, to relate this to the preceding economic corollary, we can say that we sensibly should look for a potential value return (*A* measures) before we inquire into the cost of the investment (*B* measures).

The sense of this second corollary may seem obvious. But its good sense has little currency in most present-day programs for the assessment of performance. Unfortunately, most of these programs set about to measure the individual's behavior (and therefore *B* measures) without making any attempt to determine just *how* (or even *whether*) this individual is deficient in accomplishments.

This leads us to a third corollary, which I shall give in two parts. The first part says: *Quantitative expressions of behavior (B measures), except for special purposes, are often misleading indices of performance.* Which is to say that most[4] test scores are misleading. What we want as a result of measuring the behavioral side of performance is a list of deficiencies that are significant only because they lead to important accomplishment deficiencies.

That test scores are usually misleading can be illustrated by the performance of two children with an equal "amount" of arithmetic behavior deficiency. Dorsey cannot subtract zeros from other numbers. (Dorsey's reasoning is, "You can't take 'nothing' away.") Thomasina cannot subtract from zero. (The reasoning here is, "You can't take something from nothing.") Yet Dorsey gets most of his long division answers correct, since relatively few zeros occur as subtrahends in division. On the other hand, Thomasina gets most of her answers wrong, because zeros repeatedly appear as minuends whenever the quotient has a fraction ("bring down the zero"). So, Dorsey may get a score of 90 on the test, whereas Thomasina gets only 10. Yet these scores give not even the faintest clue to the problem of either child, or to their nearly equal abilities. In fact, they obscure the real difference between the children, which has nothing to do with the "amount of knowledge" either one has.

To make matters worse, tests—especially verbal tests—are usually constructed so that differences among people are arbitrarily emphasized. Say you answer twice as many questions about vocabulary as I do; that does not mean that you have twice my vocabulary. Indeed, the real ratio of our differences must be very small, or else we wouldn't be able to communicate. This is one of the reasons that many tests unfairly discriminate against minority groups in a culture: They magnify really small, insignificant differences in behavior, and give them excessive weight. This greatly advances the cause of social prejudice, which itself is an inevitable product of the behavior cult. For example, among those whom we call the "disadvantaged," we would probably find that there are relatively few behavior deficiencies, but these deficiencies can have disproportionate effects on the majority culture. I know of a student from a poor black college who learned never to dangle participles, but he spelled the word *because* as *BECAWSE*. His mastery of participles seems somehow quantitatively a much greater achievement than that of his white counterpart who dangles participles all the time but has mastered the spelling of *because*. Indeed, we could say that the black student has even mastered six-sevenths of the spelling of this word, because he misses only one of the seven letters. After ridding ourselves of dangled participles (you will, of course, recognize this as a dangled participle), the world's response to our improvement is very small; yet when we change the way we spell *because*, we may be transformed in the world's view from illiterates to acceptably educated people.

The second part of the third corollary says: *It is frequently useful to quantify measures of accomplishment, and these measures should have economic correlatives.* There are many different behaviors that cause performance failure, and these should be listed for identifica-

tion, not obscured by summations. The "number" of them does not matter. But failures of accomplishments are directly correlated with the loss of value to someone. For this reason, it is often useful to quantify accomplishments. Indeed, measures of accomplishment have no real validity until they reflect value to someone, and the dollar currency is one excellent way to express this value. We can show, for instance, that it is valuable to learn to read by showing that literate employees are better compensated or that literate people will buy books.

Problems in household plumbing provide a good example of why we should want to quantify accomplishments, but not behavior.[5] If a water faucet is not working, we report to the plumber essentially quantifiable facts about the running water. We say that not enough water is coming through, or that it is coming through too slowly, or that it is not hot enough. We could attach a value to the volume, rate, and temperature of water; and we could even specify how much of each of these quantities we want—and how much we are willing to pay for them. Water is the output, the accomplishment.

But when the plumber comes to fix our water pipes, we expect the expert to identify the precise cause of our problem. We would be angry indeed if this expert inspected our pipes with a list of true-false questions (T-F "The elbow joint is leaking," etc.), and then gave us an achievement score as a measure of our system. "Sir, your plumbing system scored a 68, which is not passing—it needs a complete overhaul. I was hoping it would score a 75 and not cost you so much to repair." You see, we don't care how many things are wrong, or how the plumber scores the severity of the troubles. We simply want to know exactly what is wrong that can be changed to supply us the water we need. We want the plumber to isolate a "list" of problem behaviors and tell us how much it will cost to fix them.

It is the accomplishments we value and pay for. The utility company charges us for the actual number of gallons of water we get out of the tap, not for how smoothly our tap works. This means that accomplishment measures, although they are direct performance measures (e.g., targets hit, cases won in court, successful students, number of qualified sales prospects), must eventually be translated into economic terms if we are to establish their true value. And I will do this in Chapter 2.

NOTES

1. Accomplishment carries the connotation of "competence." For example, we speak of an "accomplished pianist."

2. Some readers will miss the function sign. Properly written, the equation should read:

$$W = f\left(\frac{V}{C}\right) \quad \text{or} \quad W = f\left(\frac{A}{B}\right)$$

I have left out function signs simply because I have found that they confuse many readers. Sophisticated readers can supply their own function signs.

3. The definition shows that leisure is the product of time and opportunity. In shorthand:

$$L = T \times O$$

Without opportunity, there is no leisure, just as there is no leisure without time. Dead time, then, or time we don't know what to do with, is not leisure at all.

Next, to show the relationship between leisure and worthy performance, we can make some substitutions in our definitions. If opportunity is the potential for accomplishment (pA), then leisure can be described as

$$L = T \times pA$$

Now we need only one further substitution. We need to see that behavioral inefficiencies consume the "time allowed before it is too late." "Time allowed" (T), therefore, is inversely proportional to the behavior required, or

$$L = \frac{1}{B} \times pA = \frac{pA}{B}$$

From our First Leisurely Theorem, then, leisure (or human capital) becomes the potential for worthy performance:*

$$L = pW$$

By the same simple substitution process, we can see that, conversely, worthy performance is the potential for leisure—if we define *accomplishment* as the potential for opportunity. And indeed we must, to be consistent with the way in which we actually live and strive for goals. Practically all the goals we set for ourselves we see, on analysis, as subgoals aimed at some greater opportunity, and the accomplishment of each goal opens up opportunity for new accomplishments. The very purpose of competent human performance, then, is leisure itself.

Thus, leisure, or human capital, is not only the goal of worthy performance; it is also the starting point—or, better, the point at which we begin again. It is a renewal—the rebirth of hope. To equate leisure with, say, an orgy, is to forget that one of the most hopeless and forlorn human experiences is to discover that the party is over and all resources for a new one have been used up. Leisure is not only the end of worthy performance; it is a necessary condition.

---

*This derivation makes use of the famous German *Zunge-in-Wange* method of mathematics.

4. In Chapter 2, we shall see that this is an important qualifier, but it does not detract from the main argument.

5. This does not mean that we never take measures of the input system. The plumber may take a measure of the force of a pump in the system to determine if it is below some critical value. We might reasonably find a number to express a behavior input, such as the force with which a logger applies the ax. But we are not served by counting the number of different behavior elements in a logger's repertory. Most psychological testing—and the worst of it—counts up a number of diverse behaviors, truly adding apples and alligators.

   Special education teachers are well aware of the value of a "list" rather than a number. Several of these teachers have remarked to me that they wished that all tests were scored that way.

Chapter Two
Measuring Human Competence

Meter what your Fancy will;
She'll doubtless conjour Joyous Hour.
My Love—she's more audacious still—
Challenged me to fathom Flower.

But I have measured everywhere,
By magnum at night, by minim at morn,
And neither Rose nor Vine compare
As cadent, sharp, and true as Thorn.

T.F.G.

THE SECOND LEISURELY THEOREM

I begin this chapter with an assertion that many people will at first find hard to accept, yet it is one in which I believe wholeheartedly: Any kind of performance can be measured—reliably and with considerable precision. We can measure the performance of poets, managers, teachers, physicians, lawyers, research scientists, psychotherapists, composers, and politicians—not just that of production workers and athletes. The belief that the more complex forms of performance are not subject to measurement and quantification arises simply from ignorance about how to do it. Once you get the knack, performance that you once thought unmeasurable will usually be not nearly so difficult to measure as, say, the radiation of Martian soil or the fertility of farm land. I hope to convince you of this here.

But performance alone is not what I have set out to measure, because performance alone is not competence. Competence is a social concept, a comparative judgment about the worth of performance. In order to convert measures of performance into measures of competence, we require a social standard. Once we find that standard, competence will be as easy to measure as performance.

The First Leisurely Theorem gave us the basic "dimensions" of competence (valuable accomplishments and costly behavior). But we get the competence of any one person, institution, or culture only by comparing the very best instance of that performance with what is typical. Mark Spitz, the Olympic swimmer, was (at his best) only about 20 percent faster than the average high school swim-contest entrant, which means that the average high school entrant is exceptionally competent. Mark Spitz, of course, was a perfectly competent swimmer, because he was the exemplar. I call this measure of competence, the ratio of the exemplar's performance to typical performance, the PIP (*potential for improving performance*); and it doubly serves us. First, it tells us how much competence we already have; second, it tells us how much potential we have for improvement.

I define *exemplary* performance as the worth of the historically best instance of the performance. And notice that we need not accept mediocrity as a standard. For example, if a greenhorn's acre yields $1000 in grain at a cost of $500, the typical worth index (W_t) is 2. If the best green thumb yields $2000 in value at a cost of $250, the exemplary worth index (W_{ex}) is 8. Then the greenhorn's PIP is 4, meaning that the greenhorn has the potential for doing four times as well. (Dollars are convenient units, but the PIP is by no means restricted to them.)

Human competence, then, is further defined by the Second Leisurely Theorem (or the Measurement Theorem), which states:

> **Typical competence is inversely proportional to the potential for improving performance (the PIP), which is the ratio of exemplary performance to typical performance. The ratio, to be meaningful, must be stated for an identifiable accomplishment, because there is no "general quality of competence." In shorthand, this theorem states that:[1]**
>
> $$\text{PIP} = \frac{W_{ex}}{W_t}$$

There is also an interesting corollary: *The lower the PIP of any person or group, the more competitive that person or group is.* Now, the word *competitive* is a delight to some people; to others, it signals unpleasant things. But that is because the cult of behavior has us confuse certain behavioral properties, such as greed, aggression, determination, and the expenditure of energy, with competing. All I mean by competing is performing with comparative competence.

CHARACTERISTICS OF THE PIP

You will note that the PIP is a measure of opportunity, the very stuff human capital is made of. The PIP does not assign feeble limitations to people as the IQ does, but takes the humane *and* practical view that poor performers usually have great potential. Also, our measurement theorem does not posit competence mystically inside people's heads, but places it in performance. People are not competent; performance is. People have opportunities, which the PIP can express with precision and validity.

Indeed, the PIP can be measured as precisely and as accurately as we choose. Competence may vary from time to time, but our methods of measuring it need not. I have devised practical methods of measuring the PIP, and they need not be validated against criterion measures, because the PIP, when properly used, *is* the performance criterion. And, naturally, when applied in the world of work, the PIP yields accurate measures of the economic potential for improving performance.

The PIP is principally a conceptual tool, which gives us a basis for comparing potential opportunities to improve performance. In general, the smaller the PIP, the less possibility there is to improve performance and the more difficult it is to reduce the PIP to 1.0. It is easier to reduce a PIP from, say, 4.0 to 1.5 than it is to shrink a PIP of 1.2 to 1.1. This rule is no longer true, however, if two circumstances hold. One is if we have full knowledge of why the exemplar is a superior performer, and we also have *full* control over those variables—that is, when we can give typical performers the training, information, tools, or motivation they require to emulate the exemplar. The second circumstance is even more important: when we can improve on the exemplar. Thus, the PIP is a "dynamic" measure, because new exemplary standards can always be set.

But here is something more to be considered. Even if we gave all performers the information, knowledge, tools, and so on, of the exemplar, some variance in performance would remain—someone would still manage to shine as the best performer. In a "perfectly" competitive world, where we have arranged for everyone to have everything necessary in order to emulate the exemplar, such inherent characteristics as quickness, strength, "intelligence," and ambition will give some people a slight edge. In athletics, that slight edge is the critical distinction, but in the world of work or in the world of schools it would usually be of no special economic significance at all. It is, I believe, virtually impossible to reduce PIPs to 1.0, simply because someone will always discover a better way of doing it, have some natural superiority, or possess an unusual degree of motive to excel.

What I am saying is that, in general, the more incompetent a person or a group of people are, the easier it is to improve their performance. This contradicts the way we often think. But that is because we rarely think as performance engineers. Left to "nature"—to uncontrolled and unplanned events—exemplary performers are likely to improve themselves, setting new standards of exemplary performance. But as a situation becomes more "unmanaged," PIPs will grow—with the result that management has more potential for realizing them. Although large PIPs may discourage the uninitiated, they are a welcome opportunity to performance engineers.

The size of the PIP, of course, only indicates potential for improving performance—not how economically valuable that potential is. To put an economic value on a change in a PIP, we must translate it into what I call "stakes." (Stakes are the money value of realizing the PIP.) A PIP of 4.0 in the speed at which janitors clean a building, say, does not translate into as much economic potential as a PIP of 1.5 in the speed of the production line. Later, I shall discuss the relatively simple techniques of translating PIPs into stakes; meanwhile, it is important to see the use of the PIP as a conceptual measure, pointing us in the direction of engineering opportunity.

A case history, based on real events, illustrates how the use of the PIP can be a solid clue of great economic importance to a performance engineer faced with a really unfamiliar performance system. In this case, we shall see a performance engineer, Frank Roby, face an unfamiliar situation and find opportunities to improve it greatly—opportunities of the kind that experienced management misses every day.

The manufacturing vice president of Surfside Seasonings, Inc., Willis Angel, is dissatisfied with the performance of his plants. He is determined to find some way to improve that performance, and he assigns three groups of people to conduct independent studies to tell him which programs he should invest in. Two of these groups are the corporate training and organizational development departments of Surfside. The third group is a consulting firm specializing in management development. When Angel reads the three reports, he can hardly believe that the studies were independent because their recommendations are so similar. All three reports finger the first-line supervisors of the work force in the processing area as the culprits most responsible for the poor showing in the plants. The once stable, but aging, hourly workers have been largely replaced by young women from the ghetto. All three reports agree that the old first-line supervisors simply don't know how to manage the new breed. A training program in new styles of supervision, and in human relations, will be required; and the management consulting firm offers to develop one for $78,000. For a $400 million business, this does not seem too large an investment in good supervision.

Angel, of course, is impressed by the substantial agreement of the three studies he has commissioned. And the arguments have a certain face validity: The culture of the work force has changed, and there is no doubting that. But the $78,000 training-development cost for an operation that has been losing money gives Angel trouble. He can't quite make up his mind, and he decides to get another opinion. He has heard of a consultant named Frank Roby, a man with a mixed reputation. Some say that Roby is completely without professional qualifications and imply that he is a charlatan. Others insist that although his methods are truly unorthodox, Roby gets results. The word *results* sounds sweet to Angel, so he hires Roby at $750 a day.

Because of Roby's reputation, Angel decides to watch him work. Roby shows up one morning and makes the mandatory tour of a manufacturing plant, seemingly without noticing a thing. He then spends the rest of the day talking with the corporate accountant, the plant production manager, and the chief quality-control inspector. To Angel's surprise, Roby appears in his office at 5:00 p.m. saying that he is ready to deliver his report and suggests that they conclude the study in the nearest bar over Vidalia Specials, a mixture of orange juice and sour mash bourbon.

While Angel begins his adaptation to this curious blend, he asks Roby if he has ever been in a manufacturing plant like Surfside's. "Not exactly," Roby replies, "but I once helped some folks in a chewing gum factory."

So much for Roby's credentials. Angel begins the audition with deep suspicion, but after an hour Roby has completely convinced him that the best way for Surfside Seasoning to waste its time and money is to train first-line supervisors; and that, indeed, the company has an extraordinarily competent corps of foremen in the processing areas. (Mind you, Roby never so much as interviewed a supervisor.) Besides, Roby tells Angel exactly where he thinks the problem is, why it is there, and what can be done about it. He is so convincing that the next morning Angel seeks authorization to spend the $150,000 that Roby said would be required for the program.

Only 18 months later, Angel has sufficient data to prove that the adoption of Roby's program is netting the company a return of several million dollars a year in greatly increased labor productivity, decreased waste, lower employee turnover, and fewer grievances. And Angel finds himself taking all the credit—not that he's that kind of guy. But how could he ever convince anyone that a man could walk into a seasonings plant for the first time and after a day tell you how to turn the plant around—and against all the advice of seasoned professionals?

We can look at just a sample of the data that Roby studied to reach his conclusions: Table 2-1 shows some production data for three* representative supervisory groups at Surfside Seasonings. (Of course, Roby didn't depend on these data alone, but they contributed far more than anything else to his remarkable conclusions.) In examining these data, Roby could see at once that

*In the real case, there were 32 groups. Three are chosen here to simplify the argument.

TABLE 2-1 COMPARATIVE MANUFACTURING PRODUCTIVITY

Supervisor A		Supervisor B		Supervisor C	
Employee no.	*Hrly. prod.*	*Employee no.*	*Hrly. prod.*	*Employee no.*	*Hrly. prod.*
1	163	11	194	21	172
2	149	12	138	22	137
3	118	13	137	23	136
4	108	14	131	24	135
5	106	15	110	25	127
6	93	16	89	26	100
7	60	17	61	27	56
8	57	18	49	28	52
9	42	19	48	29	41
10	30	20	41	30	28
Average	92.6	Average	99.8	Average	98.4

the potential for improving the performance of the hourly employees was considerable, but that the differences among supervisors was small. Even though Supervisor B had the best supervisory performance in the company, getting other supervisors to perform as he does would not improve matters greatly. If the situation were reversed and there were large differences among supervisors, his conclusions would have been quite different.

The average production is 96.93, and the best employee produces 194 units; so the employee PIP (assuming that costs and quality are the constants) is

$$\text{Employee PIP} = \frac{194}{96.9} = 2.00$$

This employee PIP shows that the average hourly employee has the potential for doubling productivity. But the supervisory PIP is negligible—unusually low, in fact. Roby looked at these variances and then noticed that the job the employees had to do was to operate complex low-tolerance equipment. A lot of learning is required to master it. He also heard people say that it simply took a lot of experience to get maximum production. And he learned that the hourly employees got no formal training—mostly because production managers didn't think that formal training was as good as on-the-job experience. He considered this nonsense, of course, and he advised Angel that $150,000 invested in proper training in the theory and troubleshooting of the equipment could get any new employee producing at about 150 units an hour, reducing the employee PIP to less than 1.3. Roby proved to be right—and the most important information he had was the PIP measures. Management had hidden the data in its books, but not in the form of Table 2-1.

Frank Roby is a real person, and this is an almost true story. It is true in every important respect except for the time it took—Roby has never met anyone as open minded as Willis Angel; it usually takes weeks or

months to build up sufficient appearance of credibility for his advice to be taken seriously. Roby has no magic, no mysterious capacity for insight. Indeed, his methods are so simple that when people watch his behavior, they cannot help but be unimpressed. Roby has learned to observe measures of competence and to make sense of them. Those simple measures can be powerful instruments in our pursuit of competence if we can set aside our behavioral biases long enough to see how they can be used.

WHOSE PERFORMANCE CAN BE MEASURED?

The Roby example deals with relatively simple performance that can be measured quite easily—in units of production. You might argue, however, that much of the world of human performance is not so simple; and you might reasonably question whether other kinds of performance can be measured to yield neat units like the PIP. At least consider my proposition that any kind of performance can be measured.

Oh, the thrill when we first broke through what seemed to be the dense underbrush of John Donne's poetry. But if Donne was a competent poet, how can one measure that competence? Is there any way to say precisely that Donne is 2.3 times the poet that Herrick is, or 3.0 times Lowell? The obvious answer comes much too easily: There is no way to quantify beauty or spiritual power.

But trying to measure the poet's competence illustrates the problems. First of all, it is clear that we cannot measure Donne's behavior—he is dead. Similarly, we can deduce nothing of Shakespeare's competence from his behavior, because we know next to nothing about it. But it doesn't matter. Even if someone could prove that Shakespeare and Donne had reliably measured IQs of only 90, that couldn't reasonably affect our judgment of their competence.

All we can measure is exactly all we need to measure—the poems a poet produces. (For the exercise, we shall assume that the cost of behavior is a constant.) Now, how do we measure poetic performance by looking at the poems? When we think about it, the problem is not that we cannot measure Donne's performance, but that there are so many different ways we might measure it. We could, for example, measure the effect his poems have upon people's emotions by various means—by questionnaire, interview, or even by hooking electrodes up to readers and taking polygraph measures of changes in blood pressure and heart rate. Or we could measure how often his poems were reread by the people who had learned to read them. Or how often they were quoted or anthologized. We could measure metric characteristics, or we could have present-day poets rate them for quality. This only begins the long list of possibilities.

The problem is not *whether* we can measure Donne's performance, but what it is we expect from poetry—what we consider a valuable poetic contribution. Measuring noncreative competence seems to be easier than measuring the competence of creative artists—but only because people can more easily come to an agreement about what is expected of noncreative performance. Anyone's performance can be measured in many different ways, and those measures become measures of competence whenever we can agree on what it is about the accomplishments that we value. In Chapter 4 I shall describe a method for helping us arrive at those agreements. For now, however, it should be sufficient to say that we can measure any kind of performance. And to argue that performance is too difficult to measure is, it seems to me, the luxury view of things. If most people did not live in poverty and abject servitude, this view would be easier to accept. Indeed, in that distant day (should it arrive) when all people have broken the bonds of ignorance and need, and we sit sipping mint juleps on some warm veranda, poetry itself may become the currency of the land, and all the absurd numbers will be safely confined to the computers. But until that time I for one must believe that it is possible to measure performance and competence, even John Donne's, and to make those measures mean something. It may not always be easy, but the stakes are reasonably high. Indeed, if we cannot measure competence, there is very little reason to talk about it at all.

The widespread feeling that many of the important characteristics of human conduct resist measurement is a result, I believe, of the familiar confusion between behavior and performance. There are at least two reasons why behavior is often difficult to measure satisfactorily: much of it is covert and not easily observed; and it is often hard to specify exactly what behavior is required for exemplary performance, because two exemplars may behave in considerably different ways.

Table 2-2 shows two lists of descriptions of parts of several jobs. The A list describes accomplishments, and the B list describes hypothetically related behavior that clients of mine have seriously attempted to measure. I list these particular examples because, in each case, I found that the exemplar (on the accomplishment measure) did poorly on the behavior measure.

By the way, I would gladly accept the challenge of providing a measure of Donne's competence if more of my readers cared for poetry. But simpler materials will better serve to instruct in the methods I have devised. If I were to build a scale of poetic competence, be assured that I would not start by observing the *behavior* of poets. Donne's poems speak for themselves—clearly to a few, not too clearly for most. No end of analysis of his behavior would add one scintilla to a proper assessment of his performance. Besides, as I have said, Donne's behavior is

TABLE 2-2 EXAMPLES OF JOB MEASURES

Job	List A	List B
Salesperson	1. Sales prospects (quantity and quality)	1. Knowledge of the community (ratings)
Salesperson	2. Sales closed (volume)	2. Rapport with customers (ratings)
Dock loader	3. Trucks loaded (rate)	3. Hustle on the docks (ratings)
Teacher	4. Students' design of energy system (quality)	4. Engineering vocabulary (vocabulary test)
Product representative	5. Sales displays (volume and quality)	5 Sales presentations to store manager (number and ratings of quality)

no longer available. And behavior is not competence any more than an eight-cylinder engine is a Sunday drive in the country. Once we lock that concept firmly in mind, it becomes much easier to measure human competence.

APPLYING EXEMPLARY STANDARDS

Consider Dalton Windsor, who is a stone carver and chisels cornices, friezes, and gargoyles for the Bednarsh Cathedral Company. As we watch him, we cannot help but be impressed by the adroitness of his gnarled hands. But regardless of how those hands fly, they tell us nothing about the degree of Windsor's competence, since, for all we know, he may have never completed a figure. As with Donne, we do not need to observe Windsor himself in order to establish his worthiness. Perhaps we should try to construct a means for quantifying Windsor's competence, because the methods we use should be perfectly universal and as applicable to a manager as to a clerk—and applicable even to John Donne himself.

Obviously, we want rules of procedure that honor the fundamental logic of our subject matter, and that are as elementary and agreeable as we can make them. At least one rule of procedure is, I think, clearly established: We must begin by looking at performance and not at behavior. But before we proceed beyond this, refinements in the definition of competence are required.

If Windsor were the only stone carver who has ever lived, the evaluation of his competence might be fairly direct. He creates a product (gargoyles and the like) in some quantity, and to some standard of quality; his efforts also cost something, in labor, granite, tools,

energy, and the space to work. The simple formula $W = V/C$ (remember the First Leisurely Theorem) would require us only to measure these things. So, if Windsor created 25 figures a year with an average market value of $500, and at a cost of $10,000, we could say that he has netted $2500. Or, expressed as a ratio:

$$W = \frac{V}{C} = \frac{\text{Productivity} \times \text{Quality}}{\text{Cost}} = \frac{25 \times \$500}{\$10,000} = 1.25$$

This simple measure tells us that Windsor's accomplishment has a value that is 1.25 times the cost invested in it. We might use this worth index to conclude that Windsor has some degree of competence. If Windsor were the only stone carver in the world, we could hardly conclude anything else. But since he is not the only stone carver, we need a standard of comparison.

This number (1.25) is disturbing. We cannot sensibly compare it with the number we would get if we similarly measured, say, a stockbroker whose accomplishments were valued at $1 million at a cost of $100,000. We would then be comparing different accomplishments, and competence has to be stated as relative to a given end. Then with what do we compare Windsor's "score" of 1.25?

All Windsor's 1.25 score says, so far, is that the institution (Bednarsh Cathedral Company) in which we view his performance got a return of 1.25 times what it invested in Windsor. We can make sense of Windsor's score only by comparing it with scores of other stone carvers whom we have measured by identical instruments. If we find from the worth formula that the average stone carver has a score of 2.5, then by comparison Windsor's performance looks poor. Possibly he accomplishes the same value at twice the cost, or maybe half the value at the same cost. His *relative* return (or rate of return) is only half that of the average stone carver.

Although we shall not adopt the relative return measure, it has some advantages over the mere score of 1.25. It adds the necessary social dimension to the definition of competence, by stating *competence* comparatively. And by doing so, it reaches to the very heart of why we would ever want to measure competence other than as a parlor game. This comparison of worth yields a measure of *potential* for the improvement of performance. The discovery of such potential, and the fruits of realizing it, are, more than anything else, the reason for measuring human competence. This *kind* of measure will tell us as managers, teachers, parents—even as individuals—what relative impact we might have on worthy performance when we try to improve it. It is the basic measure of human potential.

But our example is flawed. The ratio of Windsor's worth index to the average worth index sets average performance as a standard. Such a standard is simply not worthy of us. We can reach higher; if we are to survive, it may be that we *must* reach higher. Too often in commerce, and more often in government and schools, the average performance of a group of people is established as the standard. The result is inevitable: mediocrity. We shall therefore adopt exemplary performance as the standard of comparison. Why?

It is time to recall the story of Mr. Sloe and Mr. Quik. Quik was the very best at accomplishing the things we were measuring, and Sloe's accomplishments could not have been poorer. Yet, when we viewed Sloe's repertory of behavior, we saw that he was not very far away from Quik's achievements. The ratio of their worth indices—as an accomplishment ratio—would tell us that Sloe's potential was virtually infinite. Yet we know, by observing Sloe's behavior, that we don't have far to go in order to realize that potential. A large PIP may require (and usually does) small remedies. But this is only an expression of the observation fundamental to this book: "There are great differences in what people accomplish, but small differences in their repertories of behavior." These small differences in behavior, more than anything, require the use of exemplary standards of comparison. A ratio using exemplary worth as a standard can tell us whether we have potential for improving performance, and it can help us set priorities. But a corresponding "behavior ratio" is useless. We do not need to know the "amount" of behavior missing from a repertory; rather, we wish to know which specific behaviors are required to fill the accomplishment potential. And when we look at it this way, we often find the key to realizing the potential that the PIP represents.

We see that Dalton Windsor exhibits low competence, even when compared with the average stone carver. His potential for improvement is really much greater than a comparison with the average would suggest. But no manner of behavioral quantifications will tell us what must be done to realize this vast potential. Perhaps all we need to do is discover that Windsor's tools are old and dull, and he needs to replace them. Then he becomes the finest stone carver in all of history—far better than the average.

To establish a really worthwhile standard against which to measure Windsor's comparative performance—his potential for improvement— why not set our sights high? We may, indeed, find it no more difficult to reach the high standard than the average one; but even if we do, the stakes will be more than worth it.

Windsor's story is oversimplified, but the point should be clear: Once we escape the notion that the best performers carry some deep,

mysterious secret—rather than, say, a set of sharp tools that look very much like everyone else's tools, only the least bit sharper—we shall not hesitate to establish the best performer as a standard. But when we confuse behavior with accomplishment, we are apt to conclude that performance deficiencies represent bottomless, empty pits. Naturally, we despair of filling them. However, if we are assured that correcting the tiniest defects in behavior can achieve the vast potentials in accomplishment, we shall eagerly try to establish the best as our standard.

To set the best performance as the basis for measuring competence—and therefore the potential for competence—implies that all people could achieve what the best has achieved. Aside from certain obvious physical limitations, I find the implication satisfying, and by no means an abandonment of reason. My own experiences, both in the world of work and in teaching, have convinced me that this standard is practical.

WHO IS THE EXEMPLAR?

But who is the exemplar? The exemplar must always be defined in terms of a particular accomplishment, because a person whose performance serves as an exemplar in the pursuit of one accomplishment may not be the exemplar in the pursuit of another.

I shall define exemplary performance as the most sustained worthy performance that we can reasonably expect to attain. This need not be the performance of the historically best performer, because we may have reason to believe that we can improve on the exemplar. But if not, we should take exemplary performance as the standard, because it usually is reasonable to expect that others can be brought to achieve that standard. Sometimes, the highest performer works under some advantage that we cannot reasonably expect others to have. For example, the fastest stone carver may have access to a quality of stone that it is impossible to provide for other carvers. If that is so, we must pare our standard accordingly. But we should never pare our standard unless we are certain that it is impossible to meet.

The worst misconception about exemplary performers is that they work harder, know more, and are more highly motivated than others. These things sometimes may be true. But in years of observing exemplary performers I have discovered that the opposite is generally true: *Exemplary performers do things more easily than others do them.*

To explain what I mean by an exemplar, we can consider the class of organizations whose principal goal is to construct cathedrals. Presumably, we could identify the exemplary organization—the one that

builds the finest cathedrals relative to the cost. Suppose we discovered that this was the Bednarsh Cathedral Company, the outfit that employs Dalton Windsor. We can assume that Windsor makes some contributions to the magnificent performance of Bednarsh Cathedral; but we need not accept him as the exemplary gargoyle carver, although gargoyle carving is one responsibility that must be discharged in creating really nice cathedrals. Indeed, the exemplary gargoyle carver may be in the employ of the very worst cathedral builder. If Bednarsh's management wishes to find the gargoyle-carving exemplar, it should not confine itself to its own craftsmen. Or suppose that Dalton Windsor does turn out to be the gargoyle-carving exemplar. We still cannot assume that he is the exemplar of all the duties required to fulfill that responsibility. One such duty is the selection of the right block of granite. Perhaps Windsor does not perform this duty as well as the very worst gargoyle carver, who turns out to be the exemplar of stone selection. The point is that the selection of a standard of measurement, the exemplar, must be done relative to the particular accomplishment we wish to measure.

Once we have identified the exemplar for any given accomplishment, we can quantify the potential for improving the performance (PIP) of that accomplishment by any person or group. The PIP is expressed by comparing two worth indices; and if we use the exemplar as our standard, the exemplary worth index must be the basis for the comparison. So, to measure the PIP of stone carvers in the Bednarsh Cathedral Company, we could establish the average worth index of the carvers and compare it with the worth index of our exemplar, Windsor.

Suppose that the average stone carver produced 40 gargoyles a year, with an average sales value of $800 each, and at a cost of $20,000. The average worth index would be

$$\frac{40 \times \$800}{\$20,000} = 1.6 = W_{av}$$

On the other hand, if Windsor created 80 gargoyles a year of identical quality, and at the same cost, then his index is

$$\frac{80 \times \$800}{\$20,000} = 3.2 = W_{ex}$$

Then we can express the stone carver's PIP in Bednarsh as

$$PIP = \frac{W_{ex}}{W_{av}} = \frac{3.2}{1.6} = 2.0$$

This tells us that average stone carvers have the potential for at least doubling the worth of their gargoyle performance. Windsor is twice as good as the average on an important dimension of worthy performance: productivity. Later, I shall introduce worksheets that will make the efforts to measure competence practical. The PIP, as I am discussing it here, is primarily conceptual—an idea of how much improvement we can reasonably expect when we set out to engineer a performance system. A PIP of 5.0, for example, tells us that we could improve typical performance fivefold, and, in doing so, increase the value of accomplishments or decrease the cost of attaining them by a similar degree. A PIP of 1.1 tells us that the exemplary performer is only 10 percent better than the typical performer, and that there is not much possibility of achieving a lot of improvement—unless we can improve the exemplar's performance and therefore establish an even higher exemplary standard.

PIPS I HAVE KNOWN

How big are PIPs, and what do they mean to us? I have observed many PIPs—in government agencies, commerce, schools, and elsewhere. A PIP as large as 5, or even 10 or 20, is not uncommon. But a rather small PIP can have considerable significance.

In 1954, the Cleveland Indians baseball team won 111 of 154 games, compared with an average team's wins of 77. This performance gives a PIP of 1.44, a high one for any sport. For individual players, the PIP for getting on base (as crudely measured by the batting average) is 1.61. Back in 1901, Napolean Lajoi hit 0.426, compared with an average of about 0.265 in those days. In 1921, Babe Ruth scored 177 runs, the most in modern times, compared with an average of 87.5, giving a runs-scored PIP of 2.02 for that season and one of the highest PIPs I have found in athletics. In medium-distance running, Jim Ryan in 1967 completed 1500 meters at a rate of 7.039 meters per second, compared with something like 5.5 meters per second for the average competitor at that distance, and giving a PIP of only 1.3. Mark Spitz in the 1972 Olympics swam the 100-meter free style at a rate of 1.953 meters per second against an average competitor of about 1.7 meters per second. This swimming PIP is 1.1, showing that the 100-meter swim is intensely competitive. If the average duffer completes a round of golf in 110 strokes, compared with a course record of 64 strokes, the PIP is 1.72; but compared with the average professional competitor who makes the round in 75 strokes, the PIP is only 1.17, showing that golf is one of the most competitive of contests.

So, measures of athletic productivity reflect the intense competition, and the greatest degree of "natural" selection. At work and at school, PIPs run considerably higher, showing much more potential for increased competence than we find in sports. My figures are not exact, but here are some PIPs I have observed:

Insurance sales by salespersons	14
Packaging machine production	2.5
Reading teachers	10
Printing shop management	6
Grocery store management	5
Individual clerical productivity, microfilm reading	1.75
Departmental clerical productivity, telephone book entries	1.6
Encyclopedia sales	12
Training material development	25
Metal fabricating plant management	3
Coverage of safety inspectors	4
Teaching certain mathematics topics	30
Lawyers, damage awards	20
Sales of advertising space	12
Filling a cosmetic order (accuracy)	1.3

In general, I can say that in athletics, PIPs almost invariably run less than 2, and usually less than 1.5, whereas in the world of work PIPs of 5 or more are very common. The PIPs of individual sales performance are among the high ones—usually over 5, and often over 10. Management PIPs, measured by comparing similar department stores and plants as profit or cost centers, tend to run around 3 or more, suggesting that management is not nearly so competitive as it would like to think. Routine jobs, like clerical work, normally display PIPs between 1.2 and 3.0. When a world-of-work PIP is low (around 2, or even less), it is because the jobs are either very routine, exceptionally well managed, or extremely competitive and demanding. For example, airline pilots, measured by the number of miles flown safely, will have PIPs near 1; less competence would not be tolerated.

DIMENSIONS OF PERFORMANCE MEASUREMENT

Performance can be measured in many ways, and we need to sort them out first to make sense of them. So far, I have treated performance measures in a rather abstract way, in order to establish the concept of

the PIP. But in practice, a performer may be defective in production along many dimensions; and to find solutions to a performance problem we need to make fine distinctions within the measurement classes.

We shall examine these distinctions shortly. But first, I want to caution you not to be misled by all the arithmetic in the examples. When we analyze competence, we try to *classify* the conditions of performance rather accurately; yet we seldom require precision in quantifying it. Scientists and physical engineers must demand a high degree of precision. In fact, they try to manipulate forces in order to achieve very precise results. But in the pursuit of competence, we are looking for opportunity—the opportunity to improve our own or someone else's performance. And because opportunities are so ample, there is no need to use a micrometer to find them. If we observe performance systematically, keeping our eye on accomplishments, the opportunities will jump out and seize us. This point needs to be stressed, since I have too often seen my students become so immersed in the arithmetic of PIPs that they lose sight of variances so large they hardly need quantifying. As an example, we might examine the differences in productivity between the two imaginary groups in Table 2-3. The individual PIP is an unusually low 1.09, and the group PIP is 1.06. Clearly not much room to improve performance here (assuming that the figure of 75 is the true exemplar). (Such low PIPs are rare in the world of work.) Yet the difference between the average of each group is "statistically significant"—meaning that this difference is probably not due to a chance error in sampling. Within our perspective, then, we are seldom looking for differences so small that we would have to confirm their significance statistically. To the contrary. Mathematical precision is not required to

TABLE 2-3   PRODUCTIVITY DIFFERENCES

	Group A	*Group B*
	67	72
	75 (apparent exemplar)	64
	69	67
	72	65
	73	68
	69	61
	74	66
	69	63
	66	74
	73	65
Average	70.7	66.5

discover truly significant differences, except in rare instances. So, as we examine the dimensions of worthy performance, we need not worry greatly about having precise instruments for measuring along these dimensions.

And since I use the word *dimension* loosely here—not in the same fine sense as it is used in physics—I need a new word suitable for this subject. The word I shall use for these classes of measurement is *requirements*. There are three: *quality, quantity* (or *productivity*), and *cost*. And it so happens that each of the three major requirements of worthy performance consists of three requirements itself:

1. Quality
   (a) Accuracy
   (b) Class
   (c) Novelty
2. Quantity (or Productivity)
   (a) Rate
   (b) Timeliness
   (c) Volume
3. Cost
   (a) Labor (behavior repertories)
   (b) Material (environmental support)
   (c) Management

When we measure an accomplishment, any one or more of these requirements may be relevant, and one of our principal tasks is to identify them. As an example, for the stenographer's accomplishment of "typed letters," rate and accuracy will be relevant, and sometimes timeliness; but certainly not novelty, class, or energy. For a sculptor, class and novelty will be relevant, but not rate. To help you make these distinctions, I shall briefly define each dimension.

1. Quality
   (a) *Accuracy.* The degree to which an accomplishment matches a model without errors of omission or commission.
   (b) *Class.* Comparative superiority of an accomplishment, beyond mere accuracy. For example, two short

stories may both be technically accurate; but one is more effective, appealing, or sells better. Several kinds of units may be used to measure *class:*

(i) Market value, or simply what something sells for: High-quality (class) furniture is likely to bring a higher price.

(ii) Judgment points; show dogs are judged and given points—so many for erect ears, and so on. Olympic acrobats and skaters are similarly judged. It is a system widely used, both formally and informally.

(iii) Physical measures: Chemists and engineers often rate accomplishments by simply measuring some quality. A batch of rubber that is too soft is assigned to lower-quality lots to be used in an application that does not require high quality.

(iv) Opinion ratings: In these, people are polled and can respond as they like. A film wins an Oscar, or a ballplayer's performance is judged "most valuable" by people who are not given a point system or market criteria to follow.

Each of these measures of class can have its usefulness, but the definition of *class* is inherent in the method of measurement adopted.

(c) *Novelty.* Inventors, artists, and designers often strive to achieve this. For inventors, the measure that might be applied is useful variance along some important dimension—such as gas mileage in an auto engine. If an inventor develops a system for getting 100 miles per gallon without sacrificing other qualities, the accomplishment is truly novel. For artists, we probably have to resort to a judgmental point system or an opinion rating.

(d) *Quality combinations.* Sometimes, quality is clearly the product of more than one quality requirement. The great gasoline engine inventor must preserve accuracy and produce novelty; if either is missing, the quality is zero. The dimension we assign to these accomplishments would be expressed as requirement products, such as $Q = f(a \cdot n)$.

2. Quantity (or Productivity)

   (a) *Rate.* This is the most common measure of productivity, and it applies when "bulk" is time-sensitive: "pieces produced per hour" or "time to completion."

   (b) *Timeliness.* It applies when time, not bulk, is the key consideration: "getting Cinderella home before midnight"; "a letter mailed before sundown"; "a manufacturing line running by the time the night shift arrives."

   (c) *Volume.* This applies when bulk is important but is not time-sensitive. "How many fish did you catch?" or "How many sales did you make?"

3. Cost

   (a) *Labor.* The amount expended on purchasing all the necessary labor to make an accomplishment, including direct overhead, benefits, wages, insurance, and taxes.

   (b) *Material.* All material costs required to make an accomplishment, including supplies, tools, space, energy.

   (c) *Management.* By this I mean supervision, its supports, public taxes, and internal allocations of general and administrative costs associated with an accomplishment.

Table 2-4 shows several examples of performance requirements that are both relevant to an accomplishment and reasonable. For example, we would hardly consider *accuracy* a requirement of a man running a 50-meter dash, because we assume that he will run in the right direction. Accuracy, or any other requirement, is relevant only when people's accomplishments will vary significantly with respect to them.

Table 2-4 might also show that jobs which seem unmeasurable are actually measurable once we identify their accomplishments and relevant requirements. Many jobs that people say cannot be measured ("you can't measure show-horse breeding—it's an art") seem that way only because we are thinking of behavior rather than accomplishment. How would we measure the behavior required in selecting good breeding stock? I haven't the faintest idea. But we can measure results, provided that: (1) we identify them; and (2) we establish some requirements for them. Fashion (behavior) will never replace class (accomplishment).

TABLE 2-4 EXAMPLES OF PERFORMANCE REQUIREMENTS

Job or Role	Accomplishments	Measures	Relevant Requirements
Telephone operator	Customer connections	1. Average work time per call 2. Answering time 3. Error performance 4. Freedom from supervision	1. Rate 2. Rate 3. Accuracy 4. Management
Chewing gum factory manager	Inventory demands filled	1. Cost efficiency (or profitability)	1. Accuracy 2. Timeliness 3. Rate 4. Cost
Chewing gum factory manager	Job assignments	1. Job failures and successes: how often and how big	1. Accuracy 2. Rate 3. Cost
Fashion designer	Style designs	1. Manufacturing constraints 2. Ready for season	1. Accuracy 2. Timeliness

	Output	Criteria	Standards
Show-horse breeder	Show prizes	3. Manufacturing costs	3. Cost
		4. Fashion competitive	4. Novelty
		5. Price competitive	5. Class
Show-horse breeder	Stables clean	1. Size of prizes	1. Class
		2. Frequency of prizes	2. Rate
		3. Budget performance	3. Cost
Insurance salesperson	Insurance sales	1. Sanitary standards	1. Accuracy
		1. Sales quota	1. Volume
		2. Travel costs	2. Materials
		3. Product mix	3. Accuracy
Vocational teacher	Job-prepared students	1. Kinds of jobs	1. Class
		2. Job performance	2. Accuracy
		3. Number of students successful	3. Volume
Vocational teacher	Homework assignments	1. Relevance	1. Accuracy
		2. Coverage	2. Accuracy
		3. Student interest	3. Class
		4. Coordinated with training	4. Timeliness

UNITS OF MEASUREMENT

Like physical dimensions, requirements can often be translated into different units of measurement. And we must do this before we can begin to measure performance.

Velocity, for example, is a dimension in physics. Even though we have identified it as the relevant dimension, we are not yet ready to measure. We next have to establish a measurement scale with some units. We can measure velocity as miles per hour or as kilometers per second. The same dimension can be measured in many different units—in fact, in as many different units as we might choose.

Similarly, with requirements. For example, we can measure sales volume as "number of policies sold" or as "sales revenues." Once we establish that quality, say, is a significant requirement, we must then decide on the units to measure it. This problem becomes further complicated when we combine certain requirements into a single measure. For example, if we set both sales volume and cost as requirements of a sale, we may want to express them as a ratio in dollar units:

$$\frac{\text{Revenues}}{\text{Sales Costs}} = \frac{\text{Volume}}{\text{Cost}}$$

There are no special rules for choosing units of measurement other than the common rules of arithmetic, but there are some guides to help us make the decisions. The first decision is determining how we need to use the measurements. Performance analysts have somewhat different needs than, say, first-line supervisors. Analysts, acting as consultants or specialists, approach performance that frequently has not been measured properly, if at all. They must therefore establish the relevant requirements of an accomplishment and useful units of measurement before they can discover any standards of performance. So, if they are to measure sales of insurance policies as an accomplishment, they must ask themselves some basic questions. For example: Is the cost of selling a relevant variable? Is the rate of selling relevant? Is the product mix an important quality requirement? If only the total sales revenues are important (for example, if sales costs are reasonably fixed), they can take as their performance measures this simple unit: "dollars of revenue per month."

Next, it is important to determine if we have units to measure everything we want to measure. It is easy to overlook measures of important requirements. To avoid this kind of oversight, there is no substitute for checking each accomplishment against each of the nine possible requirements. An example will help describe the recommended "checklist" thought process.

Suppose that we want to measure the clerical performance of pro-

cessing an insurance claim. We begin at the top of our list, as in Table 2-5. By this step-by-step process, we arrive at five possible measures, only three of which apply to the clerks, and four to the supervisors. These five measures can be expressed by a summary measure for the branch:

$$\text{Department Efficiency} = \frac{\text{Claims Completed}}{\text{Processing Costs}}$$

Another decision to make is to whose performance does our measure apply. One question can settle it: "Who has control over variations in the measure?" Obviously, it is unfair to apply the "department efficiency" ratio (above) to the clerk, because the clerk has no control over many of the costs of processing claims, like overtime and supervisory costs. The clerk does have responsibility for the rate of processing claims, but so does the supervisor and the branch manager. In short, we must never apply a measure to a performer who cannot be held accountable for that performance.

Finally, there is the decision of determining whether we have measured the same thing twice. Measures of rate and labor costs are tricky, because the greatest effect that high-rate performance *often* (but not always) has is to reduce the cost of productive labor. As we go through our list of requirements, we need to ask, "Have I already measured this?"

A subtle cause of measurement redundancy may occur, too, when we fail to separate accomplishments properly by levels of generality. For example, suppose that we describe two of a salesperson's responsibilities as:

1. A list of sales suspects (unqualified prospects)
2. A list of qualified prospects

We might list these as two independent accomplishments, simply because one occurs first. But when we measure the rate at which these two things are accomplished, we may find that we are essentially measuring the same thing twice—since the rate of getting suspects may be the largest determinant of the rate of getting qualified prospects. When this redundancy occurs, we have probably ranked the responsibilities poorly—confused accomplishments with subaccomplishments. A better way of describing this part of the salesperson's job would be:

Accomplishments	Subaccomplishments
Qualified prospects	1. List of suspects
	2. Qualification data

TABLE 2-5   UNITS-OF-MEASUREMENT GUIDE

	Questions	*Units*
QUALITY QUESTIONS		
Accuracy:	What are the effects of errors in processing claims?	
	a. They can result in overpayments.	a. Percentage of overpay-ment
	b. They can result in costly adjustments if the claim is underpaid.	b. Percentage of claims re-quiring adjustment
Class:	Are there degrees of quality in processing claims beyond the standards of accuracy?	
	a. No.	None
Novelty:	Can claims be processed in original ways?	
	a. No.	None
QUANTITY QUESTIONS		
Rate:	Is it reasonable to expect significant varia-tions in the rate that claims are processed?	
	a. Yes	a. $\dfrac{\text{Claims Processed}}{\text{Labor-Hours}}$
Timeliness:	Are there likely to be damaging delays in processing claims—and what would the damage be?	
	a. No. Even in the poorest offices, claims are processed in sufficient time.	None
Volume:	Can a good performer process a larger vol-ume of claims—independent of the rate of production?	

*Volume is not a time-sensitive measure. A salesperson may vary in the rate of rates (sales per day) and also in the volume (revenues per sale). Aside from sales, volume requirements are rare.

Now we see that getting a list of suspects is simply a part of the responsibility for getting a list of qualified prospects; and the rate of one will depend on the rate of the other. The discovery, then, of a redundant measure in a list of accomplishments should lead us to reexamine the way we have described the job.

COMPARATIVE PIPS

The question of whose performance a measure fits is not a simple one, and requires some discussion. Obviously, if clerks in, say, a government agency have a large PIP, we may best be able to improve their

Questions	*Units*
a. No. There is a fixed input of claims to be processed, and it is as valuable to process one claim as another.*	None

COST QUESTIONS

Labor: Are there likely to be significant variations in labor costs that are not wholly reflected in the rate measure?

a. Supervisors can permit too much overtime, but clerks have no control over this.	a. $\dfrac{\text{Overtime}}{\text{Straight Time}}$ (for supervisors' performance only)

Materials: Are there likely to be significant variations in the wear and tear on equipment used to process claims; or variations in material scrapped or wasted?

a. No.	None

Management: Would appreciable variations be expected in the amount of supervision or other indirect costs (overhead and the like)?

a. Branch managers can use too many supervisory hours. b. Branch managers have some small degree of control over the office rents paid—but too small to take seriously.	a. $\dfrac{\text{Supervisory Wages}}{\text{Total Wages}}$ (for branch managers only)

performance by working directly with them. Or we may have a greater economic impact by improving the performance of their supervisors or managers. To find the real locus of economic opportunity, we often need to make comparisons of PIPs at different levels in an organization—for example, different levels of management having essentially the same mission. The average employee in an office may be only a third as productive as the exemplar. Yet the cause of this PIP of 3 may not lie in the employee, but in the supervisors. Study Table 2-6, the clerical productivity figures for three selected supervisory groups. It is not unlike the data Frank Roby examined. (Like most data in this book, these are derived from real materials, and only rounded off or otherwise simplified.)

TABLE 2-6   COMPARATIVE CLERICAL PRODUCTIVITY (units per hour)

Supervisor A		Supervisor B		Supervisor C	
Clerk	*U/hr*	*Clerk*	*U/hr*	*Clerk*	*U/hr*
1	65	11	62	21	141
2	65	12	61	22	137
3	63	13	61	23	137
4	60	14	60	24	134
5	60	15	59	25	130
6	58	16	50	26	130
7	56	17	50	27	126
8	54	18	50	28	121
9	51	19	45	29	120
10	48	20	40	30	119
Average	58.0	Average	53.8	Average	129.5

The average for all 30 clerks is a productivity of 80.4 units per hour. The *clerical* PIP is then (assuming quality and costs are constant):

$$\text{PIP Clerk} = \frac{141}{80.4} = 1.75$$

This is an appreciable PIP.

Of much greater significance, however, is the supervisory PIP (calculated here by taking the average of all groups *except*[2] the highest):

$$\text{PIP Super.} = \frac{129.5}{55.9} = 2.32$$

Clearly, the difference between ordinary supervisors and the exemplar is much more significant than that between the ordinary clerks and the exemplary clerk. The largest clerical PIP *within* a group is 1.15. This tells us immediately that what we should do to improve clerical performance is look first to the supervisors. Two of the supervisors are relatively incompetent. But Supervisor C is doing something right, and we should find out what it is.

If we merely take averages and compare them with the exemplar, the PIP between groups often will not be so great as the total PIP for individuals. That is why a relatively smaller PIP between groups can have considerable significance. For a more precise treatment of data such as these we can resort to statistical methods, like the analysis of variance. If there is a statistically significant difference between the group averages, then we should look to the performance of the manager of that group for the reason, as well as to individual employees.

Comparisons of PIPs can sometimes be rather complex. Suppose I have two groups of people who perform as those in Table 2-7 do (the nature of the units doesn't matter for the purpose of this discussion). Supervisor A's group is greatly superior to Supervisor B's group. We can assume that if we could get B to perform as A does, B's people would improve their performance fivefold. But notice employee 11. This person is three times as good as the average of the B group, but not nearly so good as the worst employee in group A. Yet employee 11 might be the true exemplar and might perform even better than employee 1 if transferred to group A. Perhaps employee 11 has a technique superior to anyone else's—one that has three times the potential of employee 1. But the superiority of this technique might not be apparent simply because of the disastrous ways Supervisor B schedules the work of that group. The true exemplary standard would be 600 units, although the data do not show this. Examples of this kind are rare, and there is no substitute for close observation to reveal them. Of course, PIPs can, and often do, reveal themselves at higher levels of management than the first-line supervisor.

Table 2-8 is a stylized, simplified representation of some real data for four different automobile metal fabrication plants. Average fender production in these four plants is 23 units per hour, giving a PIP of 1.54, which is very significant when such large units as plants are being compared. But the average supervisory line PIP, taken one plant at a time, is only 1.2. Actually, most of the variance can be attributed to differences in productivity between companies. With Universal Motors used as the exemplar, the Specific Motors PIP is 1.59. The hourly employee PIP in factories like these is extremely low, because each employee, like a mule, is attached to an assembly line that determines

TABLE 2-7   COMPARISONS OF GROUPS

Supervisor A		*Supervisor B*	
Employee no.	*Performance*	*Employee no.*	*Performance*
1	200	11	120
2	199	12	30
3	199	13	29
4	196	14	28
5	196	15	28
6	196	16	28
7	195	17	28
8	192	18	27
9	191	19	27
10	191	20	26

TABLE 2-8   MANUFACTURING PLANT VARIANCES (units per hour)

| | Specific Motors, Inc. | | Universal Motors, Inc. | |
	Plant A	Plant B	Plant C	Plant D
Average fender line production	15	19	24	30
Best fender line production	19	25	27	33

the rate of production. The mass of incompetence in this business can be found in company management at a level above the plant management. Naturally, this management finds it more comfortable to lay the blame on low worker productivity.

It is of course quite possible to find considerable PIPs at all levels—in hourly employees, supervisors, and middle and top management. But, as you will see later, it makes the most sense to begin a program of improvement at the highest level where a significant PIP exists. Yet, in my experience in the world of work, management tends to think in the other direction. If things aren't going well, put the blame on the hourly employee; and if that argument cannot be made to stick, try the first-line supervisor.

SPURIOUS PIPS

People confronted by PIPs in which they are involved commonly dismiss them: "You can't really compare these departments; they are much too different." And so, every chewing gum factory is said to be completely unlike any other; even clerical units performing the same work are declared hopelessly incomparable. But no serious analyst of human competence will take these assessments seriously, unless there really is a difference: for example, one plant is automated and another is not. What these people *are* saying is that PIPs represent spurious differences—differences resulting from some condition that has nothing to do with human performance. I say this is nonsense, as this case study illustrates.

One division in Waldo, Inc., a national company that compiles and prints city directories, does all the clerical work required to handle new directory entries or changes in the old ones. Each department of the clerical division handles one or more directories. Waldo's Personnel Department has employed a consultant to help develop a course in human relations for first-line clerical supervisors. Fortunately for Waldo, Inc., the consultant, Dolly Moulton, is a

long-time associate of Frank Roby, and she asks to look through production data of clerical departments—particularly the daily records of individual clerks. People in the Personnel Department are certain that she has the wrong approach to human relations training. And because no individual production data are available, Moulton has to collect her own. Table 2-9 is a simplified representation of what she found (a unit of clerical production is called an *entry*).

After studying these data, Moulton points out to her client that the difference between Books (departments) seemed rather large.

"But," her client says, "there is no way to compare departments; they are all so different. They have widely differing procedures, and some of them are partly mechanized—they have computer help. Besides, what does this have to do with human relations or supervisory rapport?"

Moulton is quite willing to believe that different departments have different procedures—at least that could account for some of them being so incompetent. She calculates her PIPs like this:*

Clerical PIP	3.1	(Data are not in Table 2-9.)
Supervisory PIP	2.1	
Book Manager PIP	1.8	
Divisional PIP	3.0	

These PIPs are all quite sizable, indicating great potential for improvement in competence. But the client has insisted that these variances are spurious and are caused by factors that have nothing to do with human performance— factors like computerization and different procedures. So Moulton must investigate these claims. Beginning with computer mechanization, here is what she finds:

Book I	Computerized	24.0	
Book II	Noncomputerized	16.8	Entries per hour
Book III	Noncomputerized	8.1	
Book IV	Computerized	5.4	

*Actual PIPs were calculated differently, but these relationships make the point. In the example, it must be assumed that cost and quality are constant, which is reasonable.

TABLE 2-9   CLERICAL PRODUCTION, WALDO, INC. (Entries per hour)

	Carolina Division		Georgia Division	
	Book I	*Book II*	*Book III*	*Book IV*
Supervisor A	28.0	23.0	11.1	7.2
Supervisor B	24.1	16.9	8.4	4.9
Supervisor C	19.9	10.4	4.7	4.1
Average	24.0	16.8	8.1	5.4
		20.4		6.8

So much for the computerization argument, although Moulton has other reasons to believe that the difference between Book I and Book II might genuinely be caused by computerization. But computerization is clearly not the biggest factor. What about the difference between Books III and IV? She also finds little to support the claim for other spurious sources of variance—all except one: different procedures. She discovers that the Georgia Division uses different general procedures, and these are clearly inferior. And Book IV, she finds, has even more inefficient variations on these procedures.

Clearly the greatest and most important PIP is divisional. One division is downright incompetent. When she suggests to her client that perhaps they ought to begin by improving divisional management rather than first-line supervisors, the client responds with dismay: "But that's not what we were asked to do. We're responsible for clerical and supervisory training."

It seems a shame to Moulton that a company with so many troubles should pursue some will-o'-the-wisp called human relations training. The really poor conditions for production in the Georgia Division, in her opinion, generate more troubles for human relationships than a dozen tactless supervisors. When Moulton examines the organizational chart of Waldo, Inc. (Figure 2-1), she gets a new idea about where to attribute some of the large PIP.

Clearly, the lowest level of management that could be responsible for common divisional practices is the President of the company, Monty Bloomfield himself. A regional V.P., for example, is responsible only for the divisions in one region, and decisions at the regional level would not affect divisions in other regions. So, if someone wanted to change anybody's performance in order to accomplish common divisional clerical procedures, that person whose performance needs changing would be the head of the company.

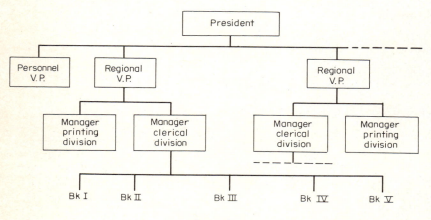

FIGURE 2-1   Partial organization of Waldo, Inc.

When Moulton reports this to her client, the response is immediate: "Me go to Monty Bloomfield? Not on your life! I don't even get to see my own vice president."

Once we try to trace the PIP to its source, it can lead us to unexpected places.

Of course, PIPs can be inflated by spurious factors, too. The exemplar of insurance sales may live in a place where people just naturally love to buy insurance. The high-PIP chewing gum factory may be located in an area where the humidity makes it hard to package gum. Such factors need to be taken into account; but even then, the analyst of competence will discover that the major sources of the PIP are the much more easily controllable factors that impinge directly on performance. An exemplar may have the luck, but luck is more even-handed than we would like to admit. Far more likely, the exemplar is simply doing something right; and if we are not afraid to acknowledge the existence of an exemplar, we can find out what that is. (In Chapter 6, I discuss a way of taking spurious factors into account in measuring performance.) These examples should make it clear that the measurement of performance in an institution requires a considerable amount of sorting things out.

MEASUREMENT AND THE PERFORMANCE AUDIT

Measurements of performance require some care in keeping things straight, because most performance situations are complex and "multidimensional." They are also "multilevel." For example, if we want to measure the performance of the Bednarsh Cathedral Company, we can look at several aspects of the company's total performance (sales, production, purchasing, etc.). We can also look at the performance of stone carvers, salespersons, and purchasing agents; at that of managers and supervisors. We can observe the performance of certain tasks, such as a stone carver's selection of stone or the salesperson's list of prospects, at an even more narrow focus. Naturally, all of these are accomplishments and not behaviors, and each represents a different potential for improving performance. Further, each of these accomplishments, at whatever level we focus on it, may have several significant requirements. The study of even a small institution, then, offers the possibility of quite a number of performance measures. This could be a formidable task except that we have methods and principles to guide us toward measuring only the performance that has real economic potential.

One principle that is extremely helpful is to start with general measures before going to more specific ones. Remember, our only

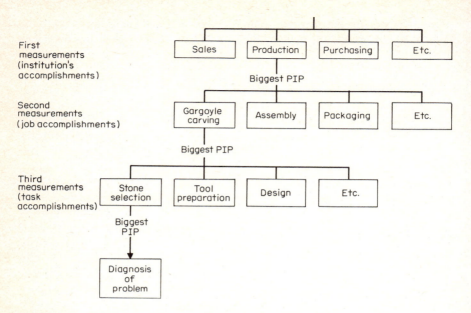

FIGURE 2-2   Advantages of measuring from general to specific.

reason for measuring is to discover our opportunities for performance engineering. If I begin by measuring the accomplishments of Bednarsh rather than those of stone carvers, I may find that my greatest opportunities for improvement are in sales, not in production. But if I begin by measuring the performance of a task such as stone selection, I have no way of comparing stone-carving opportunities with others. The performance of the institution provides a context for interpreting the performance of people.

As Figure 2-2 shows, if we were to proceed from the specific to the general, we could get hopelessly lost—and we would surely waste a good deal of time and effort. That way, we would have to look at all of the specific details in turn to discover where the problems are. But even when we found specific deficiencies, we would be hard pressed to interpret their meaning. Only by knowing that production is a significant problem are we able to see that poor stone selection is a significant cause. So by proceeding as we do in Figure 2-2, we avoid the necessity for measuring much performance where there are relatively small PIPs. (In Chapter 6, I discuss this procedure in greater detail.)

To make performance-measurement procedures as simple and systematic as possible, I have devised a method that I call the *performance audit*.[3] One useful tool for conducting a performance audit is a worksheet that I call a *performance table*. Keep in mind that to measure performance we must do several things, and in this sequence:

1. Identify accomplishments.
2. Identify requirements.
3. Identify exemplary performance.
4. Measure exemplary performance (W_{ex}).
5. Measure typical performance (W_t).
6. Compute the PIP.
7. Translate the PIP into "stakes"—into economic potential.

These steps constitute the performance audit and make up the columns of the performance table, as the following case study illustrates.

David Wise is asked by the Northernmost Gas Company (a utility known locally as NoGas) to develop a training course for upgrading the skills of the people who sell residential gas-fired air conditioning. It seems that the company is losing money on air conditioning, and the management assumes that the salespeople are the culprits. Wise sagely convinces the management to let him look first at the performance of the company as a whole. His subsequent analysis reveals an unusually low sales PIP of only 1.1—meaning that sales performance could be increased by 10 percent if all salespeople could do as well as the exemplar. Many other observations confirm Wise's suspicion that the problem lies elsewhere, and that NoGas salespeople are, as a group, exceptionally competent. He takes a clue from these salespeople, who say that builders and homeowners are buying less because they can't get satisfactory service. So Wise makes an analysis of air-conditioning service personnel.

Wise seeks the exemplary service employee, who turns out to be the only woman on the service force. According to all known measures and opinions, Marilyn Blue is by far the best serviceperson. The local mythology is that she is smarter than the men—and, after all, she is the only service employee with substantial college credits.

Wise constructs a performance table to examine service at the first (departmental) level of analysis—asking how well the service mission is performed as a whole. Table 2-10 summarizes this analysis, beginning with the primary accomplishment of the Service Department,* and describing exemplary performance as a standard. He finds three areas of service with economic potential:

1. Rate (productivity)—the number of service calls made a year. Blue makes 1500 compared with an average of 900—a PIP of 1.67. If the typical serviceperson could perform as well as Blue, a theoretical savings of $448,056 per year is possible.

---

*Table 2-10 is a somewhat simplified version. The patient reader may laboriously trace through the computations.

TABLE 2-10   PERFORMANCE TABLE: CENTRAL HOME AIR-CONDITIONING SERVICE PERFORMANCE—FIRST-LEVEL ANALYSIS

(1) Accomplishments	(2) Standards		(3) Impact of PIP	Actual Value or Cost of Performance			(7) Total	(8)* PIP	(9) Value of Correcting PIP
	Requirement	Exemplar		(4) Typical Performance	(5) Unit Value or Cost	(6) No. of Service-persons			
Operating central home air conditioning	Number of service calls (productivity)	1500 calls per year	Excess labor costs, etc.	900 per year	$17.78 per call	70	$1,120,140	$1.67 = \dfrac{1500}{900}$	$448,056
	Minimum replacement of AC units (quality)	Only one replacement in 5 years (0.2 per year)	Cost of equipment	0.5 per year	$2500 per AC unit	70	$87,500	$2.5 = \dfrac{0.05}{0.02}$	$52,500
	Minimum callbacks (quality)	20 per year	Excess labor costs, etc.	30 per year	$17.78	70	$37,338	$1.5 = \dfrac{30}{20}$	$12,446

etc.

*To get column 9, multiply column 7 by $1 - 1/PIP$ for costs or $PIP - 1$ for values.

2. Quality, so that units don't have to be replaced. The larger PIP of 2.5 is impressive, but it doesn't translate into as much money. Only $52,500 could be saved by making the department exemplary.

3. Quality, by decreasing callbacks because the job wasn't done right the first time. Here, a PIP of 1.5 translates into only $12,446 a year—which is surprising, because NoGas management had said that this was the significant area in which service could be improved.

Wise concludes that priority attention should be given to speedy service. Why is Blue so much more productive than the other service personnel? The service manager and the personnel V.P. agree on two reasons:

1. She is smarter.
2. She takes more pride in her work.

Wise considers these typical examples of behavior cultism to be nonsense. If such explanations are valid, the cause is lost, because it is just too hard to make people smarter and prouder than they already are. Management agrees, and asks him to reconsider sales training. But Wise goes to the second (or job) level* of analysis—looking at the major accomplishments of the service job. Table 2-11 summarizes a performance table describing, at the second (job) level of analysis, two of the major outputs of a service employee:

1. Trouble diagnosis
2. Trouble correction

According to the table, the major reason why Blue is more productive is because she diagnoses problems faster (not more accurately) than other people. It takes her 20 minutes to find out what's wrong with an air conditioner, whereas the average serviceperson spends 70 minutes at it. This has a potential worth of $410,299 a year to NoGas—or roughly 40 percent of its service costs. Once a problem is diagnosed, speed of correcting it is not a big factor.

Wise wonders, "Why is Marilyn Blue faster at diagnosis?"

"She has a real feel for the equipment," the service manager says. "It's uncanny—not something you can teach people."

"Behavior cult mythology," Wise says to himself, and proceeds in his analysis to the third (task) level, looking at the component tasks of each job accomplishment (see Table 2-12). He finds that Blue does three things to diagnose problems. She (and every other serviceperson) inserts thermometers into seven wells in the air conditioner and takes their readings; she then records

---

*For a discussion of different *levels* of analysis, see T. F. Gilbert, *Levels of Performance Analysis* (Morristown, N.J.: Praxis Technical Publications, No. 1, 1974).

TABLE 2-11 PERFORMANCE TABLE—SECOND-LEVEL ANALYSIS

(1) Accomplishments	Require- ments	(2) Standards Units of Measurement	Exemplary Performance	(3) Impact of PIP	Actual Value or Cost of Performance (4) Typical Performance	(5) Unit Value or Cost	(6) No. of Service- persons	(7) Total	(8) PIP	(9) Value of Correcting PIP
AC equipment trouble diagnosis	Accuracy	Percent ser- vice calls not requir- ing callback	98%	Trouble not cor- rected (callbacks necessary)	96.7% (30 callbacks per year)	$17.78 per call	70	$37,338	1.5	$12,322
	Speed	Hours spent in diagnosis of service call	0.33 (20 minutes)	Increased service time	1.17 hours (70 minutes)	$7.84 labor costs per service hour	70 × 900 calls	$577,886	3.5	$410,299
Trouble correction	Accuracy	Percent cor- rectly diag- nosed prob- lems not corrected	99%	Callbacks	99%	—	—	—	1.0	—
	Speed	Hours spent to repair	0.67 (40 minutes)	Increased labor time	0.72 (43 minutes)	$7.84	70 × 900 calls	$355,622*	1.05	$17,781

*These figures do not add up to the $1,120,140 in Table 2-10 since travel time is not figured into these times.

TABLE 2-12 PERFORMANCE TABLE—THIRD-LEVEL ANALYSIS

(1) Accomplishments	Requirements	(2) Standards — Units of Measurement	Exemplary Performance	(3) Impact of PIP	(4) Actual Value or Cost of Performance — Typical Performance	(5) Unit Value or Cost	(6) No. of Service-persons	(7) Total	(8) PIP	(9) Value of Correcting PIP
1. AC temperature readings	a. Accuracy	Percent correct	100%	—	100%	—	—	—	1	—
	b. Speed	Minutes	About 2 or 3 minutes	—	About 2 or 3 minutes	—	—	—	1	—
2. AC temperature interpretations	a. Accuracy	Percent correct	100%	Speed up diagnosis	0% not done					
	b. Speed	Minutes	2 minutes	—	Not done— see problem 3b below					
3. Confirmation tests	a. Accuracy	Percent correct	100%	—	100%	—	—	—	1	—
	b. Speed	Hours	0.25 hour (15 minutes)	Labor costs	1.12 hours (67 minutes)	$7.84 per hour	70 × 900 calls	$553,190	4.48	—

*For net savings you would subtract the labor costs of diagnosing temperatures (about $16,000).

these readings on a company form (because the manufacturer requires this). But next, unlike other service personnel, she interprets the relationships among these seven temperatures and can tell within 2 minutes, and with 100-percent accuracy, what is wrong with the air conditioner. Finally, she performs several required but needless tests to confirm the diagnosis. Other service personnel, not knowing how to diagnose by temperatures, use these lengthy confirmation tests to make their diagnoses.

"If we just kept thermometers in the wells and asked the customer to give us the readings on the phone, I could diagnose the problem without even looking at the equipment," Blue says. "Half the time the customer could correct the problem without any help from us."

So, any time something isn't right, the temperatures inside the air conditioner change in a way that is consistent with the problem. Wise finds it remarkable that no other serviceperson in the company even knows this, and therefore must use the confirmation tests, trial-and-error fashion, to find out what is wrong. Wise has now located the source of the problem. Indeed, the only reason Blue makes confirmation tests, and wastes an additional 15 minutes, is because the company requires the results to be recorded on a form.

Through the careful analysis of PIPs, level by level, Wise targets the principal service problem of NoGas. Why does Blue know how to interpret temperatures? She says: "It tells you how to do it in an appendix in the back of the service manual. I guess I just like to read things like that. I used to look it up in the manual, but I finally memorized it."

I won't insult the reader's intelligence by describing the utterly simple solution to the main problems of NoGas service. Suffice it to say that it cost a total of about $5000 to devise and print a guide for all the servicepeople to use. Alas—and it is significant—the unnecessary paper work on the confirmation tests was not abandoned. Management PIPs are not that easy to realize.

The performance tables led NoGas away from a request to retrain salespeople and to a contract to develop a simple job aid for troubleshooting equipment instead. This rather surprising (to NoGas) turn of focus is characteristic of the kinds of disclosures performance analysis leads to. The performance table seldom verifies management's hunches about where the problems lie. My colleagues and I have used performance tables in the analysis of everything from manufacturing automobiles to teaching history; from the design of training materials to medical diagnosis. Surprise has been the rule, not the exception. Performance tables simplify analysis and, indeed, would make it routine except for one unfortunate circumstance: Management seldom has sensible information about performance readily available—not because it is difficult to get, but because management, unfortunately, does not think this way as often as it should. Profit-and-loss statements do not tell

us much about human performance. Data are plentiful, but data are not information until they tell us something.

Although I call this kind of analysis a "performance audit," the name should not imply that the precision of accountants is required. If you work with data requiring accounting or statistical precision to reveal reliable variances, you usually are looking in the wrong direction. The potential for improving human competence is ample enough. If the performance audit is conducted in the proper fashion, opportunities will leap out.

I shall show later that the most valuable single source of treatment for the ills of incompetence is the very data that clearly show its existence, its size, and its meaning. The 100-meter freestyle swim event has a low PIP for a good reason: The people engaged in this activity know immediately how well they are performing, and what it means to them. If the same were true in the world of work, PIPs would inevitably become much smaller. One of the great values of the performance table, then, is to show us what data we should collect.

HOW NOT TO MEASURE COMPETENCE

The very act of measurement is a powerful tonic for the condition of human competence—provided that we use the right kind of measures. Unfortunately, all too many common measures can have the opposite effect—measures like the standardized (store-bought) tests of behavior.

But if these tests are not at all useful in telling us something about human competence, why do so many seemingly smart people use them? I have been asked this reasonable question many times, and I shall try to put my answer in perspective. First, I am not saying that such tests are completely useless. They can be of limited use in certain situations, provided that we are willing to pay a price for their use—a price that extends beyond the cost of purchasing and administering them. Let us see what that additional price can be.

Hickory George runs a manufacturing plant and employs machine operators who, to do their job well, must become troubleshooters of rather complex equipment. They must frequently find out why their machines are not running well and correct the problem. When these operators first come on the job, they are assigned to a machine and given close supervision and on-the-job training (OJT). George notices that after 3 months on the job, there is considerable variation in the ability of different operators to diagnose machine trouble. So he decides to measure the performance of new operators after 3 months to see just how well they do perform. To do this, he sets up a test machine in which he can "dial" in any one of 20 common problems (an electrical failure, a clogged valve, a pressure maladjustment, etc.). Then he

asks each operator to troubleshoot these problems, and he records the accuracy and speed of their performance. He finds that 30 operators, after 3 months on the job, diagnose an average of 8 of the 20 problems.

George then decides to use a test battery ("Mechanical Aptitude," "Numerical Reasoning," etc.) as a key to selecting new operators. Someone in the Personnel Department explains that these test scores might account for as much as 10 to 15 percent of the variation in on-the-job performance after 3 months.

When his carefully selected operators have been on the job 3 months, George measures their performance and finds that they can diagnose an average of 10 problems—and significantly faster than the earlier group. He also measures what seems to be a significant improvement in productivity and machine downtime.

Were George's selection tests useful to him? Probably, because such tests can often account for as much as 10 to 15 percent of the variance in job performance—seldom more, and frequently less. The increases in performance attributable to the use of selection tests *might* pay for the cost of these tests in the first year of their use.

George is disturbed by one thing, however. His turnover has increased since he introduced the selection tests. He isn't sure, but he believes that it might be because he is selecting better-educated people who aspire to better jobs. It also disturbs George that many of the people his test battery rejects would probably have gone on to become good operators, whereas many who are selected don't work out so well. George dislikes treating people statistically when it comes to their means of making a living. But he also knows that the competence of his plant significantly affects the cost of his goods, and therefore the price he must charge consumers. He hopes that this will offset the injustices to the people he refuses to hire because of their test scores. But then Sarah Barton comes along.

Sarah B. is a performance engineer whom George meets at a cocktail party. George proudly tells her about his selection system, but Sarah B. is not impressed. She asks George why he doesn't select only the people who fail his tests, since they are almost all really disadvantaged people. Then, she insists, he could arrange for them to become crack diagnosticians in, say, a month's time. "It would greatly cut your turnover, and it would surely improve plant performance much more than those wicked tests."

George's curiosity is aroused when he finds that Sarah B. has a great reputation for making good on some of her boasts. Just 6 months later, he hires her and turns over to her the responsibility for selecting and preparing his machine operators. But he warns that he wants measurable results.

Sarah B. demands that an independent person measure the results. She wants no accusations that she doctored the data. She then selects 30 machine operators from the "bottom of the deck"—those who would have failed George's selection tests. After 1 month on the job, she gets measurements that George can hardly believe. Her 30 operators can diagnose an average of 19.5

of the 20 machine problems. They also rank among the top 10 percent of all operators in average productivity, machine downtime, and scrap. Moreover, her poorest operator gets 18 of the 20 diagnostic test problems correct—which is all the *best* of George's selected crew would do.

These results are no surprise to Sarah B. She began her study by measuring the PIP of machine operators, and it never occurred to her to aim for anything less than exemplary performance. The fact that the operators she selected were said to be "poorly qualified and not likely to succeed" only meant to her that there was even greater potential for improving performance.

Sarah Barton's results are not imaginary, nor are they unusual. How did she do it? Rather than selecting "bright" people and throwing them into a comparatively disorderly environment, she selected so-called "dummies" and engineered their world into an orderly and sensible place. First, she developed a 2-week course that thoroughly taught them the theory of the machines (hands-on, as well). And she mounted a troubleshooting guide on the side of the machine—a guide that nearly anyone could follow with a minimum amount of training. She also posted production, machine downtime, and scrap performance data for every operation every 4 hours so that the operators could know how well they were performing. Furthermore, she introduced bonuses for good performance. She did nothing magical at all. Moreover, 12 months later, 28 of her 30 operators were still on the job.

This example can help us place statistical tests of behavior in some perspective. Are they useful? They can be, because they are capable of making predictions *slightly* better than a toss of a coin, provided that we don't tamper with the performance we are trying to predict. Using such tests is exactly like finding a correlation between soil color and fertility. If we didn't know anything else about farming, we would sensibly choose the black patch of ground to grow okra instead of the light patch. But as soon as someone comes along and properly waters and fertilizes the light patch, our okra won't compete on the market any longer.

Hickory George's test battery was slightly useful to him until he decided to go into the performance engineering business. His tests did not predict the performance of Sarah Barton's operators, so performance engineering made them useless. It is clear that to engineer worthy performance, we need an entirely different approach to measurement. Quantifiable tests of behavior will seldom, if ever, be useful to the performance engineer. They can be interesting, even useful, tools for the sociologist. The sociologist wants to describe the world as it is; the performance engineer wants to turn it into something else.

Furthermore, whatever usefulness IQ tests and the like have for those concerned with human competence is far offset by the social cost.

Behavior tests can be slightly correlated with *some* forms of competence under *certain* social conditions. But the correlation can completely disappear when the social conditions are changed. It is equally
true that skin color, the state of people's health, accent, and the like are
slightly correlated with *some* forms of competence in *certain* social
conditions. How is it that enlightened people react to these "measures"
of behavior as useless, socially unacceptable devices that discriminate
against people, and yet do not reject the use of test-taking peculiarities
for the same purpose? Because the tests are developed "scientifically?"
Why wouldn't a test battery consisting of measures of skin color, health
ratings, voting records, accent, height, home location, and the like, be
just as "scientific" if I applied the same statistical techniques as IQ
testers and administered this battery with complete "objectivity?" It
would be; and it would also show a *slight* correlation with *some* forms
of competence under *certain* social conditions. It would not only be
just as "scientific"; it would also be equally useless to people who take
their responsibilities for engineering human competence seriously. I
therefore reject these behavioral tests on both social and pragmatic
grounds.

This does not say that all behavioral "measures" ought to be
rejected. As we have seen, the kind of diagnostic test that gives a *list* of
specific behavioral deficiencies can be very useful. An example would
be a test that identifies a student's inability to multiply by zero, or to
borrow in subtraction. But such tests are useful if we have a contract
with people to help them improve their performance, and if we use the
results for specific diagnostic purposes rather than for discriminating
against them socially. And with these kinds of behavioral tests, we
needn't summarize people into numbers entered on their permanent
social records.

When we engineer performance, then, we need quantifiable measures of performance, not of behavior. Both the PIP and the IQ purport
to measure human potential, but beyond that they diverge completely.
The IQ, for example, assigns the greatest potential to those who score
highest on the test; the PIP assigns the greatest potential to those who
show the poorest performance. They therefore represent two opposing
views of a human's capacity for performance. The IQ concept says that
some people "have it" and some don't, and it doesn't get much more
specific than that. The concept of the PIP says that competence is
external to people; that is, competence is an effect they can have upon
the world, and any person with normal faculties has the potential for
accomplishing the effects that other people have shown possible.

I maintain that the second view is the humanistic one—the view that
sees people for what they can do, and not for their limitations. More
important, however, the PIP is a practical measure that people can put
to use to improve their condition. The IQ only discourages average

people because it labels them as inherently and irretrievably average. If your IQ is only 100, then how can you expect to achieve very much? Your excuse is branded indelibly on your record. But if your PIP is 15, and clearly specifies a goal you care to achieve, you know that you really have somewhere to go; and perhaps your performance can establish a new standard. The responsibility is yours. The IQ is, then, a point of view invented by the necessity for class consciousness. But the PIP is a "vector" that must always be stated in terms of a direction along which potential lies for any person. We have a choice between these points of view. And the one we should choose, I think, is not merely a matter of philosophical taste. Rather, it seems to me, our leisure capital depends on our choice: between seeing people for their potential or for their presumed limitations. Table 2-13 compares some of the qualities of the PIP and the IQ.

TABLE 2-13   COMPARISON OF PIP AND IQ AS MEASURES OF HUMAN PERFORMANCE POTENTIAL

Qualities	PIP	IQ
1. Content	Performance	Behavior
2. Interpretation of low performer "scores"	High potential	Low potential
3. Relativity to real world	"Vector"—relative to a given accomplishment	General—a "scalar" that states no relative conditions
4. Real-world validity	A criterion measure of real-world performance	Zero to 25% common variance with real-world performance
5. Reliability	As reliable as the real world	50% to 75% common variance on repeat measures
6. Implications for human potential	Potential is opportunity	IQ is limitation
7. Philosophical implications	Supports view that people are responsible	Supports view that people are limited by forces beyond their control and are not responsible
8. Social implications	Discriminates narrowly, and only on the basis of true performance	Discriminates socially against low test scores
9. Economic implications	Uncovers economic opportunity	Has the most limited economic use
10. Implications for performance engineering	A principal diagnostic tool for the engineer	Has little or no use for performance engineering

Psychologists are fond of telling us that we use only a small part of our "brain" capacity. These are the same psychologists who are so fond of indexing our potential with the IQ. These two notions, however "metrically independent" they may be, simply don't match as points of view about human potential. To suggest that John Doe has a sort of "generalized PIP" of 100 seems to say something diametrically opposed to branding him with an IQ of 100. But then, as long as we view the competence of psychologists by *their* behavior—how impressively they talk—and not by their accomplishments, we can expect such spectacularly dazzling contradictions.

Finally, we may abandon the IQ test on its most fundamental assumption—that people's IQs state the limits of their ability to learn. This not only is empirically unsupportable, but its contrary can be demonstrated. Jack Findley[4] has trained pigeons and monkeys to perform tasks requiring discriminations so complex that people of IQs of 150 could not perform them unless they were first similarly trained. These are tasks requiring intricate combinations of double-alternation problems that psychologists have said cannot be learned at all by people of low-average IQ. I shall gladly accept the challenge of training "average IQ" people to score "genius" on independently devised IQ tests. Whatever correlation the IQ testers find with hereditary factors can be overcome by well-designed opportunity. If psychologists would spend equal energies in designing such opportunities, they would happily negate their constricting tests.

NOTES

1. We could, of course, invert the ratio: PIP $= W_{av}/W_{ex}$. It would make no difference except that the larger number tends to emphasize potential rather than deficiency.

2. Normally, we should include the highest in the average. I have not done so here because, for the illustration, I have selected only 3 of some 20 supervisory groups—and to include the highest would greatly inflate the average.

3. I have been using this term for some 15 years, and it has been popularized through workshops conducted by Praxis Corporation. The first published use of the term, so far as I am aware, was by my student, Edward Feeney, in a paper entitled "Performance Audit, Feedback and Positive Reinforcement," *Training and Development Journal,* 26 (November 1972). I include this note because I have heard arguments about where the expression originated.

4. Personal communication. A variety of Findley's fascinating work appears in *The Journal of the Experimental Analysis of Behavior.*

Chapter Three

The Behavior Engineering Model

One rule of heart that must be obeyed:
You can peddle the poem, but the poet's to be paid.

T.F.G.

THE THIRD LEISURELY THEOREM

The first two Leisurely Theorems tell us how to recognize and measure human competence—and more: They provide the base for actually engineering worthy performance. Nothing is more critical to creating competence than establishing clear, valuable, and measurable goals, and determining the potential for accomplishing them. The emphasis in the first two chapters has been on accomplishment, not behavior. But to engineer performance well, we must be able to deal with behavior, which is what this chapter is all about. And when we examine behavior we need to be exceptionally careful to keep it in perspective, because efficient behavior[1] is only one component—and often not the component that is most critical—for achieving worthy performance. Imagine the "world's greatest" team of bridge builders working smoothly to create the most beautiful and nearly indestructible bridge at the lowest possible cost. Is the team competent? The distinction between competence and efficiency would be very clear if we should learn that our "world's greatest" team built the bridge across the wrong river. Obviously, efficient behavior applied in the wrong direction can be even more incompetent than bumbling efforts in the right direction. Throughout the remainder of this book, this point is made in many examples from the real world. Over and over, we shall see that only when we have made a proper analysis of accomplishments and their measures will we have any sensible reason to concern ourselves with behavior.

Suppose that I sell typewriters, and I have a credit department that views its function as keeping me from incurring any bad debts. It does

its job very well—at least by its own measures. It refuses to give credit to any but extremely good risks, and it uses high-pressure tactics as soon as a debtor falls behind in payments. Unfortunately for my business, I am losing sales to less-than-perfect risks—and losing customers among the good risks who become angry at my tactics. The credit department is proud of itself, because practically no past-due accounts are outstanding.

Yet this credit department is really incompetent, not because it lacks the behavior required to do the job well, but because it misconstrues its mission. The first thing I must do—perhaps the only thing—to make this department more competent is to redefine the accomplishments it is responsible for. I do this by establishing a new goal: *credit contracts*, and as many as possible within certain liberal limits of constraint. So I say that I want (within limits) as many debtors as possible, not as few as possible. Now the credit department becomes competent, and greatly improves my sales while only slightly increasing my sales costs. And I improve competence without attempting any direct manipulation of behavior.

But the tendency to focus too narrowly on behavior is not the only great barrier to performance engineering. Often we focus on the wrong aspects of behavior—especially those aspects that free us from responsibility for worthy performance. For example, ask anyone why someone else doesn't perform well, and you might get either of these answers: "She doesn't care," or "He's just too dumb." Most often, these answers are wrong. They are favorites of the behavior cult, however, because they place blame directly on others, and therefore free either the manager or the teacher in charge from any real responsibility. Variations on these answers have the same result: "He has hang-ups." "They have the wrong attitude." "Her morale is low." are common explanations.

If a person really "doesn't care," the manager or teacher can do little about it. But to turn the judgment around and say "I haven't provided enough incentive" puts the manager or teacher on the spot. Similarly, to switch from "He's stupid" to "I didn't teach him very well" is more than a little troublesome to the conscience. No wonder the common explanations are so popular.

Here's another common reply: "It's hard to say, because every case is different. No two people are alike." This response buries not only responsibility, but even the possibility of action—except, of course, "clinical analysis," the ultimate tool of the cult of behavior. "Psychoanalysis" may take years, and its success is said to depend ultimately on the desire and powers of insight of the patient. The analyst cannot fail.

But people who take on the responsibility for engineering human performance cannot shift that responsibility to others. At the moment we assume the role of manager—whether of a business, a classroom, a

hospital, or a home—we are saying, in effect, that we know how to control a significant number of the conditions required for competence. All managers, whatever their titles, are in the business of engineering human performance. If they are to fulfill their responsibilities, they not only must be able to identify and measure competence, but they must also have a method for identifying its behavioral causes. What is really needed, then, is a model—a system—that will guide us in creating competence through more efficient behavior: first, for troubleshooting behavior, and, second, for arriving at strategies that will produce greater efficiency.

When we first think about it, the task of developing such a behavior engineering model seems forbidding, because the events that can impede competence are innumerable. An upset stomach, anxieties created in childhood, defective tools, a hot day, poison ivy, fatigue, ignorance, things that compete for attention, ennui, forgetting, and obsessive jealousy—these only begin the endless list. So, when we discover any instance of incompetence, any PIP, and when we are certain that the impediments lie in behavior, where do we start to discover the potential remedies? To answer this question, we need a clear definition of behavior, one that clearly distinguishes those components essential for competence. An example will illustrate what these components are.

Suppose that I want to start a simple weaving business. Immediately, I am trying to engineer competence. The accomplishment side is easy: I set objectives and develop standards of performance. But what do I do on the behavior side?

First, I get myself a weaver—one Carl Birdrock. Carl is just an ordinary person, except in at least one unique aspect: He has a repertory of weaving behavior. This means that he can understand patterns and weaving specifications; he can make many specialized responses, such as sewing. Furthermore, if he is a reliable weaver, he will find this weaving activity reinforcing. People's behavioral repertories are part of their personal characteristics, those they bring to their jobs. We designate a *person's* repertory of behavior as *P*.

But Carl and his repertory of weaving are not sufficient for me to get the behavior my business needs. I also require a weaving environment (E),[2] and this environment is just as fundamental a component of behavior as Carl's weaving repertory. I must supply Carl with the information he needs, such as patterns and specifications; and I must also give him the tools he needs in order to weave. Finally, I must supply certain incentives to reinforce his activity—in the form of wages, recognition for good work, and the like. If I am missing any of these things, I shall fail to achieve the accomplishments (A) that I want.

So, the behavior repertory (P) of the weaver interacts with the weaving environment (E) to produce the finished cloth—the accom-

plishment (A) that I am looking for. It is also axiomatic to this view of performance that I am standing the costs of behavior (B). And these costs consist of at least two parts: I am paying for the weaver's repertory (P), and I am paying for his working environment (E). My total behavior costs are therefore the sum of these two payments:

$$B = P + E$$

With this understanding that at least two aspects of behavior are important components of competence, I can now restate the definition of worthy performance:

$$W = \frac{A}{B} = \frac{A}{P + E}$$

This definition says that I must pay for both a behavior repertory and its supporting environment. But my costs do not end there. I, the manager, also expend energy in a useful direction, and so I have a management cost (M) since I, too, can be a source of incompetence in my weaving business. It requires only a little common sense to see that if my weaving business is defective in some way—if suits are manufactured too slowly or if they come apart at the seams—I must look to weaving behavior to find the cause. Perhaps the weaver doesn't know what standards I have in mind, or perhaps his sewing machine is defective; or perhaps I am not paying him enough. Maybe he doesn't know how to sew well, or he has arthritis, or he just doesn't like to sew. In any event, I will find the problem as a deficiency in either (or both) his own repertory (P) or in the environment (E) that supports it. And whatever the most immediate cause of the poor performance, I, as the manager, have no one to blame but myself. The cause of the incompetence is my management. I have selected the wrong weaver, bought a defective sewing machine, failed to convey to the weaver the acceptable standards of performance, or something.[3]

I think that the weaving example is generic and can be the basis for the Third Leisurely Theorem, which I also call the Management Theorem. This theorem identifies in a general way where it is we have to look in order to find the causes of competence and incompetence:

For any given accomplishment, a deficiency in performance always has as its immediate cause a deficiency in a behavior repertory (P), or in the environment that supports the repertory (E), or in both. But its ultimate cause will be found in a deficiency of the management system (M).

A rather remarkable case history dramatically illustrates how incompetence in a seemingly tiny task can be traced to the failure of management to establish the standards for performance. For the want of a nail, the battle is lost; but, somehow, "top management" must see itself responsible for this critical nail. Management gets paid too much to justify anything else, as Micah Battle's experience will tell us.

Micah Battle has been made the new acting chief of the State Forest Service's Bureau of Parks and Recreational Areas. He knows that his job is temporary until they can replace the old boss, Birch Lobby, with another politician; but he's determined to do the best job he can.

Micah begins his new job by conducting a performance audit of his department. He shows each of his managers how to use performance tables, and he gives them a couple of weeks to do the job. He is particularly pleased with the work of Bo Valentine, his Supervisor of Recreational Rangers. The Rec. Rangers, as they are called, manage the camping areas of the State's parks and forests. However, Micah notices that Valentine has not followed through on one of the accomplishments he has listed for the Rec. Rangers.

"'Head counts,' you've got here, Bo; but you haven't done anything with it. What's a 'head count'?" Micah asks.

"Well, that's not very important—didn't want to bother you with it," Bo assures him.

"But what *is* a 'head count'?" Micah persists.

"Uh . . . the Rec. Ranger is supposed to count and tally the number of people who visit his area each day, and he turns the tallies in once a month. Just a little thing—not very important—didn't want to bother you with it." Bo says.

"Let's make sure," Micah persists. "We'll work it through the performance table. What are the requirements for a 'head count'?"

"Accuracy—and timeliness, I suppose. They're supposed to hand them in once a month."

"And what is exemplary performance?"

"Well, a conscientious ranger should be able to count nearly 100 percent accurately and get all the tallies in at the end of the month. It's not hard."

"What's typical performance?" Micah asks.

Bo doesn't know the answer, but he does recall that someone actually studied this performance once. After searching his files for an hour, he produces the answer.

"A couple of years ago, when we checked, our guys were only counting about half the people who visited the areas. We sent out a memo saying they ought to do better, but I don't think anybody paid attention to it. Most of them think it's just a lot of busy work."

"O.K., so we have a PIP of 2. What shall I put in the 'impact' column? What the hell difference do these head counts make? *Is* it just busy work?"

"Well, I don't know for sure," Bo muses, "but the state law says that money will be allocated to the recreation program on the basis of how many people use the recreation areas—so many dollars per head. Come to think about it, I guess head counts are important."

"My God!" Micah yells, nearly coming out of his seat. "You mean to tell me that money is appropriated to us on the basis of the head count, and we only count half the heads?"

"Well, that is about the size of it, Mr. Battle. I really hadn't thought of it that way before."

"Tell me," pleads Micah, "didn't you ever point this out to your old boss—Birch Lobby?"

"Well, sir, he was always so busy with the legislators that he didn't want to be bothered with the details of how things were done," Bo says a bit sadly.

"I'll get Lobby on the phone right now and tell him about it. This might help him raise more money than likkering up a bunch of legislators."

After talking to Lobby, Micah Battle puts the phone down and stares blankly at Bo Valentine.

"What did he say?" Bo asks.

"Will you believe it? He asked me to leave things alone. He said, 'What would the legislature say if we suddenly doubled the head count?'"

"You mean 'doubled since he left the job'?" Bo demurs. "Well, I didn't think he'd want to be bothered."

Micah Battle's problem beautifully illustrates the Management Theorem. First, it shows an example of incompetence that results from the failure of management to define all of its important accomplishments—and to assign responsibility for them. Next, we see that the immediate cause of failure lies in the simplest form of behavior—marking tallies on a sheet of paper. Now we ask what behavior changes Micah must produce to get worthy performance. Surely, no fundamental changes in anyone's repertory is required, because people know how to make tallies. But a change in the environment is needed. Someone now must provide the stimulus and the incentives for getting the head counts made; and that, like much of performance engineering, requires the simplest kind of action: setting head-count standards, and communicating them to the rangers. Management has failed to define all the purposes of the rangers' jobs and to provide the environmental supports to see that the rangers perform accordingly.

The Management Theorem is just another expression of a saying

promulgated by B. F. Skinner, and repeated religiously by the people who work in his animal laboratories: "The animal is always right; only the animal trainer can fail." If Skinner's rat (or pigeon) did not perform to expectations, it was rightly assumed that:

- P. It had not been properly trained; or, if it were ill, not properly selected; or perhaps not motivated (deprived of food).
- E. Something was defective in the Skinner box (lights, lever, etc.).
- M. In either case, the animal trainer or the control panels (management system) had to change.

But for Skinner to know how to change his management system, he must first locate the intermediate problem: Is it in the environment or in the behavior repertory?

If the answer is not immediately obvious, Skinner would look into the records of the animal. How has it been trained? Has it been deprived of food? Is it sick? If he finds no problem with the animal, he then looks to the Skinner box itself. Are the lights in the box working? Are the food pellets all right? Is the lever stuck? And so on. The answers to these questions give him a good idea of what he must do to change his management system. If the animal isn't trained, let's train it; if the lights aren't working, let's check the light-control system.

The Third Leisurely Theorem puts us on our way toward the construction of a behavior engineering model. We are not looking for "scientific" explanations of behavior, but only for an orderly guide to asking the questions an engineer must ask. But before defining such a model, I shall develop further the ways in which we can usefully look at behavior.

WHAT IS BEHAVIOR FOR THE PERFORMANCE ENGINEER?

People have studied behavior at great length, and there are hundreds of systems for classifying it—some of them simple, some complex, and some of them exotic. Indeed, there are about as many systems for classifying behavior as there are people interested in doing it. Unfortunately for our purpose, most people who have studied behavior have made it their focal subject matter—they have been interested in it for its own sake, rather than for the sake of engineering competence. They have tried to define behavior, measure it, explain it, and manipulate it. There have been great disagreements even about what it is. Does the study of behavior include "mind," "personality," "motive," or merely

"observable reflexes"? The various systems of psychology have divided themselves on hundreds of such questions. There are also many schools of thought about how to manipulate behavior—from simple conditioning to abstruse psychoanalytic theories, from behavior modification to psychotherapy. Yet these various systems have not especially advanced our capacity to engineer human performance, although we can learn something from some of them.

For the performance engineer, behavior is only one of the conditions for human competence—*not the focal subject matter itself.* And our model of behavior should, of course, be a simple one. We need not become involved in debates about the time structure of the mind or the nature of the reflex. As a matter of fact, we haven't even succeeded in using the rather vast amount of information all of us already have about how to engineer performance efficiently. By the time we are 12 years old, we know far more about behavior than we are effectively able to use.

Because our purpose is to design a system of engineering, a useful behavior engineering model will deal with events that we can manipulate. It cannot be useful if it points to conditions of competence over which we have little or no control. There may be a chemical somewhere that, when taken orally, inevitably results in exemplary performance. But until someone discovers, refines, and packages it, we shall have to be satisfied with what we do have to work with. Thus, we are not looking for a model that tells us about the ultimate causes of behavior. What we are looking for is a simple and useful way to identify the kinds of behavioral conditions we can manipulate—and at a cost that is less than the value received. But to do so, we need to clear up some common confusions. Despite our considerable and intimate experience with it, and despite the frequency with which we discuss it, there is much confusion about the word *behavior*. To some people, it means only the more overt actions of people, in contrast to thoughts, feelings, and the like; to others, behavior means all the direct actions of people (or other animals), ranging from eye-pupil dilations to mathematical problem solving, and from agonizing over a lost love to typing a letter.

I shall use the word behavior in this second, wider sense. Even so, the possibility of confusion does not end there. When I try to alter behavior, it is not always clear whether I am altering the repertory of behavior or something else. For example, if a carpenter is not performing well and I give some skill training to improve performance, few would question that I have altered behavior. This carpenter now holds the saw differently and moves the hammer through quite a different arc. Suppose, however, I find that the carpenter already has great skill, but

the saw is dull and I have provided no sharpener. In that case, I sharpen the saw and get better performance. Have I altered the behavior? I have certainly done nothing *directly to the carpenter;* rather, I have manipulated the saw. Nevertheless, the carpenter's behavior is somehow different.

Because there are so many ways we can alter behavior, directly or indirectly, this question needs to be answered: Which part of behavior, if any, is the saw? Then we can pick our way through the seemingly infinite thicket of complexities that compose behavior. And the answer is compelling: The saw is as much a part of the carpenter's behavior as skill or muscle movements.

Or how should we classify the movements of a fish? We observe it moving its tail in water, and we do not hesitate to call this swimming behavior. But suppose we toss the fish onto the beach, and observe that it makes identical movements with its tail. This is no longer swimming, but thrashing. In other words, the mere movements of the organism taken in isolation of its environment do not have the full force of behavior. Nor is it very useful to confine our meaning of behavior within the skin of the animal—to its repertory.

We can say that all instrumental human behavior—all behavioral components of performance—have two aspects of equal importance: a person with a *repertory of behavior* (P) and a *supporting environment* (E). The person's repertory and the supporting environment together form a transaction that we call behavior. The saw and the hand, the light and the perceiving eye are merely two sides of the same coin. We can therefore define behavior (B), in shorthand, as a product of both repertory *and* environment:

$$B = E \cdot P$$

For the performance engineer, this definition is invaluable.[4] It tells us immediately that when behavior is inadequate for competent performance, we may alter it either by altering a person's repertory or by changing the supporting environment; or, of course, we might do both. So, when we try to improve human competence by altering behavior, we need to decide which of these two strategies is more effective. I can elect to improve the information, tools, or the incentives that support performance (environmental supports); or I can choose to modify *directly* the person's repertory of behavior through training or dozens of other devices; or I can do both.

What we need, then, is an orderly method to look at all of these approaches that we might use to influence behavior. But first we need to identify more closely the components of behavior which we shall use.

COMPONENTS OF BEHAVIOR AND THE BEHAVIOR ENGINEERING MODEL

To refine the ways we can look at behavior, I shall use some convenient shorthand symbols that will be familiar to many but not all readers. It is the shorthand of "stimulus-response" used by psychologists of almost all persuasions.

In the elementary psychological model, all behavior can be described in terms of stimuli (S) and responses (R). Behavior occurs when some event—a stimulus—occasions a response (R). We step into a dark room and turn on the light switch, which we can describe as here:

$$S \longrightarrow R$$
Dark   Throw
Room   Switch

But this description of behavior is still incomplete. If we throw a switch in a dark room and nothing ever happens, we shall soon stop doing it. For behavior to be maintained, it must be reinforced (or "rewarded," to use a simpler but more troublesome term). In this example, behavior is reinforced by the light's coming on. But this light is itself a stimulus, informing us that our response was successful. So we can see that stimuli have dual functions: They tell us what to do, *and* they tell us whether we have responded correctly. Psychologists use some distinguishing notation to separate these two functions of a stimulus. When we talk about a stimulus as an occasion for a response ("evoking" a response), we shall use the symbol S^D. The superscript D denotes "discriminative," meaning that the person must be able to discriminate an event in order to respond to it appropriately. For example, we must be able to recognize (discriminate) that the room is dark; otherwise we would not respond differently. When we talk about the reinforcing aspect of a stimulus, we shall use the symbol S_r, meaning "reinforcing stimulus" or "reinforcer." We can now describe our simple example of behavior in shorthand, like this:

$$S^D \longrightarrow R \quad \cdot \quad S_r$$
Dark   Throw   Light
Room   Switch On

Keep in mind that the reason we complicate the symbols with subscripts and superscripts is because all stimuli can be both reinforcing (S_r) and discriminative (S^D). The light that comes on in the room reinforces our throwing the switch, *and* it sets the occasion for us to make the next response. This diagram represents the dual role of stimuli:

$$\text{------}R \quad \cdot \quad S_r^D \longrightarrow \quad R\text{ - - - - - -}$$

Throw	Light	Go to the
Switch	On	Bookshelf

To simplify all of this now, we can say that behavior has three aspects, or components:

1. Information comes into the person telling him or her what to do (S^D).
2. The person responds in some way (R).
3. The action, that of responding to the stimulus, becomes reinforced (S_r).

Now add to these three components of behavior the two aspects we considered earlier: the person's repertory (P) and the environment that supports it (E). We can see that the discriminative stimulus (S^D) has an environmental component (the light), *and* it requires something of the person's repertory (perceiving the light). Also, the response requires an environment that contains a switch *and* a repertory of hand-eye movements. For reinforcement to occur, the environment must light up *and* the person must have a motive—he or she must "want" the room to light up. All six of these things occur together in a single transaction. They are not isolated, independent events, but simply six ways of looking at the same event. And with these six vantage points, we can create a useful model for helping us engineer an important component of performance.

These six aspects of behavior can be summarized in a simple matrix, as in Table 3-1. Shortly, this matrix will develop into the behavior engineering model we need to help us order our thinking about how we can alter performance through changes in behavior. First, however, it is important to realize that I do not mean to imply that behavior is some kind of disjointed sum of six mechanical parts, just because the matrix itself consists of six little cells. The only purpose of separating

TABLE 3-1 COMPONENTS OF BEHAVIOR

	S^D *Information*	R *Instrumentation*	S_r *Motivation*
E	Data (dark room)	Instruments (light switch)	Incentives (light on)
P	Discrimination (perceives darkness)	Response capacity (flips switch)	Motives (likes a light room)

out the parts of the whole, unitary transaction is to get a better understanding of what we can most economically manipulate in order to achieve the behavior we want. A sale is a transaction involving seller, goods, and buyer. And with any of these parts missing, there is no sale nor any selling. But we can focus on the parts of this transaction separately in order to know what we must do to increase the probability of the sale. Is the seller making the wrong pitch? Are the goods defective? Does the buyer need them? We can ask this: Is the defect we

1. (S^D) Stimulus (information)

2. (R) Response

3. (S$_r$) Reinforcement (motivation)

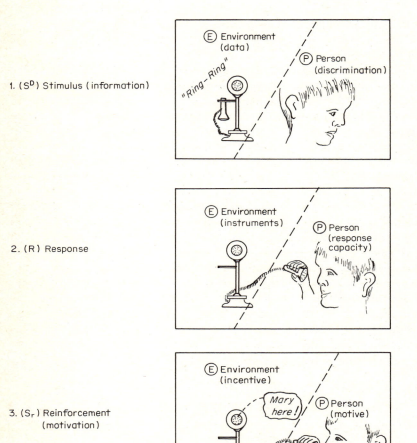

FIGURE 3-1   Behavior from six points of view.

can best correct in the environment or in the person? And, in either case, we ask if it is in the stimulus (information), in the response (instrumentation), or in the reinforcement (motivation).

Of course, when performance is imperfect, none of the six aspects of behavior is likely to be perfect—or all of them could be improved. We could improve both the data needed for performance and the person's ability to absorb the information; we could improve both the tools and the capacity to handle them; incentives could be applied more effectively and motives heightened. For the performance engineer, the question then is: "Where can we get the greatest leverage; how can we have the biggest effect at the least cost?" I shall discuss this issue of "leverage" later in more detail. But first we should examine these six manipulable properties of behavior more closely. As an example, we can look at the simple behavior of answering the telephone. Figure 3-1 illustrates both the repertory and environment sides of stimulus, response, and reinforcement.[5] It should also be clear that all six conditions must hold if telephone-answering behavior is going to occur. (See Table 3-2.)

The very simplicity of this example might obscure its point, because the Telephone Company goes to great lengths to see that nothing goes wrong with this particular performance system. Suppose we consider an example of a performance system in which many forces work to make it go wrong: a soldier firing a rifle. The soldier may fail to hit the target because the target is obscure (data failure); or because he can't tell friend from enemy (knowledge failure); or because the rifle may not be made true (instrument failure); or because our soldier may not have a strong enough thumb to cock the trigger (capacity failure); or because the enemy may keep coming (incentive failure); or because our soldier may abhor killing him (motive failure). The army takes special care to see that these things don't happen too often. It uses flares so the soldier can see the enemy (data), and trains him carefully to fell an enemy

TABLE 3-2   CONDITIONS FOR BEHAVIOR TO OCCUR

	S^D Information	R Instrumentation	S_r Motivation
E *Environmental* *supports*	1. Data The phone's ring must be loud enough.	2. Instruments The receiver must be removable.	3. Incentives The calling party must be audible.
P *Person's* *repertory of* *behavior*	4. Knowledge The answerer must have the ability to hear the ring.	5. Response capacity The answerer must be able to reach for the phone.	6. Motives The answerer must want to talk to people on the phone.

when he sees one (knowledge). It is careful to design the rifles so that they are true (instruments), and to select people strong enough to handle them (capacity). It pins medals on those who kill the enemy (incentive), and tries to recruit those who believe in the cause of the war (motives). The winning army is the one that excels in each of these six things.

We can return now to the happier example of the telephone. The Telephone Company engineers telephone-answering behavior by manipulating three of the six variables, all of them environmental. It has done much research to get the right tone and the right loudness of ring (data), to make the receiver easy to handle (instruments), and to minimize obscene or threatening calls (incentives). The Company generally avoids manipulating the customers' repertories directly—except for commercial messages about the glories of the telephone, designed to heighten our motive for using it. In concentrating on environmental variables rather than on our behavior repertories, the Telephone Company shows good sense; it has learned that the environment is easier to manipulate than people's repertories. It could have used obscure rings (data failure), and made an effort to teach us to discriminate their meanings (knowledge); or it could have made the phone set difficult to use (instrument failure), and provided us with prosthetic devices or exercise programs to shape our ability to use it (response capacity). It could also have made an instrument with loud, crackling, painful noises (incentive failure) and spent millions of dollars promoting the importance of taking the punishment (motives). Although these tactics seem absurd, they are nonetheless frequently adopted elsewhere—sometimes even by the Telephone Company. A great deal of money is spent unknowingly by management each year to guarantee the creation of unfavorable conditions for performance.

Let us examine our six-celled table again—this time, to see what management can do to make behavior inefficient. Then ask yourself if these things aren't often done—almost as if there were a conspiracy to create incompetence. Table 3-3 outlines six kinds of performance tactics commonly used to engineer incompetent performance. Anyone who studies Table 3-3 and doesn't see that most of these tactics are the rule, not the exception—and that *at least* one of them is vigorously employed by almost every place of work or by every school—simply hasn't had much experience.

However, by reversing the tactics in Table 3-3, we can arrive at a suitable behavior engineering model against which managers, teachers, and others can compare their own methods of managing other people's performance. Table 3-4 is a generalized description of the behavior engineering model, which identifies almost all the kinds of things we

TABLE 3-3   A BEHAVIOR MODEL FOR CREATING INCOMPETENCE

	S^D Information	R Instrumentation	S_r Motivation
E **Environmental** **supports**	Data 1. Don't let people know how well they are performing. 2. Give people misleading information about how well they are performing. 3. Hide from people what is expected of them. 4. Give people little or no guidance about how to perform well.	Instruments 1. Design the tools of work without ever consulting the people who use them. Keep the engineers away from people who use the tools.	Incentives 1. Make sure that poor performers get paid as well as good ones. 2. See that good performance gets punished in some way. 3. Don't make use of nonmonetary incentives.
P **Person's** **repertory of** **behavior**	Knowledge 1. Leave training to chance. 2. Put training in the hands of supervisors who are not trained instructors. 3. Make training unnecessarily difficult. 4. Make training irrelevant to the students' purposes.	Capacity 1. Schedule performance for times when people are not at their sharpest. 2. Select people for tasks they have intrinsic difficulties in performing. 3. Do not provide response aids (e.g., magnification of difficult visual stimuli).	Motives 1. Design the job so that it has no future. 2. Avoid arranging working conditions that employees would find more pleasant. 3. Give pep talks rather than incentives to promote performance in punishing situations.

might do to achieve greater competence through the improvement of behavior efficiency. Any job that could be characterized by the descriptions in Table 3-4 would surely carry a guarantee of high competence, provided, of course, that management was structured so as to really deliver these things and had a clear focus on the mission of the job in the first place. Similarly, any school that could be characterized by these descriptions would have few dropouts and a great market for its graduates.

But, you might say, behavior costs money. And programs to get more efficient behavior can also cost money. The question is, then, will these programs pay for themselves? The answer is a decisive "yes"—always, and not just in most cases—provided that we are working with the really important PIPs.

First, the costs of these programs are usually (with one exception)

TABLE 3-4   THE BEHAVIOR ENGINEERING MODEL

	S^D *Information*	R *Instrumentation*	S_r *Motivation*
E ***Environmental*** ***supports***	Data 1. Relevant and frequent feedback about the adequacy of performance 2. Descriptions of what is expected of performance 3. Clear and relevant guides to adequate performance	Instruments 1. Tools and materials of work designed scientifically to match human factors	Incentives 1. Adequate financial incentives made contingent upon performance 2. Nonmonetary incentives made available 3. Career-development opportunities
P ***Person's*** ***repertory of*** ***behavior***	Knowledge 1. Scientifically designed training that matches the requirements of exemplary performance 2. Placement	Capacity 1. Flexible scheduling of performance to match peak capacity 2. Prosthesis 3. Physical shaping 4. Adaptation 5. Selection	Motives 1. Assessment of people's motives to work 2. Recruitment of people to match the realities of the situation

ridiculously small. The exception is training, which can be very expensive. But, as we shall see, the greater part of the cost of training will have to be borne anyway, whether it is carefully designed to match the situation or not. This being the case, Table 3-4 represents six kinds of reasonably small investments that can yield great returns in improved performance. Remember the economic principle of Chapter 1? A small investment in behavior can yield great returns in accomplishment.

Obviously, not all six kinds of programs will pay off equally well; nor do all of these areas always require improvement. Which one or more of these programs is useful in any given situation requires analysis. And that analysis is simply a matter of diagnosing why deficiencies in performance occur in the first place. Why is typical performance less than exemplary? What behavioral defect causes the PIP? When we have a deficiency in performance, we usually have a deficiency in behavior—in either its environmental supports, or in a person's behavior repertory, or in both. Where do we look to find out? The behavior engineering model will help us answer this question.

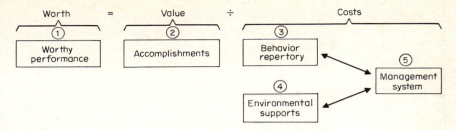

FIGURE 3-2 Economics of the behavior engineering model.

But before we examine how we can use the behavior model, we can place it in the perspective of the larger model of performance. Figure 3-2 illustrates the economic relationship between behavior as cost and accomplishment as value.

DIAGNOSING PERFORMANCE DEFICIENCIES

As I have noted before, the two causes of poor performance most commonly espoused are motives ("they don't care") and capacity ("they're too dumb"). But these are usually the last two places one should look for causes of incompetence, simply because they rarely are the substantial problem. I make this assertion without hesitation. Except for a few strange individuals, people generally care a great deal about how they perform on the job, or in school; and defects in capacity—mental or physical—are the exception, not the rule. Because, whatever defects in motives or capacity exist, their consequences can usually be minimized by careful attention to the other variables in the behavior engineering model. Improvements in training can do wonders for most people we consider slow-witted; better incentives can usually obliterate all evidence of defective motives.

When we use the behavior engineering model as a diagnostic tool, we must look at it in perspective. First, no person or environment is likely to be perfectly designed for the accomplishments expected. Even under ideal circumstances, *some* improvement in behavior will be possible. Then the question is not *if* we can improve this or that aspect of behavior, but which strategies will yield the most worthy results: the greatest improvement in accomplishment with the least cost of behavior. The question is, Where is the greatest *leverage?* I am saying that most people have both sufficient motive and capacity for exemplary performance in almost all circumstances of work and school. So, we should look to these variables only when we have exhausted other remedies. If you have done a great job in correcting defects of information, tools, incentives, and training, and you still have not achieved

exemplary performance—and if the PIP is still economically significant—then you can sensibly worry about the selection of people who have greater motives or capacity. I think athletics is the only significant exception to this rule. If I wanted to develop a fighter to win the world title, I would worry at the beginning about his natural physical endowments and his "killer" instincts. But other pursuits seldom demand the capacity and motives that most of us cannot meet. Yet athletics provides much of the model that managers (and, to a lesser extent, teachers) use in coping with employees. And perhaps this helps explain the incompetence of management. Many managers see their jobs as fitting their concept of a football coach: It consists of careful selection of "talent" and "leadership," which usually means pep talks and tough stances that threaten punishment. Capacity and motives are the chief variables with which they work. And such posturing gets heavily reinforced by other managers—if only because this is the behavior we have come to equate with management.

Unfortunately for the athletic model, it doesn't hold up too well even in athletics. I once knew a great college football coach—a man who is widely considered to be an exemplary athletic manager. Many sports writers tout him as the best. He has a national image as a man who puts the fear of God and a great desire to win into his players, and for shrewdly selecting the best of talent. But, according to my observations of his techniques and his own descriptions of the variables he attends to, capacity and motives are low on his scale of considerations. "Coach" (as I'll call him) says in private that he does three things to account for his success. The first is to give training (knowledge); the second is to provide frequent and detailed reports for each player on his progress (data); and the third is to make certain that the players get rewarded, both financially and otherwise (incentive)—with awards, for example.

Coach says, "If the boy don't want to play [motives], he quits anyhow; and unless he's lame [response capacity], he can play football. I've even had some lames ones play pretty well."

In my observations, Coach never gave pep talks or went out of his way to be "inspirational." And he took all comers into his tryouts. He spent most of his time managing his assistant coaches as they viewed thousands of feet of film; he also reviewed the films with the players, and taught them how to block and tackle. The rest of his time he spent, as he said it, "in politics"—getting the alumni to provide the incentives, both financial and other (awards, dinners, etc.). It makes me suspicious that most of our managers who use football coaching as their management model played on mediocre or losing teams.

If motives and talent are overrated sources of the PIP, where do we look for significant deficiencies in behavior—those that account for most of the PIP? We look first to the environmental variables, because

we are most likely to find powerful strategies there that cost very little to implement. From my own experience, I have concluded that the behavior engineering model itself gives the order in which we should look diagnostically to behavior.

Begin with the data. Ask if they are a sufficient, informative, and reliable guide both to how one should perform *and* to how well one has performed. Improper guidance and feedback are the single largest contributors to incompetence in the world of work, and a principal culprit at school.

Next, examine the tools and materials people have to work with. If these can be improved, much training might be saved. Managers who seriously examine the tools of the jobs they manage don't *look* as much like the behavior cult tells us managers should look. But they no doubt are doing a better job of managing.

Next, look at incentives. How can incentives be improved and made more directly contingent upon good performance? This most funda-mental and simple concept of engineering competence seems to have been virtually abandoned, even in the most capitalistic of cultures. The athletic analogy tells us that "winning is its own reward," but Coach doesn't attribute his success to such a concept (even though he publicly promotes it). Oil company management, for example, advertises the importance of incentives for drilling for oil, but few oil company employees are differentially rewarded for superior performance.

Finally—though not least in importance—look at training as a means to achieve greater competence. It is often a powerful strategy, but usually very expensive. It is well to make sure that we don't end up training people to use tools that could be redesigned, or to memorize data they don't need to remember, or to perform to standards they are already capable of meeting and would meet if they knew what these standards are. But if the PIP is still large after we have tried manipulat-ing the environmental variables, we can conclude that we really do have a knowledge problem, and that *perhaps* improvement in training will be worth it.

The behavior engineering model, then, is really an outline of a performance troubleshooting sequence. Significant PIPs invite us to proceed step by step to diagnose the kind of deficiency in behavior, as in Table 3-5.[6] This sequence is, I maintain, the most efficient one, because it is most likely to get the greatest leverage for the performance engineer. But it should not be misinterpreted as a sequence of impor-tance. Motives are surely just as important to performance as good data, for example. But an attempt to correct motive deficiencies (cell 6) will seldom pay off as well as an attempt to correct data deficiencies (cell 1); nor are they as likely to be as significant in their effects. In most situations, it is no doubt possible to stimulate such great motives to

TABLE 3-5 SEQUENCE FOR DIAGNOSING BEHAVIORAL DEFICIENCIES

	S^D *Information*	R *Response*	S_r *Motivation*
E *Environmental* *support*	(Data) ①	(Instruments) ②	(Incentives) ③
P *Behavior* *repertory*	(Knowledge) ④	(Capacity) ⑤	(Motives) ⑥

perform that people will simply find a way to overcome deficiencies in data. But why try? It will surely be more difficult and more costly, and its promise of success more ephemeral. And, besides, as I will show later, an improvement in data will almost certainly produce an improvement in motives.

The point can be made more convincingly, I think, by an example. A simple troubleshooting worksheet applied to almost any job will reveal that environmental changes will almost inevitably yield greater results in performance. Any example will do, but it is best to begin with a simple one: the job of an operator of a packaging machine in a convenience food manufacturing plant. (Later, after I make the method clear, we shall look at such diverse groups as teachers and managers.)

Table 3-6 illustrates an analysis of the typical packaging-machine operation at Potatoes, Inc. The company manufactures potato chips—and there is a large PIP. Why? Table 3-6 is, of course, a highly simplified form of the worksheet. But even by putting the questions in such general form, we begin to clarify what we must do to improve the performance of our packaging-machine operators. We need to provide them with some feedback, that is, some measures of how well they are performing against standards. We should pay them more as they perform better. And we should teach them the "secrets" of exemplary performers.

The questions asked in each of these categories can, of course, be expanded (I shall elaborate in Chapter 5 and elsewhere). In fact, as the questions get more specific, you will see that the answers get easier to make. These answers should give the reader an appreciation of the behavior engineering model as a troubleshooting model.

An important point to note, too, is that although the behavior engineering model is a guide to locating the cause of a performance failure, it does not necessarily indicate the best strategies for correcting the problem. For example, a failure of knowledge does not necessarily mean that training is the most *worthy* solution. To understand this lack

TABLE 3-6   THE BEHAVIOR ENGINEERING MODEL AS A TROUBLESHOOTING WORKSHEET

Variables	Questions	Answers
I. Environment		
1. Data	1. Do typical operators know how well they are performing against the production standard?	No
2. Instruments	2. Do they have the tools and facilities to package well?	Yes
3. Incentives	3. Are their incentives made contingent upon how well they package?	No
II. Repertory		
1. Knowledge	1. Do they know enough to operate the packaging system as well as the exemplary performer?	No
2. Capacity	2. Do they have the intelligence, physical ability, etc., to perform as well as the exemplar?	Yes
3. Motives	3. Are they willing to work for the available incentives?	Yes

of a one-to-one relationship between problem and cure, we must understand two concepts: one I call "diffusion of effect," and another I call "leverage."

LEVERAGE AND THE DIFFUSION OF EFFECT

"So you don't really believe in motivation!" I have been told on several occasions when I discussed the importance of information feedback in supporting competent performance. I might as well confess to believing that oxygen is not important to sustaining human performance. Of course I believe in the existence of motives, just as I believe in the existence of ventilation, love, aesthetic feelings, and violent hatred. And I believe that variations in these things, and many more, can greatly affect human conduct.

But I suppose I am so often barred from the pigeon holes of motivation because of the neat cellular nature of the behavior engineering model itself. In short, I have probably asked for it. And, unfortunately, I have seen a tendency in some of my students to use the behavior engineering model in a rather rigid way—even to say that motivation is *not* important. This conclusion results from a fundamental misunderstanding of the model. The behavior engineering model is merely a way to organize empirical data. And if we use it as if it says that motives,

information, knowledge, response capacity, instruments, and incentives have empirically independent lives, then we have truly become pigeon-holers who miss the point of the model.

I reiterate: The behavior engineering model classifies different ways to *look at a single phenomenon* we call behavior. Performance cannot exist at all unless all six aspects of behavior are present. So all are equally important to performance, but not equally likely to be important to the performance engineer. For example, people revolted by the sight of students learning (motives) won't teach well; nor will those who don't know how to teach (knowledge). But in these matters, since revulsion is more improbable than ignorance, the performance engineer is more likely to train people how to teach than to soothe their revulsions.

So the question is never whether information is more or less important than motivation to competent performance. Rather, the question is: In what way can I achieve the greatest *leverage* when I attempt to establish better behavioral conditions for performance? Or, what aspects of behavior are most deficient?

These questions are further complicated by the unitary nature of behavior. Here is an empirical fact: Whenever I change some condition of behavior, I may indeed—and often will—have a significant effect on some other aspect of behavior. So, if I improve the incentives for performance, people may learn more, even though I have made no effort to teach them better. And when we give people better information about their successes, we may have also improved their incentives to perform well. A history of excellent incentives for working will change one's motives—one's attitudes—toward work. Improving one's response capacity by prosthesis, scheduling, medical treatment, or rest can have marked effects on how well people learn and on their attitudes. It is also possible to make an inefficient tool acceptably efficient just by training people how to use it.

There is no way to alter one condition of behavior without having at least some effect on another aspect—often, a considerable effect. And usually it is difficult, if not impossible, to determine the degree of the diffusion of the effects. For example, suppose that I employ people to design equipment, but I never let them know how well their designs work. I surely cannot expect exemplary performance. Then I introduce a system in which they can test immediately the efficacy of any design change they make, and suddenly I get exemplary performance. Part of the reason for this improvement is purely informational—"technical." But part of it is certainly motivational—I have made the job more pleasant. How do I tell the difference?

The answer is, "It's hard to do." Fortunately, the answer also is, "I needn't." If, for example, my designers show a sudden and dramatic

drop in turnover, I must conclude that the feedback I introduced also had a considerable motivational effect. But the behavior engineering model (since it is a rational, not an empirical, classification system) cannot tell me whether I actually had a motivational effect or not. What the model did for me was lead me to ask certain questions, such as: "Do people have the data that will inform them how well they are doing the job?" For my designers, the answer was "no." Suppose that I had first asked, "Do my designers care whether they perform well or not?" (motives). Knowing my designers, I would have guessed, "yes, indeed." They already have a storehouse of motives. Then I can ask, "Does my new feedback system appeal to those motives?" My answer here must be presumptive: If I now get exemplary performance— extreme quality in design sustained over long periods—I must presume it does. Indeed, until I find it reasonable to establish a new exemplary standard, I must presume that the motivational conditions of the job are now ideal.

But what did the behavior engineering model tell me about the adequacy of my designers' motivation? Nothing. What did it tell me about the information they received? Again, nothing. The model only told me to first *look* to see if the data are adequate, and to begin by correcting the obvious defects if I could. These defects were obvious, and I could correct them. It also told me to examine motives, and to correct their obvious flaws. No flaws were obvious; and even though I half suspected some, I wasn't sure how to correct them.

The behavior engineering model serves one purpose only: It helps us to observe behavior in an orderly fashion, and to ask the "obvious" questions (the ones we so often forget to ask) toward the single end of improving human competence. Indeed, its purpose is to put behavior into some perspective, with reference to what we might do to engineer superior performance. By using the model to direct our questions, we can often avoid plunging into performance improvement programs that have relatively little leverage. It has the tremendous advantage of reducing, to a basic few, the myriad questions we *could* ask about behavior. The model, of course, does not *answer* these questions. But it has been a source of great satisfaction to me to see how easily we get reasonable answers when we pose the questions in a simple way.

THE BEHAVIOR ENGINEERING MODEL AND OTHER IDEAS

The behavior engineering model has another advantage: It can help us to see where and how the many "experts" on human behavior might serve us. Some people have learned a good deal about training, motivation, engineering the tools of work to better fit people's needs, and so on. At least, some people *might* know more about some of these things

than you do. But my own experience is that great strides can usually be made in performance engineering without applying any specialized knowledge of behavior at all. This is especially true with human motives, despite the profusion of "experts" on the "inner person."

I am arguing that the performance engineer will usually find the greatest leverage in other aspects of behavior than attempts to directly influence the motives of people—especially when engineering the performance of adults. This in no way says that people's motives are not important; nor does it say that changing people's motives is not very effective. Rather, it says that *direct* attempts to manipulate people's motives, to deal with the "inner person," are not likely to be as useful as attempts to alter other aspects of behavior. This conclusion is simply pragmatic and empirical, and does not deny that people may have very complex and intricate "inner lives." It simply says that in engineering human performance, the "inner person" usually is not the most efficient place to look. To search the "inner person" for the causes of performance problems has a number of appeals, and only one of them is to avoid responsibility. For example, it often sounds more impressive, and other approaches are said to be too superficial. Or, some people just like the opportunity to peer into other people's private lives and thoughts. But no matter how appealing, the "inner person" approach seldom meets pragmatic tests.

The fundamental difficulty with the "inner person" point of view is that it fails to tell us which actions to take. When you explain to me why a piece of equipment is not working, I should then know how to fix it. But when you tell me that a person is not performing well because he has "underlying hostility," "free-floating anxiety," or "a strong need to be loved," then unless you are suggesting that I make a pass at the person, or perform a lobotomy, you haven't really told me what to do about it. Competent explanations of incompetence should prescribe a program of action—or at least point in that direction.

To the extent that managers (and, to a lesser degree, teachers) come to see their jobs as largely manipulating the environment in order to achieve greater competence, they will become more competent. Managers may like to think of themselves as having terrific insights into human motives and capacities, but so do some poets. To the extent that managers *do* have these insights, they will probably be better people to work for—if only because they will be "nicer" people. But being nice and understanding, while surely admirable and desirable, is not the principal technique for engineering worthy performance. Managers who let their employees know what is expected of them, give them adequate guidance to perform well, supply them with the finest tools of their trade, reward them well, and give them useful training will probably have done their jobs well. If they are also sensitive to the

"inner selves" of their employees, that is a plus. But sensitive managers who fail at these first four accomplishments will certainly have unhappy employees, and nonproductive ones as well.

Furthermore, our "inner lives" resist direct manipulation. Many kinds of specialists concern themselves with our "inner lives," including psychoanalysts, psychiatrists, and clinical psychologists. But there is no concrete evidence that any of these specialists can actually engineer more worthy performance. As far as I am concerned, your "inner self" is rich and complex. But it is neither in my realm of expertise, nor is it any of my business.

Behavior Modification

Not everyone in psychology is concerned only with the "inner person." Many are interested in modifying more overt manifestations of human conduct. In recent years, for instance, there has been a growing interest in behavior modification, largely stimulated by the work of B. F. Skinner. "Behavior mod," as it is often called, has enthusiastic supporters and a voluble opposition. Perhaps I can help put the issues it raises into some perspective, with the assistance of the behavior engineering model. What the model tells us is that we can change performance in one of two ways: by modifying the behavior repertory itself or by modifying the environment. Behaviorists would probably say that in either case we are modifying behavior, which means that such activities are fundamentally the subject matter of behaviorism. Then, by extension, they say that the fundamental principles we must understand are the laws and rules of behavior—specifically, reinforcement theory. But I think this is not completely true, and that such a view overstates the role and importance of behavioral principles in the engineering of performance.

Suppose that I employ 20 people to squeeze oranges for me by hand, and I sell the orange juice. At some point, I become dissatisfied with the performance of my company, Citrus, Inc. My competitors are turning juice out faster and can charge less for it. I am intent on improving the competence of my operation, so I apply the behavior engineering model. Table 3-7 lists the questions I ask and my answers. Given these answers, I clearly need to do one thing to get greater competence—I must provide my employees with a mechanical orange squeezer. When I do, I get performance superior to that of my competition; I get exemplary performance. Have I modified behavior? Of course. Have I applied the principles of behaviorism? Of course not—at least, not in any serious way.

Now I go one more step. I design an automation system that will mechanically cut oranges, squeeze the juice from them, and clean up

TABLE 3-7   QUESTIONS AND ANSWERS

Behavior Repertories	*Environmental Supports*
Q. Do my people have all the information and knowledge needed for exemplary performance? A. Yes.	Q. Do they have all the data they need for exemplary performance? A. Yes.
Q. Do they have the capability to make the responses required of exemplary performance? A. Yes.	Q. Do they have the best tools to use for exemplary performance? A. No.
Q. Do they have the motivation to give me exemplary performance? A. Yes.	Q. Are the incentives I give them sufficient for exemplary performance? A. Yes.

after itself. For this, I need only one employee, to push the buttons and monitor my machinery. Have I modified behavior? Surely. Did I do it scientifically? Naturally—I used all the science of automation available to me. Did I apply reinforcement theory? Of course not.

When I built my mechanical squeezer—before I automated my factory—I certainly took into account certain characteristics of behavior. I designed it so that it could be used by either right- or left-handed people. I built a grip that would fit a hand. And I employed the very scientific principle of the lever—a long grip and a short fulcrum. In doing these things, however, I was viewing my employees less as repertories of behavior than as mechanical constructions themselves. Indeed, I would not have designed my squeezer any differently had my employees been mechanical robots shaped like people. The principles of behavior that I applied—if any—were at most trivial. I directly manipulated the environment, and I achieved a change in accomplishment. That I also may have modified behavior repertories is of no fundamental interest to me. Behavior repertories were not the variables I manipulated most directly, and their modification was not the change that I had to pay for.

The practitioners of behavior modification hold as their subject matter behavior itself (and, chiefly, behavior repertories), and they can bring some useful skills to certain performance problems. They can help us achieve good results in toilet training, the control of "bad habits" like smoking and overeating, and other problems in which behavior seems resistant to change and requires a specialist's help.

But the subject matter of the performance engineer is not behavior. Behavior modification differs from performance engineering in three ways. First, the modification of behavior repertories is only one of many techniques we might use to improve performance. I could, for example,

find the methods of compensation specialists, doctors, or industrial engineers equally useful, depending on the nature of a PIP. Second, behavior modification, as it is usually described and practiced, is largely a direct extrapolation from the animal behavior laboratory. But, however important the scientific principles found in that laboratory, laboratory experience does not even suggest most of the techniques needed to design intelligent performance systems. Engineers need handbooks that guide them in orderly and sensible ways, and I believe that behaviorism falls far short of giving us even the basis for such practical procedural steps. Third, theories of behavior modification have simply avoided the central questions of value that any engineering discipline must begin with. And, as we shall see, this is no mere matter of oversight—values are avoided because that is the "scientific," as opposed to the engineering, point of view. These major differences deserve some elaboration.

Note first that I am not saying that behavior modification, as the behaviorists speak of it, is an unimportant and useless discipline in achieving more competent performance. Because it is in its infancy *as a discipline,* it has a lot of yet unrealized potential, as you will see in some of the chapters that follow. But performance engineering—or teleonomics—is also in its infancy *as a discipline;* and those interested in it should not narrow their views to behavior modification as the sole, or even principal, technique for achieving their goals. Human behavior is always required in achieving human competence, but so is human genetics and physiology. Selective breeding and the administration of drugs *might* some day prove to be useful techniques for engineering some forms of competence. And when and if this happens, their proponents will no doubt announce the arrival of the millennium. But we shall, hopefully, be prepared to pigeon-hole these methods into their limited place in the behavior engineering model (in the cell for response capacity, most likely), and simply add them to our bag of techniques—along with behavior modification, human factors engineering, otology, and Archimedes' principles.

B. F. Skinner has, of course, provided the principal philosophical arguments in favor of behavior modification as the central tool of performance engineering. But I simply cannot live with his easy extrapolations, however exemplary I find his scientific work.

I am an old behaviorist, apprenticed in Skinner's laboratories. And I cannot doubt the evidence of my own eyes and my own experiments that the behavior of animals is, indeed, subject to control and conditioning in lawful, orderly ways. Nor do I reject the proposition that people also are animals and subject to these laws of reinforcement. What I do object to is the notion that these laws are the *only* things underlying the most important performance engineering strategies.

We all know that people consist of a few dollars' worth of chemicals, and that a person will fall like a stone if tossed into a vacuum. But when we observe human beings as a subject matter, they emerge as more than mere physical things. The laws of the physical sciences account for a great deal of our characteristics, but certainly not all of them. But just as we are not merely a collection of chemicals, atoms, cells, and electric currents, we need not assume that we are merely animals (in Skinner's sense), with our behavior subject *only* to the laws of reinforcement. There is no authoritative document that says that we are totally explained and controlled by the laws of physics, chemistry, and reinforcement. Indeed, to generalize that this is true is to invite widespread disbelief.

Of course, some of that disbelief can be discounted as romance or religious superstition, but certainly not all of it. It seems to me that there is a characteristic of human beings which simply begs to be taken as a serious subject matter and which defies reduction to the laws of reinforcement and the physical sciences. One thing that distinguishes people from other animals is their enormous variety of vantage points (points of view) and values—and their incredible capacity to change these vantage points and to manipulate them to their own ends.

To extrapolate and say that vantage points and values are nothing more than behaviors, even verbal behaviors, subject strictly to the laws of conditioning, is to assert far more than is evident. To show that values and vantage points can be shaped by reinforcement, and can be conditioned and learned, does not fully account for them—any more than we can fully account for vantage points to show that they can be shaped by drugs or physical disruptions of the brain.

Skinner once made an astonishing remark on a TV talk show, on the occasion of the publication of his book *Beyond Freedom and Dignity*. He said (and I can only paraphrase from memory, so I may be doing him a disservice) that if management would take reinforcement theory seriously, industry could, *within the space of a year*, become a model of human competence, productivity, and happiness. (He also ventured that the schools could as easily solve most of their problems in the same way.) A remark like this makes it unnecessarily difficult to take behaviorism as seriously as it should be taken. It is a leap of the imagination, unsupported by the realities of nonlaboratory life.

Finally, and most important, behaviorism fails as an engineering discipline because it fails to face directly the issue of cultural values—except to discard them. And this seems to me to violate the first and most fundamental requirement of any system of engineering. It is this one act of Skinner's—the rejection of values as an important issue in engineering human performance—that gives rise to most of his critics. Once, I looked upon Skinner's critics as closed-minded anti-scientists, and I could not listen to them without scoffing at their "romantic"

pigheadedness. But more recently I have listened with more respect, and I think I hear what at least *some* of them are saying. (Not all their arguments make sense.) They are saying that to make behavior the focal concern, when we try to design a better world, threatens to toss aside human values as a serious issue. And they are right—it does threaten to do just this. Skinner seems to tell us that values—except as we cast them in behavioral terms—are misleading, even superstitious, ideas; and that only by making behavior our focal subject will we be able to achieve the good life. Indeed, he says, "When we can design . . . cultures with the confidence we bring to physical technology, the question of value will not be raised."[7] Value judgments, he asserts, are the guesswork we do when we do not understand the underlying conditions of behavior.

But values *can* be treated systematically, as I shall show in the next chapter, and the amount of agreement we have about them is enormous. Indeed, these agreements are what bind us together as a culture. We can measure these values, and we can measure how well we are achieving them. Human values are there as a subject matter as real, as measurable, as predictable, and as attainable as human behavior.

I do not like the way Skinner wants to design a culture for the very reason that he rejects the values of accomplishments as the starting point. Without that starting point, I would not know where the cultural designers would be taking me—except into some contingency system in which things would work out well for me—in which I would be " . . . happy, secure, productive, creative, and forward looking."[8] Skinner asks, "What is wrong with it [a behaviorally engineered culture]?" Then he accuses his critics of finding only one true flaw: "Someone planned it that way."

But Skinner does not adequately explain why a conscious plan should be so aversive to people, and so threatening. I don't believe it is; nor do I believe that this is what people object to about his program of behavioral modification. I think that *almost all* of us know that human beings exert control over each other's behavior—and that we often plan it that way. The notion that we all do that never seems to bother people; nor does the act of talking about it and openly plotting it. Yet there is something about Skinner's planned society that does seem to bother nearly everyone I know (including Skinner's most thoughtful students—and I consider myself one of those—and even the most hard-bitten business people, who openly plot the most undemocratic forms of behavior control every day). What is that "something?" It is simply the notion that we can create a culture "scientifically" by making behavior the focal subject.* It is not the scientific methodology, or the

---

*It's disturbing, in this context, that behaviorists, in their labs, simply kill the animals that resist their training.

idea of planning, that bothers us; it is the choice of subject matter. It is beside the point whether the "scientists" who direct the cultural design act from afar and only as the catalytic agents, or sit upon a throne and direct it with a scepter. The problem is that the controlling system, however benign, begins its process of engineering on the assumption that what is good for the culture can be found in *my* behavior. But I would prefer the quality of the culture to depend not so heavily on our behaviors, but on our accomplishments. Too many different behaviors can lead to the same accomplishments, and some unexpected variations lead to even greater accomplishments.

In Chapter 1 I told the story of Barton Hogg, who had engineered a culture—one that dug for lead. The fact is that if Barton Hogg had sufficiently perfected a system of reinforcement so that he could easily get any behavior he wanted by what Skinner would consider the most scientific means, he would have failed by an even wider margin. He would have used his powerful techniques to get the college boys to dig in cadence from the very beginning. But if Hogg had been a good performance engineer, instead of a poor behavior modifier, he would have begun the design of his culture by focusing on what he wanted to accomplish, and he would have established the standards required for that little culture to survive. If he had then conveyed these standards to those who had joined it, he certainly would not have found it necessary to manipulate anything else.

Skinner assures us that a scientific approach to behavioral control will eventually find the best way—the way with the greatest survival value. But what do I have to convince me of that except Skinner's assurances and his appeal to the prestige of science? This is exactly as our parents treated us: They assured us that if we developed certain basic "good habits," these habits would in the long run pay off. Skinner is not just asking us to be reasonable, sensible, "scientific" people; he is asking us to make the particular methods and focus of operant conditioning the principal value of our culture. It will, he seems to say, make everything all right. When that everything-is-fine state happens to me, I will possibly be sufficiently reinforced to come around to his viewpoint.

Skinner, of course, has been enormously reinforced for pursuing the methods of science in manipulating behavior. That kind of behavior led him to discover far superior ways to control the behavior of others and to organize behavioral data. His science is a significant contribution to the cause of engineering human competence. But his successes, I fear, have caused him to overgeneralize—to believe that the scientific methods he used in the laboratory will, in extension, be the behaviors appropriate to the engineering of cultures. No values—no valued accomplishments of the rat—were involved in his experiments. For him, then, engineering a culture will require no concern for value:

> . . . value judgments take up where science leaves off. *When* we can
> design small . . . cultures with the confidence we bring to physical
> technology, the question of value will not be raised.[9]

This statement underlines the sharp differences between behavior modification and performance engineering as a way to design a culture. Skinner talks as if his science will take us somewhere we have not been, but here he is short on facts. Small cultures called businesses— from manufacturing plants to research laboratories—are designed all the time. The engineers are called "managers" or "businesspeople." Many of them are not very good at designing, but some of them are. The manufacturing plant is a genuine culture, and one usually designed with the same confidence that "physical technologists" display.

But such confident engineering does not set aside the question of value; *it begins with them.* The good engineer of these cultures performs teleonomically: He begins by ordering the accomplishment intended for the culture; establishes a scale of values for these accomplishments; and then learns how to measure them. Everything else— including the behavioral contingencies and incentives—flows from this initial analysis of goals and value. *Some* of these cultures work with surprising efficiency, full of " . . . happy, secure, productive, and creative" people who know very well that their culture has been carefully planned and are proud of it.

My own laboratory, since I left Skinner's, has been these very cultures. And I have found repeatedly that a culture that does not work well—in which people are unhappy, insecure, unproductive, and uncreative—was designed by a manager who did not begin with careful analysis of its goals and values. This analysis, this teleonomic engineering, pursues a method astonishingly different from that of the sciences. Not that there are no similarities between the method of science and that of engineering: Both depend heavily on detached observation, measurement, and orderly procedure. But beyond that, the similarities fade. The serendipity that Skinner finds so important in the laboratory is certainly not a reliable experience in engineering, because the engineer starts at a different point: The engineer knows in the main what the goal is, and begins by making a design of that end point. The engineer tries to create what certainly can exist, but the scientist tries to discover what we don't even know exists. And it is, I believe, Skinner's failure to make the important distinctions between these two methods that causes his overgeneralization and his peculiar concept of how to design a culture. That Skinner does not really see the critical differences is evident in this description of his:

> Most people would subscribe to the proposition that there is no
> value judgment involved in deciding *how* to build an atomic bomb,

but would reject the proposition that there is none involved in deciding *to* build one. The most significant difference here may be that the scientific practices which guide the designer of the bomb are clear, while those which guide the designer of the culture which builds a bomb are not.[10]

Skinner makes an assumption that we need to examine: When scientific practice (engineering) becomes effective (advanced), values disappear from its consideration. He has chosen an excellent example, because I can use it to show that those who designed the bomb made fearsome value judgments in deciding *how* to build it. And I can show that their method was much closer to those of the factory manager than those of the scientific laboratory.

William Manchester gives an excellent account of these value judgments.[11] The designers knew that a chain reaction would take place when they split the atom, but they did not know how great it would be. In testing it out, they built a screen that would decelerate the buildup of the chain. Listen to Manchester (italics mine):

> So great a prospect of success raised new questions ... it was impossible to gauge the efficiency of decelerating techniques. The [reaction] might defy their checks and restraints, might break loose and take all of Chicago, or even Illinois, with it. To *reduce* the risk ... strips of cadmium and ... boron steel ... were passed completely through the pile ... no one could be sure that would be successful. ...

The designers even formed a suicide squad of two young scientists who would make one last try to stop the reaction if it got out of hand. The value judgment—that the risk of the destruction of Illinois was offset by the prospect of success—is in the very nature of engineering. Any engineering system begins with an economic base, and strives to create results in which the values exceed the costs. When engineers design a bridge, *how* they design it is conditioned by the weighing of values and costs. How much of a safety factor should be built into it? To make it perfectly safe would cost too much money, and would defeat the purpose of the engineering, which is to find a more economic way to cross the river. So they balance the risks; they weigh the values of safe transport with the costs of construction. So vital are the value judgments of decisions about *how* to design the bridge that the state will not permit engineers complete freedom in making them, and it sets up careful regulatory codes to constrain the engineering judgments. The physician, who uses the method of engineering and not that of science, weighs similar values every day; and *how* the doctor treats a patient will be conditioned by personal judgments (which sometimes the

patient must make). The engineer of physical things does not have the freedom from value judgments that the "pure" scientist has. Indeed, every engineering effort is conditioned by the values that initiated the project.

And you can also be sure that "physical" engineers often proceed with far less competence than the cultural engineers we call managers. The men who built the bomb were flying by the seat of their pants. And far more so than the exemplary designers of work cultures.

The point is this. Great knowledge about the science of behavior does not qualify us as performance engineers. The orderly application of knowledge to create a desirable end—engineering—is quite a different method from the pursuit of knowledge not yet born. Or, to put it another way, the performance required to use scientific knowledge efficiently is not *necessarily* the same as that required to develop that knowledge.

In fact, fundamentally the method of engineering (as I described it in the beginning of the book) is the opposite of the method of science. The good engineer begins by creating a precise model of the result; then explores for techniques to help in achieving those results. And any techniques will do, provided that they fulfill the value criteria—that they work. The "pure" scientist proceeds just the other way: not knowing what the results will be, nor their value, but having a set of techniques for getting these results. The scientist, armed with a technique, explores for results, whereas the engineer, knowing exactly what the desired results are, explores for the techniques to produce them.

And that is why the subject matter of teleonomics is not human behavior. The systematic modification of behavior is only one of the kinds of techniques that the cultural engineer—the manager or teacher—will explore. But it is not the end result.

When I first left Skinner's laboratory and went eagerly to try my hand at engineering competent cultures, at work and at school, I was armed with what I thought were two powerful tools: the techniques of operant conditioning, and an open mind about results. These were admirable behaviors for the laboratory. But they became extinguished in those subcultures I presumed to be able to redesign, and replaced by a new set of behaviors: a technique for identifying results and their value, and an open mind about operant conditioning.

NOTES

1. We need to distinguish between efficiency and effectiveness. A performance engineer is more than an "efficiency expert." *Effectiveness* refers to accomplishments, and ultimately to their value. *Efficiency* refers to behavior (the denominator of the worth formula), and ultimately to its costs.

Teleonomics is concerned with both effectiveness and efficiency, but ultimately with worth, their ratio. We can pursue stupid goals efficiently; or we can be effective at too great a cost. In this and later chapters, we shall see many instances in which concern for efficiency without regard for effectiveness results in unworthy performance.

2. We are very sloppy in our use of behavioral terminology. Even "professionals" do not often distinguish clearly between behavior (which must include an environment) and the behavior repertory, which is only a component of behavior. As this chapter will make clear, the distinction is critical for the performance engineer.

3. It is simply a matter of one's vantage point whether we call something less than exemplary performance a "deficiency" or a "potential." We are so used to seeing incompetence as "failure" and "deficiency" that it is difficult to call it "potential." But if we take the vantage point of a performance engineer, it is surely potential. If we could more clearly separate our view of people as animals (which they are) and as humans (which they can be), we would be more careful in our language. When a person's animal fails, it is natural enough to say that it has "potential." After all, we can "train it." But when we see the failure as a "human" one, we are tempted to call it a "deficiency," i.e., a defect in the human. There is more about how to keep these vantage points straight in Chapter 11.

4. The confusion about the components of behavior is widespread among professional psychologists. Some speak as if the stimulus were totally in the environment and the response in the person (or "organism"). An example is this absurdity: "He didn't respond to the stimulus." How can an event be a stimulus if there is no response to it? Another example is found in the so-called circularity of the law of effect: "The rat presses the lever *because* the food it gets is a reward. How do we know the food is a reward? *Because* it presses the lever to get it." This seems to be an absurdity only when we see the motive and the incentive as two separate things rather than two different ways to look at the same thing. Chapter 6 elaborates this point.

    B. F. Skinner, of all people, makes these things confusing when he leaves the laboratory and speculates on the larger world. He says, for example, that we should "credit" the environment, not the "behavior" with the "success" of organisms (B. F. Skinner, *Beyond Freedom and Dignity*, New York: Knopf, 1971). Somehow, behavior exists "within" the organism. But in the laboratory, he is more careful. What is at issue is the confusion between "behavior" and "behavior repertories." Skinner—and some of his followers even more—do not always keep the distinction clear.

5. A common behavioral model is written (in shorthand) as

$$S^D—O—R \cdot S_r$$

The O stands for the "intervening organism," and sometimes is written P to stand for "person." There are at least two faults to be found with this model. The first one is abstract: To separate the "organism" from "stimulus," "response," and "reinforcement" implies that these things are somehow

"outside" of the person, which is nonsense. The second is practical: We could say that S^D, R, and S_r stand for the environmental aspects of behavior. That's fair enough, but we would lose some of the power of the model.

6. For years, I promoted a simpler distinction between "deficiencies of execution" (D_E) and "deficiencies of knowledge" (D_K). This distinction later was popularized by Robert Mager. By D_E's I meant what I now call "deficiencies of environment," and D_K's recognized that knowledge deficiencies were the most important problems of the behavior repertory. The behavior engineering model is obviously an improvement over this old and now widely used distinction. See T. F. Gilbert, "A Scientific Approach to Identifying Training Needs," *Management of Personnel Quarterly* (now *Human Resource Management*), Vol. 6, No. 3 (Fall, 1967). Also, see Robert Mager, *"Analyzing Problems, or "You Really Oughta Wanta"* (San Francisco: Fearon, 1970).

7. B. F. Skinner, "The Design of Cultures," in Roger E. Ulrich et al. (eds.), *Control of Human Behavior* (New York: Scott, Foresman, 1966).

8. Skinner, "The Design of Cultures."

9. Skinner, "The Design of Cultures." (Italics mine.)

10. Skinner, "The Design of Cultures." (Italics mine.)

11. William Manchester, *The Glory and the Dream* (Boston: Little, Brown, 1973), Vol. I, pp. 380–382.

Part Two
MODELS OF
PERFORMANCE
ANALYSIS

People often have a much harder time deciding where they want to go than they do in figuring out how best to get there. And, as I shall argue in Part II, mistakes in decisions about goals are the greatest single cause of human incompetence. This judgment is no mere whimsy, but comes from years of observing people perform in a number of institutions.

As an example, it should be obvious, although it generally isn't, that the mission we set for a school will condition even the details of its curriculum. Suppose that I began a school with the one interest of teaching students to become devotees of some sublime god, and I defined an educated and competent person as one who could most completely pay homage to that god. Would reading be in my curriculum? Probably not, unless I found reading useful in paying homage. Indeed, I might conclude that reading could prove great harm to my cause since it would only distract my students.

Or I might decide that the truly educated person is one who lives independently—that is, not dependent on others in the least for survival or comfort. Would reading be in my curriculum? Certainly not, since reading is principally a way of getting help from others—materially or emotionally. But gardening would, of course, be central to my curriculum, as would self-defense and carpentry.

Our own educational system has a commitment to a few small goals, but not to any mission that I can

detect. Trying to find out *why* a school teaches its students about the Treaties of Utrecht, and does not teach them how to buy insurance wisely, is nearly a hopeless task. This aimlessness surely does more to cripple our educational system than all the inefficiencies in teaching that we could point out. The real question is: *Why* do we teach Johnny to read? If we had begun with a focus on some purpose, I am convinced that our curriculum would look much different.

In Chapter 4 we shall observe institutions that behave with great *efficiency,* but that are nonetheless grossly incompetent—either because they have set the wrong accomplishments as goals or because their subgoals do not match their ultimate goal. We shall examine a method for avoiding incompetence by clarifying our goals and making them compatible with the goals of others. We have already (in Chapter 3) examined a system for creating greater efficiency—but one that will not be useful unless our goals have been well defined. Because efficiency applied in the wrong direction is merely a way to maximize incompetence. The "greatest" woodcutter in the world—the most efficient—who, by misreading the assignment, chops down all the valuable fruit trees and leaves the lumber pine standing, is far more incompetent than the bumbling clod who takes a day to level a single pine. People who boast of their efficiency terrify me when I don't know to what ends they are applying it.

Part II has just two chapters. Chapter 4 describes a system for analyzing our goals, from the highest to the smallest subgoals; for placing values and standards on these goals; and for determining what must be done to attain them. The performance matrix—the central tool described in Chapter 4—is a way to organize our points of view so we shall set first things first when we design a performance system. It is also the most general and valuable method of troubleshooting existing performance systems.

Chapter 5 details specific troubleshooting techniques for assuring ourselves that we have, indeed, described our goals properly; for discovering where our greatest potential for improvement lies; and for pinpointing actions that will give us the greatest leverage in engineering improved performance.

Chapters 4 and 5 will also synthesize what has gone before. In Part I we examined the three most basic assumptions of the system. Now I shall try to show how they are put together into a single method of engineering.

Chapter Four

The Performance Matrix

O civili, si ergo,
Fortibus es in ero!
O nobili, deis trux.
Vatis enim, causan dux.

ANONYMOUS

COMPETENCE AND VANTAGE POINTS

Latin students are well advised not to attempt a translation of the bit of
verse we owe to Anonymous, unless they wish to waste hours on the
futile assumption that the verse is truly Latin. Anyone can translate it in
an instant, however, by assuming the correct point of view. And the
translation nicely illustrates the impetus for this chapter. I have provided a "translation" below,* but the reader may first want to try. I warn
you, however, that it is a simple matter only if you assume a simple-
minded vantage point.

The translation illustrates that language cannot be understood from
its syntax, vocabulary, and orthography alone, but is conditioned as
well by the way we look at things. Similarly, much of our disagreement
and confusion about human competence results from conflicting or
unclear vantage points, more than from the details of what we are
viewing and talking about. And many subjects that appear to be
abstruse can soon be reduced to utter simplicity by a slight shift in our
viewpoint, just as the imposing pretentiousness of the "Latin" verse
becomes reduced to banal doggerel.

Human performance often seems imposing in its complexity, and
disagreements about it unresolvable. But mystery, like beauty, is in the

---

*O see, Willie! See 'er go!
Forty buses in a row.
Oh No, Billie, they is trucks.
What is in 'em? Cows and ducks.

111

eye, and has no objective existence. If we are to make sense of human performance, it will be because we develop simple and useful vantage points when we discuss it. But first a communications network is required. Since both the pillage of New York City and the preservation of Central Park can be valuable accomplishments depending on one's point of view, we must have a way to sort out our viewpoints and weigh our values if we are going to communicate.

Suppose I design a furnace that burns oil more efficiently. Is this a valuable accomplishment? Perhaps not in the context of an institution that sells furnaces only so that it can sell more oil. But in the context of a society that is attempting to conserve fuel, it is truly competent.

Such conflicts of interest are of course common, and they complicate the evaluation of competence. But very often (not always) these conflicts can be resolved to the satisfaction of all parties if we look to some higher aim. We have already seen the "competent" credit department that hurt the sales department until the goals of the two departments were reconciled. And there are countless situations just like that one.

Some conflicts of purpose can be reconciled completely; others, only compromised. In any case, an efficient system of analysis is required to know which is possible—and also how to do it. Furthermore, the values we place on accomplishments depend on the larger contexts in which we view them. The furnace company that bends all efforts to increase the demand for oil so that it can sell more of it is just like the moron who rips the siding off his house to keep a fire in his hearth. For the sake of immediate aims, both the furnace company and the moron may be performing with high efficiency. But at some point their performance will prove disastrous—not only to others who must eventually pay, but also to their own larger aims. So we see that another reason for a system of analyzing purposes is to resolve hidden conflicts within the same set of interests. Our greatest sources of incompetence lie in inconsistencies within our own hierarchy of values. And our hierarchy of values begins with a philosophy of life, whether or not it is well articulated.

We need a system for sorting out the levels—the scope—of our viewpoints when we talk about values and accomplishments. To design that system, I have begun with an assumption that I consider axiomatic—what I call the Fourth Leisurely Theorem.

> We can view human accomplishments at several levels of generality, and the values we assign to these accomplishments at each level will be derived from the level just above them.

When we talk about the manufacture of a gas stove as an accomplishment, then, we need to identify whether we are talking about it in the context of, say, the conservation of natural resources, the context of a salable or useful commodity, or as a practical way to cook food. An accomplishment may contribute to competence at one level and not at another; but if the values at one level are not consistent with those at a higher level, competence is voided.

However, I believe that most of the disagreements people have about values and competence are not a result of applying different standards of value, but of observing the same things from different (or not clearly stated) points of view. As an example, suppose that we have agreed to discuss the competence of the rebellious Virginian, Robert E. Lee. Where would we begin, and what would be the rules guiding us to agreement?

Summer nights in the South encourage talk, especially when mixed with bourbon and good friends on a porch. A child can lie on the steps and listen to the quiet, drawling voices just rise above the whir of the cicadas and the chatter of crickets. And sometimes there is a sorcery in the sounds and sensations, and the conversation becomes as indelibly imprinted as the unforgettable odor of the yellow jessamine and the creak of the old swing.

It is such a moment of magic that I recall long ago on some now-forgotten veranda. The retired Colonel Broadview, as I shall call him, orated rather pompously about General Robert E. Lee and about how the General was the most competent warrior in all of history, recorded or otherwise. The Colonel seemed most to admire the way Lee had outsmarted all the Yankee generals time after time, as he kept a war alive that he should have lost long before.

"He wasn't too smart at Gettysburg," objected old Xavier Cooting. He had been in the army, too, and was gassed in France, which gave him credentials enough (though it was not as if a Southerner needed credentials to engage in debate). "Lee should have been cashiered," Xavier went on. "He trusted men like Longstreet too much, and he should have sacked Jeb Stuart. And Pickett's Charge—what a damn fool Lee was."

"Oh, come on, Xavier," the Colonel replied, rocking a bit more vigorously. "Lee was brilliant, and he didn't really lose at Gettysburg, you know. He fought a bigger enemy to a standstill on its own ground. The whole idea of coming up through Pennsylvania and getting above Washington was the damnedest bit of daring, and marvelous strategy. He drew the Yankees out of Virginia and came close to making them wash their hands of the whole affair."

"But the point is, he didn't succeed. Any damn fool can be daring. I'm not saying he wasn't brave and clever—just that he was an incompetent general," Xavier grunted. "How about another drink, Polly?"

Polly Seay, the veteran Southern belle on whose veranda we were assembled, was nothing if not soft-spoken.

"Old Bob Lee only made one mistake, Xavier. He fought on the wrong side," Polly said to everyone's amazement. At least her daughter, Ethel Good, was amazed.

"How can you say that, Mama?" Ethel said. "You of all people! Lee had his home and people back in Virginia, so he had to fight on their side even if he didn't agree with them about slavery and secession. I'd call him a noble man."

"Noble, my ass; he was a damn chauvinist—just another militant bastard," Abby Stracht interrupted. Abby was Polly's cousin, and a feminist of local notoriety.

"Killing people was his hobby. If he had been really noble, he wouldn't have gone to war at all. If he had been a decent man, he would have stayed home and helped his wife wash the dishes. People who fight wars are incompetent by any definition," sneered Abby.

And so the argument went, through the night, with no minds changed until Tony Logisti, the visitor from up North, finally tried to switch subjects.

"What's the big argument all about? Maybe he didn't wash dishes, Abby, but he did take good care of his men. That's what I always admired about Lee; he worried all the time about feeding and clothing his troops. I thought that's why he came up through Pennsylvania in the first place—to supply his army. You can't be a competent general if you don't tend to the details. Besides, that war is over," reasoned Tony.

Although I have long forgotten exactly who those people were on that magic Carolina evening, the arguments have never faded; partly, no doubt, because it was the first time I had heard anyone question the competence of General Robert E. Lee, paragon of Southern virtue and skills. But there was a deeper reason—one that obsessed me in my youth: curiosity about why seemingly intelligent adults, having much the same information, disagree on anything. It seemed to me then that logic must be so simple and commanding that no one could escape its conclusions. And when I asked, I was always told, "It all depends on your point of view."

Years later, I heard two great generals of World War II revive the Lee argument, one attesting to Lee's competence at Gettysburg, the other sharing Xavier Cooting's opinion that Lee should have been cashiered. Surely these men, equally expert in military science, and both scholars of Lee's war, had no room for dispute.

Slowly, I began to see that each of the six friends of that warm Carolina night was correct in assessing Lee's performance, as were the two generals. And we can reconcile the differences. Because they did

not really dispute each other—they only seemed to. It wasn't as if they were viewing the same thing and arriving at different conclusions. Rather, they were viewing different things—different aspects of a person's performance—and arriving at quite reasonable though different conclusions. It can be very instructive to sort out their viewpoints and make some sense of them.

Problems of philosophy and analysis are problems of the vantage point. And the problem of vantage points is getting them organized so that we can assess what it means to stand in one place or another. Three of our six friends thought Lee's performance worthy, and three others thought him a fool. So our first sorting of these viewpoints looks like Table 4-1.

But we should examine the six judgments of Lee's competence more closely. One characteristic of these several judgments that seems to differentiate them is the degree of "generality." Abby Stracht is concerned with the philosophical Lee; Tony Logisti, pleased by the General's attention to the supply of soldiers' shoes. Indeed, we might say that each of our six friends is looking at Lee's performance with a different scope and from a different level of generality, as Table 4-2 shows. Here we see six people—six perfectly intelligent and knowledgeable people—looking at the same performer and unable to agree with one another, because they are standing in completely different vantage points.

For its purpose, each level of view is legitimate and useful, and there is every reason to be able to stand in each. Difficulty arises mostly when we get our levels of view confused, and when, in talking with one another, we fail to make our vantage point clear. The Colonel and Xavier are not really in disagreement at all about Lee's competence;

TABLE 4-1 ASSESSMENT OF LEE'S PERFORMANCE

Competent	*Incompetent*
Ethel Good: Against great temptation to do otherwise, he chose to fight for home and family.	*Abby Stracht:* His philosophy was such that war and killing were among life's acceptable tools.
Colonel Broadview: As a general, his strategy was innovative, spectacular, and ingenious. With luck, it would have won for him.	*Polly Seay:* As a sheer matter of policy, he was untrue to himself. He gave up the chance to fight for policies he believed in—indeed, he fought against them.
Tony Logisti: He went to great lengths to supply his men and care for their needs—and this was his strength.	*Xavier Cooting:* He let personal loyalty and trust interfere with the proper execution of battle, and therefore he failed his people.

TABLE 4-2 LEVELS OF JUDGMENTS OF LEE

Viewer		Level of View	Judgment of Lee
I.	Abby Stracht	Philosophical (philosophy of life)	Negative
II.	Ethel Good	Cultural (cultural values)	Positive
III.	Polly Seay	Policy (institutional goals)	Negative
IV.	Colonel Broadview	Strategic (planning)	Positive
V.	Xavier Cooting	Tactical (execution)	Negative
VI.	Tony Logisti	Logistic (supply)	Positive

nor do they dispute each other's "facts." They are simply talking about two entirely different and independent things. The Colonel admires Lee as a planner, a strategist; Xavier deplores Lee's failures in execution, his tactics. Polly and her daughter Ethel are not in conflict either; they, too, are simply talking about different things: Polly despairs of Lee's pursuit of his political aims, and Ethel toasts his devotion to a larger culture. Yet they all speak as if there were only one judgment to make of Lee's performance.

LEVELS OF VANTAGE

We may fail to agree with each other about facts ("that did happen"; "no, it didn't happen") or about tastes ("I love anarchy"; "I hate anarchy"). But we really cannot sensibly disagree when we are standing in two entirely different vantage points.

A vantage point is like a scientist's microscope or telescope—an instrument that sets the range of our observations, and separates and highlights events in which we are particularly interested. To view performance from no vantage point, or from an ever-shifting vantage point, is really to see nothing of import, and leads only to a collection of confused impressions, no matter how clear and articulate our descriptions may sound.[1] Presumably, we always wish to look within a context and to a purpose (unless, of course, like a poet, we merely wish to absorb "passively" the delicious sensation of a sunset—and even that passivity could be called a viewpoint, within an emotional context and to a sensuous purpose).

Once we have chosen our vantage point—set its context and stated its purpose—we shall be looking through the same scope as anyone else who assumes the same outlook. We may disagree about what we see once we look through that scope (is this event a fact or an illusion?),

or about our taste for what we see (I hate it; I love it). But at least our disagreements will now be intelligible, and not a result of using different lenses to look through.

The disparities of view about General Lee that we found among our six friends are universal, I believe. They represent ranges of scope, or breadth of generalization of viewpoint, from the most abstract to the most specific. In Table 4-3, I have summarized these "levels of vantage point," showing the context and purpose that define each position. The accomplishments at each level tell us what we must look at to distinguish performance when we are viewing from that level.

When we view from the *policy level,* we are generally standing in the context of a fairly well-defined institution, such as a corporation, a school, the rubber industry, the Department of Agriculture, home, or the Boy Scouts. This institution need not be physically well defined but may be a group in a "drug culture" or just "independent voters." Once we have identified the context—in this example, the institution and the subculture—we begin to look at the purpose of the institution for further definition. At the *policy level,* we look to see how the institution attains its cultural goal. Because, by my definition, this is what characterizes institutions. Then, to distinguish between institutions, or to evaluate performance within one, we look at their *missions.* What is constant about any institution is that it is pursuing a specific cultural goal. What is different about institutions is the mission each tries to accomplish in order to achieve that goal. For example, if the cultural goal of an institution is the distribution of good food, it may pursue that goal by dedicating itself to the accomplishment of a variety of missions—as different as packaged potato chips or the sale of health foods.

The generality with which we view and evaluate accomplishments depends on the level at which we view things. If we are asked whether there is competence within a certain corporation, our answer will depend on the level at which we view its performance.

Suppose that I am asked to evaluate competence in the manufacture of potato chips. I may reach a variety of conclusions. For example, I may report back that in potato chip plants, the scheduling and supply of potatoes, oil, wrapping paper, and labor are unmatched by any other manufacturing institutions: I am viewing at the *logistic level,* looking at *supplies, implementation,* and other supports.

Then I may continue to report that the packaging departments have problems in wrapping the chips, because too much paper is wasted when operators mount the rolls of paper incorrectly on the packaging machine. Now I am reporting from the *tactical level,* looking at the execution of *duties.* But I may conclude that, in the end, the packaging departments are really quite able, because they meet high standards of

TABLE 4-3 LEVELS OF VANTAGE POINT

Vantage Level	Accomplishment Variables	Constants		Accomplishment Examples
		Context	Purpose	
I. Philosophical	*Ideals* that relate to the quality of life, transcend specific cultures or politics, and require specific goals if they are to be achieved	Human identity	*Raison d'être*	Physical pleasure
II. Cultural	*Goals* of the particular culture that give performance its meaning, and require policies if they are to be reached	Culture, the State	Fulfillment of ideals	Good food
III Policy	*Missions* that define the basic purpose of institutions and subcultures, and require programs of action	Institutions, organizations (subcultures)	Attainment of specific cultural goals	Tasty snacks manufactured and sold
IV. Strategic	*Responsibilities* that define the roles of the members of an institution, and require plans for fulfilling them	Roles, jobs, etc.	Completion of missions	Potato chips put in packages
V. Tactical	*Duties* that must be fulfilled to discharge the responsibilities of any role or job, and require tools for execution	Tasks, skills, etc.	Discharge of responsibilities	Wrapping paper mounted on packaging machines
VI. Logistic	*Supplies* of resources needed to execute the tasks required by a duty	Implementation schedules	Execution of duties	Quantities of wrapping paper available

getting the chips packaged; in spite of many tactical blunders, they discharge their *responsibilities* well, because if we look at them from a *strategic level,* they follow good strategies and exhibit good planning.

Next, I may report that their policies are inadequate to meet their sales quotas, telling you as I view from the *policy level,* that too often the company is not completing its *missions* very well. Perhaps its sales policies are inept.

Then I may report that the company is doing a great job in supplying the world with large quantities of "good food," even if its sales profits are too low. I am saying that the company is fulfilling a highly regarded cultural *goal,* because members of the culture obviously place great value on potato chips. Now I am viewing, from a *cultural level,* the larger environment in which the company exists.

Finally, I conclude my report quite equivocally. From the *philosophical level,* I must conclude that the company is helping people fulfill at least one widely held *ideal,* "physical pleasure." But if "physical health" is the ideal the company set out for, it didn't do a great job of promoting it, since an ounce of mashed potatoes has 50 percent more protein and only two-thirds the fat content of an ounce of potato chips.

So when we question its competence, our potato chip company is very much in the position of Robert E. Lee: It all depends on our point of view—on the levels from which we view things. And this is equally true of any conclusions we draw about human competence anywhere.

The analogy between vantage points of viewing performance and the scopes employed by scientists is a good one. Because unless we choose the same scopes, we will be viewing different things. Scientists tell other scientists whether they are using a microscope, a telescope, a magnifying glass, or the naked eye. But when we talk to others about human performance, we usually leave it to them to discover which scope we use. And even when we make it understood which level of outlook we stand in, we are still likely to confuse our listeners unless we also communicate how we calibrate our scope. Two scientists looking through the same microscope will see two different things if they set the magnification at different powers. The wing of a bee at $30\times$ looks like something completely different when it is viewed at $1000\times$. Similarly, our "levels of vantage" scale is a relative one, for which we must establish a focal length. You and I could seem to agree to view an institution at the policy level, yet actually view it from a different scope. You may be looking at the potato chip company as a whole, and I at the sales department; you at American home life, and I at home life in a neighborhood; you at education, and I at the local school.

Table 4-3, which summarizes the six levels of vantage point, merely identifies six kinds of outlooks, and not the fine calibrated adjustments we must make to focus within each one. When we speak of the "larger

culture," we may mean Western culture, Americans, Southerners, or Appalachian Mountaineers. One way to focus any instrument is to take a fixed reference point and to adjust from there. We first identify a field of view, and then find our focal point by successive adjustments. So, one way to calibrate our viewing instruments is to begin by agreeing on the *philosophical* context in which we view, then on the *cultural* and *institutional* contexts. In any event, a little thought should convince you that it would never do to begin at too fine a point. We could both agree to look at Robert E. Lee's performance at the strategic level, but we shall probably come to different conclusions if I choose as my cultural context the nineteenth-century South, and you the industrial-age Western world. The best strategies for manufacturing "physically pleasurable" food may, indeed, differ from able strategies for processing "healthy" food. Obviously, we must begin our mutual focusing at the philosophical level.

To illustrate, we may deplore the performance of Adolf Hitler—but from what level of vantage? In the context of World War II and relative to the values and ideas *he* was trying to achieve, we might have to admire his strategies and even his policies as efficient. But in the context of Western cultural goals and philosophical ideas, his strategies were catastrophic. And because competence is worthy performance, we must condition each instance of competence by the value context in which we view it.

In Chapter 1 I argued that the proper sequence for analyzing human performance entails moving from context through purpose to means— from culture through accomplishment to behavior. The arguments of this present chapter should reinforce that position and expand it. What I am now saying is that at whatever level we ultimately wish to draw conclusions about performance, we must begin by identifying the context at a higher level. And even to identify that high context appropriately, we need at least to understand *its* context. If we cannot agree on the philosophical context of our conclusions, we may never agree at all.

Nevertheless, if we *can* agree on philosophical context, we can communicate quite well, even if we cannot agree on the ideals themselves. So it is that an esthete who believes it evil to seek physical pleasure can hardly disagree that the potato chip company employs excellent strategies for manufacturing pleasurable foods; nor, presumably, can the most zealous humanist refute the awful efficiency of Hitler's tactics for disposing of Jews.

To summarize, I have said that human competence, when seen as worthy performance, is relative to the level of abstraction and the range and scope of the viewpoint we adopt in order to observe the perfor-

mance. To communicate with each other, then, as well as with ourselves, we must know from what level of vantage we are viewing. Our
analysis may lead to totally different conclusions about competence
when performance is viewed at one level rather than another. And the
disparities in the conclusions need not be contradictory, because at
each level of generality we are really looking at something different.

FOCUSING THE PURPOSE OF ANALYSIS

At any level of view, our purposes may differ. To complete our "communication matrix," therefore, we need to distinguish the kinds of
purposes we can pursue. For example, we may be discussing accomplishments with the purpose of deciding what our goals are. Or our
purpose may be to determine how poorly we are meeting our goals
(what our PIPs are). A third purpose of analysis may be to determine
what we should do to improve our performance. These different purposes, combined with the levels of vantage, can form a matrix of
performance analysis, as you will see in the illustration that follows.

Mendham University has enlisted the nearby Burdsal Pharmaceutical Company into its cooperative graduate program. Each semester, selected students
are assigned to work alongside the executives of Burdsal. They are given a
task to do, and results of their performance are reported to their advisors. O.
D. Searls, Vice President for Sales, luckily has drawn three especially bright
students. Scott Audrey studies sociology; Ross Paul, industrial psychology;
and Beth Kirby is in the Graduate School of Business Administration. Searls
gives each of the students an identical assignment: to study the company's
salespersons, called drug detail men (superstition has it that only men can do
this job); and to write a report entitled, "Performance of District Detail Men."
Searls very carefully structures the vantage point from which the analysis will
be made. Each student is to work at the strategy level, and be concerned with
the accomplishments characterizing the job of drug "salesmen."

All three students begin this task by accompanying salesmen on their rounds.
Burdsal salesmen, they discover, go from one physician to another, leaving
behind samples of the company's prescription drugs, and sometimes explaining these products. That's what they do every day; and when they have
covered their territories, they begin all over again.

When the three students write their reports, they make a big hit with Burdsal
management—such a hit that the reports are circulated as required reading.
Then the major conclusions of each student are published in condensed form
in the company's executive publication. Here are excerpts from these
conclusions:

I. Scott Audrey

Actually, there are many different kinds of salesmen. Some are principally *prospectors*, who achieve their best results by wisely qualifying potential customers. . . . If you're selling swimming pools, the most important thing you can do is to make sure you call on people who are already primed to buy.

Other salesmen are chiefly *pitchmen*. If you sell life insurance, almost everyone is a prospect; the principal problem is to present the product and to meet the objections so well that sales resistance is broken.

Many of the people who sell highly technical products are essentially *teachers*. Their job is to get engineers, say, to understand the product so well that they will make purchases that exactly fulfill their needs.

But Burdsal drug detail men are none of these, really. Every doctor is a prospect for the company's drugs. And these doctors mostly resent the hard pitch, nor do they have time for it. Furthermore, they all understand the product—or at least they need no in-depth instruction.

What should a Burdsal salesman be doing? He should be promoting. His essential job is to serve as advertising space in the flesh. His mission should be to bring our brand names to the attention of the customers as often as possible, and in as pleasant a context as possible.

This model of what a Burdsal salesman should be has many implications for how he might be doing his job differently. . . .

II. Ross Paul

The most important deficiency I found in Burdsal salesmen is in their rate of calling on physicians. Good detailers see 30 or 35 doctors a week, but the average salesman in the district I studied saw only 10 to 12 a week. The longer they linger with doctors, the more the doctors resent them—and the fewer the doctors who actually see the product.

The principal cause of this problem is, I believe, an absence of any standards about the number of physicians to be approached. The salesman, in effect, is never told how many doctors he should see each day, nor why it is important to see so many of them. . . .

III. Beth Kirby

Three programs need to be developed to improve sales performance:

1. Establishment of a physician call-quota system, with bonus incentives for meeting and exceeding the quotas.
2. Development of a formal course for sales managers that communicates the correct role of the salesman and how it should be fulfilled.
3. Design of a tracking system that will follow each salesman's performance, and rapidly feed back the results to every level—from detail men to Vice President. . . .

Now it becomes obvious that even when intelligent people view performance at the same level, they can reach a variety of conclusions. Sociology student Scott Audrey idealizes the job of the drug salesman— she looks at performance from the standpoint of what it should be. Ross Paul, with the biases of a psychologist, observes what is defective about sales performance. And Beth Kirby, the practical student of business, gets right down to a program for improving the management of salesmen.

From these excerpts we can see that people can reach a variety of conclusions because they can set for themselves somewhat different purposes. Although the general purpose that defines a view from the strategic level is to comprehend the accomplishments of a role (or job) within an institution, one can nevertheless adjust the focus of that view to different stages. Scott Audrey looks for a theory of the salesman's job; and when she finds it, she derives a *model* description of the proper responsibilities of a salesman. Scott's effort is an invaluable—indeed essential—step toward the discovery of competent performance, although it by no means completes the analysis.

Clearly, these students have coordinated their efforts, because Ross Paul uses Scott's model of the salesman's job; and by putting it against reality, he *measures* how well real salesmen fit the idealized model. He finds significant deficiencies, and finds at least some of the reasons they exist. By doing so, he has taken the next essential step in the pursuit of competence.

Then Beth Kirby, with Ross Paul's findings at hand, searches for *methods* that might remedy the deficiencies in sales performance; and therefore takes the third step required to achieve worthy performance.

Obviously, the analysis of these three students, although necessary, is not sufficient, because all they have done is to work out *strategies* for creating competence. To bring their analysis to fruit, someone must next proceed to the tactical and logistical levels of work. Strategies require execution and implementation. Besides, however correct and logical the students' analysis may appear, it has absolutely no validity unless it is consistent with discoveries made at the policy level. And it is assumed here that someone properly concluded that Burdsal's drugs can really be sold effectively through contact with physicians. Naturally, the analysis should have begun at least at the policy level.

At whatever level of analysis we work, we can usefully follow the pattern our three students have set for us. First, we begin with *models* of what is desirable performance for the accomplishments we wish. Next, we take *measures* of how existing performance deviates from the models, and why. Finally, we look for *methods* for correcting the deviations. And we follow these three stages at any level of vantage, as Figure 4-1 shows.

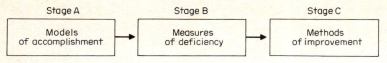

FIGURE 4-1 Three stages of analysis.

Now, if we combine the stages of focusing our performance analysis with the scope of vantage levels, we produce a matrix—a table of rows and columns. Table 4-4 illustrates this.

EXPLANATION OF THE PERFORMANCE MATRIX

There is a word in each cell of Table 4-4 summarizing the activity which would occur at that point in the analysis. Each of these words may require some explanation.

I. Philosophical Level

A. The *Ideals* of people, which are common to more than one culture, are the accomplishments we view at the philosophical level.

B. When we assess performance against the scale of ideals, we are measuring *Integrity.* Other words, like *virtue, goodness, purity of heart, morality,* or *rectitude,* could be used—even *righteousness.* It

TABLE 4-4   SKELETAL PERFORMANCE MATRIX

	Stage		
	A. Models	*B. Measures*	*C. Methods*
I. *Philosophical Level*	*Ideals*	*Integrity*	*Commitment*
II. *Cultural Level*	*Goals*	*Conformity*	*Policy*
III. *Policy Level*	*Missions*	*Worth*	*Programs*
IV. *Strategic Level*	*Responsibilities*	*Value*	*Strategies*
V. *Tactical Level*	*Duties*	*Cost*	*Tools*
VI. *Logistic Level*	*Schedules*	*Material needs*	*Supplies*

depends on our connotations. Naturally, whether we judge performance to have integrity or not depends on the *models* of *ideals* we take to the inquiry at this level.

C. The first *method* we would recommend at this level of vantage would be to adopt a *Commitment* to a set of principles (tenets, convictions, beliefs) compatible with the model of ideals. Of course, doing this here does not make us people of integrity; the commitment must proceed all the way through the tactical and logistic levels.

II. Cultural Level

A. The accomplishment we are concerned about here is the purpose, aim, or *Goal* of the larger culture in which the performance occurs. We must be careful to identify this culture and create a model of its values before we can conduct an inquiry at this level. If we view the performance of General Lee, we have to decide whether we will measure it against the values of Southerners, or Western culture, fathers, or older people—to name but a few possibilities. That the values of the various cultures in which we live often come into conflict only makes analysis more interesting, and careful procedure more important.

B. With a model of the culture goal, we measure how well the performance conforms to this goal—its *Conformity*. The kinds of nonconformity we often admire may merely be instances of performance conforming to certain goal models that we assign to cultures like "creative people" or "pioneers." Sometimes, we admire what we call nonconformity because the nonconformist's performance actually is closer to our model of the goal for a culture than that of the conformist. By "conformity," I mean the degree of adherence to some *model* of values set up to analyze performance. I do not mean the homogeneity of performance, and certainly not the homogeneity of behavior. The behavior cult breeds conformity in the worst sense of that word.

C. At this level of analysis, we view a set of methods to achieve cultural values I call Policy. *Policy*, in this sense, is a set of laws, procedures, or rules for running a state or organized community.[2] It is the mode of managing a larger culture. Actually, the word *polity* is more narrowly suitable to this level of analysis than *politics* or *policy*.

III. Policy Level

A. *Missions* are the accomplishments that define subcultures—specifically, institutions or organizations. How broad a subculture might be is relative to the culture in which the analysis is conducted. "Soldiers" might be viewed as a larger culture, transcending any given military organization, and the army might be an institution within that culture.

To know if we really are looking at a subculture, or institution, we must be able to construct a model of the fairly specific purpose or *mission* for that group.

B. To measure how effectively institutions perform, we look at the *Worth* of their achievements: How much greater are the returns than the costs? And the values we use to estimate worth must be taken from the cultural level if we are to be consistent in our analysis. If Lee had captured Washington, D.C., at the cost of 50,000 Confederate dead and 75,000 Union dead, we would have to evaluate the worth of this performance for the culture of the Confederacy against the comparative value of that conquest to the value placed on human life. Naturally, it is easier to estimate worth when we deal with more conventional institutions like businesses and peaceful government agencies. With these institutions, we can measure directly in dollars and cents, or in some sensible performance units.

C. When the worth of performance is less than its potential—when an institution is defective in gaining its mission—we search for *Programs* as methods for correcting the defects. And these programs embody the policies of the institution.

IV. Strategic Level

A. When we have advanced to the strategic level of analysis, we are ready to create models of critical roles. In the institution of the working world, these roles are called jobs, and the accomplishments that define a job are its *Responsibilities*. Responsibilities are also the accomplishments that define other roles, such as "mother" or "gang leader."

B. We measure performance against responsibilities by calculating or estimating the *Value* gained when those responsibilities are discharged; the value lost when they are not discharged; or the potential increase in value when performance (accomplishment) is improved. To make such estimates, we naturally require standards. But more about standards later.

C. Programs established at the policy level indicate which roles or jobs need improvement, and (in a general way) what will be done (and invested) to optimize the performance of the organization. *Strategies* for carrying out these programs are plans for improving the performance of people in a specific role or job.

V. Tactical Level

A. At the tactical level, we come closest to examining actual human behavior. But before we do—or before we can even determine that we

need to do so—we must first construct a model of the accomplishments that are required to discharge any given responsibility of a role or job that interests us. I call these responsibility components the *Duties;* and they are outputs, or accomplishments, of a task component of a role or job. Sometimes it is useful to describe certain behaviors required to perform these duties, particularly when we need to know how to train people to perform them. And then we may create a model of the knowledge required to discharge these duties—a model I call a *knowl-edge map* (see Chapter 9). Other kinds of models are relevant when training is not the route to successful performance.

B. The next logical step in our analysis is to determine what behaviors we must invest in, and how much it will *Cost* us to make these behavior changes. With some experience, an analysis of the extent and nature of costs can be projected.

VI. Logistic Level[3]

A. At the logistic level, the accomplishments we observe are the *Schedules* of people, materials, facilities, and expenditures required in order to implement performance improvement programs. Again we begin by creating a model of support services—a model that can range in complexity from simple lists to sophisticated, computerized schedules of requirements.

B. Then we merely take inventory of the *Material needs* we have yet to fill.

C. And, finally, we make sure that there is a system to *Supply* these needs. The logistic level may seem a great distance from the philosophical level, but it is just as essential to the analysis and achievement of competent human performance.

Table 4-4 is simply a summary of the 18 different classes of decisions required if a performance analysis is made at every level. As we shall see, this table does not represent as much complexity as it might appear to, partly because our analysis follows a consistent pattern at each level.

To help you understand the performance matrix, I shall give you an example of its application—one somewhat oversimplified for this purpose, although adapted from real life. Then I shall summarize the example with respect to each cell of the matrix.

The example is suggested by my experience with an extremely competent performance engineer who took on a social organization that she believed totally incompetent, and converted it to one of the most effective organizations in the country—one that has powerful influence on social legislation. We shall see how she did it, level by level, stage by stage.

Level I: Philosophical Ideals and Commitments

Kathy Jenkins is dissatisfied with people and sincerely wishes she lived in a better world. Her father convinces her that it ill becomes her to complain about things unless she is willing to do something about them. So Kathy decides to do just that—work to make the world closer to her heart's desire. She begins her crusade by making a list of the high *ideals* she holds. Since Kathy has always been very athletic and somewhat obsessed by physical fitness, the top item on her list is "physical health and vigor." For her, physical fitness is as important as religion is to some people; and she takes a dim view of most people's regard for their bodies. "Most people," she says, "don't have the *integrity* of physical fitness." So Kathy decides to make a lifetime commitment to advancing the physical health of the nation. She has many other ideals, too. But she knows that, from the standpoint of performance, there is a limit to what she can accomplish, and makes only one *commitment.* Hers is to advance the cause of physical fitness—an ideal that will determine much of the course of her life. But because there are many ways in which she can pursue her ideal, she knows that she must define more immediate goals.

Level II: Cultural Goals and Policy

Kathy, being a very serious individual, rejects certain *cultural* goals as too frivolous—goals like physical beauty. But in her list she does include "physical exercise," "nutritious diets," and "freedom from filthy habits" (by which she means almost anything enjoyable). With such interests, Kathy might have decided on medical school, but she is much too impatient to pursue her goals one person at a time. She does some research on health, and concludes that most of us are slobs largely because we abuse our bodies with poisonous food. She then decides to pursue the goal of more nutritious diets for her culture because, in her opinion, greater *conformity* to proper diets will do more than anything else to improve people's health.

But what will she do to affect national *policy* (polity) in order to promote nutrition? Kathy joins several organizations dedicated (rather strenuously) to the advancement of nutrition. These organizations aren't very satisfying to her because she has concluded that they are largely incompetent: They accomplish so little, yet expend so much energy. One reason they accomplish so little, she reasons, is that their aims are too vague. Fortunately, after working for several years for her favorite organization, the Society for Physical Perfection (SPP), she is elevated to the job of Executive Director. Now, she decides, she can set her goals more specifically.

Level III: Institutional Missions and Policies

As her first act as Director of SPP, Kathy decides to reexamine the organization's goal and the *missions* it has established as its major accomplishments.

Since SPP has never clearly stated what it was all about, Kathy publishes a memo stating that improved nutrition is the sole purpose of the Society.

One of the major missions of SPP, she notes, is the publication of information about nutrition. Indeed, Kathy concludes, this seems to be the only real mission that SPP pursues with any competence. "We are now a publishing company. But publications are not our cultural goal. They are only one accomplishment that might help us reach it," she tells her staff.

One really important accomplishment, Kathy decides, is to influence legislation related to nutrition. But then Kathy is discouraged to discover that SPP has no lobbying effort. If the investment that people make in SPP is to be *worth* it, the Society must accomplish real changes in health legislation.

Kathy next looks for the reasons that SPP is not affecting legislation. Using the behavior engineering model (Chapter 3), she finds two most important barriers: First, SPP employees don't know *how* to lobby (except by publishing pamphlets that legislators don't read); and, second, the Society is not organized for lobbying.

So Kathy establishes two important programs that will greatly influence the direction of SPP. She thoroughly reorganizes it, creating a Department of Health Legislation. In the reorganization, she provides for local field representatives who report to a Legislative Director, and these people are given the responsibility to influence the enactment of laws relating to nutrition. Her second policy requires employees to be trained for lobbying activities, including both legal instruction and field organization of public pressure groups.

The two jobs that Kathy figures to be most critical to the success of the new mission are the "field representative" (FR) and the "legislative specialist" (LS). Now she must decide on their specific accomplishments.

Level IV: Role Responsibilities and Strategies

Kathy next creates role (or job) models for the two critical roles (FR and LS). An example of a *responsibility* of the LS is

> "Lists of proposed federal, state, and local health legislation."

Kathy is wise enough not to describe these jobs in terms of behavior, but to state them as "outputs" or accomplishments. To complete her job models, she establishes the important *requirements* and *standards* of each responsibility. An example is

> "The list of proposed healthy legislation will be updated monthly."

The requirement of timeliness is qualified by a clear and attainable standard—"monthly." Against such standards, Kathy will be able to measure how well each LS performs on the job.

After her new organization has been operating for a year, Kathy takes stock. She wants to know how she might improve the *value* of what she is getting

from her employees. To do this, she must first measure actual job performance against the standards she has established. She finds, for example, that the lists of proposed legislation are updated on the average of once a quarter rather than once a month—although at least one legislative specialist manages to meet the monthly standard.

But Kathy Jenkins knows that it is useless to become disturbed about deficiencies that don't make a difference. She must next calculate what difference it makes when legislative lists are 3 months old; and when she does this, she discovers that at least 25 percent of health-related legislation is processed through various government agencies before SPP is sufficiently aware of their existence to have any impact on them. Kathy says that what this means to her is that a fourth of the $20 million annual budget of SPP is simply not being used effectively. Naturally, she is sufficiently appalled to seek out the causes of this deficiency.

She finds two. First, she discovers that her District Managers have never taken seriously the weekly requirement for updating the lists. Managers don't judge field representatives on this standard; nor do the Managers have any easy way to know whether the lists are timely or not. Next, she discovers that most field representatives don't really *know* how to do the research necessary to get the information.

So Kathy is ready to devise *strategies* for correcting the job deficiencies she finds. One of her strategies is a plan for a system of feedback so that district and national office managers will know more precisely and frequently how well the field representatives are performing; and she makes a list of every job accomplishment that such feedback would help. Another example of her strategies is a plan for the design of a job aid for helping people perform research to update legislative lists, to be accompanied by training in the theory of how that research should be done.

Level V: Duties and Tactical Tools

Kathy employs some of her staff to make a detailed analysis of those job responsibilities that give her the most trouble. Her staff analyzes the *duties* required to discharge these responsibilities—one of them being the performance of research on health-related legislation currently being proposed in various government bodies across the land. Her staff creates two kinds of models.

One of them is a *knowledge map* that identifies both the kinds of behavior one must achieve to fulfill the research duty, and the way in which one should learn this behavior. The second is an *information model,* around which a set of performance measures can be designed. When implemented, the measures will provide the feedback system Kathy is looking for, and will tell everyone how well the employees are performing.

Kathy requires her staff to report back on the estimated *costs* of implementing her programs. They make estimates by performing such tasks as assessing the

current research knowledge of field representatives; and to project training costs, they compare this knowledge with the entries on the knowledge maps. These cost estimates permit Kathy to make adjustments in the programs in her attempt to get the most for the Society's money.

Finally, with a detailed plan for job aids, training, and performance measures, Kathy assigns the task of developing these *tools* to her staff.

When the development is completed, tried out, and revised, Kathy decides to pilot her programs for one year and to assess their effectiveness.

Level VI: Logistics

Next, Kathy has to *schedule* the resources required to set her pilot program in motion. Her staff designs a computer program that will calculate performance measures. They also decide that they need a sort of quality-control inspector to monitor—by sampling—the accuracy of the information fed into the computer. A training schedule must be provided for instructors, and a method for tracking the effectiveness of training.

An assessment of existing resources shows Kathy's staff that no one is really able, nor has the time, to handle the required instruction, so they must find some way to fill this *material need*. The staff provides for instruction by finding a *supply* of local teachers who volunteer to teach the employees of SPP.

Now we can use the performance matrix to summarize Kathy Jenkins' venture into performance engineering. See Table 4-5.

Some readers will be at least faintly disturbed by the uncommon orderliness and sensibility of Kathy Jenkins. It is one thing to be Promethean (Prometheus, the Greeks tell us, was man's great benefactor); it is another to resemble Polyphemus, the one-eyed Cyclops. What makes us uneasy are the single-minded fanatics who take a point of view and apply it to all phases of life. Performance engineering is only one of many points of view people can take. So long as Kathy Jenkins restricts its application to useful ends, we can't charge her with being a fanatic. Kathy is simply a competent person paid to do a job. A fanatic is one who extends a favorite point of view to all areas of life. There are behaviorists who consciously try to condition us even though they have not been asked to, and psychoanalysts who analyze our motives gratuitously. Fanatics believe that there is only one way to look at things, and that it should be used at all times. The great challenge to people's philosophical side is to find different ways of looking at the world for different purposes. The performance matrix is no substitute for love, exploration, science, art, orgies, or churches; it is merely a way to order our vantage points efficiently when we set out to improve a performance system.

TABLE 4-5   A PERFORMANCE MATRIX SUMMARIZING THE IMPROVEMENT OF AN ORGANIZATION (SPP)

	A. Models	B. Measures	C. Methods
I. Philosophical Level	Ideals Physical well-being, etc.	Integrity People are abusing themselves	Commitment Improve physical well-being in the nation through performance engineering
II. Cultural Level	Goals Nutritious foods, etc.	Conformity Poor diets are the major cause of physical abuse	Policy Institutions needed to advance good nutrition require improvement: goal direction, etc.
III. Policy Level (Institutional)	Missions Nutrition legislation, etc.	Worth SPP is not now influencing such legislation—therefore is not serving its contributors	Programs Reorganization of SPP and training of legislative specialists (LS), etc.
IV. Strategic Level (Role or Job Performance)	Responsibilities Lists of pending legislation, etc.	Value Timeliness of lists needs improvement, etc.	Strategies Accountability and feedback system, etc.
V. Tactics Level (Tasks)	Duties Research data on health legislation, etc.	Cost Make training cost-effective	Tools Job aids, training sessions, etc.
VI. Logistics Level	Schedules Training schedules, etc.	Material Needs Need for instruction, etc.	Supplies Tapping local resources for instructors, etc.

My own interest in the study and design of competence is as a detached and objective subject matter, and only on rare occasions am I carried away with the actual living of it. The performance matrix admirably serves my purpose; it provides a steady guide for systematically distinguishing at least 18 different vantage points from which we may view performance; and it opens new avenues to the "science" of managing competence. Much of the remainder of this book is about

how we might use this matrix to practical ends, as well as about other dimensions of vantage point that we may add to these.

Several comments about Kathy Jenkins' quest are appropriate. The efficiency of her effort depends greatly on her progress in proceeding from the most general to the most specific level of analysis. If we begin our analysis at cell VI C of the performance matrix and work backwards, we have no guide for the direction we should take. Yet many decisions to implement ways of attaining competent performance are made in just such a retrogressive fashion. Indeed, many institutions—companies, homes, government agencies—begin by allotting resources for such programs as training and manpower development without first determining if these programs are needed. How many organizations have opened their doors on the first day with a live and already budgeted training department? Kathy Jenkins, on the other hand, sought no such resources until their contribution to the worth formula was fully established. By doing so, she escaped much unnecessary waste and worry.

Kathy's analysis at each level draws from the conclusions of the previous level. She has made certain that the mission of her organization drew its values from the cultural values she held paramount; the responsibilities that she assigned to the important jobs in SPP were determined by her missions. And although it may seem obvious in this example that each level depends on the level above, how many jobs in how many organizations remain as they used to be—even after the missions have changed? In a manufacturing plant, we may find packaging mechanics who are required to be able to construct such machines, even though modern engineering has made such responsibilities obsolete. How many jobs are assigned too few responsibilities to meet their new missions?

Kathy Jenkins is remarkable for her competence at every level of performance. But a review of the examples will show only that she is competent to analyze and manage at each level—not that she is necessarily capable of executing at each level. She depends heavily on her staff to execute for her. For all we know, Jenkins is temperamentally or intellectually incapable of actually doing the required work herself.

We should be able to see that individuals are able to perform better at some levels than at others. We all know a few of those golden people who are naturals at logistics and devote their lives to serving us— always at hand to fix our breakfast, or drive us to the airport when we visit them, and going each day to the office to run errands for the company. Yet we seldom seek these people to plan or execute difficult jobs, or to help us develop policy. And the good people I know who are like this usually smile back accommodatingly when we try to engage them in lofty philosophical thought.

And there are natural-born (or made) tacticians. One of the greatest I ever saw was in Stanley Kubrick's movie, "Dr. Strangelove." Slim

Pickens acts the role of the bomber pilot who manages to outwit the incredibly sophisticated military defensive machinery of both the United States and the Soviet Union as he carries his atomic bomb load to a Russian target—blindly, but irrevocably, following mistaken orders. That the discharge of his commanded duty would set forces in motion to destroy the world was no deterrent to his determination to execute this tactical maneuver.

At each level we find people uniquely competent to analyze, manage, or execute. Undoubtedly, many of us are especially qualified to supervise performance at one level, analyze at another, and execute at still another level. It might be interesting to imagine a "template," a sort of self-assessment chart, that we could lay over ourselves to identify our strengths. Such a chart of "competence" might look like Table 4-6. This particular pattern of plus marks might be the assessment of an individual who is a superb analyst, but is inevitably frustrated in efforts to get anything done without much help from others. Other people, with all their plus marks in the execution column, would possibly be frustrated similarly, because they would have great capability for getting things done, but no idea of how to use that capability. Presumably, no person could rate a plus mark at every point of this "map"; that is one reason, I suppose, that we need each other so much, and that institutions are required for our survival.

To be sure, I illustrate the "competence map" only as a conceptual device. I am all too well aware that many people will seize upon anything to support their claim to being experts on the character of others—as psychologists do with their so-called personality tests. It would only require filling the cells of the competence map with a few questions, and the publication of a couple of so-called scientific papers, and we would have yet another unwanted tool for the invasion of privacy, and another victory for the behavior cult—another way of pigeon-holing people.

TABLE 4-6 A "COMPETENCE" MAP

Levels	Analysis	Supervision	Execution
I	++		+
II	+		
III	++	+	
IV	++		
V	++		+
VI	+		++

Kathy Jenkins' rather extraordinary competence guarantees almost certain success in her quest for the spread of physical culture. But she happens to be almost uniquely single-minded. Once she has committed herself to the ideals of a physically vigorous world, she pursues them unhampered by other demands on her loyalties. Kathy is Kierkegaard's angel: "Purity of heart is to will one thing." For most of us, however, many of the accomplishments we desire are in conflict with each other.

Suppose, for example, that Kathy held in equal esteem the existential ideal that all people are completely responsible for their own destinies (making Kierkegaard even happier). Then her efforts to create restrictive health legislation, giving the government power to determine what we eat, would come into direct conflict with her commitments as an existentialist.

The only way open to her to pursue the ideals of physical vigor would be to maintain her organization as a publishing company, or, perhaps, as a private religious institution; and to use the tools of persuasion. This conflict between accomplishments is possibly the most immediate concern of everyone who manages a business—or anything else, for that matter. Manufacturing plant managers try to achieve production of the greatest worth—that is the kingpin of plant policy. But worth has two dimensions, value return and cost of investment. Production superintendents, if they are any good, will do everything they can to create the greatest value of production, regardless of hidden costs for which they are not responsible. They would, for example, build up huge and expensive inventories to minimize the likelihood of emergency demands on their production systems. In that way, they would be able to maximize the efficiency in scheduling people and machines. And if they had their way, they would get gold-plated equipment from the engineers, have materials-handling managers double their work force to serve production more quickly, and require accounting departments to double production bonuses. In short, as production managers maximize the value of their mission, they would be minimizing the accomplishments of every other mission—thus disastrously reducing the overall worth of the plant.

Similarly, marketing managers are faced with salespeople who would sell as much as possible regardless of the company's ability to service the sales. Training directors, left completely to their own devices, might keep every employee in a classroom for years. A personnel officer, judged by low employee attrition and grievance, would create unreachable recruitment hurdles. And quality-control inspectors would cheer the hearts of every consumer advocate by passing on nothing a bit less than perfect.

The competence of every manager operating at the policy level must be judged in part by that person's ability to deflate the efficiency of those operating at the strategic level. That is why Kathy Jenkins, in her

quest for her ideal, sensibly refused to authorize the best research training possible. And that is also why the final word about the competence of human performance can never come from viewing at one level in isolation.

Of course, these implications of the performance matrix bring little news to seasoned managers. What the performance matrix can do for them is to provide a tool that will help them sort out the difficult performance equations, so that they can come closer to maximizing their own worth.

A MATRIX OF DECISIONS

We are now ready to summarize a simplified performance matrix as a sequential set of decisions we need to make when we analyze—or, for that matter, construct—a performance system. This simplified version of the performance matrix deals with only three levels—policy, strategy, and tactics—because these are the levels most demanding of detailed analysis when we design such subcultures as schools or institutions in the world of work. I call the simplified matrix the performance engineering model (PEM), which is outlined in Table 4-7.

If you study Table 4-7, you will see that at the models stage (stage A), at each level of analysis, we are doing essentially three things:

1. Identifying accomplishments
2. Deciding on the important requirements and their units of measurement
3. Establishing exemplary standards

Then in stage B (measures of opportunity), we are

1. Getting measures
2. Analyzing PIPs
3. Identifying the critical PIPs that offer the largest opportunity for improvement

Finally, in stage C (methods), we are using the behavior engineering model to analyze the alternative ways we might make the pursuit of accomplishments more efficient, looking at:

1. Environmental methods
2. People programs
3. Management actions

TABLE 4-7   A SIMPLIFIED PERFORMANCE MATRIX

Levels \ Stages	A Accomplishment Models	B Measures of Opportunity	C Methods of Improvement
I **Policy** **(Institutional Systems)**	*Organization models* 1. Cultural goal of the organization 2. Major missions 3. Requirements and units 4. Exemplary standards	*Stakes analysis* 1. Performance measures 2. PIPs 3. Stakes 4. Critical roles	*Programs and policies* 1. Environmental programs (data/tools/incentives) 2. People programs (knowledge/selection/recruiting) 3. Management programs (organization/resources/standards)
II **Strategy** **(Job Systems)**	*Job models* 1. Mission of job 2. Major responsibilities 3. Requirements and units 4. Exemplary standards	*Job assessment* 1. Performance measures 2. PIPs 3. Critical responsibilities	*Job strategies* 1. Data systems 2. Training designs 3. Incentive schedules 4. Human factors 5. Selection systems 6. Recruitment systems
III **Tactics** **(Task Systems)**	*Task models* 1. Responsibilities of tasks 2. Major duties 3. Requirements and units 4. Exemplary standards	*Task analysis* 1. Performance measures or observations 2. PIPs 3. Specific deficiencies 4. Cost of programs	*Tactical instruments* 1. Feedback 2. Guidance 3. Training 4. Reinforcement 5. Etc.

Copyright © Praxis Corporation, 1976.

The PEM is an excellent guide for performance engineers, helping them to keep track of which decisions they must make—and also in what sequence. But my students have always had initial difficulties in using it. After analyzing their difficulties, however, I have found that they have several related problems:

1. Distinguishing between the levels, especially policy and strategy

2. Having a clear view of what decisions about performance can be made at the policy level

3. Bafflement, because our actual analysis doesn't always seem to reasonably follow the sequence of the performance matrix

Here is a typical problem a student will state:

> We often *measure* how things *are* before we develop *models* of how they might be. Don't we often really proceed, say, from stage B to stage A? And don't we often find it helpful to look at the jobs before we settle on the organizational models, so that we proceed from level II to level I?

The problem is well stated, and represents a misunderstanding. It is critical to remember that the PEM represents a sequence of *decisions* (*accomplishments* of the analyst), and not a sequence of analytic *behavior*. Two things are important to keep clearly in mind:

1. When first approaching an institution, we may look at many places and at many levels to learn something about the organization. Consultants, in learning about their clients, need first to get an *inductive*—to explore for an overview, and for as much information as they can get in order to become oriented to the institution and its problems. They may then observe foremen at work, observe training tactics, look to see where information is stored, get a sense of order or disorder in the atmosphere. And so on. Such "inductive" observing allows the analysts to classify the organization against their own experiences with other organizations—and simply to learn their way around. Analysts are always looking at what *is*, and must do that well before they can ever construct reasonable models of what should be. Consultants are also learning some basic technicalities of the organization—especially, the terminology of the subculture they are studying, and other of its peculiar habits.

2. In the measures stage of the PEM, the accomplishment is to measure not how things *are*, but how they *deviate* from a standard, or from the model. Analysts are always observing how things are, and must do that well before they can construct a reasonable model that will permit them to say which deviations are significant.

Furthermore, good model makers will draw from experiences about the strategies and tactics of an organization before they construct their own models—thus, *behaviorally,* analysts will observe at all levels, but make decisions at each level in turn. The PEM is therefore a guide to the sequence of *accomplishments,* not to the sequence of analytic *behavior.*

Here is another frequently stated problem:

> The performance engineering model is a good guide to strategies, and helps us make specific strategic recommendations (e.g., improved feedback for the operation). But what kind of *specific* recommendations can we make at the policy level? How do we keep from being too vague?

Recall the basic worth formula:

$$W = \frac{A}{E + P + M}$$

Here, E is the environmental supports of behavior, P is people's repertories of behavior, and M is the control (or management) system. Before we can reasonably make conclusions about job strategies, we need to understand which policies relate to these three aspects of behavior $(E + P + M)$. For example, a strategic analysis might lead us to conclude that the tools of work should be changed (say, a computer should be introduced). But before we plot such a strategy, we need to get assurance that a policy will be made committing funds and attitudes toward the change. Generally, nine kinds of policy decisions *may* have to be made. We can begin with three basic management decisions.

Management Decisions

M1. Can we make changes in the organization in order to assist performance?

Example: Early studies of the job of a telephone repair clerk indicated that the clerks didn't have much of a job, and that they could do more. But before we could develop a model of a good repair clerk, we had to get a commitment from the Telephone Company to restructure the responsibilities of the job and to direct the Methods Department to cooperate. This is a policy decision, whether it is made by those responsible for policy or not. It says, "Yes, you can change the way we are organized, and we will commit company resources to help you do it."

M2. Can we make changes in the way resources are allocated in order to improve performance?

Example: Policy-level analysis tells us that hiring building industry consultants* can pay off for a utility, but that the utility needs to take the job seriously and beef up its consulting department—appoint full-time consultants, for example. Is the utility willing to make this investment? This is a *policy-level decision;* and if it is not made, strategic analysis probably will not pay off.

M3. Can we change the standards of performance?

Example: Early in the analysis of utility consultants, we concluded that the utility should set and enforce standards of consultant performance; and if it didn't do that, nothing we did would probably be taken seriously. We were asking for a *policy decision.* In a drug company, we concluded that the rate of sales calls was a critical measure. We had to get a commitment to this standard so that the rest of our work would make any sense. Our later description of the drug detail man's job was based on the assumption that the company had accepted the rate-of-call standard.

To see the remaining six kinds of policy decisions, it will be helpful to use the behavior engineering model of Chapter 3. In that model, we identified three classes of environmental supports (data, instruments, and incentives, $E1$, $E2$, and $E3$); and three kinds of ways to create the behavior repertories needed to improve performance (knowledge, response capacity, and motives, or $P1$, $P2$, and $P3$). A decision to modify behavior in any of these ways may require a policy decision. Here are some examples.

Environment Decisions

E1. Will the company permit information about performance to flow freely? Will it commit resources to this? change standards? reorganize?

Example: Early in the analysis of a manufacturing plant, we could see that improved information flow was going to be a major strategy of change. But we had to establish that plant management was willing to get the information and see that people used it.

E2. Can the tools be redesigned?

Example: Early in the analysis of a computer operator, we could see that the keyboard was far from ideal. We recommended a change, but found too many

*Engineers who aid builders in designing utility facilities in new buildings.

policy barriers: The keyboard design was fixed; but if it could have been changed, our description of the operator job (strategic level) would have been different.

P2. Can selection improve performance?

Example: In repair clerk analysis, we found that the company actually hired people with much lower verbal skills than it said it required. Raising the selection would make training development easier. Were they willing to raise the standards? No; this was the *policy decision.* So, although our training strategies were not much affected, our tactics of training were, and we had to develop materials for poor readers.

P3. Can the recruitment be changed so that the people are better suited to the job?

Example: A manufacturing company took anyone at all off the streets for jobs as packaging machine operators—because it was an awful job. By making a *policy decision* to upgrade the job technically and economically, the company could have attracted people interested in a career as technicians. This would have of course changed our training tactics, if not our strategies.

Whenever we are analyzing an organization at the policy level, we are beginning to assess its weaknesses against the performance matrix.[4] And so we must always ask: What policy decisions must be made if good strategies and tactics can be developed? The best way to follow the performance matrix as an analysis model is through case histories. A detailed application of performance engineering is given in the Appendix.

NOTES

1. Expert debaters are masters of subtle shifts of vantage points to confuse the opposition. But you needn't attend a debating contest to observe the phenomenon. Sit in on university faculty meetings, business conferences, or, indeed, listen to almost any argument. If one person begins to make a good strategic argument, watch it be cut down by another person's sudden concern for tactical difficulties. Still another person will soar to philosophical implications. Alas, the strategist who shifts effectively to the new level is soon isolated again as, say, logistic difficulties are introduced. Somewhere in college, I was taught that all disagreements were about either "fact" or "values" (judgment, taste, and so on). I no longer believe this. Questions of fact can be resolved. Questions of taste are essentially unarguable. But questions of the level of vantage point are seldom even raised.

2. *Polity* would be a more exact word, but some people think it is clumsy. According to the *Oxford English Dictionary,* it is a "mode of administering or managing public or private affairs."

3. The word *logistic* comes from the same root as *lodge* and is not related to *logic.*

4. I have observed a close correlation between the levels of performance analysis and levels of organizational management. There are, for example, policy-, strategic-, and tactical-level managers. For the most part, the levels of management relate to the levels of analysis more or less like this:

Level of Management	Level of Analysis
Fifth (divisional heads)	Policy
Third (department heads)	Strategy
First (first-line supervisors)	Tactics

Intermediate levels of management (second and fourth) tend to be charged with facilitating the flow of information between the levels above and below them.

Chapter Five
Troubleshooting Performance

JOB DESCRIPTION

If all were artists and artisans none,
There'd be poems without paper for printing them on;
A footless Phidias, the fundament gone;
Songs and no cymbals to sing them with;
Plays seeking podia to plot them upon;
And canvas without cradles for curbing the myth.

Then, frameless painted works of heart
Would mix and meld and overheat
And, streaming through the somber street,
Consume the world in angry art.

T.F.G.

TROUBLESHOOTING AND PERFORMANCE ANALYSIS

The performance matrix and the behavior engineering model are simplifications of the ways in which we can view performance. For some, particularly students of psychology, these models may seem to be oversimplified and even superficial, because they represent none of the complexities of human motives, nor the intricacies of our neurologies and learning processes. So much the better, I say, because I present them only as aids to designing and troubleshooting performance systems. Their value, if not their validity, lies in how much they help us do these things.

To back up a little, my incentive to develop these models arose from two observations:

1. Those who take on the job of engineering human performance already know a great deal about both behavior and performance.

143

2. Few of us know how to summon our knowledge of performance in an orderly and systematic way when we set about to engineer it.

In engineering performance, most of us are in the same position as the crack mechanic who understands every detail of a piece of machinery, yet takes hours to find out what is wrong with it when it breaks down. It takes so long because the mechanic doesn't follow a "troubleshooting algorithm," a systematic order for asking questions about the machine. A troubleshooting algorithm, or model, is familiar to the physical engineer. This kind of model says very little about the nature of the system giving the trouble because it assumes that the engineer already knows the relevant details. It simply directs the questioning.

Finding the defective bulb in a string of Christmas tree lights illustrates the simplest kind of troubleshooting logic. It wasn't too long ago that strings of the festive lights were commonly wired in series (some still are), meaning that electricity had to flow through one light in order to reach another. If one light blew out, none of the lights would work, because the defective unit acted as a break in the electric line.

Suppose that you have a string of 64 Christmas lights, and a bulb blows out. And suppose you have more knowledge of electricity than you would ever need—say, as much knowledge of its details as an exemplary household electrician would have. How would you go about finding which of the 64 lights is defective? You would, of course, take a test meter—a device that measures whether current can flow. If you want to know if current can flow through a segment of an electric circuit, you merely place each of the two leads from the meter at either end of the circuit and read the dial on the meter.

With no troubleshooting logic to guide you, you would begin by testing the first bulb in the string. If the first bulb is good, you would continue to the second, and so on until you discover the bad bulb. If you are very lucky, you may have to take only a single measure; if you are very unlucky, you may have to make all 64. On the average, of course, if you tested many such strings, you would have to make 32 tests in order to find the bad bulb.

What a waste, because you should never have to take more than six measures if you follow a proper troubleshooting algorithm. The smart way to make the tests is to proceed by "halves." First test across the first 32 lamps; if current runs through this half of the line, the trouble must be in the second half. Then test across 16 of the remaining 32; and if there is a meter reading, the problem is in the last 16. Continue this "halving" down to two lamps, one of which is bad; then one more test will give the answer. Figure 5-1 is a schematic of the six tests. So, with six tests instead of an average of 32, your testing efficiency is increased

ı ı

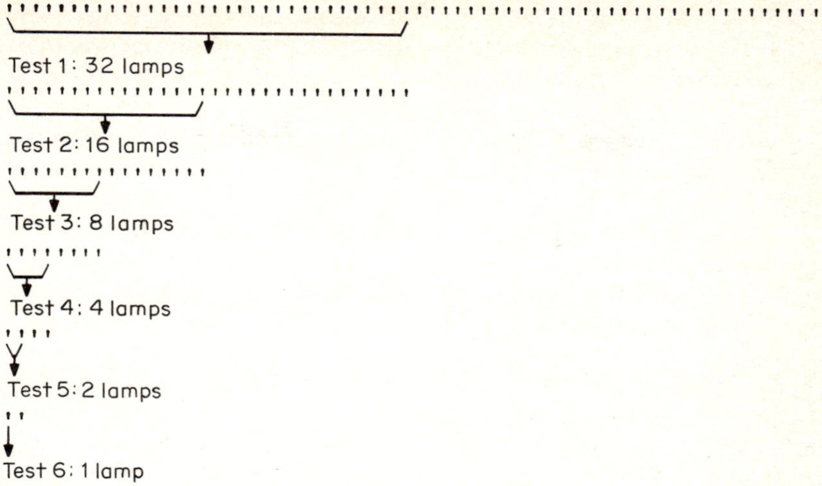

Test 1: 32 lamps

ı ı

Test 2: 16 lamps

ı ı ı ı ı ı ı ı ı ı ı ı ı ı ı ı ı ı ı ı

Test 3: 8 lamps

ı ı ı ı ı ı ı ı ı

Test 4: 4 lamps

ı ı ı ı

Test 5: 2 lamps

ı ı

Test 6: 1 lamp

FIGURE 5-1 Troubleshooting algorithm.

more than fivefold. In a 128-lamp string, seven tests are needed; and the defect among 256 lamps would be found in only eight measures. The efficiency of the troubleshooting sequence becomes exponentially greater as the system tested gets more complex.

Naturally, little of either the physical or the performance world is as simple as a set of lights wired in series. But this point should be made: Some sequences of asking questions about a complex but defective system are more efficient than others. And those who follow the best sequence are more likely to spot the trouble than those who don't. Indeed, in complex performance, we cannot even be sure what part of the system is defective, or that any of it could be significantly improved—which makes a troubleshooting sequence even more valuable.

Another point should now be clear. With a good model, one can become a better diagnostician than those who have much greater mastery of the details of a system, but no systematic way to troubleshoot it.

A major aim of performance analysis is troubleshooting—the discovery of the most important opportunities for improving competence. The previous chapters have laid the groundwork for a system of performance analysis; they also discussed the basic ways to look at human competence and how to realize the potential for improving a performance system. Now we need to see how all of the principles can be woven together into an analytic procedure.

In Chapter 3, I described the behavior engineering model, and in

this chapter I shall show how we can use this model to complete our troubleshooting sequence. I shall discuss an efficient performance analysis sequence that follows the performance matrix, level by level, in analysing our goals *(models),* our potential for improvement *(measures),* and our means of realizing that potential *(methods).* But first we can review a case history illustrating these three troubleshooting procedures.

The Waterman Finance Company maintains loan offices across the country. Each office is run by a loan officer and three or four loan agents. A district manager supervises 10 such offices in a small geographic area.

Denny Detale is the district manager for Morris County. Denny works hard, and, in 10 years with Waterman Finance, has developed a detailed knowledge of every aspect of the public loan business. But in the few years he has been a district manager, the earnings of his 10 offices have fallen steadily even though business for the company has improved. Denny's boss doesn't understand it, since he had originally recommended Denny and still thinks highly of him.

Waterman Finance has employed a consultant from Teleonomics Associates to study supervisory performance. The consultant finds that Denny Detale, rather than being a poor performer, actually represents the company's average. Waterman Finance's upturn in business can be attributed to the greatly improved performance of only a few offices, and the consultant identifies the exemplary district manager as one Jessie Dungil. The comparison of how Jessie and Denny manage their offices is quite instructive—especially since Jessie, in her short time on the job, has tripled the business of her 10 field offices.

Here are some of the puzzling differences. Denny visits each of his offices once every 2 weeks; Jessie usually sees only half, or fewer, of hers in the same time. Denny not only works 12 hours a day, but he works very hard. Jessie's boss has criticized her several times for short hours and for 4-day work weeks. Also, her employees, although they like Jessie, make jokes about her 3-hour lunches. Indeed, Jessie's boss has several times thought of giving her a bad review—but he simply isn't able to argue with her results.

What is Jessie's secret? She simply combines a systematic troubleshooting algorithm with good performance measurements. First, she sets exemplary standards of performance for each of her offices, measured in terms of the gross operating income of the office. Denny, on the other hand, always sets the company standard as a goal for his offices.

Second, Jessie, who doesn't seem very systematic, is really far more efficient than Denny, who does seem systematic. For example, every 2 weeks Denny selects a certain kind of performance to monitor. During the past 2 weeks, Denny carefully observed how everyone used the telephone to track down delinquent accounts. Next, he plans to monitor selling at the counter; then,

sales presentations to people who buy "dealer paper" (that is, the loan contracts that Waterman Finance buys from retail stores) in order to get some of the interest money for administering these loans. Denny is always monitoring some very specific performance dimension, and to Jessie this is like studying one bulb at a time on a string of Christmas tree lights. Jessie starts with general performance measures, and keeps troubleshooting until she finds a specific case of poor performance. Her troubleshooting sequence—going from general to specific—follows. (The example is oversimplified so the reader won't require much knowledge of the lending business.)

Step 1: Visit the office or offices that are farthest below standard in gross operating profit.

Step 2: If an office is below standard, there can be one (or more) of these three reasons for it:
(a) Too few loans are made.
(b) Income on the loans is too low.
(c) Office expenses are too high.
Jessie measures each of these areas in the poor-performing office, and identifies the area(s) of nonexemplary performance.

Step 3: For each poor-performing area, Jessie takes measures of the three or four ways that the area can be defective. For example, if an office has too few dollars in loans outstanding, she knows there can be any one (or more) of these three causes:
(a) The loans are too small.
(b) There are not enough new loans.
(c) There are too many payouts and payoffs.

Step 4: Once Jessie spots the next area of poor performance, she analyzes it to find its possible causes. For example, if there aren't enough new loans, she knows that one or both of two things can be wrong:
(a) Too little dealer paper has been bought.
(b) Too few new-customer loans have been made.
She takes measures of each of these, and then continues.

Step 5: Having identified an even smaller area of performance deficiency, she looks for its cause. For example, if there are too few new-customer loans, she knows that there must be one (or more) of these four problems:
(a) Advertising isn't working well.
(b) There aren't enough good new-customer prospects.
(c) Promotional mailings aren't going out.
(d) Telephone selling is not effective.

By now, Jessie has usually found the one or two performance failures causing the poor performance of the office as a whole. And because her performance

measures are so well set up, it takes her very little time to do it. For example, in her Mountainville office last week, she traced a slippage in gross operating profit to a let-up in placing advertising and to an increase in waiving late charges. Had the office placed enough ads and collected its late charges, it would have met her exemplary standards.

Jessie Dungil isn't through with her troubleshooting, even though she knows in what specific ways the Mountainville office is defective. Next, she wants to find the behavioral cause of substandard performance so that she can correct it. Jessie then asks a series of questions by using the behavior engineering model as a guide (see Table 5-1). The six cells of this model can be repre-

TABLE 5-1   JESSIE'S USE OF THE BEHAVIOR ENGINEERING MODEL

Category	Questions	Answers
E/S^D (Data)	1. Do the loan agents know how many and how good their prospects are?	1. *No.* Systematic records are not kept, nor are there measures of prospect quality.
	2. Do they know what the standards for prospects are?	2. *No.* No one ever gave them any standards.
E/R (Instruments)	1. Do they have all the tools, materials, and resources needed to prospect well?	1. *Yes.* The tools and materials are very simple.
E/S_r (Incentives)	1. Are there any incentives for prospecting well?	1. *Yes.* The agents get bonuses depending on office performance.
	2. Are the incentives scheduled well—and made contingent upon good prospecting performance?	2. *Yes.* A poor prospect is hard to sell; and, when sold, often becomes an unpleasant customer.
P/S^D (Knowledge)	1. Do the agents know the importance of good prospects?	1. *Yes.* They can tell you exactly what happens when you get poor prospects.
	2. Can they distinguish between good and poor loan prospects?	2. *No.* They are unable to describe the characteristics of a good prospect.
	3. Do they know the procedures for getting lists of good prospects?	3. *Yes.* The procedures are routine.
P/R (Response capacity)	1. Are the agents capable of prospecting—or can they learn to make the necessary discrimination?	1. *Yes.* Almost anyone can.
P/S_r (Motives)	1. Do the agents care if they get good prospects?	1. *Yes.* There is nothing they dislike more than poor customers, or those hard to sell.

sented by the questions she raises about the ability of the Mountainville office to develop new-customer prospects.

By asking these questions, Jessie has identified three principal reasons that her Mountainville agents are not prospecting well:

1. The number and quality of prospects are not measured and reported to the agents.
2. Agents are not given any standards that tell them how many and how good their prospects should be.
3. Agents don't know how to tell a good prospect from a bad one.

Jessie quickly traces these three problems to the recent retirement of the Mountainville loan officer who was accustomed to developing all the prospects himself. He was quite good at it, but he never let the agents do it. Nor did the retired officer use the excellent *Company Prospecting Manual* that clearly distinguishes good prospects from bad ones. So Jessie institutes three solutions to her problem:

1. Each month she reviews prospects and posts her measures and analyses of them.
2. She establishes clearly stated standards for prospecting.
3. She makes sure that everyone gets the *Company Prospecting Manual,* and understands and uses it.

Denny is a different sort of manager. He sees one solution to all performance problems. If he had been lucky enough in his "lamp-by-lamp" troubleshooting to discover the prospecting weakness, he would have attempted to inspire his people to higher levels of performance—using memos, pep talks, and (when those didn't work) cajoling and threats. Denny is from the "hard work and motivational school of management." He is so busy monitoring telephone selling, for example, that he misses opportunities to improve selling performance. Jessie is a graduate of the "leisure school"—first find the problem, and then fit the solution to it.

But something more than style distinguishes Jessie from Denny. No matter how open-minded Denny became, he would still have a major problem so long as he proceeds from the specifics looking for the general. Behavior is infinitely complex, and there are an incredible number of instances of it. Starting with the analysis of behavior is very much like proceeding lamp by lamp to discover a flaw in a Christmas tree string with a billion lamps. You will just never get there; it would require an average of 500,000 tests. Jessie, on the other hand, could find the problem in this string with a mere 30 tests.[1]

To understand the kinds of troubleshooting methods that people like Jessie use, we shall examine the performance matrix in detail. Recall that it identifies three stages of analysis at each level—models, measures, and methods. The matrix itself is a troubleshooting model, guiding us to observe performance at each of these three stages and level by level—beginning at least as high as the policy level, and then proceeding to lower levels in turn.

The world of performance is somewhat more complex than a string of Christmas tree lights wired in series, so no one simple performance troubleshooting model would be sufficient. Indeed, each stage of the performance matrix requires its own diagnostic model.

In stage 1 (models), we ask what accomplishments, requirements, and standards of performance are desirable. A sequence of diagnostic questions is useful in determining whether this stage has been done well. For example, we need a procedure to determine whether the right accomplishments have been identified, and whether they are properly described and understood. Performance will be defective if the wrong goals are set, regardless of how adroitly people behave in the pursuit of those goals. Indeed, the more efficiently they behave to attain the wrong goal, the more incompetent they may be.

Then how can we be sure we have set the right accomplishments as our objectives? There are many ways to find out. But here is one way that seems to me to work very well. I call it the ACORN test.

TROUBLESHOOTING GOALS: THE ACORN TEST

The first stage at each level of the performance matrix asks us to make three decisions: What are the accomplishments, requirements, and standards that define exemplary performance? And nothing in performance engineering is so difficult for beginners as identifying the first two of these—partly because they seem so obvious and it seems so easy to do. (The reader will do well to review the performance matrix in Chapter 4.) To see how difficult this task really is, we can follow an example of some people who think they know what they want to accomplish.

"I know exactly what my salesmen should accomplish," says Ike Noet. "Chewing gum sales—what else? How is that going to help me analyze their performance?"

Ike is a district sales manager for the Todd Confection Company, makers of Chucklers and other chewy confections. His employees—he has eight of them—are called territory sales representatives, and they are the people who go from store to store "selling" chewing gum, mints, and the like. Ike has just

identified the *mission* of his department as *chewing gum sales*. But Ike's description of this mission doesn't pass the ACORN test—at least, not all of it.

What is ACORN? It is just an acronym for five qualifications of every good description of the mission of an institution (at the policy level). If we can identify the mission, it is much easier to describe the accomplishments at other levels correctly. Here are the five questions to ask of the description of any mission to find out if it is truly the goal of those assigned responsibility for it:

A: Is it an *A*ccomplishment, and not just a description of behavior? If the mission has been described in behavioral terms, it has not been identified.

C: Do those assigned the mission have primary *C*ontrol over it? Or does good performance principally depend on others?

O: Is it a true *O*verall *O*bjective, or merely a subgoal?

R: Can this mission be *R*econciled with other goals of the institution, or is it incompatible with them?

N: Can a *N*umber be put on it—that is, can it be measured?

Ike's territory representatives are said to be responsible for "gum sales." This does describe an accomplishment (*A*) and not behavior. Gum sales sounds like an overall objective (*O*); at least, it is the business the company is in. It can be reconciled (*R*) with other goals of the company. And it can be measured; that is, a number (*N*) can be put on it. So it passes four of the five tests.

The problem is that it isn't realistic to assign gum sales as the mission of territory representatives because they don't have real control (*C*) over sales. Why? Because too many other things control the sale of gum—how good it tastes, how attractively it is packaged, how competitively it is priced, and how well it is advertised. Indeed, if anyone produces a tasty, high-quality, beautifully packaged gum that is priced and advertised well, every store in the country will want to buy it.

"You're saying that gum sales isn't the mission of my representatives?" Ike mourns. "What is it then—'sales orders'?" Again Ike misses the target, because even though his representatives do take orders from store managers, they are more than mere order takers. "Sales orders" doesn't pass the *O* test; as we shall see, it is a subgoal and not the overall objective of the job.

There are lots of questions: "How would you know, after they went home, which of the representatives were exemplary? Or, suppose some representatives performed their jobs *perfectly?* How would the world be different?"

"Oh, that's easy. If they performed their jobs perfectly, every available display slot in every store in their territories would be filled with Todd's gum." So, Ike has finally identified the mission of his representatives: "Gum displayed." This is an accomplishment (*A*); the representative has great—

even primary—control over it (*C*); it is the overall objective of the job (*O*); and it can be reconciled (*R*) with the other missions of the organization.

"But how would you measure it?" Ike was skeptical. Of course, first its requirements (see Chapter 2, page 43) have to be identified. And two seem to be critical here—a quality (accuracy) requirement and a volume requirement:

1. Gum should be displayed where people can see it (accuracy).
2. Todd's gum should be in every display spot possibly available for it (volume).

Both of these requirements are readily measurable. Like every district manager at Todd, Ike visits a sample of 20 stores of each of his territory representatives at least once every 2 weeks. To measure the volume requirement, all he must do is count all the available display slots in each store, and count the number filled with Todd's gum. To measure the accuracy, he can assign weights to each filled slot—3 if it is readily visible; 2 if it is not ideally displayed; and 1 if it is displayed in such a way that a customer is not likely to see it. So, he (and the company) will have a performance measure:

$$\text{Display Performance (DP)} = \frac{\text{Weighted Todd Slots Supplied}}{3 \times \text{Total Slots Available}}$$

And Ike can use this measure to begin a troubleshooting sequence. If a representative's DPs are low, Ike (like Jessie Dungil) can look at subsidiary measures to find out why. Is the representative commanding enough space? Is the space commanded but not kept in supply? Or is the quality of the display too low?

Such rethinking of the mission of this job brought about a big change in the performance of Todd Confection Company. But, of course, the troubleshooting had to be carried out to its conclusion. By taking these measures over a period of time, Todd management people discovered a large PIP in "display performance." Next, they had to locate the cause of the problem. Using the behavior engineering model to guide their questioning, they concluded that the chief culprit was the failure to set display standards and to provide feedback to the representatives about their display performance. Subsequent results bear them out. But it is doubtful if they would have improved display performance if they had not first applied the ACORN test to assess the real goals of the territory representatives.

Each of the five ACORN rules should apply to all the missions of an institution. Too many programs I have observed are based on objectives that do not conform to all of the ACORN rules. This does not surprise me, however, because I have discovered through much experience how difficult it is for people to describe the accomplishments they value. Because of this, I have attempted to articulate some subsidiary questions that I have found helpful in using the ACORN test to troubleshoot performance problems.

A Is for Accomplishment

Keep in mind that distinguishing between accomplishments and behavior is not so simple as it often sounds at first. But there is a good question we can ask to help us make certain we are describing accomplishments: Can we observe this thing we have described when we are not actually observing the performer, or when the performer has gone away? Descriptions like "a list of sales prospects" are accomplishments because we can see them even after the salesperson has gone home. If we are *not* describing behavior, then the person responsible for an accomplishment need not be present.

C Is for Control

If people do not have control over an accomplishment, it cannot reasonably be described as their mission. Territory representatives (to use an example we have explored before) who "sell" a popular brand of chewing gum to grocery stores are said to have the mission of gum sales. But do they? Remember, what determines whether people buy gum are such things as its flavor, packaging, pricing, or promotion— none of which is under the control of the representatives. And store managers are almost certainly going to buy the gum anyway. Then what *is* the mission of these representatives? "Gum displayed" passes every one of the ACORN tests. The representatives certainly have more control over it than anyone else, because their mission is to see that as many slots in the store as possible are filled with the company's gum.

O Is for the Only Objective

A mission is just that: the overriding objective or goal of any role. When we are able to ascribe more than one goal to a role, all but one (and perhaps all of them) are subgoals. We have either failed to identify the mission altogether, or we have not distinguished it from a subgoal. Consider an example of a training department for a typewriter company: The description "people trained" is a proper accomplishment of that department, but it is not its mission. Training people is necessary to maintain the requirements for good "improved skills," which is the mission of the department.

A key question to ask is this: "If this accomplishment were perfectly achieved, would performance be perfect? would anything more be desired of the performer?" This question represents the ultimate performance test. If the training department did a perfect job of keeping people in training, there would be no one working—and that surely isn't what we expect from a perfect training department. But suppose we ask this question of our territory representative with the gum

company: "If Todd gum appeared in every possible display spot in every store in a territory, could you ask any more of the representatives?" The answer is "no," which means that "gum displays" is the mission of the job.

R Is for Reconciliation

Usually when the missions of two roles within the same institution seem to be in conflict, it is because one (or both) of them is ill-conceived. Good performance in the training department only seems to be in conflict with the sales department when we mistake its mission as "people trained." The "reconciliation test" is similar to the "ultimate objective test." The key question is this: "If this mission is perfectly executed, will it be possible to execute all the other missions perfectly?"

If people are always in training, sales must suffer. But if training is perfectly executed, then either sales must benefit or training has been poorly defined.

N Is for Numbers

If we cannot measure performance—especially at the level of the mission—we have not described the mission. The head of a quality-control department once described its mission as "systems monitored." Obviously, it is difficult to say to what degree a system has been monitored without resorting to such descriptions of behavior as "10 minutes to examine each part." Remember that the ultimate test of whether we have really identified a measurable accomplishment is to determine whether something observable and measurable remains after the performer "has gone home"—after the performer can no longer be observed. When the quality-control employees go home, no "monitored" systems are left. But "errors detected" is an observable output of the quality-control job, and we can read the measurements without ever watching anyone monitor a system.

Applying the ACORN Test to Subgoals

The ACORN rule, and the five tests it represents, is especially useful for evaluating the descriptions of a mission. Once we have identified the mission of a job, it becomes much easier to derive the subgoals— the accomplishments that make up the responsibilities and duties of the role. But these lesser sets of accomplishments must also pass parts of the ACORN tests. Subgoals obviously cannot be overall objectives,

so they cannot pass the *O* test. And often subgoals cannot be fully reconciled with the mission, so they may fail the *R* test too. As we shall see in the following example of the typewriter company's credit department, we would want to get as many credit contracts (the mission) as possible, but we need to control the rate at which we collect money (a responsibility) so that we can keep our credit contracts profitable without interfering with sales.

But subgoals should pass the other three tests: They should be accomplishments (*A*) under the control (*C*) of those charged with their responsibility; and they should be measurable (*N*).

Consequences of Failing the ACORN Test

Do not imagine that separating missions from subgoals and applying the ACORN test is a mere academic exercise. We can return to the typewriter company example and examine it in more detail, because it well illustrates the economic power of these activities.

The credit department of the Cronin-McDonald Company, makers of typewriters, uses MBO (*m*anagement *b*y *o*bjectives) in managing its several district credit offices.

"What is the 'objective' of a credit office?" we asked Don Dun, the National Credit Manager.

"'Money collected.' It's a simple and measurable goal, and each credit manager is given a monthly objective," Dun replies confidently.

But Dun's objective doesn't pass the ACORN test. Listen to Lucky Salvadore, the National Sales Manager.

"Don Dun's MBO program has really hurt us. We're losing many sales because of the eagerness of the credit office to collect from our typewriter dealers. They don't understand: We are in business to sell typewriters, not to collect money."

Lucky Salvadore has just recognized that the perceived mission of one department is not reconciled with the mission of another department. But that shouldn't be; no one should have a mission that is in direct conflict with the goal of the institution. So we ask Lucky to direct us to the one credit office *he* considers exemplary.

Skinny Junkins, Credit Manager, has $1.5 million on loan to the typewriter dealers in his area, which is three times the average. From Lucky Salvadore's viewpoint, this is ideal.

"But his past-due accounts are three times the average," Don Dun protests. "He's going to have to shape up. He's worse about meeting our objectives than any credit manager in the company."

But what Dun doesn't realize is that Skinny Junkins' ability to find ways to finance dealer typewriter purchases has increased sales in his district by $2 million a year. And the cost of this loose credit to the company is only $20,000 more in interest than that of the average office.

But while "credit contracts" are an accomplishment that can be reconciled with Cronin-McDonald's true goal, the accomplishment "money collected" is not. By making credit contracts his mission, Skinny has found an objective that passes the ACORN test. Rather than being in conflict with the company's goal, it actually promotes it.

As a management theory, management by objectives sensibly recognizes the great power of feedback and reinforcement for maintaining performance. But unless the objectives are reasonably established and they pass the ACORN test, MBO can be a very efficient way to defeat the purpose of an institution, as our experience with Don Dun suggests.

TROUBLESHOOTING THROUGH MEASUREMENT

The ACORN test is a method of troubleshooting a performance system to determine whether we have successfully completed the first (or *models*) stage of performance engineering. As we shall see in Chapter 8, such troubleshooting is also relevant to establishing educational missions when we design school curricula. The power of the ACORN test lies in helping us know where we are going, whether we seek the greediest or the noblest ends. But once we know where we are going, we need a means of analyzing how well we are getting there—a method of troubleshooting the second (or *measures*) stage of analysis. This, of course, requires us to look at data.

It is important to keep in mind that data, by themselves, are not information[2] and that too much data, in fact, can destroy information.

Suppose, for example, that we wished to judge the performance of several hundred motel managers—among them Manager Carol Condit. I could give you a large file of data on these managers listing everything from the number of dirty ashtrays found in their motels to their separate laundry bills. But if I did this, your task of judging their comparative performance would be just about hopeless. Say that every week I gave you data on 100 different categories for 300 different managers. You would have 30,000 individual pieces of information to sort through for just a single week. To make the task easier for yourself, you might begin to look for the really large numbers—for those deviations that stand out. Manager Condit, for example, might show an average of 25 dirty ashtrays for the week—four times as many as for the average manager. Such deviations might invite you to rush immediately to Condit's motel to correct that problem, and this of course would be absurd. Because what you might not know is that over a period of a year, Condit's motel

excels all others in revenues per dollar of expenditures and also in percentage of occupancy. If you knew this, you would have to consider her ashtray performance a peccadillo.

You want performance information for one reason only: to help you decide how to appropriate your energy and resources intelligently to improve performance. Because no one is perfect, anyone's performance of anything can potentially be improved. If you find a manager with only one dirty ashtray a year, you could invest your efforts in reducing that manager's error to zero.

You may or may not be surprised to know how much management time is spent in equally silly ways. To avoid wasting our efforts on low-return ventures, we need a strategy for converting data into optimally useful information. Because our purpose is to troubleshoot performance, the strategy that suggests itself is the troubleshooting algorithm—essentially a procedure of going from the general to the specific in order to target the cause of a problem. The logic of the strategy is the essence of simplicity, as we saw in the example of the Christmas tree lights.

We can now apply this simple strategy to performance analysis—say, of Carol Condit's management performance. We don't begin one by one with individual items of performance, such as the status of her ashtrays. Rather, we apply the most general test first: Is her overall performance—the performance of her mission—adequate or not? We begin by applying one general measure to her performance: the ratio of her actual net earnings to her potential net earnings (what she would earn if she operated at utmost efficiency and kept the motel filled). Suppose we found this ratio to be 1, meaning that she could not operate a motel any better. Then it is useless to look beyond this to her performance. If her ratio is less than 1—say 0.80—we want to compare this ratio with the ratios of other managers. If hers is still the highest, we shall clearly want to invest our efforts in looking elsewhere. The PIP is our guide.

But when her ratio drops to the point that her overall performance concerns us, we shall want to ask the next-most-general question: Is the reason she isn't getting an adequate return because she isn't filling the motel? or because she isn't operating it efficiently? or maybe both? If our answer shows that she is operating efficiently (so far as operating cost per occupant is concerned), but is not filling the motel, our next worry is about her efforts in sales and customer relations rather than about such operating details as ashtrays and the food she is wasting in the kitchen.

Our next question could then differentiate between the quality of her marketing efforts and the quality of her treatment of her customers once they are in the motel. Perhaps our measures here will indicate excellent promotional efforts, but a low incidence of customers return-

ing. Then we shall want to look at how well she keeps her rooms, serves her food, and so on. We may conclude that dirty ashtrays and linens are driving customers away. Finally, we may conclude that her great operating efficiency is gained at the cost of employing too few people to keep the rooms in order. Such a method of transforming data into useful information not only saves time and energy but, more important, it will often lead analysts to conclusions they might not otherwise reach.

Levels of Measurement

Once we recognize our strategy for developing information as one of proceeding from the general to the specific, we use our concepts of the performance matrix and the levels of analysis to refine this strategy further. It is convenient to have names to distinguish the measures of performance at different levels of generality. To indicate these distinctions, we can use different words at each of these three levels of analysis:

Levels of Analysis	Performance Measures
1. Policy (organization)	Coefficients
2. Strategic (job)	Indices
3. Tactical (task)	Indicators

You should be able to recognize the levels in the example of Condit, the motel manager. We first looked at Condit's performance against the goal of her organization and the mission of her job (policy level). Then we looked at indices of performance, measuring how well she fulfilled the responsibilities of her job (strategy level). Finally, we observed indicators of how well she executed certain tactics of her job (tactical level). Table 5-2 summarizes these "tests" of performance. We can see

TABLE 5-2   PERFORMANCE MEASURES AT DIFFERENT LEVELS

Level	Performance Measure
Policy (organization)	$\dfrac{\text{Actual net revenues}}{\text{Potential net revenues}}$
Tests 1 and 2 (coefficients)	Operating costs per occupant *and* percent occupancy
Strategic (job) Test 3 (indices)	Promotes quality and motel quality
Tactical (task) Test 4 (indicators)	Various "Motel quality" indicators such as cleanliness of rooms and food service

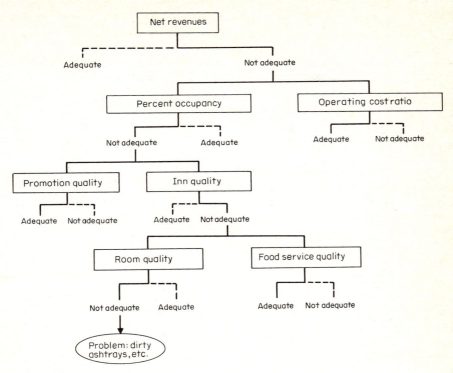

FIGURE 5-2   A troubleshooting tree.

how this progression follows the simple troubleshooting algorithm depicted in Figure 5-2. In our motel example, measures of net revenues, percentage of occupancy, and operating costs would be *coefficients;* measures of promotion quality and inn quality would be performance *indices;* and observations (not necessarily formal or quantified measures) of room quality would be highly specific performance *indicators.*

To use another example, if we examined the performance of a salesperson, we would first look to see how well the salesperson fulfills the mission of the sales job. The relevant coefficients, depending on the type of sales job, might be:

1. $\dfrac{\text{Sales Revenues}}{\text{Sales Costs}}$

2. $\dfrac{\text{Sales Revenues}}{\text{Sales Quota}}$

3. $\dfrac{\text{Sales Costs}}{\text{Budgeted Costs}}$

The first of these coefficients would tell us immediately (by comparing it with the exemplary standard) how successful our salesperson is. The second and third coefficients would give us information that would help us focus on certain aspects of the salesperson's job. For example, if the salesperson had excellent revenue performance, but excessive costs, we might look to the entertainment or promotional performance, but not to the adequacy of the prospects. If the revenue performance was poor, however, we would certainly want to look at the salesperson's prospects.

Possible performance indices to measure prospecting performance might be

1. The number of prospects per week
2. The quality rating of prospects

These are measures of job responsibilities (job-level analysis) which must be discharged in order to fulfill the job's mission. (The example cites only one such responsibility.) If the salesperson is deficient in prospecting performance, we then look to task-level measures, which might be

Responsibility: *Sales prospects*

Duties: 1. List of sales suspects

2. Qualification data

3. Prospect classification

In other words, to establish a good sales prospect, this employee needs to collect the names of possible customers (suspects); get data to qualify them as likely buyers; and, finally, establish which line of products they are most likely to buy. If the prospects are of excellent quality, but there are simply too few of them, the salesperson may be performing any of these three duties too slowly. But at this level, the experienced manager (say, the sales supervisor) may not need to make quantitative measures of how well the salesperson performs duties, but simply observe how well the employee seems to perform them. If the manager notices that the employee has very few names of suspects but excellent data on them, this may be an *indicator* of the salesperson's problem of having too few prospects. Or, if the salesperson has many names of suspects but a much too elaborate procedure for qualifying them, the manager may take this as an indicator of the problem.

TABLE 5-3   MEASUREMENT LEVELS

Level	Accomplishment	Requirement	Measure	Kind of Measure
1. Mission	Sales	(a) Volume (b) Costs	Revenue / Sales Costs	Coefficient
			Revenue / Quota	Coefficient
			Costs / Budget	Coefficient
2. Responsibilities	Prospects, etc.	(a) Rate (b) Quality	Prospects / Week	Index
			Quality rating	Index
3. Duties	List of suspects	(a) Rate	Suspects per week	Indicator
	Qualification data	(b) Quality	Supervisor's judgment	Indicator
	Prospects classified	(c) Quality	Supervisor's judgment	Indicator

Table 5-3 is a summary of the performance measures and trouble-shooting process in the example. Figure 5-3 shows what the trouble-shooting process might look like. Notice that in the troubleshooting procedure, the performance analyst (or supervisor acting as performance analyst) is observing *accomplishment* (output) measures in the first three steps. But only when the problem is isolated is there any need to look to the behavior of the salesperson. Here, using the behavior engineering model in step 4, the analyst asks such questions as: "Does the salesperson have the know-how to classify the prospects?" "Does the salesperson have the incentives to classify the prospects?" "Does the salesperson have access to the information needed to profile the customers?"

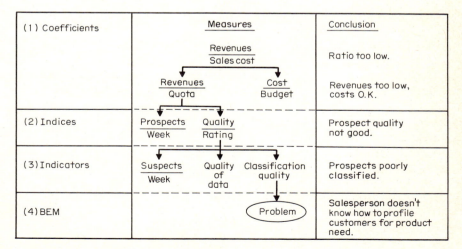

FIGURE 5-3   Measurement levels and the troubleshooting tree.

This example underlines another great advantage of the trouble-shooting strategy. A salesperson (or any other employee) has relatively few responsibilities and duties, but vast amounts of behavior. And targeting specific behavioral deficiencies is extremely difficult if we begin by trying to observe all the possible behaviors. First, there are just too many of them; second, it is almost impossible to evaluate a behavior unless we first know which accomplishment is defective and how valuable it is to correct the deficiency.

Which Performance Should be Quantified?

There is no exact answer to the question of which performance to express quantitatively. Numbers help us greatly in making compari-sons, and in translating opportunity into dollars. But we can still observe significant performance deviations without quantifying them.

The general rule is that we should try to quantify as many measures of performance as we can at the organizational (policy) and job (stra-tegic) levels. And we should seldom try to quantify measures at the task level. Why?

A number is simply a convenient way to summarize observations so that we can compare them. I make performance observations for one purpose: so that I can direct my energies in the most fruitful direction. When I observe the performance of an organization, I can be sure that it will not be perfect on any account. Unquestionably, I can improve its sales, its service, its marketing, its manufacturing, its accounting sys-tems, and so on. But to what extent? Since I cannot do all of these things at once, I must be selective. I can make such comparative decisions by taking my observations systematically enough so that I can quantify them. It is not enough to say that the organization has less than exem-plary sales and service; I need to know how much less than exemplary. And I need to know how the deviation translates into dollars of opportunity.

Similarly, when I study the performance of salespeople, I know that they are not *perfect* in discharging any of their responsibilities. But at no time am I going to try to make them perfect in all things. Rather, I want to know where the greatest return for my efforts will occur. If poor prospecting is 70 percent of their problem, I would certainly be stupid to try to improve their promotional displays until I have corrected their prospecting—particularly if I am concerned with an entire national sales force, or with all the salespeople in a branch office.

The performance of an organization's goal and job missions reflect too large a complex of events for me to make very reliable informal comparisons. I need the power of summary that numbers can give me. At the task level, however, I do not always need this power. Then I

must pay attention to individual salespeople. Rather informal observations may convince me immediately that all, or nearly all, salespeople have plenty of *suspects* to work with, but that few of them know how to qualify these suspects as prospects. Or, if informal observation shows deficiencies both in getting suspects and in qualifying them, and if I cannot tell for sure which is the more important task, I shall certainly have no trouble in trying to correct both problems without worrying about measuring the exact contributions of each.

Indeed, the only time I shall need to quantify performance at the task level is when informal observation does not almost certainly reveal the problem tasks. If informal observation leaves any doubt about how a task contributes to the larger problem, and if correcting performance on that task requires real effort, then I shall want to measure the task accomplishment (duty).

We can say that the decision to take quantitative measures of task performance is a function of three things:

1. The potential value of the quantitative information. To the extent that quantitative measurement has a chance of revealing significant performance failures, the more reason to measure task performances.

2. The cost of measurement. The easier it is to take the measures, the more reason to take them.

3. The cost of the effort to improve task performance. To the extent that it is difficult or costly to improve task performance, there is more reason to quantitatively measure it in order to be certain that the effort is not misspent.

Obviously, this decision is not founded on an exact science. But following the troubleshooting paradigm in performance analysis will greatly reduce the difficulty of the decisions about which performance to quantify.

TROUBLESHOOTING AND THE BEHAVIOR ENGINEERING MODEL

We have now discussed troubleshooting in two stages of performance analysis: accomplishment models and performance measures (recall the performance matrix). Now we want to look to the third stage—methods—particularly with emphasis on the methods of modifying behavior. And here we can use the behavior engineering model as a troubleshooting guide.

One problem some people have when analyzing behavior is a great

diffidence that they know anything about it. Don't you have to be expert of some kind to analyze behavior? Many "experts" will hasten to answer "yes." So the question is this: Do you have to be a highly trained "expert" on human behavior to be a good performance engineer?

The answer is an emphatic "no." Let us see why. Recall the story in Chapter 1 of Mr. Quik and Mr. Sloe—and its message that almost all of us know most of what any of us knows. Mr. Sloe was not a mass of ignorance about firing a rifle—in fact, he had a repertory that was only slightly deficient. Before he had received any formal training, he knew almost all there is to be known about rifle firing, long division, and selling. Similarly, when we set forth to engineer worthy performance, we can be sure we know almost all there is now known about human behavior. Then the question is: What small but significant deficiencies might we have in *our* repertories that will prevent us from performing well as performance engineers? And it will be only in these few things that we will need any training, guidance, or the aid of others. We will also have to search our skills very specifically: Do we need this help at the policy level, at the strategic level, or only at the tactical level?

We will often find that we need little specialized help at all—at least not in determining *what* must be done to improve performance. But in preparation for getting whatever relevant assistance we need, we should ask ourselves these questions about the performance system we are trying to engineer:

1. Have I clearly described the goal, missions, and responsibilities of the performance system? Am I entirely satisfied with them and with my description of them? Are they described as measurable accomplishments and not as behaviors?

If we have difficulty answering "yes" to these questions, perhaps we need some help—but not from behavior experts, because our problems here are not yet behavioral. Where do we look for help at this point? Probably from our colleagues, whether they are peers, superiors, or subordinates. We might also get useful help from such diverse sources as management consultants, industrial engineers, and philosophers (if we can locate any). But if we do look for help here, we should make sure we know the answers to these questions about goals, missions, or responsibilities before we worry about other matters. At this point, if people try to sell us training, or a motivation program, or human factors, or any other kind of system for modifying behavior, we should throw them out. The first problem is to discover for sure what we are trying to accomplish. And until we know that, no one is going to be able to tell us

how to accomplish it. We aren't going to buy a program to help us improve people's behavior if we have only a feeling that their performance can be improved. We will wait until we know in exactly what respect, by exactly how much, and with exactly what valuable returns.

>   2. Do I have sensible requirements and standards of performance that are based on exemplary possibilities? And do I have a reasonably reliable and accurate way of measuring these standards?

And if we are not sure of our answers here, we better not ask for help from people who are specialists in measuring behavior, because behavior is not what we are trying to measure. Help can come from diverse sources, such as management consultants, systems engineers, industrial engineers, controllers, and even some personnel specialists; but we can't count on it. Many of these specialists have not had real experience with the measurement of human performance.

>   3. Have I found where the greatest opportunity for improving human performance lies? the greatest PIPs with the biggest stakes?

Presumably, those who helped establish the system of measuring performance can also help make the measurements—provided that the people who do the helping don't have a vested interest in what the measurements might show. And, again, we are not ready for behavior specialists, because behavior is not what we are measuring.

Only when we have answered "yes" to these three sets of questions are we ready even to consider seeking assistance with behavior. And the behavior engineering model can be the guide, inviting us to pose these questions:

I. Information:

>   1. Do people know what accomplishments are expected of them and what the standards are?
>
>   2. Are people informed as quickly as possible—and with high frequency—about how well they are performing? Are they truly informed, and not just given data that are difficult to understand? Are the data accurate? Are the data tied to performance, so that they measure only the performance over which people have real control? And do the data tell the people in what respect they are not

performing well? Is there an enforcement system that ensures that the information will be dispersed as it should be?

If we cannot answer "yes" to these questions, and we think we have neither the time nor the skills to create such feedback ourselves, we might, again, get help from diverse sources. There are a number of performance specialists and management consultants who really believe in the importance of feedback, and who have been successful in applying it. But if the people being managed are students, then we had best become the authority ourselves.

3. Does the incoming information efficiently guide performance? Is it free from confusion and a model of clarity? Are there adequate guides as how to perform a job so that memory isn't critical? Are these guides models of simplicity and clarity?

When the stimuli of a job are confusing, an industrial engineer or a human factors specialist might be able to help. But it is wise to be careful here. For example, the engineers who designed the new telephone operator's computerized "switchboard" (TSPS) built it so that a light goes *on* to signal that the customer has hung up. This is just contrary to what we are used to: A light usually goes *on* when someone's on the line. And this confusion is difficult to overcome when one is being trained to become a telephone operator.

As for manuals and other job aids, a few training development specialists have done excellent jobs in designing them well. But in general it is best to avoid subject matter experts, because they will want the manuals and guides to be models of detail rather than of simplicity.

II. Response: Instruments

Are the tools and materials people have to work with designed mechanically to fit human beings? Are better tools available? Are they optimally arranged and made available for use?

Industrial engineers and human factors specialists can pay off handsomely with special equipment problems. But many of the solutions here are simply a matter first of common sense and then a decision on whether or not to invest the resources. Industrial engineers may sometimes help us determine if the return on the investment is worth it.

III. Motivation: Incentives

> Is there something in it for people to perform well? Are
> the incentives made contingent upon good performance?
> Do people know that? Are there competing incentives to
> perform poorly; and, if so, is the balance of consequences
> in favor of positive performance? Are the incentives
> scheduled well enough to protect against discouragement
> and extinction of performance? Are all the available
> incentives being used?

Again, a good, hard, unbiased look at the incentives available to people
should answer these questions for us without much expert help. If poor
performance persists in spite of all we have tried, perhaps some incentive specialists can help. But it is a good idea to begin simply by asking
the people we are managing.

The fact that a good performance system is being engineered will in
itself remove many of the negative incentives for poor performance.
People find it more pleasant and rewarding when their responsibilities
are well defined and measured, and results are fed back to them. Self-
management becomes possible when the management is accomplishment oriented, and when supervisors are not constantly monitoring
behavior. Indeed, the need for supervision can be greatly reduced
when realistic accomplishments, requirements, measures, and standards are laid out for people. When these things are done well, punishing forms of paternalism are no longer needed.

IV. Information: Knowledge

> Would people fail to perform to exemplary standards even
> if their lives depended on it—even when they have ade-
> quate information, instruments, and incentives to do so?
> Does the exemplary performer seem to know something
> that other people don't?

If we can answer "yes" to these questions with fair certainty, training
probably should be considered as a useful strategy. An expert is seldom
needed to help us answer these questions. But once we are assured that
training is indicated, a good training specialist—one who is oriented
toward performance analysis and the economics of training—can help
us determine both the needed content of training, and also its costs and
probable returns. A good training specialist might also help identify
when an alternative to training, such as guidance, can be used because
it will pay off even better.

V. Response: Capacity

> Is it certain and proven that one must have special apti-
> tudes, intelligence scores, verbal skills, manual dexteri-
> ties, and so on, in order to perform in an acceptable, if not
> exemplary, manner? Is the proof so sound that there are
> virtually no exceptions to it?

The answer to this question probably should be made by almost anyone
except experts on testing, IQ, and the like. If the answer is an unequivocable "yes," experts may be able to help in developing a selection
system. But a "yes" answer here is not likely.

Of course, talent, ability, and special skills become increasingly
important in poorly designed performance systems. Poor training methods give naturally quick learners a big advantage over other people. But
excellent training will greatly narrow the gap between the gifted and
the slow.

Of course, there are people of unusual talent who become exemplary
performers under the very worst of conditions. All kinds of unaccounta-
ble things can happen. But the challenge to the performance engineer
is to discover what the exemplary performers do that is so different, and
then to arrange for the average performers to do as well. To the extent
that the success of a performance system depends almost wholly on the
unusual characteristics of a few, the system must be poorly engineered.
To the extent that a system depends on the selection of people for its
success, the system must fail to realize a great deal of human potential
for performance.

All this is just as true in the schoolroom as it is at work. Really well-
designed instructional systems, which you will see (in Chapter 9) are
possible, would greatly reduce the variance in student performance.
The best instructional tactics will transform many students whose tests
say are doomed to failure into performers superior to those who now
make the highest marks with our common training tactics.

VI. Motivation: Motives

> Is the performance system inherently so dull, unreward-
> ing, or punishing that people must have special motives
> to succeed in it, even when the incentives provided are
> excellent?

If we can honestly answer "yes" to this question, and if we cannot
redesign the performance requirements to make the tasks more rewarding or more challenging, then recruitment of people on the basis of
motives may be an effective performance strategy.

Some people like dull, monotonous work; some even like punishing work. But in most situations in which the performance system is otherwise well designed, natural self-selection will provide all the motivation required for exemplary performance. Inspiration is the only legal tactic I know of, besides recruitment, that will produce exceptional motives. What about leadership? Unfortunately, in poor performance systems the effects of inspiring leadership are likely to be only temporary.

The greatest effect we can have on people's motives comes through indirect means, by improving the environment: improving incentives, information, work tools, and the assignment of greater responsibility or the redesign of the job. The direct manipulation of people's motives seldom has important leverage. In fact, people who are directly trying to improve the attitudes of employees and students are usually looking in the direction of the *least* leverage.

I have treated these questions about behavior here in a rather general, even superficial, way because I just wanted to introduce you to them here. Part III of this book is devoted to questions of behavior in far more detail—not *all* the questions of behavior, but those that in my opinion usually offer us the greatest leverage in engineering performance.[3]

NOTES

1. The number of tests (t) that you must make to discover the defect in N items is given by this simple formula:

$$2^t = N$$

Therefore, $2^6 = 64$, meaning that six tests will isolate the problem in 64 items. And 2 to the 30th power is a bit over a billion.

2. For the distinction between *data* and *information,* see Chapter 6.

3. For another treatment of these subjects, see Thomas F. Gilbert and Marilyn B. Gilbert, *Supervising Worthy Performance* (New York: John Wiley & Sons, 1978).

Part Three
POLICIES, STRATEGIES, AND TACTICS

I began my own professional career experimenting with and measuring learning, both in human beings and lower animals. When I left university teaching more than 15 years ago, it was to apply what I knew about human learning in practical settings. I approached the practical world with the firm conviction that all the problems of human performance could be solved by my small bag of tricks, which mostly included a good understanding of reinforcement theory and some unusual (although rather meager) experiences in applying that theory to problems of training people. It was deeply frustrating to discover that my own tactics of instructional design had severe limitations as a panacea for human incompetence.

One of the earliest limitations I discovered is that people often know how to perform far better than they actually perform, but that they often do not know what is expected of them, or if they are performing to those expectations. Clearly, there were other things I had to learn than neat ways to design teaching systems.

Another discovery was even more surprising. The principal reason I left the university was a deep sense that I was being reinforced more for being impressive than for being effective. It seemed to me that too many of my academic colleagues cared less about engineering competence in students than in the impressive symbols of competence. Surely, I

thought, the "real world" would be different, and there I would be judged only by what I could accomplish. Alas, it was not true. I soon discovered that I could be a "successful" consultant indefinitely by employing the same brand of "impressive" techniques that had made my academic career seem promising. Counterfeit symbols of competence were as real a currency in the world of work as they were in the world of schools, though perhaps not so exclusively so. I had, then, little option except to establish procedures for measuring my own effectiveness. This was especially difficult for me, because I found great relish in impressing people.

This forced self-discipline was fortunate, because it gradually turned my head away from behavior and toward accomplishment. And as my bag of behavioral tricks grew larger, the discipline of measuring accomplishments allowed me to put these tricks into some perspective. In this part of the book, I hope to share some of that perspective with you.

Quite properly, to cover the subject of human competence, Part III should consist of 18 chapters, 3 devoted to each of the 6 cells of the behavior engineering model. There would be, for example, chapters on policies, strategies, and tactics of human factors engineering—in the design of instruments to be suitable for human use. And chapters on incentives and motives would be as long as the chapters on knowledge and data. But I have not followed this format because this book is an act of creation, not an anthology of scholarship. Although I have had experience in human factors engineering, for example, I have little new to contribute to that approach for improving human performance. Similarly for motivation. In my small chapter on the subject, I have tried to say only enough to share my perspective of the subject.

Part III, then, is principally devoted to the policies, strategies, and tactics of information and knowledge—because it is in these areas that I have had some exceptional experiences. Not all I say will be totally new to every reader, but much of it will be new to most.

There are four chapters on knowledge, two of these dealing with knowledge policy: one treats the world of work; the other, the world of schools. I handled policy this way because considerations in the two kinds of cultures, work and school, are fundamentally different. But there is just a single chapter on knowledge strategies and tactics. That chapter does not distinguish between work and school because I believe the basic principles are much the same for both. I do want to point out, however, that the design of conditions for creating efficient knowledge is really a technology in itself, and it deserves a superior technical treatment that is beyond the scope of this book. My objective here is to show the great untapped potential of instructional design. I

do this primarily by illustration rather than by in-depth discussion of the principles, because readers are not likely to be convinced that instruction can produce the enormous economic returns I argue are possible unless I also present convincing examples of truly superior instructional techniques.

Chapter Six
Information and Competence

HAYSTACKS

Data, like the hay, is usually dry
And piled in stacks and measured by the bit.
But how like the needle information is: It
Always has a point and needs an eye.

T.F.G.

WHAT IS INFORMATION?

Improved information has more potential than anything else I can think of for creating more competence in the day-to-day management of performance. But, as the behavior engineering model (Chapter 3) points out, we can improve information in two general ways:

1. We can improve the clarity, relevance, and timeliness of the data designed to inform people.
2. We can improve people's ability to use the existing data.

Training is an attempt to create a permanent change in people's repertories—most often, in their ability to process difficult data. As an alternative, we can work on the *data*—try to make them simpler and clearer, thus easier to understand without extensive training. Obviously, I am not restricted to one or the other of these solutions, and intelligent planning will require that I weigh both alternatives. Perhaps a little change in the clarity of the data can be combined with a little training on how to use them to get cheaper or better results than a lot of either. But, in my experience, one strategem tends to pay off more often—and pay off dramatically: to improve the data designed to support performance. And even if training is the central solution for improving performance, redesigning the data will nearly always make the training simpler and easier to achieve.

175

The purpose of manipulating data, of course, is to convert them into information. Data and information never need to be confused, although they frequently are. People often point with pride to the great stacks of data their computers produce. But if the printouts don't really tell us anything, we cannot classify them as information. This confusion of information and data is an example of what a turn-of-the-century psychologist (Edward Tichener) called the "stimulus error." We make the stimulus error when we confuse the stimulus with its source. It is, then, contradictory to say: "He didn't respond to the stimulus." A stimulus is defined as an event that evokes a response. If "he didn't respond," the event wasn't a stimulus. It is a similar absurdity to say: "I gave him the information, but he didn't understand it." Rather, we should say, "I gave him the data, but the data didn't inform him." Data are not information until they get through to a person.

The stimulus error misleads us even more when we begin to qualify or quantify data. Psychologists will often say, for example, that one stimulus was strong, or twice as strong, as another stimulus, when what they are really doing is quantifying an event independently of any response it might evoke. Tichener posed this question: Suppose that you look at a board with 100 lights, all burning very brightly except one that has burned out. Which light is the strongest stimulus for our attention? The obvious answer is the one with zero candlepower—the least intense light is the most intense stimulus.[1] Yet psychologists will speak of increasing the intensity of the stimulus when what they mean is making the light more intense.

Similarly, we may become satisfied that our information is orderly and clear even before we establish that it occasions orderly, efficient actions. It is a near certainty that if you write a clear and effective set of instructions in a manual telling people how to perform a task, some expert at the task will say to you, "You don't have all the information there." And if you follow that expert's line of thought, your manual will soon become so cluttered with minutiae that it will inform no one. If you don't believe this, just look at the manuals of instruction that fill the shelves at work and school. What you should be able to say to the expert is, "You mean that I don't have all the data here. But notice that I have arranged the data so readers can get all the information they need." Remember Mr. Quik and Mr. Sloe in Chapter 1? Mr. Sloe already had so much data that he needed only the slightest bit more to convert him from a stumblebum to competence.

The stimulus error is so important in formulating information that it deserves a name of its own—one I shall call the "telling" error. You commit the telling error when you think you have told people something, but when all you have really done is say something to them. If they don't hear what you've said, you haven't really told them anything.

Telling errors are very common symptoms of the cult of behavior, and are painfully obvious to consultants in the world of work. My wearisome search for a few kernels[2] of useful information lead me directly to the sources of data. What I found was that the more data available, the greater pride in the "information" service. Yet, as a rule, the more complex the system of data, the more difficult it is to extract useful information from it about human performance. The business of processing data, too, has recently grown tremendously in sophistication, but useful information about human performance is about as hard to get as ever.

What difference does it make? I can give you my own opinion: On the average, we could dramatically reduce at least three-quarters of the PIPs in the world of work by applying relatively simple procedures for transforming data into useful information. And these procedures are almost always far less expensive and less troublesome than training. I believe that the improvement of information in the world of work can be nearly as powerful in its effects on competence as the improvement of teaching in the world of schools.

KINDS OF INFORMATION

We could find hundreds of ways to classify kinds of information, but our engineering purpose will simplify the task and narrow the classification to the two ways in which data can function to support performance. This distinction is elementary, as an example will show.

Suppose that you are driving a car, in a hurry to get to Mountainville, and you see the road sign for it (Figure 6-1). This sign does two things simultaneously: It gives you a direction; it also confirms that you are on course and are making good time and need not speed up. In stimulus-response notation, every stimulus serves two information functions, as Figure 6-2a shows. This can also be expressed graphically, as in Figure 6-2b, with notation[3] I have used before.

A bit of the data can direct us what to do next, or it can confirm that we have been acting correctly, or it can do both. The problems of engineering human competence by improving information therefore center around these two functions: direction and confirmation. And they tell us two ways that we can manipulate the environment to assure

FIGURE 6-1

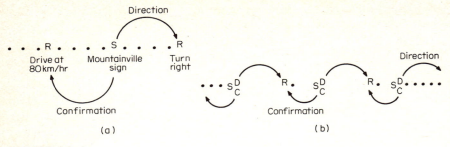

FIGURE 6-2

more competent performance. We can do a better job in showing people what to do, and we can improve our methods of letting them know how well they have been doing. So there are at least two different ways that we can, without training, improve the information required for competent performance:

1. We can improve what is often called "feedback" by manipulating the data so that they effectively confirm performance.

2. We can improve the ways in which we direct or guide performance.

More than half the problems of human competence can be traced to inadequate data. Although both direction and "feedback" (as confirmation is often called) can be greatly improved, feedback has, I think, even greater potential. In years of looking at schools and jobs, I have almost never seen an ideal confirmation system. Managers, teachers, employees, and students seldom have adequate information about how well they are performing. This, I believe, is often the most important reason for the large PIPs we find.

This defect in performance confirmation is so prevalent that almost any human performance system will serve to illustrate. I shall give specific examples, however, because such an easily correctable defect wouldn't exist if people were more aware of it and its consequences. But first I shall explain the curiously simple principles of information as a support for performance, because the examples can be better appreciated against this background.

PRINCIPLES OF INFORMATION FLOW

The requirements of an information system sensibly designed to give maximum support to performance are absurdly simple, and they can be summarized in eight steps:

1. Identify the expected accomplishments: mission, responsibilities, and duties.

2. State the requirements of each accomplishment. If there is any doubt that people understand the reason why an accomplishment and its requirements are important, explain this.

3. Describe how performance will be measured and why.

4. Set exemplary standards, preferably in measurement terms.

5. Identify exemplary performers and any available resources that people can use to become exemplary performers.

6. Provide frequent and unequivocable feedback about how well each person is performing. This confirmation should be expressed as a comparison with an exemplary standard. Consequences of good and poor performance should also be made clear.

7. Supply as much backup information as needed to help people troubleshoot their own performance and that of the people for whom they are responsible.

8. Relate various aspects of poor performance to specific remedial actions.

These steps are far too simple to be called a "technology," but it may be that their very simplicity helps explain why they are so rarely followed. I suppose that people tend to look for more complex reasons for seemingly complex performance problems, and therefore more complex solutions.

I have said that these steps are seldom followed, but let me make it stronger. Although I have taken no "statistically representative" samples, I have studied several hundred performance systems—both at work and in school—and I have never observed even a close approximation to these steps. Never, that is, until some systematic engineering was applied.

EFFECTS OF INFORMATION

Even though the principles of improving information are simple, their application requires very systematic care and analysis. But the effects of a good information system can be staggering. Whenever my students and I, or my colleagues, or my clients have engineered one, we have invariably been able to achieve a substantial improvement in measured performance—never less than a 20-percent improvement, often a 50-

percent change, and sometimes improvements as high as sixfold. Indeed, I can safely assert that a properly engineered information system should reduce the PIP of a group of people from whatever it is to as low as 1.2 or even less. There is one substantial exception, however: When people have not been trained adequately, the feedback of data alone obviously will not have such dramatic effects. But it is important to know that very often people are judged to perform poorly because they do not know *how* to perform; in reality, however, they simply do not know *when* they are performing well. In my own experience, more than half the clients who request help with training need very little or no training at all, just better confirmation of their performance. And even if training is needed, this is hardly an excuse to release trainees into a world that fails to confirm the value of what they have learned.

The training exception obviously includes schools. Of course, the kinds of results I am describing cannot be realized there merely by programming the flow of information. Still, engineering simple information at school could have dramatic effects, in my opinion, even without improving the instruction. Few students ever know what accomplishments their efforts are directed toward, how those accomplishments are measured, what exemplary standards are, and how well they are performing against those exemplary standards. (I shall discuss this problem in greater detail in Chapter 9.)

Confirmation and Superstition

If the effects of good information flow can be powerful, however, the consequences of shoddy information can be devastating. Ill-designed information systems not only fail to support superior performance, but they also actively promote incompetence. One of the principal ways they can do this is by creating superstitious behavior. Usually when we think of superstition, we think of black cats and salt over the shoulder, but there is nothing mysterious about it at all. And its power to mislead us is so great that we need to examine it more closely.

Some years ago, B. F. Skinner walked into his pigeon laboratory one morning to find his pigeons behaving in most peculiar ways. One bird, for example, repeatedly turned counterclockwise in its cage; another repeatedly tossed its head high; another had developed a habitual pendulum motion of head and body; and so on. Skinner quickly realized what had happened. The pigeons had been put on a schedule of reinforcement such that they would get food delivered to them at regular time intervals *provided that* they pecked a window after each interval. But the electrical circuitry didn't function properly, and it delivered food at regular intervals *whether or not* the pigeon pecked

the window. So, if the pigeon happened to be turning in a circle when the food hopper "clicked" and presented itself, that circling behavior was immediately reinforced. As Skinner so well knew, if a behavior is reinforced just once, it keeps some strength for a period of time—and several occurrences of the response without reinforcement are not sufficient to extinguish it. As the pigeon continued circling for a while, the food hopper again appeared coincidentally, further strengthening the circling behavior. Skinner recognized this kind of behavior as superstition. When we exhibit superstition, we act as if some form of behavior has a causal relationship to other events. For example, we toss salt over our shoulders as if that bit of behavior will ward off unhappy consequences. Or the baseball player will go through a ritual of jerking and adjusting his cap as if that will increase the likelihood of getting a hit. Skinner's pigeons were doing just that—one was circling, as if that would bring on the food.

So, superstitious behavior is produced by accidental reinforcement. And, as with other behavior, once superstitious behavior is reinforced on several occasions—even though accidentally—it can be tremendously resistant to extinction. Indeed, human beings can verbalize the "causal" relationship between behavior and the unconnected consequence, thus further supporting the superstition. And, as many experiments have shown, the reinforcement effect is even greater if the early accidental payoffs do not occur consecutively, but are spaced out a bit. Once the behavior is established, only very infrequent reinforcement is required to maintain it.

I shall describe a real case of human superstition, unaccompanied by magical totemism, and readers can reach their own conclusions about how often superstition occurs in the rest of us—even without our being aware of it. Readers will also see how the information fed back to a person is the most powerful agency of superstition, and how the redesign of the information system could overcome it.

Lars Lucky sells advertising space for the Fenntown City Directory. His boss, Pete Privati, has carefully described a procedure for making the sale—a procedure that includes an admonition: "Always make an appointment before going to see a customer." Lucky's boss has been at this kind of work for years, and he once made a careful study of the importance of certain factors on the probability of a sale. Among other things, he found that making an appointment with a customer, instead of walking in cold, doubled the probability of a sale. But Privati fails to share this information with his salespeople because he prefers admonition to information.

Lucky had not been on the job long when, driving to his office, he noticed a filling station manager sitting in a chair in front of the station. Lucky had tried making an appointment, but couldn't reach the manager. Instead of obeying

the rule, Lucky pulled into the station. Ten minutes later, he had made a sale. "So much for the advice of bosses," mused Lucky.

Five of the next 16 cold calls Lucky made also resulted in sales. He no longer believed in making appointments. From then on, he made all his calls cold. Unfortunately for Lucky, at year's end his sales performance was among the lowest on the staff. But neither he nor Privati ever saw the relationship to cold-calling.

Lucky exhibits the classical symptoms of superstition. The cold-call technique accidentally got reinforced early, and after that it required only an occasional reinforcement to make it extremely resistant to extinction. To this day, despite his poor sales record, he openly pooh-poohs making appointments.

If you ask him why he has such low sales, Lucky displays another bit of superstition—the kind that immensely aids ethnic prejudice (as well as other kinds). He will tell you, "I get assigned all the Jewish customers." Coincidentally, of course, his first five sales were all to Italians, and his first five failures were all with Jewish businesspeople.

Eventually, one of the regional managers of Fenntown Directory decided to install an information service in his region. He asked his sales managers to plot both sales successes and sales failures under different conditions. In this way, each salesperson could see what happened to sales made with and without appointments, among other things. The effects on the regional sales performance were electric. But this does not influence Lucky—his superstitions are too thoroughly engrained.

Sales performance, possibly more than any other kind of job, is especially prone to superstition because of the chancy kinds of payoffs. But other examples abound. Go into any factory, and watch a machine maintenance engineer kick and tap a machine in a ritualistic manner. From this we can conclude two things. First, the mechanic is exhibiting classical signs of superstition. (How many times have you made something work by kicking it? Not often, but the desire to do it is irresistible.) More important, we can usually conclude that the mechanic has been inadequately trained to perform a troubleshooting sequence, or that little feedback existed in the plant to connect machine performance with the mechanic's performance—and probably both of these things are true.

Management, of course, is not free of superstition. Furthermore, it is my experience that management is more likely to develop a language of magic than the less articulate mechanics. The president of a company will boast to me about how well he selects his managers. "I look for creativity," he says. I don't know exactly what this looking-for-creativity behavior consists of, but I can be certain that it is superstitious behavior

accompanied by the language of magic. And this is true whether the president's company is doing well or not.

There are only two cures for superstition, and both have to do with improving information. One is to supply feedback that connects truly effective behavior with the results; the other is to make training so effective that people comprehend the rational nature of the causation in a situation. But one thing is certain: The cure has to be mighty, because superstition, once established, is an extremely tough habit to kick.

Confirmation and the Hawthorne Effect

I think one more example is needed to prove the great power of confirmation on performance, but its power can easily be overlooked. When we peer at the world of performance problems through the lenses of complexity, these problems seem very complex too, and therefore subject only to complex solutions. Nothing better illustrates this than the "Hawthorne effect."

Some 50 years ago, a study took place at the Hawthorne (New Jersey) plant of the Western Electric Company, which became the most famous and influential investigation ever conducted on worker productivity. In fact, the "Hawthorne effect" has become the name for the effect of extraneous variables on the result of an experiment on human performance.

Briefly, the Hawthorne investigators attempted to study the influence of several factors, such as illumination and rest periods, on the productivity of people assembling electrical relays. Employees serving as subjects were removed to a special experimental room. And, to the surprise of the investigators, the employees' assembly rates rose regardless of the variables the experimenters introduced, even when illumination and rest conditions were poor. For many years, the findings of this study have been widely cited as evidence that "more humane" working conditions will result in greater productivity. The subjects, it has been repeatedly pointed out, became—by the circumstances of being experimental subjects—a coherent social group who were given very special attention. And interpretations that performance was improved because of social identity, attention, and interactions with management set a new style in industrial relations—or, at least, in the way people talked about industrial relations. After that, anyone who introduced new conditions in an industrial setting was almost certain to be asked, "How do you know that what you did really helped? Did you take into account the Hawthorne effect?"

A half-century later, H. M. Parsons[4] reexamined the original study—including investigations that are not usually mentioned in the Hawthorne discussions—and demonstrated that two things happened in the

experimental room that had not happened at the regular work stations: (1) The subjects were given regular and frequent information about how productive they were; and (2) the system of paying them was changed so that they had greater control over how well they got paid. In short, for the first time, the employees in the experiment were told how well they were performing; and, also for the first time, were far more likely to get paid for above-standard production. Why shouldn't they do better? These two variables had been ignored up to now. If Parsons had done the original experiments, there would be no Hawthorne effect as we know it today. Or else it would refer to the effects of information (feedback) and incentives on performance. Perhaps the course of industrial relations would have been different; over the years we would have worried less about such complexities as social identity and morale, and worried more about such simplicities as telling employees how well they are doing and paying them accordingly.

I computed (from Parsons' report) the assembly performance PIP and found an interesting sidelight of the Hawthorne data. The subjects averaged 50 assemblies per shift at their regular work stations; the exemplar was producing about 75 at the end of the experiment, giving a PIP of about 1.5, which, as I noted in Chapter 2, is typical for routine tasks. But the average experimental subject rose to about 68 assemblies per shift, which shows that the PIP was reduced to approximately 1.1— a PIP characteristic of highly competitive athletic events.

Confirmation and "Complex" Performance

Discussion about the effect of easily manipulated performance usually centers around the jobs of hourly industrial employees, and not around those employed in management and professional jobs. I believe this is just another symptom of the behavior cult. There is a decided bias that the competence of those in more advanced jobs somehow wells from within, and is not easily affected by mere events in the environment. To make matters worse, it is usually thought that professional and managerial skills are too complex to be measured anyway. So how can anyone ever give professionals and managers relevant information about their performance?

This bias clearly confuses behavior with accomplishment. No doubt the mind of Archimedes was complex beyond description; but his principle is a thing of simplicity—in fact, this is one of its beautiful features. I wouldn't care to have to describe the behavior of good medical diagnosticians; but their accomplishments—their actual diagnoses—can certainly be evaluated for their accuracy, timeliness, clarity, and costs. Because an accomplishment has profound and far-reaching implications, or requires great training and experience, in no way

proves that it should be difficult to measure or that we cannot easily confirm its competence.

If we described the accomplishments of both a first-line supervisor in a manufacturing plant and the President of the United States, we would not find them so different. Among each of their accomplishments might appear: "Employees selected for jobs." That the President is selecting a Supreme Court Justice, whereas the supervisor is selecting someone to sweep up the shavings, does not substantially affect the measurability of these accomplishments. Were both the justice and the sweeper qualified? Were their appointments timely? acceptable to management (or Congress)? We don't have to know a thing about the President's behavior to judge whether his appointment was competent or not; nor about the supervisor's behavior.

I could go on spinning examples like this almost endlessly. But if one example doesn't do it, hundreds won't, because a sort of "Catch-22" is operating. If you don't have the sort of information system that exposes these incompetencies, then you can insist that such things don't happen to you and your friends, or else you would surely know about it. If you do have such an information system, it is likely to be self-curative, and you won't see these kinds of defects in performance. A good system of confirmation is such a powerful remedy for incompetence that the only time you can really observe its dramatic effects is when it is first instituted. Lack of information about the effects of confirmation on performance is no doubt a major reason why its potential is so seldom realized.

PROBLEMS IN CONFIRMATION SYSTEMS

Will people begin to install elementary information systems once they see that these more parsimonious approaches are effective? Probably not, because the most important cause of poor information systems is an inherent resistance to information that springs from many forms of self-interest and self-doubt. I shall briefly summarize, then discuss, them.*

1. *Technical ignorance* of how to measure performance well is extremely widespread and can be found everywhere— from data technologists to top management, from personnel and training specialists to the finest scientists. In short, most people don't believe that we can measure performance well simply because they don't know how to do it.

*There are other reasons ("too expensive," etc.), but these are the principal ones.

2. *Every case is different,* people will tell you. And because the circumstances of performance vary so greatly, it is unfair to report performance measures since the data fundamentally cannot be compared.

3. *Vested interest* in not having performance measured and reported is, in my opinion, the most pervasive and intractable reason why confirmation systems are not standard. And, often, when the other two technical reasons are given, they are merely excuses to cover up the real reason of vested interest.

Technical Ignorance As a Barrier

Ignorance of how to measure performance is not merely lack of knowledge, but it stems from a competing viewpoint and one that I have so often discussed: that the quality of performance is found in behavior. As long as we think that descriptions of behavior are necessary measures of competence, we shall remain at a technical standstill. And even when we agree that accomplishments are the central objects of our measures, we still have to agree on which standards should be applied to them.

The technical problems become quite manageable, however, once we agree that worthy performance is a function of accomplishment, and that the only sensible and worthy standards are exemplary ones. Then, to determine the information we need in order to confirm competent performance, we need to conduct a performance audit, level by level. In this way, seemingly unmeasurable jobs, such as that of a plant manager or a teacher, become easily measurable (Table 6-1). In describing the plant manager's job, for example, we may decide that one responsibility is to establish job standards for department managers. And when we have identified the standards, we have a method of measuring the performance.

The performance audit leads to measures that will confirm competence. These confirmation measures, as we saw in Chapter 5, can serve as a troubleshooting device, obeying the rules of information theory— or, less technically, operating like the game "Twenty Questions." For example, if we are concerned with how well the plant manager is performing, we look first to the level above—to the measures of the mission (policy level). If the yield and quality of the plant's production are exemplary, there is no reason to look further. If they are less than exemplary, we must look at measures of the plant manager's responsibilities to find out why. Perhaps the standards set for the departments are less than exemplary. If so, we then look at the duties required for that responsibility. Or, perhaps, after failing to find a true exemplar, the plant manager sets lower standards than are necessary. Indeed, it is

TABLE 6-1 DERIVATION OF PLANT MANAGEMENT MEASUREMENTS

POLICY LEVEL

	Mission	*Requirements*	*Standards*	*Measures*
A.	Exemplary production	Yield	$X output $X input	Yield index
		Quality	X points of quality control	Q.C. points

STRATEGIC LEVEL

	Responsibilities	*Requirements*	*Standards*	*Measures*
A1.	Job standards set	Quality of standards	Exemplary	Difference between actual and exemplary standards
		Communicated	All responsible know the standards	Percent of people who are aware of standards
		Coverage	All critical jobs at each level of performance matrix	Percent of accomplishments given standards
A2.	etc.			

TACTICAL LEVEL

	Duties	*Requirements*	*Standards*	*Measures*
A1(a)	Exemplars identified	Quality	None better (PIPs = 1)	PIPs of chosen exemplars
	etc.			

quite possible that this is the only reason that the yield of the plant is not exemplary.

We can examine the performance of teachers in a similar way. In auditing the performance of teaching "energy systems design," for example, we would first measure the quality of the curriculum; then we would determine how many students met standards of good design. Finally, we would examine more specific aspects of the instruction.

The nature of the technical barrier to developing information about performance becomes clear in discussions with managers and professionals. Doctors quickly concede that the accomplishments of lawyers can be measured, but never those of doctors. And lawyers think it is easy to measure the accomplishments of doctors, but not lawyers.

Industrial engineers know that the performance of the personnel department can be measured, but not their own. And personnel people hold a similar broad view. A supervisor once agreed that I could measure the performance of his company's president, but hotly argued that it was not possible to measure the performance of his clerks.

Another technical barrier to competent information systems is the difficulty in agreeing on what aspects of performance to measure. Is the quality of an engineering design as important as the economies it makes possible? How should these aspects be weighed? There is no good substitute, I think, for a careful performance audit, level by level, to answer these questions. Without systematic analysis, we are likely to become attached to measures that are easy to get but highly misleading.

There are no better examples of attachment to misleading measurement than in the great American sport, baseball. In 1974, Joe Morgan of the Cincinnati Reds won the Golden Glove Award for his fielding at second base—meaning that he could field a baseball better than anyone else in his league at this position. A fielding average is calculated as the ratio of the successful chances that the fielder handles to his total chances. (Whenever a ball is hit to a fielder, he has a chance to either catch it and put a man out, or to assist another fielder in making the putout.) Morgan had 741 chances to put out a runner or to assist in putting him out, and he made 13 errors. This gave him a fielding average of 0.982. No question about it—Morgan didn't drop the ball often that year.

Rickie Stennett of the Pittsburgh Pirates, on the other hand, had a fielding average of 0.980, and made 19 errors at second base—six more than Morgan. The difference is tiny enough to make us wonder if Morgan might have been just luckier. However, some sports writers will tell us that we really have to watch Morgan play his position—that he is the more exciting player.

But suppose we back up a bit and ask this: What do we expect a second baseman to accomplish? Naturally, to get as many opposing players out as he possibly can. There is a direct and simple measure of this accomplishment: the total number of chances the fielder handles. Unless the ball is hit directly to a player, he has to have a certain amount of quickness and speed to get to the ball and turn it into a chance. Stennett averaged 5.95 chances per game; and Morgan, 5.1. That means that in a season in which they played 150 games, Morgan would get 123 fewer opponents out than Stennett. No wonder Stennett made a slightly higher percentage of errors (2% vs. 1.8%) than Morgan. When a player is good enough to get his glove on balls that other players can't reach, he is going to drop some of them because they are harder chances. In any case, Stennett's contribution to his team's defense was greatly superior to Morgan's. Why didn't he win the

Golden Glove Award? Because the system for measuring the performance didn't result from systematic analysis.

Some people may think that baseball is just a game and that such stupidity cannot occur in serious professions. But they would be wrong. In my experience, measurements of baseball performance are far superior to most measures of "serious" performance, both in schools and at work. There is tremendous public interest in baseball. This interest invites more sensible measurements, in fact; where that interest does not exist, the measures are usually even less sensible, if, indeed, they exist at all. If the public took a similar interest in the performance of those who manage factories and teach their children, we would all have more time to go to ball games.

The "Every Case Is Different" Barrier

"We can't really measure people's performance, because no two cases are alike." We saw this as a common complaint in Chapter 2, and how it arose from confusion between behavior and accomplishment.

But the confusion of behavior with accomplishment is not the only source of this disbelief. People also believe that the circumstances of each person's job are so different that comparisons are meaningless. There is no question that data from the real world are subject to many more extraneous variables than those from the laboratory, but real-world comparisons are not that difficult if the measurement system is developed with care. Much of the argument that no two jobs are alike simply cannot be supported. People who manage the work of others are naturally more aware of differences in the circumstances their employees face than they are of the similarities. After all, perceiving exceptions is part of what a manager gets paid for. But where there *are* genuinely important differences in the conditions of a job, all we need to do is to establish separate standards for those conditions. If a salesperson with a rural territory cannot be expected to do as well as the big city vendor, for example, we must establish a separate set of tables of exemplary standards.

This is not to say that the measurement of performance is always easy; only that it can be done and that it is well worth doing.

This every-case-is-different argument is so popular, and the remedy so easily overlooked, that it needs the clear illustration that the following case history provides. This is an example of measuring the performance of a rather complicated job—one that requires selling, consulting, and engineering.

Adam Knight is a manager in the Confederate Telephone and Water Company, locally known as Contel. The group he manages are "telephone design

installation engineers," or, in company parlance, "Teddies." The Teddies are supposed to locate architects and builders *before* their plans are completed, and persuade them to provide space for closets and conduits for telephone equipment. They also must take the building blueprints and actually create designs that the builders will use. The job requires several accomplishments. Teddies must locate building plans while they are in the making, sell the builders on providing space, and create actual architectural designs. They are really both salespeople and engineers.

Adam is especially interested in finding a way to measure the performance of his Teddies because this is his first management position. He reasons that if he can tell how well his people are performing, he can be a better manager. But he discovers that no one has ever measured the performance of the Teddies. When he asks his boss why not, he is told that there is no sensible way to do it.

"There's too much about the job," Adam's boss tells him. "Besides, every building is different. An office building takes a lot of work, but a library is simple. I don't know how you could put numbers on this kind of job."

But Adam isn't discouraged, because he has a firm belief that anything that exists in some quantity can be measured. He begins to resolve this problem by taking measures of the time that exemplary performers require to design telephone space for different kinds of buildings. He finds that designing space for a 20,000-square-foot office building takes about as much time as designing for a 50,000-square-foot library. As a result, he is able to devise a table apportioning different weights to different kinds of buildings. Table 6-2 illustrates this.

Adam Knight then constructs a simple performance index from these data. He finds that the exemplary Teddie can design space for the equivalent of 100,000 square feet of multioffice space per month. According to Table 6-2, this performance merits 1000 points (10 × 100). This then becomes his standard, and any Teddie's performance can be measured as a PIP (or, inversely, as a ratio) by comparison with the exemplary standard. A Teddie

TABLE 6-2   PERFORMANCE MEASUREMENT WEIGHTS

Space	Credit points per 1000 square feet	Space	Credit points per 1000 square feet
Single-office building	8	Hotel	9
Multioffice building	10	Motel	7
Public library	4	Fast-food restaurant	6
Court house	9	Drive-in restaurant	5
Nursing home	5		
Hospital	8		

who designed space for a 50,000-square-foot library and a 100,000-square-foot nursing home in a month would have a PIP of 1.43:

Library	$50 \times 4 = 200$
Nursing home	$100 \times 5 = \underline{500}$
Total	700 points

Such information would confirm the Teddie's moderately low productivity.

Of course, productivity is not the only requirement of a Teddie's job, and by careful performance analysis, Adam was able to construct a set of performance coefficients, indices, and indicators (such as those described in Chapter 5). He knows that there is no aspect of a Teddie's performance that cannot be measured, and these measurements can be made reasonably comparable if the work is done systematically.

We can construct a similar weighted point system for almost any kind of variation that affects performance, whether the measure is of quality or of productivity. It merely takes a commitment to getting performance data, a complete understanding that we want to measure accomplishments (not behavior), and a systematic performance audit to reveal the significant performance variables. Statisticians and data systems specialists can often help in devising the system, but not in the absence of the commitment to, and understanding of, performance analysis. Moreover, we must be wary of the "numbers" specialists, and be sure that they understand the economic purpose of the measurement.

The main point is not to be put off by technical arguments. The work of confirmation can be simply put: In general, no other strategy for improving performance costs so little and returns so much. And (again in general) no strategy requires so little technical expertise. Indeed, when we consider all the technical arguments against installing effective confirmation systems, they simply fade away and leave us to confront the greatest barrier of all: vested interest that is supported by secrecy. As a matter of fact, the technical barriers are often the rational excuse of those who have a personal interest in not letting information flow freely.

Vested Interest in Management Incompetence

Who has such vested interest in incompetence? Surprisingly, much of it seems to be found in our most advanced and "noble" professional groups—doctors, lawyers, and teachers, for example. Shortly, I shall discuss their vested interest in not letting other people (and themselves) know how well they perform. But the heart of the resistance to confirmation is really in the most unlikely group—the professional managers.

In a perfectly designed, perfectly competent performance system, the manager would not have to work very hard. This is a basic conclusion from the First Leisurely Theorem, and one that should make the management of a competent system all the more desirable. But the desirability of leisure is offset by two important factors, both products of the cult of behavior.

First, because many managers have put great store on the value of hard work, this excuse for their higher salaries would disappear. A manager of a truly competent system might have to come to work only once a month. Such a manager could of course point to his accomplishments, but that would invite lesser employees to request the same treatment.

But the second reason is more important. If managers are privy to all the important information that makes a system work at all, however less than exemplary this system might be, they can place a higher value on their work. The guide who leads us through a dense jungle can place a higher premium on this service than one who shows us around a well-ordered museum. Similarly, managers who have learned to cope with a noisy world will seem to justify greater returns for their efforts than those who are required only to monitor a smoothly working, nearly autonomous system.

Indeed, the managers who are assigned to straighten out clearly shaky operations may have much the same contradictory motives as a monopolist. The monopolist has reason to produce in some quantity, or else there would be insufficient revenues. But there is also an incentive for restricting production to create artificial scarcity, thus keeping prices high. A manager who could straighten out any poorly performing system with great simplicity, and showed everyone else how to do it, would create "unnecessary" competition and drive down the value of the management service. By creating just enough improvement in an operation to impress other people, but not enough to sweep away the system's total reliance upon it, a new management can put itself into the most favorable position.

In general, then, the perfect flow of information would create two threats to management. First, it would threaten to remove the aura of magic about the achievement; and, second, it would threaten to let others know how to achieve the same results.

One of my more unpleasant surprises in working with managers in all kinds of organizations has been to learn how many of them do not want their new information systems known outside their own departments—even by other managers within the same organization who might benefit from the exchange. The urge to perfect competence is not without its limitations. But the misuse of such a powerful tool as information serves no one well. Information, when poorly used, of

course fails to support worthy performance; but it also acts in a positive way to reinforce incompetence. (One of the most powerful but subtle ways it does this is through the promotion of superstitious behavior, as I have shown earlier in this chapter.)

Certifying Professional Competence

Managers are not the only people with a vested interest in the poor flow of performance information. And nowhere is this resistance to information better seen than in the ways in which professionals are certified as "competent." First we shall examine how certification is handled and then how it might be handled.

Suppose that we decided to certify or license plumbers, and we devised a test to determine their eligibility. What kind of test should we construct? Here are sample items, one each from two different kinds of tests. Which kind of item do you think is clearly superior for certification purposes?

Test A

Connect two 2-inch pipe joints.

Standards:
  a. Water-tight
  b. Correct cement application
  c. Three minutes to completion

Test B

Which tool is best for connecting 2-inch pipe joints?

  a. Stilson wrench
  b. Monkey wrench
  c. Sprocket wrench
  d. Pocket wrench
  e. None of these

Obviously, test A is far superior, simply because it is a test of accomplishment. Test B measures a certain repertory of verbal behavior that might be helpful, but it certainly isn't necessary for doing a good plumbing job. Quite conceivably, one could make 100 percent on test B yet completely fail test A; or vice versa.

Suppose we now devise a third test:

Test C

1. Has five years' experience as an apprentice with a certified plumber.
2. Has completed a certified plumbing course.

Test C seems severe indeed. But is it equal—even superior—to test A? Hardly. The only way to know if test C is adequate is to give test A to those who pass C. By any logic, test A is the criterion measure, and test C is a measure of behavior history. Even if everyone who passes test

C can also pass test A, we could not be sure of the validity of test C, because those who fail it may pass the criterion test.

What kinds of tests are actually used to certify or license plumbers, physicians, lawyers, psychologists, and the like? They are almost always tests of the B and C type. Professionals are judged by a combination of verbal behavior and behavioral histories, and little or no attempt is made to measure actual performance. Indeed, in some professions it isn't at all clear what actual performance would define competence. For example, who is willing to say what mission would define a good clinical psychologist? Cured patients? That mission would never pass the ACORN test. Nevertheless, clinical psychologists are certified in most states.

Of course we can measure performance directly, either in real life or in simulated situations—even the performance of, say, a psychotherapist. We could, for example, make a list of "problems of living" that people have, and sample therapy patients to determine whether there has been a reduction of such problems during or after a course of therapy. Are there reductions in nightmares, suicide attempts, job absenteeism, drug usage, arrests, divorces and separations, hysterical reactions, phobias; or increases in productivity, the number of friends, socialization, or the like? Professional therapists will say that these are unfair measures—that *they* treat the "inner person." But if the treatment of the "inner person" has no noticeable influence on overt adjustments to the world, we could reasonably wonder what business a state has to license such therapy.

Naturally, in a fair certification program, standards of accomplishment would have to be established. This might be easier to do for, say, diagnostic physicians than for psychotherapists, but it can be done for both. With proper, independent measures of the number of successful diagnoses (weighted, perhaps, by kind—as Adam Knight weighted the performance of Teddies), exemplary standards could be established and published. Since the expressed (if not actual) purpose of state certification is the protection of the public, how better can the state serve this purpose than by publishing information—not only about the standards, but about the actual performance of diagnosticians, or surgeons, or psychotherapists, or lawyers?

Professionals will protest such measures and their publication on many grounds. But the real basis of their protest must be held suspect, because, above all, they have a vested interest in the use of behavior-based tests of certification. Only "experts" can say which behaviors are necessary for certification, and such tests give great power to the associations to which these experts belong. This power is useful in many ways—and none so important as to fix prices and to limit entry into the association, thus inflating the demand for services and the

prices charged. But not the least effect of this power is to protect incompetent professionals. If physicians have the degrees, and can certify that they talk the language of medicine, and if their accomplishments are never measured—who could ever charge them with incompetence? Malpractice, yes. Incompetence? No. Indeed, since the courts are the only way the public can find to protect itself from medical incompetence, malpractice suits are invited. With true performance standards and ratings of individual professionals, an entirely new and more rational set of malpractice standards could be established. With one's competence truly measured and published, the public is forewarned and can accept less than exemplary standards if it is willing to take the risk: *caveat emptor*. If the state's interest is to protect the public, why shouldn't it want to publish the probability that a physician will correctly diagnose my disease or repair my spine?

Measuring Professional Performance

Besides being the only truly fair (to the public) basis for certification, published performance measures would serve another purpose that I have already mentioned: They would greatly improve performance. Not only the public has a poor idea of how well the certified professionals perform, but the professionals themselves have little way of knowing. Consider a simple case.

A patient reports to Dr. Clup complaining of low-back pain. The doctor examines him and recommends certain treatments—rest, prescribed exercises, and certain precautionary measures. After a few visits, the patient, feeling no better, goes to a second physician, who correctly diagnoses the problem as a form of spinal osteomyelitis. The second physician prescribes antibiotics, and the patient makes a complete recovery. The patient never returns to Dr. Clup, so why shouldn't Dr. Clup imagine either that his prescribed exercises worked or that the patient was a hypochondriac who probably adopted another ailment? Because he lacks information about his failure, he will never improve his diagnostic skills. If Dr. Clup had some way of knowing that he was failing with certain kinds of patients, he would probably find ways to improve his own performance. Should both his colleagues and his patients know this, he would certainly improve his performance—or change his practice.

I am talking here about the confirmation of professional performance as a *policy*. But most arguments I hear against it are at the tactical level: It is too hard to do, or it cannot be done with precision because every case is different. Without the proper precision of measurement, it is argued, the results would be unfair to the physician. One doctor may

fail with a patient because the disease was not sufficiently advanced, whereas a second doctor succeeds because the disease has become obvious. Another frequent argument is that a sample taken of a physician's work may be a poor one, and a good physician may therefore be deprived of a livelihood.

These are all legitimate *tactical* concerns. But they also have *tactical* solutions—solutions unlikely to be found until the policy is adopted. For example, such things as the age of the illness can be factored into the measurements. And samples need never determine a physician's future. If a sample measure suggests that a doctor is a substandard performer, a more complete measurement can be taken before any judgments are made. In the age of the computer, the tactics of tracking the disposition of patients with large samples and great precision become tremendously enhanced.

Indeed, the computer[5] could defeat many of the tactical arguments against performance measurement. The real purpose of a confirmation policy is not to "catch the villains"—the incompetent—but to serve as a means for improving performance. To illustrate, we can look at a hypothetical possibility in the teaching profession.

Students in American schools are not learning how to follow written instructions as well as they might, or to perform arithmetic combinations. If a computerized test were installed in every school to measure the ability to follow instructions and the ability to add and subtract, immediate information could be made centrally available showing the comparative performance in every classroom—not only present performance, but progress in improving that performance. We could know immediately who were the exemplary teachers of addition and subtraction. Students could be classified so that the performance of children from socially deprived communities would be separated out. The aim of the exercise is not so much to spot incompetent teachers, but to find the exemplars. Who is doing the best job of teaching ghetto children to add and read? With this information, the methods of these teachers (in comparatively similar classes) can be reported to the teaching community. The computer could then feed back to teachers a great deal of diagnostic information to help them correct their performance.

To get an idea of the potential, look at this sample problem in arithmetic:

A student who can perform that arithmetic quite well may not be able to do this problem:

$$
\begin{array}{r}
26 \\
+34 \\
\hline
60
\end{array}
$$

Why not? In the second problem, adding 6 and 4 gives 10. Many students learning to carry have a problem with the "hidden zero." The advice "put down zero and carry 1" is interpreted as: "Hey, that's zero and you can't put down *nothing*." One student may then put down the 1 and carry nothing; another perhaps may squeeze the 10 into the unit spot. But a computer could make such differential diagnoses with great precision. Because there are many causes of failures, the computer printout would serve as a marvelous diagnostic tool for the teacher. (Or it could be used by itself to correct the defect.) The printout would tell the teacher how many errors students are making because of hidden zeros, carelessness, improper setups, inability to carry, incorrect combinations, and the like—and would give this information on a comparative basis. It could even print out the teaching tactics most useful to correct the deficiencies—those tactics used by exemplars. The computer could make similar precision diagnoses of verbal and social skills, and skills of measurement, speaking, and logic. Much of the confirmation would serve to be self-corrective. For example, the teacher whose students made too many "hidden-zero errors" would soon correct that deficiency. Other failures that teachers are unable to correct would signal the need for new strategies for the teachers, or even new policies for the school system.

Tactically, the problems of performance confirmation are always subject to solution. Most of the solutions, although they may require much work and thought, should prove to be fairly straightforward. The principal problem is not tactics, but policies that will commit managers of performance to the great corrective power of confirmation. It is simply never true that you cannot measure performance directly—with adequate precision, and with great consequences. The barriers are not tactical; they are political.

The age of the computer must herald the performance engineer, because all the data in the world will not improve human competence until these data are carefully selected and systematically ordered with the requirements of performance in mind. The computer will greatly reduce the plausibility of the tactical arguments against confirmation, but it certainly will not overcome the political opposition.

DIRECTING COMPETENCE

At the beginning of this chapter I distinguished two kinds of information: confirmation and direction. If the potential for improving perfor-

mance through improved directions is not so great as through new confirmation systems, it is nevertheless substantial. And the return can be found in two dimensions: not only by improving the value of accomplishments, but also by reducing the cost of behavior. As you will see in the next chapter, the cost of training is far higher than most people think. One way to reduce that cost is to create much better directions to perform; this can, in turn, reduce much of the need for training. Just writing a set of directions for people to find your home is an art that few have mastered well. Buy a swing set from a mail order firm, and try to follow the directions for assembling it. You would never know that they are written by professional technical writers.

But improving the writing of directions is not the greatest potential. A great deal of training, for example, could be replaced by well-designed job aids. More than once I have designed a troubleshooting guide for operators of complex machinery. Simply following the questions in such a guide, and in a sequence much like that described in Chapter 5, can convert a novice to a level of troubleshooting efficiency surpassing that of the best experienced operators. Yet such guides are rare.

There seems to be something faintly disreputable about job aids. The cult of behavior tells us that "really worthy people" don't need such crutches. Performing well without directions gives a person the appearance of superiority. Of course, this is behavioral nonsense. People who can use a guide avoid hours of training, and accomplish more as a result; they are simply more competent than those who bumble through on their own. Indeed, the field of guidance tools and job aids is so neglected that I have thought it worthy to make a special study of them. I shall describe three important kinds of directions I have designed, which, if widely used in the world of work, could greatly improve average performance.

The Query

Readers might admit that such results are possible for routine jobs like machine operation, but then ask whether more "complex," "advanced" jobs can benefit. Because of this natural doubt, I shall begin by describing the most complex form of direction—*the query*—which is used only for complex jobs. And the best way to describe it is through a real, if disguised, example of its application. The problem in the example is to help people in very "advanced" jobs, in which they must consider an "endless" number of factors, to make decisions worth millions of dollars.

The Humble Home is a leading magazine written for women and do-it-yourself devotees. For years, it has occupied a familiar spot on coffee tables all over North America. Unfortunately, its advertising revenues have been in steady decline for the past 3 years. Candy Cowen, the new advertising director of *The Humble Home,* is completely perplexed that her chief competitor, *Lady's Life,* is thriving while *her* magazine sinks. Demographic data from the rating services tell Candy that her magazine's readers earn more money, spend more money, do-it-yourself more, own bigger homes, and in almost all respects should be more attractive to advertisers.

But as Candy thinks about it, she begins to understand the reasons for the success of *Lady's Life.* She knows that although advertising account managers (the people who buy media space for their advertising clients) take pride in their "scientific" approach to making decisions, they are really victims of superstition themselves.

"Look at the average account executive," Candy invites her boy friend, Webber James. "He's a man with an apartment on Park Avenue and a house in Southhampton. He may make $100,000 a year. He thinks he's hardheaded, scientific, and guided only by 'real' data. But the truth is, the schmo listens to his wife and the other girls in Southhampton. *The Humble Home* is *never* on their coffee tables—they read *Lady's Life* because it's 'neat.' Our mag's readers are older people who stay home and do-it-yourself. They are stodgy and square; and they shop at Gimbels and Macy's. *Lady's Life* readers are younger and poorer; they buy less, but they buy it from Bonwit Teller or Lord and Taylor. Our account executive is afraid of all that Nielson data, and bows to the snobbery of the crowd he drinks with. If he really looked at the data, he would be begging for more space in *The Humble Home.*"

"So how do you defeat the myth?" Webber asks, knowing that Candy won't come up with a platitude.

"We've got to show them how to make the right decision," Candy says heatedly, and a little scornfully. "If we can make them look at the data, they will have to forget the mythology."

"But," Webber asks, "how are you going to 'make' a guy who takes in a hundred grand hook onto your leash?"

"I'll have to think about it," Candy says leisurely.

How do you guide people who are highly paid to make judgments that require the weighting of many factors? If it were so simple that all you needed was a checklist, they wouldn't be so highly paid.

"It's got to be something different, that's for sure," Candy tells herself. Then she thinks about how media people usually sell space to account executives.

Normally, a *Humble Home* media salesperson will approach the Leech advertising firm expensively prepared. Storyboards, flip-charts, impressive layouts, lots of data, and a team of experts are all wound up to prove to the Leech account executive that *The Humble Home* is the ideal place to sell the

new Lopez 100, say, the failed-millionaire's Mercedes. Sometimes the presentation is so rich, so astonishing, so "creative" that the account executive is swept away. But not often—just often enough to maintain the superstition that $10,000 is needed to make the pitch.

"We're fighting superstition in every direction," Candy reasons to herself. "Let's strip the presentation of all the totems and see what happens." So she devises a *query*, the performance engineer's candidly sneaky tool to get people to persuade themselves of the value of competence.

"What product are you going to pitch with your new guidance system?" Webber grins.

"A breakfast cereal—Torn Wheat. The Nauer Cereal Company has decided to try magazine advertising again. They haven't put space in a mag in years. And Leech had about decided to get Nauer to experiment in *Lady's Life*. I've talked them into a chance to make a competitive presentation. And this is the real challenge: The gals who read *Lady's Life* don't eat breakfast, and their husbands probably don't either. But Torn Wheat is just the right kind of breakfast for the middle-aged squares who read our mag."

Candy produces her presentation at a cost of about $500. It consists of a mimeographed booklet with no pictures—just words. "This will never work; it looks like junk, Candy," puzzles her boss. "I hope you know what you're doing, sweetheart. But it doesn't matter—we'll never get the Torn Wheat account anyhow."

Candy is pleased with her boss's reaction. It is exactly what she wants. She has reasoned in this way about Jack McKee, the Leech account executive she must face:

1. He is used to the hard sell. He fully expects phony arguments dolled up in expensive wrappings. When he gets them, he responds by yawning.

2. He is proud of the "knowledge" that only the "hard facts" can persuade him.

3. He completely distrusts the facts that salespeople give him. He knows that he has access to the same data, and he is paid better because *he* makes the decisions and resists the phony pitches.

"So," thinks Candy, "Let's surprise him. We're going to present him a soft sell, wrapped in cheap clothing. We'll give him the hard facts. And we'll let him make all the judgments—we won't say a thing."

"But that's never been done," her boss feigns surprise.

Jack McKee, the account executive, yawns even before the presentation begins. "We've just about made up our minds, Candy," Jack drones in his Harvard accent. "But let's see what you've got."

Candy drops her cheap-looking mimeographed booklet in front of Jack. "Jack, I don't know whether Torn Wheat ought to advertise in our rag or not. How about working through this booklet; then you tell me."

Completely surprised by Candy's approach, Jack opens to the first page with curiosity. Here is what he sees (the shaded circles are holes that go through the book):

Argument: The more income people have, the more likely they are to eat

Torn Wheat rather than some other breakfast cereal.

☐ Agree   ☐ Disagree

If you agree, read below. Otherwise go to the next page.

Read the data below, and decide which magazine it favors:

Income Data

	Magazine	
	A	B
$50,000 & up	3%	2%
$25,000 to $50,000	38%	28%
$15,000 to $25,000	46%	43%
$10,000 to $15,000	10%	19%
Below $10,000	3%	8%

Data Favor

⊘ A   ⊘ B   ⊘ Neither

Jack reads the page and puts a check mark in the hole labeled "neither." He looks at Candy with amazement. "Are you kidding me?"

"Go on," she urges with a smile. Jack turns to the next page, equally simple:

Argument: The less a magazine's readers watch TV, the more likely their major exposure to <u>Torn Wheat</u> will be in the magazine's ad.

☐ Agree   ☐ Disagree

<u>If you agree, read below. Otherwise, go on.</u>

TV Exposure Data

	Magazine	
	A	B
6 hours or more	5%	10%
5-6 hours	9%	15%
4-5 hours	16%	22%
3-4 hours	35%	33%
2-3 hours	18%	10%
1-2 hours	7%	4%
Less than 1 hour	10%	6%

Data Favor

◍   ◍   ◍
A   B   Neither

Still disbelieving, Jack checks magazine A, because he believes the data clearly favor that magazine. He continues through another 20 pages, checking A, B, or neither. Then he comes to the "backing" page, where all his check marks are recorded. It looks something like this:

	Factor		
Here is how you voted the magazines on quantitative data	A	B	Neither
22	✓		
21			✓
20	✓		
19	✓		
18	✓		
17			✓
16			
15		✓	
14			✓
13		✓	
12	✓		
11	✓		
10			✓
9			
8			✓
7	✓		
6			
5	✓		
4	✓		
3			
2	✓		
1			✓

Check in one of the holes below which magazine the quantitative data favors overall (or check neither)

A ⊘   B ⊘   Neither ⊘

Jack makes the obvious decision, although he is not guided merely by the number of checks. Candy encourages him to weight his decisions as he likes. Then he turns to the next section of the booklet—qualitative data:

Argument: The more editorial matter that a magazine has about food, the more likely a reader will see a food advertisement.

☐ Agree ☐ Disagree

If you agree, study the data below. Otherwise, go on.

Food Editorial Data

Magazine

	A	B
1976	24%	8%
1975	21%	6%

Data Favor

◍ A   ◍ B   ◍ Neither

He finishes eight such pages and reaches another backing sheet. And again he judges the data to favor magazine A. Then he goes to the next-to-the-last page:

Here are your judgments on qualitative and quantitative data. Weight them and decide which magazine you would favor.

	A	B	Neither
Quantitative	✓		
Qualitative	✓		
Your decision?	✓		

Now you have tentatively decided on one magazine. What price differential would lead you to change your mind?

If my choice cost this much more per inch, per thousand readers, I would definitely change my mind (check the hole).

1. less than 10¢
2. 10¢ to 25¢
3. 25¢ to 50¢
4. 50¢ to $1.00
5. $1.00 to $1.50
6. $1.50 to $2.00
7. $2.00 to $2.50

He clearly favors magazine A, but decides that if he could get his space for a dollar or a dollar and a half less, he would change his mind. So he turns the page and this is what he sees:

If you checked above the line, you have changed

your mind because magazine A costs 25¢ more per

inch than B. Your final choice is?   A   B

                                              ☐   ☐

✓

Magazine A is   The Humble Home

Magazine B is   Lady's Life

"What the hell is this?" Jack exclaims. "Magazine A is your rag."

"I know," purrs Candy. "But all the decisions were yours."

"You're right, Candy. Damned if you aren't right. What do you call this kind of presentation?"

"A 'paper computer,'" Candy responds. "Computers don't do anything but organize someone else's data, and we figured that you have all the relevant data. We just wanted to help you process it."

So Candy Cowen has guided the expert through a rational sequence—without once telling him what is right or wrong. When you know better than someone else how to perform, another form of guidance is useful—a more direct one. But the query, whether in the form of a "paper computer" or not, is an excellent form of guidance for those who alone must make decisions. I have used it in various forms and to guide a variety of performances, ranging from management decisions to selling.

For example, insurance salespeople will usually try to make all the decisions they can for their customers: what product is best for them, how much coverage they need, and so on. But a paper computer similar to the one used by Jack McKee can be given to customers to instruct them about the nature of each important decision, but letting *them* make the decision. The backing page has a clear description of the insurance product and price the customer chose.

It is difficult to sell the paper computer to many insurance companies, however, because a customer who makes a rational decision will usually select a product that isn't very profitable to the company. Candy, in our example, had one thing going for her—she could win only if the customer made a rational decision.

There are many and varied vested interests in other people's incompetence. But it always struck me that an insurance company that adopted queries as sales instruments could greatly reduce its huge sales staff. The paper computer would therefore cut the cost of selling, would sell a more useful product, and would sell it at a lower cost. Surely, there could be profit in such an arrangement—particularly since most insurance companies are now largely in the business of managing marginal performers.

Other Forms of Direction

The query is useful to guide people in performing those tasks for which only they can make the decisions. There are two other kinds of guidance, however, that can greatly improve the performance of other tasks: One I call an *ensampler;* the other, a *directory*. Directories are the most familiar forms of guidance. They may be as simple as the checklist that airline pilots use to check out their cockpits. Or they may be more complex "branching" directories, which carry a student through, say, a troubleshooting sequence. But a directory will give direction to performance when all the steps and all the conditions of performance are known.

The ensampler differs from the directory in that it is applied when the exact nature of the problems a performer faces is not known. An example is the problem of showing secretaries how to prepare a telegram. We know that the messages given to them are going to be too long, and that they must shorten these messages to save money. But because each message is different, we can only prepare samples to help users generalize the procedure. In its most common form, an ensampler will be a booklet with pairs of pages for each performance step. The left-hand page will give the general rule of performance and any aids needed. The right-hand page will give examples for the performer to follow.

Although this example is for a simple job, one that any reader can understand, this form of guidance can be used to direct far more complex performance as well. In fact, I have designed ensamplers for such diverse activities as medical diagnosis, sales management, and even performance analysis itself.

One secret of designing an effective ensampler or directory is to keep it simple. It should not be a substitute for a detailed handbook and manual. If some performers need more detailed guidance, it is best to indicate a reference to other material rather than to clutter up the guidance book by inserting the material there.

When Guidance Is Better

Guidance tools of the kind I have described can greatly reduce the need for training, just as they will reduce the need for memory. Indeed, once people are taught the importance of a task, and then provided with a theory of it, actual skill training will often be unnecessary and a guidance device can be used instead.

In general, guidance will be superior to procedural training on several counts other than lower costs:

1. The greater the complexity of a task, the more superior guidance is as a technique, because it reduces the probability of error and the need for training.

2. Tasks of low-frequency occurrence, or those requiring low rates of performance, favor guidance. For example, we cannot guide someone to play the piano because guidance would interfere with the high rates required. But most tasks are not of this nature.

3. Where error-free performance is extremely critical, guidance is favored because memory is not so reliable. Airline pilots checking a cockpit—also, lab technicians performing certain tests—are required by law to follow a directory.

As you will see in the next chapter, training costs are extremely high—and higher than most people think. The development and use of guidance can not only greatly improve much performance, but guidance has the potential for cutting training costs by billions of dollars. We shall examine these and other strategies and tactics for improving performance and cutting the high cost of training. But, as you will see, we need to start at a higher level of the performance matrix, and consider critical policy decisions that need to be made—first, policies at work.

NOTES

1. Tichener spoke of stimulus *attensity*.

2. A "kernel" might be a useful unit of information's effects. We might establish a kernel of information as that which reduces the PIP by one-tenth, say from 4 to 3.9. Bits are nice quantities for describing how computers talk to each other. But what about how well they talk to people?

3. The notation S_C indicates the confirmation function of the stimulus. It may also be "motivational" or reinforcing (meaning that it will increase the probability of responding—or maintain the probability). An S_C, then, may also be an S_r, or reinforcement.

4. H. M. Parsons, "What Happened at Hawthorne?" *Science, 183* (March 1974).

5. The computer-assisted instructional system called PLATO has already reached the stage of development that it could drastically change our educational system. One day it will; but profound policy decisions, defeating many vested interests, will have to be made first.

Chapter Seven
Knowledge Policy at Work

SUPPLY AND DEMAND

Yesteryear, when knowledge was in short supply
And hidden well, enlightenment was sought
With eagerness, and often purchased at
The standard offer: A penny for a thought.

But now that novelty's gone and supplies abound
And next to every pleasure dome's a school,
The tariff is a crippling interest rate—
For knowledge knows no economic rule.

T.F.G.

THE HIGH COST OF KNOWLEDGE

In 1977 alone, the American people spent over $100 billion[1] to educate youth in formal schooling. I have never met anyone who actually resented this expenditure, although there are a few people who still worry that we are not getting our money's worth. These worries about public schools are often expressed in rather vague terms, sometimes in sharp criticism, but seldom as practical programs that can be readily adopted to improve the value of education. And, surprisingly, questions about the value returned from our investment in university education are seldom raised—at least, I don't often hear them. By and large, the public is unquestioningly generous in its support of the schools. As we shall see in the next chapter, it can hardly afford to be more generous, because the money simply isn't available.

But the issue of the value of the schools should be raised here in this chapter because the investment is heavy indeed. And because few people recognize that after spending $100 billion a year to train our children, we turn right around and spend at least another $100 billion to prepare them for adult jobs, in the form of training in industry and government.

It takes little arithmetic to realize that we spend more than twice as much to train people as we spend on defense. I think that given this sum, it can be reasonably argued that adult training is one of the most promising single areas for fighting inflation. In short, we are spending over $200 billion a year, half of which we probably don't even know we are spending. And, besides, we haven't the faintest idea what we are getting for our money, or whether we could get a great deal more. Yet we have all the good reasons to be interested, because every cent of this money comes out of the public pocket, either in the form of taxes or hidden in the prices we pay for goods and services.

A few additional figures will perhaps add perspective to these training expenditures. They are all approximations, but support for them will be found in recent publications:[2]

1.	Amount spent per employee per year	$1100
2.	Amount spent per school student per year	1200
3.	Training costs as a percentage of net income, for the 20 largest U.S. industrial corporations	30%
4.	Ratio of all training costs to defense expenditures	2.2
5.	Ratio of all training costs to advertising expenditures	8

Given that we spend so much on training in our attempts to achieve competence, the stakes are high for finding a way to account for what we spend and what we get for it, and for devising programs to decrease training PIPs, which I shall later show are among the highest PIPs anywhere. In the world of work we have a double potential—for getting more value while spending less money for it.

Any program for attempting to realize this great potential must deal with it at three levels of vantage at least: policy, strategy, and tactics. In this chapter and those that follow, I shall approach the issue at all three of these levels, distinguishing between work and school only at the policy level. At the lower levels I do not distinguish sharply between work and school because the demands are much the same in both worlds.

THE STATUS OF KNOWLEDGE IN THE WORLD OF WORK

The following, rather lengthy, case study is a composite of several real cases. I present it to underline the major policy decisions waiting to be made in the world of work, and some of the major barriers to making

them. Marilyn Blue, our heroine, has been trained in performance analysis and takes her first job in training. Her experiences are in no way unusual for those who approach training from the point of view of improving performance.

As Marilyn Blue enters the large conference room, she wonders why all government buildings look alike. "I suppose," she thinks, "it saves money to buy all this standardized stuff. But does it really save that much?"

The conference is the monthly meeting of the central training staff of the Social Programs Administration. Her boss, Eliot Empire, had asked her to observe and take notes—a way to break into her new job as staff analyst. (Marilyn isn't yet sure what this is.) The objective of this meeting is to approve the new revisions in many of the courses offered to SPA personnel, and Marilyn observes that no one even mentions the possibility of disapproval. The principal revised course is for the "program monitor," a sort of superclerk who is the chief foot soldier of SPA. A program monitor—and there are 6000 of them—processes all applications for SPA assistance. There is very little talk about the content or style of the course, but Eliot questions whether sufficient time is allotted for it.

"We've always given these clerks 13 weeks of training," Eliot points out. "And while I'm sure the revision is more efficient, I always thought a 13-week period wasn't long enough. This proposal for 6 weeks doesn't sound adequate to me."

After some discussions in which 9, 13, and then 17 weeks are discussed, the consensus is that the agency should keep the 13-week span. Marilyn is puzzled that all the proposals are for such odd numbers of weeks. Why not 10? 12? or 16? Then she realizes that 13 weeks is a quarter of a year, and 9 weeks is 2 months. What is really curious, Marilyn thinks, is how the final decision is made: by a sort of informal vote, as if it were a matter of taste.

"Suppose," Marilyn muses, "that 22 days were the ideal time for a course like this. How would anyone know?"

Back in her office, she takes out a sheet of graph paper and the catalog of SPA courses. She then plots this graph (Figure 7-1). The first thing that strikes her

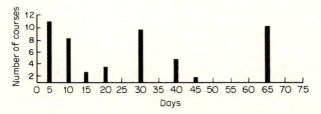

FIGURE 7-1 Typical distribution of course lengths in SPA.

as peculiar is the disjointed distribution of course times. Except for 1-day courses, all others are multiples of 5. Why? Marilyn then takes out her calculator and does some figuring. "What if they had accepted the original proposal for 6 weeks instead of 13 weeks? What difference would it make in costs?" she asks herself.

Here are Marilyn's calculations:

	6 Weeks	13 Weeks
1. Student hours	240	520
2. Hourly student cost°	8.50	8.50
3. Annual number of students	2000	2000
4. Total annual operation, costs	$4,080,000	$8,840,000
5. Difference	$4,760,000	
6. Difference per student	$ 2380	

Marilyn is appalled. The committee has just decided to increase the operational costs of conducting a single course by 116 percent without even discussing the costs. And it is clear from her graph that the length of all courses is decided arbitrarily with no thought to the cost of adding another day or another week. Now she suddenly resents the absence of draperies on her window. After a little calculation, she concludes that the extra money that Eliot just tacked on to the taxpayer's bill would curtain a million government windows, and in good style. Besides, she calculates further, making that many draperies would supply jobs for maybe a thousand or more people for a whole year. Marilyn Blue sets her jaw—she will talk to Eliot Empire.

Eliot, naturally, has a ready answer. "Look, we're not responsible for that money; it's not in *our* budget. And who can say we aren't getting that much additional value out of the extra 7 weeks?"

"But that's real money, Eliot. Does it matter that it's not in *our* budget?" asks Marilyn.

"You don't understand," Eliot says, "I have 50 instructors to teach that course. If I cut the course length in half, what would I do with them? I'd have to fire 25."

"No you wouldn't," Marilyn reasons. "You could cut the student-teacher ratio in half—to 5-to-1. Then you'd have higher-quality instruction, keep your instructors, and save most of that money, too."

"Cut the student teacher ratio to 5-to-1? My God! I'd be canned for the extravagance," exclaimed Eliot, polishing his "Beat Inflation" button.

*Wages + benefits + overhead + instructor allocation + facilities allocation.

Then he introduces her to his favorite ploy for disposing of troublemakers: Send them down the labyrinths of busywork. Back in her office, Marilyn ponders her new assignment—to make a study of methods for determining the ideal course length. But in her ingenuousness, she sets herself to the new task with eagerness, admiring Eliot for being so reasonable.

Marilyn begins by constructing a performance matrix for the SPA Training Department. Starting with the cultural level and the model stage, her first question is, "What, ideally, is the cultural accomplishment of a job-training activity, regardless of the particular institution it serves?" Her answer: capability for exemplary job performance.

Next, still at level II, she proceeds to the measures stage. "How well is the accomplishment being achieved?" she asks. "How worthy is the performance of job-training agencies?" Her answer:

> *Value returned:* Job PIPs are large, typically 2 or greater. Obviously, training has much potential to tap.
>
> *Cost invested:* In the United States, the cost of job training is $100 billion a year.

So, realizing that the stakes are high, Marilyn decides to make an informal study of the "national training PIP." To do this, she must find a training exemplar.

Eliot is more than happy to get her out of his hair, and he is quite willing to pay for the travel her search requires. After some investigating, she discovers the Mathetics Corporation, a small training-development company operating out of Conway, South Carolina. Eve Darling, President of Mathetics, states flatly that her company can take any course of training in industry or government and double the value achieved from it (in job performance) while cutting its cost, on the average, to a third. Besides, the Mathetics Corporation has a record that seems to support its claims, having devised large-scale training programs for a number of businesses and government agencies. Mathetics has a policy: Before it will develop a training course, it must establish that training is genuinely needed, and its clients must cooperate in measuring the change in job performance and training costs. This policy satisfies Marilyn, and she computes the "national training PIP" like this:

1. She assumes, just for a handy reference, that existing training is a breakeven operation.

    Value = $100 billion annually
    Cost = $100 billion annually
    Worth = 1

2. Mathetics Corporation, as the exemplar, seems to promise this.

    Value = $200 billion annually
    Cost = $33.3 billion annually
    Worth = 6

3. Given these assumptions, the "national training PIP"[3] is 6—very large indeed. Translated into dollars, if the job-training effort of the entire nation could perform as well as the Mathetics Corporation, the returns would look like this:

	Present	Possible
Assumed value	$100 billion/year	$200 billion/year
Cost	$100 billion/year	$ 33 billion/year
Potential worth (net gain)	—	$167 billion/year

These data leave no question in Marilyn's mind that, culturally at least, the improvement of job-training efficiency should be national policy.

Marilyn, still working at the cultural level and the measures stage, decides to do some performance troubleshooting at that level. She knows that she must look at three classes of variables to discover the cause of the large training PIP: environmental supports, behavioral repertories, and management systems. So she sets up a "troubleshooting worksheet" (Table 7-1). With the help of Eve Darling, Marilyn fills out the worksheet.

"Notice something funny?" Eve asks. "Our 'yes' answers are directly opposed to common explanations of the problems of training. The usual story I get about how to improve training is, 'give us better facilities, give us smarter people who really care, and give us more money.' But we're saying those are the things that aren't needed. Interesting."

Marilyn Blue decides to write a report of her study to this point, and present it to Eliot Empire. Her report reads, in part:

These are the reasons I found for the large national job training PIP:

1. Virtually no training agencies in the nation have any way to directly measure their impact on performance. They usually administer tests—measures of behavior. The kind of information training departments could get, but seldom do, are measures describing the impact they have on the performance system.

2. No incentives are typically meted out for good training performance. Since good training performance (by my definition) means improvement in the job performance of others, an improvement in training could bring great returns. If all the people working in United States training agencies could become 10 percent more efficient, the return on that increment would be worth maybe $17 billion[*] a year. That's an awful lot of money.

3. Of course, the training people themselves don't know how to tap the potential. The Mathetics Corporation uses a sophisticated system for the

*Based on the calculations extrapolated from the data of the Mathetics Corporation.

TABLE 7-1   TROUBLESHOOTING WORKSHEET

	Variables	*Questions*	*General Answer*
I.	**Environmental**		
	A. Information	1. Do people in typical training agencies have any way to know how well they are performing in terms of their real effects on job performance?	No
	B. Response supports	2. Do they have the physical facilities and tools to perform well?	Yes
	C. Incentives	3. Are their rewards made contingent upon their performance?	No
II.	**Behavior Repertories**		
	A. Knowledge	1. Do they know how to perform well? Could they perform well if their lives depended upon it—without getting any further training?	No
	B. Response capacity	2. Do they have the physical and mental capacity to learn to perform well?	Yes
	C. Motives	3. If they could, would they be willing to work well for the available incentives?	Yes
III.	**Management System**		
	A. Standards	1. Do managers know how well the training is performing, and does it have any standards for its performance?	No
	B. Organization	2. Are training agencies organized for optimal performance?	No
	C. Resources	3. Are the resources available for improving the performance of training agencies?	Yes

development of training programs. I believe that if other training people are to be capable of exemplary performance, they must learn this system, too. If 100,000 course developers were given 6 months' training in this system, the cost would only be about $1 billion. And then there probably is some justification for amortizing that cost over, say, 5 years. That's peanuts, however, compared with the potential return. In fact, it may be the finest business investment available anywhere today.

4. The changes naturally must begin with management. As a start, management will have to establish some standards for evaluating a training agency that do not include such things as college degrees, association membership, test scores, and—most particularly—the size of the training

effort. The more labor-hours a training department ties up in a classroom, the more successful it appears. But that is the opposite of what we want. Until management sets realistic—preferably exemplary—standards of job performance as a measure of training performance, the potential will never be tapped.

5. The typical organization of training in any agency is self-defeating because it supplies only one function: It supplies behavior improvements. To make a training staff into a complete staff function, it should really be turned into a performance department. A performance department would supply performance improvement, not just behavior improvements; and it would control by constantly monitoring the performance needs of the agency, as Figure 7-2 shows. At present, the training department is looked upon as a little red schoolhouse. We send people over there, and the "bright" ones come out with A's and the "dumb" ones fail. The training department is never said to fail—nor to succeed very much either. No one expects much from it or measures what it gives, or even asks what is possible for it to give. Management gets pretty much what it asks for—almost nothing.

To summarize, these are the five principal causes of the large "national training PIPs":

(a) No way of knowing what training is accomplishing.

(b) No special incentives to perform well.

(c) No mastery of the technology available for training competent performance.

(d) No performance standards established by management.

(e) An antiquated, nonfunctional organization structure.

Eliot puts off responding to Marilyn's report for several weeks. When Marilyn finally corners him, his response is unclear. "Interesting," Eliot muses. "But I disagree with you on two fundamental points. First of all, the money paid in

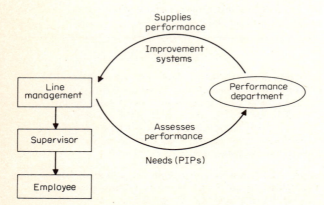

FIGURE 7-2 A functional staff organization.

student wages would be paid whether we scheduled them for training or not. So it's false money you're talking about."

"How is it false?" Marilyn demands. "It doesn't matter whether you put them in a classroom or let them learn on the job. You are still paying them real dollars when they are not producing. That's the whole point. The agency is paying for training whether it has a training department or not. The training department presumably is an investment made to cut that training time, or to get better performance, or both. Those are real dollars—not false ones, Eliot; and the question is how are we influencing them? If you say those are false dollars, then you would probably not worry if your car broke down. You could always say, 'I would have to walk anyhow if I didn't have a car.' What's the other thing you disagree with, Eliot?"

"Well, all of this is very idealistic—and good, mind you. But you can never get people to change their ways for ideals."

"Idealistic!" Marilyn exclaims. "What's idealistic about it? I assume that people fundamentally work in their own interest, if they know what that is. I assume that people like to make money, and I'm just trying to show how money can be made. What's idealistic about that?"

Next, Marilyn moves to the methods stage of her performance matrix, still at the cultural level of analysis. She asks herself what is to be done to capture the great potential for improving training performance. Because the issue is larger than any one government agency or corporation, it obviously invites national policy. "What," she wonders, "could the government and industrial associations do to further a program for capturing the potential?"

She reasons that the government should have tremendous interest, because a successful program could have a huge impact on inflation. Business associations, too, should be interested in the large profit potential in improved training. Marilyn decides that the greatest impact that government could have on training in the world of work is to begin at home and to adopt a policy for its own training. The government would be taking leadership, she reasons; and through the experience it would gain, it could show other agencies how to make similar policies work. Table 7-2 summarizes the policies she thinks the government should adopt, and she includes this in her second report to Eliot Empire.

"Interesting," Eliot replies. "But who's going to pay for it? You didn't think about that, did you?"

"What's there to pay for?" Marilyn asks. "The bonuses would come out of money saved, so nobody has to put up any substantial front money. The training would cost something, but we already pay $200,000 a year to train people on the training staff. And as for the quality-inspection staff, we already have a lot of people around here who say that their job is to assure quality training. I figure the net cost of this program would be zero, with a potential return of over $150 billion. That ought to appeal to somebody's interest."

"Yeah, but whose?" Eliot sniffs.

TABLE 7-2   POLICIES FOR IMPROVING TRAINING PERFORMANCE

Deficiencies	*Suggested Policy*
Information about training performance	1. Establish an independent quality-inspection system that measures the impact of training on job performance.
Incentives for performance	2. Provide bonuses tied to the efficiency of the trainees' performance.
Skill in course development	3. Provide training in course development, and create a certification program.
Standards for training	4. Adopt performance standards for both course developers and instructors.
Organization	5. Reorganize training departments as performance departments with three functions: (a) Assessment of performance problems (b) Development of performance systems (c) Delivery of performance systems
Resources	6. Budget the performance department for training time.

Marilyn might have made her argument more convincing if she had stuck to the training course for program monitors. That one course encompasses, in microcosm, the entire problem of buying knowledge, and it is worth examining more closely later. But, first, let us look at some basics.

When we buy knowledge, we pay for three things:

1. Analysis and development of the training program (lectures, films, books, etc.)
2. Delivery of the training program (instructors, facilities, management, etc.)
3. Trainees (wages, benefits, overhead, etc.)

The distribution of costs across these categories varies somewhat, but not much. Although no one knows the exact national average, Table 7-3 shows the typical distribution of the training dollar. The strange charac-

TABLE 7-3   DISTRIBUTION OF TRAINING COSTS

	Trainee Costs	*Delivery Costs*	*Development Costs*
Typical institution	90%	9%	1%
U.S. company with the largest developmental costs	85%	12%	3%
Institutions with little or no formal training effort	95%	5%	0%

teristic of this distribution of costs is that trainee costs seldom appear this way in anyone's budget; they are usually completely hidden. And, so far as I know, they never appear in a training department's budget. This leads to several economic anomalies.

First, the largest cost factor hardly enters into management decisions about training. It is as if a company, faced with the decision to construct a new building for its headquarters, looked only at the architectural costs. Indeed, it is even more absurd, because far more dollars are involved.

Second, the other two items, delivery and development, are budgeted and therefore come under periodic scrutiny. They therefore have to be justified. And because training is never (so far as I know) structured as a profit center, and because its values go unmeasured, the easiest way to justify it is to show that the budgeted money is kept busy—to demonstrate that you have used it to get as many people as possible to spend as much time as possible in a classroom. This is the measure demanded by the "subcults of knowledge and work": If an extra dollar is budgeted for training, there must be a corresponding increase in the amount of behavior expended. If the behavior cult stated its own training theorem, it would read like this:

> The value of training is the ratio of student costs to the budgeted costs of training.

or

$$\text{"Value" of Training} = \frac{\text{Trainee Costs}}{\text{Development Costs} + \text{Delivery Costs}}$$

This remarkable absurdity goes a long way toward explaining why training costs are so high, and training budgets run low. It is not because training professionals are irresponsible spendthrifts, but because the organization of training departments is self-defeating and designed to reward people for conforming to the behavior cult's training theorem. Indeed, a few training professionals are aware of the

dilemma, but they don't know a way out of it because they have trouble getting the attention of their management.

The solution to the problem, in part, entails investing more money in training development. What must be done to make the design of a training course more efficient will simultaneously reduce the amount of trainee time as well as increase its impact on job performance, as the next two chapters will show. Take the course for program monitors that Marilyn Blue agonized over. Here is a description of how that course is presently operated.

Each year, 2000 program monitors are trained in a 13-week course (520 hours), during which time the trainees engage in very little or no productive employment. Their classrooms are cramped; the seats are hard; and the space is not air conditioned. The instructors are the lowest-level supervisors. They are assigned to training either because of their inexperience, or because of their ineffectiveness as supervisors; and few of them have ever had any training in instructional methods. The primary instructional medium is a droning lecture. The materials are 8 years old, badly dog-eared, and written by untrained writers. Worse than that, 80 percent of the materials relate to problems that account for 10 percent of the job's problems. (This doesn't describe the worst of instructional situations, but one that can be found everywhere.)

The cost of this course is $9,840,000 a year, and its value is untested and unknown. These costs are broken down as follows:

Trainee costs	$8,840,000	(90%)
Delivery costs	1,000,000	(10%)
Development costs	0	(0%)
Total	$9,840,000	

Naturally, the budgeted amount for this course is only part of the $1 million, because most of the classroom facilities and some of the instructor salaries don't appear in the training budget.*

Now let's suppose the agency takes Marilyn Blue seriously and replaces Eliot Empire by a smart manager, Rob Goodale, who follows the recommendation of the Mathetics Corporation to change the balance of costs. Goodale employs a group of professionals to develop new materials for the course: highly self-instructional, supported by as many aids as needed, and answering to real job accomplishments. He puts up $200,000 for this development (or $40,000 a year, amortized over 5 years). In addition, he promises the development group a bonus of 2 percent of the total savings if they can prove that they achieve significantly better value from the new course.

---

*In many places, the only budget items are salaries for the training director and his or her staff, and expenses.

Next, Goodale doubles the investment in instructors and facilities, getting experienced and successful managers to teach the course after they have received instructional training. He spends part of this money to improve the physical facilities for the course. He also offers the instructors a bonus of 1 percent of the savings—on the provision that proof of increased value can be given to an independent assessor.

The new course, lasting only 5 weeks, goes into operation. This is the revised annual cost picture:

Trainee costs	$3,400,000	61%
Delivery costs	2,000,000	36%
Development costs	40,000	3% (plus bonus)
Subtotal	$5,440,000	
Gross savings		$4,400,000
Bonuses @ 3%	132,000	
Total costs	5,572,000	
Net savings		$4,268,000
Total additional investment		
Development	$ 128,000	
Delivery	1,044,000	
	$1,172,000	
Return on additional investment		364%

This is a remarkable return on the investment. But it is only part of the story. The new course also proves to yield greater value: An independent study shows Goodale that under the old course, employees required 9 months after training to reach median productivity; and during those 9 months, they averaged 60 percent of median productivity. He takes a conservative figure and estimates that the median experienced employee's productivity is worth only $10 an hour. In a year's time, then, the value of his trainees' productivity would look like this:

	First 13 Weeks	*Last 39 Weeks*	*Annual Total*
Per-hour value	0	$6.00	
Number of hours	540	1500[*]	
Number of employees	2000	2000	
Total of value	0	$18,000,000	$18,000,000

With his new course, Goodale's trainees are on the job after 5 weeks. Besides, his independent assessor shows them to be 30 percent more productive than the average experienced employee a month after they leave training; and in the first month, they are as productive as the average experienced person:

*Corrected for leave time.

	First 5 Weeks	Next 4 Weeks	Next 43 Weeks	Annual Total
Per-hour value	0	$10	$13	
Number of hours	48	40	1600°	
Number of employees	2000	2000	2000	
Total value	0	$800,000	$41,600,000	$42,400,000

So, in one year Goodale has gained $24,400,000 in productivity from his additional investment of $1,172,000. This gives him a total return of $28,268,-000, or 2412 percent. There just aren't many of those kinds of investment opportunities around in the world outside of the world of training.** Goodale, to be on the safe side and to ensure that he maintains this performance, could easily afford to take 10 percent of his new return and mete it out as bonuses to the trainees for maintaining their performance. This $1500 annual bonus would sharply reduce turnover, saving further training costs as well.

But many managers, suspecting that the real costs of training are high, reach the opposite solution. "Don't invest anything in formal training and instructors and we won't have any training costs." This is

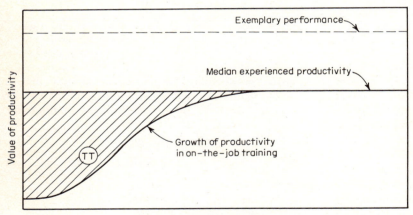

FIGURE 7-3 True training costs in on-the-job training. (Reprinted from T. F. Gilbert, "The High Cost of Knowledge," *Personnel*, March–April 1976.)

*Corrected for leave time.

**These figures (time saved and productivity increased) are not invented; they represent a true case, though freely rounded off.

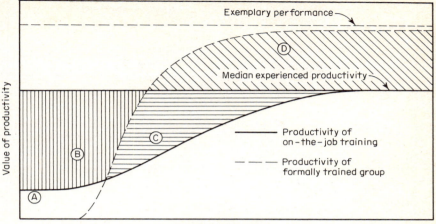

FIGURE 7-4 Differential training costs and value: design versus on-the-job training. (Reprinted from T. F. Gilbert, "The High Cost of Knowledge," *Personnel,* March–April 1976.)

pure nonsense. Figure 7-3 is a graph of the growth of productivity when employees are left to learn on the job and by themselves. The shaded area (TT) represents true training time; it doesn't matter that the training methods are informal. Employees have to learn anyway, and the true costs of that training are a function of the paid nonproductive time while they are reaching average productivity. The formal design of training can greatly decrease that cost and increase the value, as Figure 7-4 shows. In this figure, the area labeled (A) represents the fixed costs of formal training. The areas (A) plus (B) are the true costs of formal training. And (B) plus (C) are the true costs of on-the-job training (OJT). The added value of formal training is a function of the areas (C) plus (D), and area (D) is a value that continues over the years.

But formally designed training is seldom so efficient. Figure 7-5 represents a more typical case, in which formal training may not pay off because the costs of development, delivery, and classroom time cancel out any early gains in productivity. In this figure, area (A) represents fixed costs of formal training; (B), the value from earlier productivity resulting from formal training; (A) plus (C), the cost of formal training; (B) plus (C), the cost of OJT. You can see that gains could be tremendous if we just shift the curve to the left by reducing training time. What, then, is to be done—specifically—to realize the great PIPs in the training industry? What steps must we take?

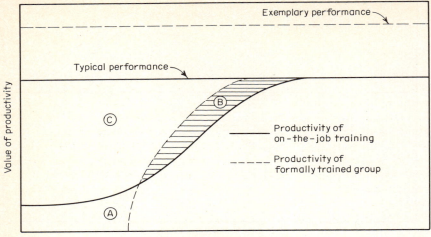

FIGURE 7-5   All too frequent result of formal training. (Reprinted from T. F. Gilbert, "The High Cost of Knowledge," *Personnel*, March–April 1976.)

STEPS FOR REDHEADED STEPMOTHERS

Training is the stepchild of the world of work, usually relegated to the lowest order of things, viewed as a convenient place to employ the less ambitious, or less productive managers and supervisors, and seldom discussed by top management. This is not surprising, given the budgetary practices of work agencies. Top management, indeed, often seems to consider it an indignity to concern itself with such mundane affairs, and this is the most inflationary and unprofitable posture that management could possibly take. But the potential is enormous. Many agencies could easily double their profit, and some unprofitable ones could become profitable, if smart investments were made in human performance. Of course, as we shall see, training is only one of the strategies for improving competence, and it is frequently applied to situations where it isn't relevant at all. The question is, then, how can management realize the great potential of training for improving human competence? And before I answer that question, I shall describe one method some serious companies use that does not work too well because it is a piecemeal effort.

Some large institutions rotate their young management in different jobs, including a 2- or 3-year stint as a manager of training. Suppose we briefly follow the career of one Trumbull Anderson, a rising middle manager in

mammoth Rural Life Insurance, Inc. He has just been assigned the job for 2 years as Training Manager, Technical Training Services Department (non-sales). His department is in charge of training everyone—from application clerks to data-processing technicians.

Rural Life is very "serious" about training, and on the whole does a good job. (The company even has an Assistant Vice President in charge of all training.) Trumbull was selected because he is considered a promising prospect for top management. But his first day on the job he discovers that he is not fully in charge. A resident Ph.D. (in psychology) has been in the company's training department for 15 years—one Dr. Ivan Knowall, a man with top credentials and an impressive variety of knowledge about this and that. Bearded, brilliant, charming, and intimidating, he actually outranks Trumbull and has a fancier title. He is situated in this department because he didn't get along too well with the Assistant Vice President when he was on his immediate staff. Dr. Knowall is responsible for most of the existing courses, which, under his "technical" tutelage, have gradually grown in length and coverage over the years.

Also on Trumbull's staff are a number of lower managers who quickly impress him that they work hard, love their jobs, and seem to be utterly confident that they know what they are doing.

To top all this off, when Trumbull was given his assignment, no one even suggested what he was expected to accomplish. So he decides, wisely, that his first task is to learn as much as he can about training, a subject totally unfamiliar to him—he thinks. During his first week on the job, his know-nothing feelings get amply reinforced; he didn't realize so much technical language was associated with training: "critical incident techniques," "analysis of variance," "behavioral objectives," and so on, until Trumbull is dizzy.

But immediately he is caught up in a myriad of details. A new course is being tried out—a longer, more sophisticated revision of an old one. The training staff leans heavily on him: "You've just come from the field; you've got to get them to cooperate with us in introducing this new course." That means traveling and selling something he doesn't fully understand. . . . "It's going to cost $100,000 to set the first draft into type, and we're only budgeted for $60,000. You're on good terms with the regional Vice President. Can't you get us the money?" "We want to hire two great consultants, and we need your approval." "There are three coordination meetings this week, and you're supposed to chair them."

Trumbull Anderson doesn't stand a chance. But after responding to the many pressing stimuli for over a year, he begins to get a glimmer that something is wrong. He can see that the value of training is never measured against its impact on job performance, and that all of his most "successful" efforts serve to increase the amount budgeted for training and the number of hours people spend in classrooms. The more new training opportunities his department turns out, the more people seem to praise it. And Dr. Knowall is a fountainhead of ideas about new things to train people to do.

As Trumbull's 2-year stint comes to an end, he reports to his boss, Crystal Tower, for a review of his performance.

"Trumbull," Crystal smiles, "you have just been voted Young Manager of the Year in Rural Life. We're all very proud of you. Ivan Knowall is brilliant, everybody knows; but he has always rubbed people the wrong way. You've been able to deliver on his programs and sell them too. In 2 years you've increased the number of courses in the department 20 percent, and really beefed up the big courses. And you've built up the training budget by 50 percent. We like what you've done so well that we're going to make you Manager of the Sales Training Department—at a big raise, of course."

How can you argue with success? You can hardly blame Trumbull—or his managers, either. They are all poor, unfortunate victims of the behavior cult.

How do we combat the behavior cult and capitalize on the opportunities that lie at our feet? It will not be done by writing a memo affirming one's belief that opportunity is there. Radical surgery must be performed.

I believe these are the six steps to success:

I. *Reassess our existing training operation.* A good way to begin would be to abandon the belief that existing training departments are necessarily manned by professionals who know how to get the most out of training. They are probably excellent at two things:

1. The logistics of training
2. The tactics of delivery

Beyond that, their careers probably have discouraged them from developing the policy and strategic skills that are needed.

So we need to ask these kinds of questions about our existing training operation:

1. Has training been installed to meet a proven and measured performance need?
2. Are there performance measures to show that training is working for us?
3. Are the measures taken independently, or do we have only our training staff's word that training works?
4. Is exemplary performance the standard for training? And does the trainee reach the standard?
5. Are the people in charge of training competent, or is training relegated to those who just aren't very good at other jobs?

6. How long is our training, formal or OJT? How long does it take for a trainee to become a top performer on the job? If it takes more than, say, a month or two, we are probably missing great opportunities.

7. What are the true costs of our training, formal or OJT? There is little excuse not to know.

8. Are trainee costs budgeted?

9. What is an estimate of the value we are getting for our training?

10. Are our course lengths arbitrary or determined only by the time required for training?

11. Do we have access to really expert training development skills? (Chapters 9 and 10 best answer this question.)

12. Do our training people know how to conduct a performance audit?

If we can't answer these questions "yes," we no doubt have a great economic potential for improving training.

II. *Reorganize the training function;* convert it into a performance department that operates as a "profit" center. The training staff is probably as good a place as any to get into the performance-engineering business in a systematic way, because few others have as much experience with as wide a variety of performance problems. But the performance department must have real responsibility. I suggest that it report directly to the chief officer of the institution and have full power to institute all performance-improvement programs, as long as it could show a measured effect on performance. Of course, it will take some time to create this reorganization, but a good beginning is to set up a pilot organization that can expand (and absorb training) as it learns to be successful. Several of my clients are doing this, with great results and without upsetting people. And these performance departments are gradually absorbing other groups concerned with performance quality, such as industrial engineers and OD people. It doesn't matter what this department is called. Sometimes the lead organizer has been a personnel officer, an industrial engineer, a training specialist, and even a sales manager. What is important is the performance, not the titles.

III. *Develop a performance staff.* It takes a little time for performance engineers to learn their business. And while there is some training available, the staff will have to learn largely in its own way. The activity should be budgeted handsomely for the first year or two, and payback arranged for the effort. The advantage of beginning with pilot projects is that the performance engineers would have a chance both to learn and to prove their capability.

Generally, a performance department should have three areas of responsibility, which can be reflected in its own organization:

1. Assessment of performance opportunities
2. Development of performance systems (including training development)
3. Delivery and implementation of performance systems

IV. *Establish a performance-measurement system* (such as I have described in Chapters 2 and 5). It is important to create an independent group of people who are in charge of performance measurements and organize them in the same way as a quality control. For example, production supervisors should not report on their own quality of production. Independent reporting of performance measures requires the same lack of vested interest to assure objectivity and reliability. The best strategy is to have the performance-engineering department develop the kinds of measurements to be taken, but to keep collection and reporting of ongoing data an independent function.

V. *Establish performance measures for performance engineers*, and measure each of their three functions (as I described in III). Training, in particular, should be measured as a separate operation, and the return on the investment calculated.

VI. *Develop line managers* to be able to understand and read performance audits—and even to conduct them. Line managers are the real performance engineers, and the performance department should be there only to help them do the work.

These steps are not difficult. A few organizations have already taken them. What they have learned is that improved strategies and tactics of training, once so difficult to achieve, tend to develop naturally once good performance policies are adopted.

NOTES

1. *Statistical Abstracts of the United States, 1977,* Washington, D.C.: U.S. Department of Commerce.

2. Parts of this chapter originally appeared in these publications: T. F. Gilbert, "The High Cost of Training," *Personnel* (March–April 1976); and T. F. Gilbert, "Training: The $100-Billion Opportunity," *Journal of Training and Development* (March 1977).

3. This is my own "experienced" estimate.

Chapter Eight
Knowledge Policy at School

True learning's a moss that grows in darkened places
In gardens of wort and lichen, a growth antique
And constant. It is no flower of happy faces,
No profligate that spends its lust to seek
The sun and husbands too late to last through dread
Hibernal nights; but nourished by our tears,
It forms a pallet beneath an anguished head—
An herb enriched with potions for the years.

So when, my child, you seek this book to measure,
You ought not gauge its wit nor mental power,
Nor plumb its depth, nor draft its dizzy pleasure;
But rather calibrate its lingering hour,
And by this timeless scale you'll be assured
That through your wearying winter it has endured.

T.F.G.

SCHOOL HOUSE ECONOMICS

A school system is also a performance system, and the way to begin looking at any performance system is to view its economics: What is it designed to produce? How much is that worth? How much does that cost? Most educators I talk with tend to focus on the third of these questions—what are we spending to educate our youth; or, why can't we spend more? The general opinion seems to be that, although education has its problems, it is headed more or less in the right direction and principally needs more money to get there. Scrutiny, I think, will deflate this view and lead us to conclude that our educational systems are not at all clear about where they are headed and what they are trying to produce. It will indicate that the educational PIP is very large; we are not getting nearly what we could for our money. And, finally, it will disclose that we can hardly afford to spend more money

231

on education, and that we must learn how to realize the great PIP with the money we are now spending.

First let us review the economics. Keep in mind that in 1977 we in the United States spent over $100 billion to educate our youth. That is a very large sum, and certainly enough to lead us to ask what we got for it. The immediate answer one educator gave me was that the illiteracy rate of American adults is extremely low, and that alone says a lot. Unfortunately, this educator was using the propaganda of the great cult of behavior.

According to a recent study[1] supported by the U.S. Office of Education, 20 percent of adult Americans are functionally illiterate. This figure contrasts sharply with earlier traditional statistics in which the illiteracy rate was described as being only 1 percent. Why the sudden leap? Is our nation just forgetting how to read? The explanation lies elsewhere, of course. Up to 1969, literacy was measured by reading *behavior;* but in the 1970s, the investigators administered tests of reading *accomplishment* instead. And nothing could better illustrate the difference between the behavioral (achievement) and accomplishment views of education.

Before the 1970s, literacy was measured by simple behaviors such as writing one's name and pronouncing the words in a simple-to-read passage. These were behavior criteria that virtually every American could pass. But the new tests base functional literacy on such accomplishments as the interpretation of simple want ads and grocery advertisements. With these tests, only 80 percent of adult, noninstitutionalized Americans can reach the minimum standard of literacy.

But the news is even worse. Another third of American adults (39 million) are functionally *inadequate* (not proficient) in such accomplishments as determining the unit price of various-sized boxes of breakfast cereal. Indeed, only 46 percent fell in the highest category of being unquestionably proficient in such accomplishments.

We should worry about the competence of a system that keeps our children for at least 8 years, more usually 12, and yet one-third of the population it turns out gets little or no use from the simplest forms of reading. And there is every evidence that the situation is getting no better—and perhaps even worse. The value of our educational system is far less than we might hope for. These astonishing statistics invite radical new policies for education.

You might say that this only provides further proof that we need more money to overcome the deficiencies. I seriously doubt this.

Not only did the United States spend over $100 billion a year to educate its youth in 1977, but the amount we are spending grows rapidly. Besides, it is not the absolute amount but the relative effect of these expenditures that is so disturbing. In the three decades following

World War I, the United States spent a little over 3 percent of its gross national product (GNP) on school education.[2] After 1950, the proportion began to rise rapidly—to 5.1 percent in 1950; 6.4 percent in 1960; 7.1 percent in 1970; then a rapid jump to 8.2 percent in 1972; and over 9 percent in 1975.[3] Obviously, educational expenditures cannot keep rising at this rate, because we would reach 25 percent by the end of the century—and 40 percent a mere 50 years from now.

And what are we getting for these increased expenditures? Hardly anyone will agree that the value of education has increased proportionally with the expenditures; and many insist that there has been a steady (some would even say dramatic) decline in value.

What is amiss, and what can be done about it? How can we increase the value we get from our schools, and at the same time curb the ever-increasing costs? The answer surely lies elsewhere than in more public funds.

WHAT ARE THE GENERAL DIMENSIONS OF THE PROBLEM?

Our first clue to finding the answer to this question is buried in the illiteracy data. Our schools seemed to be performing with at least minimal adequacy so long as we were judging their performance on the basis of student *behavior*. Only when we began to measure *purposeful* performance did the evidence of failure become too uncomfortable to ignore.

To identify the opportunities for improving our school system, we need to look at it systematically as a performance system. And to do this, we must first ask what accomplishments it is designed to create. As with any other performance system, we need to know if it produces something of value before we ask if it is efficient; we need to ask what it *should* accomplish before we can ask how well the system is behaving.

Keep in mind that the ultimate goal we choose for an education would determine the particulars of the curriculum. Should we take that goal seriously? We might not teach children to read, say, if we decided that total social independence was the desirable end condition. To evaluate the performance of our schools, then, we need to know what they are intended for, and here is the first great difficulty. How do we find this out? The obvious approach is simply to ask those in charge of our educational institutions.

I have done this. I took a sample of 12 of the 50 United States and wrote two letters to the education department of each, asking for an explanation of their curricula and for literature describing their content. I also asked how their curricula came into being. Half of these 24 letters were written under the letterhead of a professional research organization and signed by a Ph.D. (me), who requested the information in the

interest of research. The other 12 letters were sent from parents who lived in each of these states.

The results: Six of the 12 professional requests were answered, and only three of the parents' requests. The answers given the professional consisted entirely of documents and catalogs offering practically nothing about the curricula. And seemingly relevant items I bought from the catalogs uncovered no special intelligence. The answers to the parents were brief, vague, and guarded letters, two of which invited them to meet with some school official. When these meetings were rejected and published—or unpublished—written descriptions again requested, the second requests were ignored. The total information gained from 24 requests? None. The conclusion: You can't easily find out why they try to teach Johnny to read just by asking.[4]

Another approach, of course, is to ask the client—the public who pays for the school system. Beginning by asking which accomplishments the client values is precisely how we proceed in a performance audit in industry. For example, if a manager asks me to train people to master electrical wiring diagrams, I must first know what the accomplishment is to be. Should students produce wired electrical circuits using the diagrams as an aid? Or should they draw diagrams of actual circuits? What this subject is and how I teach it could be determined largely by which accomplishments the client values.

I have done this in a simple experiment, using history as the subject matter. But first I asked myself what accomplishments a public school education in history should make possible for its students. I identified four possibilities:

1. Successful students of history might produce an orderly record of past events. Such students would be *archivists.*

2. The students might be able to create a written or oral account of past events. They would be *raconteurs*—or perhaps propagandists, essayists, or even novelists.

3. Or, if we define history as the accomplishments of those who make history, we would teach our students to be warriors, playwrights, politicians, and the like—*history makers.*

4. Finally, we might define history as a source of predictive power: a set of experiences permitting us to deduce the variables that determine the events in the future so that we can account for current social developments, forecast their direction, and visualize how events could be altered. With this definition in mind, our students would produce *predictions.*

And then I asked 34 people between the ages of 23 and 56, both men and women, which of these four history accomplishment models they valued most. Although my group was in no way a properly drawn statistical sample of the American public (all were students in a seminar), the result invited a generalization. All 34 people chose the "predictor" model, and discussions with them revealed sensible reasons for this choice. Let us examine the possibilities more closely.

The first two models, that of archivist and raconteur, represent valuable vocations. But they are certainly not vocations that the public would wish all of its children to follow. In fact, only a few people are needed to serve here. We should therefore be able to reject these mastery models for a public school education right off, although we might want to adopt them for graduate history departments in universities. The probability is small that these accomplishments will significantly affect later competence outside of school.

Unfortunately, if we look at our public school curriculum in history, we realize that somehow these two models must have been adopted already. Because there is little evidence that the public school curriculum in history has much relation to teaching people either to make history or to make predictions about the course of current events. Instead, we seem to be trying, however feebly, to train our children for vocations as archivists and raconteurs—vocations for which few jobs exist.

The third possible ultimate master—one who makes history—is difficult to adopt, mostly because, again, only a few seem to be needed for this role. Besides, the role itself is so diffuse and so often surprising that it is not easily defined systematically as a subject matter. When we look for what is common to those who make history, we may emerge with a list of behavioral characteristics that tell us little: for example, perseverance, creativity, boldness, and ambition. The public might like to set up programs to develop more of these behavioral characteristics in its children. But, careful—those who make history also tend to be troublemakers, and a public school system that increased the number of troublemakers might be frowned upon.

The fourth ultimate master—one with a source of predictive power, who can use this power to make predictions about the course of events—would seem to fit more closely to what the public seems to value. And what could people value more than a child who, through the study of history, could view the confusing events of our time and both make sense of them and tell us where they are likely to lead; a child who could sweep aside the irrelevancies and put a finger on the essential variables that are making things work as they are? If we could brush away the cobwebs from our archaic view of teaching history, we might find that this, indeed, is what the public really values. Such an

accomplishment in school should aid the cause of greater competence away from school in all manner of performance areas, from voting to being a statesman.

But how did our history curriculum get like it is? To answer that question, we might look at who is actually responsible for creating that curriculum. First, there are the archivists and raconteurs themselves— the professional historians—who write the books the schools use and whose displays of virtuosity in learned matters so intimidated us, the public, when we were in school that we were graduated too timid to doubt their authority. Nearly everyone knows secretly that the curriculum is somehow wrong, but feels too dumb to question it. And we are dumb about history, largely because those who are responsible for the curriculum made it so confusing and irrelevant.

We might look to the curriculum department, to the teachers, to the teachers' colleges, or to the textbook publishers. But how does it help us to attach blame anywhere? There are those who believe that a conspiracy is afoot, but the evidence for this is flimsy. To have a conspiracy, people must be talking to each other. And there is not the slightest evidence that publishers and teachers communicate, or that the college professors who write the books ever listen to the teachers. Indeed, the publishers and their authors barely speak to each other.[5]

All parties can put up a plausible defense. Publishers of textbooks can say that they publish what the schools demand; teachers can say that they simply teach the material the publishers give them; and teachers and test makers can use the same excuse about how education is measured. It is not easy to tell who is responsible for what.

Exercises in Futility

What is clear is that there is no well-defined set of goals to guide the schools as performance systems. By default, a rather arbitrary set of behaviors becomes not the means, but the *de facto* aim, of school education. Of course, the absence of public purpose to guide our schools might be stoutly defended on one ground and one ground only: the importance of diversity. We could argue that it is in the public good to let each school community establish its own objectives. But this defense holds no water. We need only to observe the school programs in such far-apart places as Northern Vermont and Southern Texas, as Harlem in New York City and Horry County in South Carolina, to see that diversity is not really a significant characteristic of the educational system. The similarities between these places in student exercises, tests, texts, programs, and so on, is impressive. Paradoxically, American schools seem to be headed in exactly the same direction, yet headed in no real direction at all. They wander aimlessly in lock-step formation.

This aimlessness penetrates the very fiber of the educational experience given to our children. Suppose we drop our sights for the moment, from lofty history to the simplest daily language exercises. When purpose is ill defined, our education suffers—not only in a global way, but in the moment-to-moment activities of each of our students. Not sure of where we want them to go, we have them mark time and work exercises characterized more by their drudgery than by any accomplishment. A simple, isolated exercise, taken from a workbook widely used in schools, will illustrate.

The reader should study the exercise in Figure 8-1; indeed, it will be

---

Dividing an unfamiliar word into syllables can often help you figure out what it is. Suggestions A and B may help you divide such a word.

A. In a word in which two or more consonants come between two vowels, divide after the first consonant.

For example: or/bit

B. In a word in which one consonant comes between two vowels, divide before the consonant and make the word long. If the word does not sound familiar this way, divide after the consonant and make the first vowel short.

For example: gro/cer fin/ish

Use suggestions A and B to divide the word below. Draw a line like this: / between the two syllables. Then put the letter of the suggestion you followed in the space beside each word. The first has been done for you.

_A_ Cam/el   ____ Proceed   ____ Tenant   ____ Anguish

____ Survive   ____ Salad   ____ Female   ____ Pretzel

In the sentences below, draw a line between the first and second syllables of each underlined word. The first one has been done for you.

1. When Mom burned the bis/cuits, Dad told her not to pan/ic.

2. There is a discount sale of jerseys in the bargain basement.

3. Formal dinner parties are the usual practice at the palace.

4. Voters may compare the platforms of the candidates for the senate.

FIGURE 8-1 Exercise from a school workbook.

even more interesting if you work the exercise *before* you read my analysis of it. It is sufficient that you know only that it is reprinted verbatim from a workbook used in certain schools. Try to guess for which age group.

If I saw this exercise in isolation, I think I would guess that it was written for a typing course for teenagers or adults: The proper division of words is an important achievement for a typist. But I would be wrong. The exercise appears in a workbook[6] designed for third- and fourth-grade children. It was produced by a major publisher to be sold in as many schools, public and private, as possible. It is used by students in affluent, so-called advantaged schools, as well as by poor children in ghetto area schools. Busing to more affluent neighborhoods will not help children escape the exercise—nor will enrollment in private schools.

I am confident that you will sense that something about the exercise isn't right. But what? We have to make a detailed "clinical" analysis to find out.

First, what is the purpose of the exercise? To what accomplishments, worldly or unworldly, is it relevant? We can examine a few of the worldly possibilities. I have given it some thought, and here are the five possibilities I have identified. (It requires this kind of analysis, because the teacher's manual does not say.)

1. Spelling
2. Guessing the meaning of unfamiliar words
3. Pronunciation
4. Dividing words in typing or printing
5. Interpreting confusing instructions

I shall examine each of these possible purposes separately.

1. The exercise could be designed to help students in the spelling of words. Correct spelling is considered an important accomplishment in Western culture.

There are certain rules that can help us spell—such as "*i* before *e* except after *c*." Another one, and the only one that might be relevant here, is the rule of "double the consonant when adding a suffix to a stressed, short syllable." "Mate," then, becomes "mating" and "mat" becomes "matting."

If you examine the exercise, you will find it only indirectly relevant to this rule. Indeed, with only the rules that were given in the exercise, the children would have to be quite accomplished linguists to infer this spelling rule; and no exercises that follow give it.

Judging from what the exercise asks, we could not state that it is

directly relevant to spelling as an accomplishment. If it were, why not give the phonetic rule for spelling and have the students apply it?

2. It could be designed to help students discern the meaning of unfamiliar words. Breaking down words into roots, suffixes, and prefixes is one aid in comprehending the meaning of a complex word. But it happens only occasionally that splitting a word into syllables separates roots from prefixes and suffixes, and the examples given do not support this purpose. (Anyway, is a *palace* a "friendly card?" or "embroidery for father?")

3. Just as the analysis of vowels and consonants can be a help in spelling, it can also be a help in the pronunciation of written words—an important accomplishment. For example, students who know the spelling rule "double the consonant" should be able to pronounce *canning* with a short vowel. But the sample exercise actually assumes that students already know how to pronounce words (e.g., *salad*). So we can eliminate pronunciation as a relevant accomplishment.

4. Division of typed words is an accomplishment requiring the application of a rule similar to that in the exercise. Indeed, close analysis can lead us to believe that this may be the direct relevance of the exercise. But the rule is misleading—downright erroneous. Students who followed it ("Suggestion A" in the exercise) would split the word *stable* like this: *stab/le*—which is incorrect.

We are then to infer either that the exercise was designed to aid typing accomplishments and gives an erroneous rule—or we are at a loss to know what relevance it has. Typing comes closest to the known relevant accomplishments; and if it is the one that the writers had in mind, we can ask why. Of all the worldly accomplishments we might prepare a third or fourth grader to produce, I would imagine that typing would be low on the list. This is confirmed by the observation that no actual practice in typed, or even written, splitting of words is regularly required in the third grade or in the grades that immediately follow. Typing is a useful skill, and I have often wondered why we rarely teach it to young children. But why develop one of the lesser skills of typing (dividing words) without developing the more important ones?

5. The authors might have had other accomplishments in mind. Interpreting badly written rules is surely a major accomplishment in life—and one expected of the truly educated person. But I seriously doubt that any of the parties approving this book, including the authors, intended to aid this noble accomplishment. Nor (strangely enough) does it occur in any curriculum I have seen. And why expose the student to an erroneous rule if the purpose is only to give practice in reading one that is poorly written?

But we should not pick on the writer's error in constructing the rule, and overlook the main point. Assume that the rule were corrected. What

could then be the purpose of the exercise? Our analysis seems to leave us with only one possibility: In order to prepare a written page (especially a typewritten one), the student will apply the rule for dividing words syllabically.

The next step is to ask how well the exercise is designed to fulfill its purpose. This is, of course, hard to say if we don't know what the purpose is. But given the purpose I have inferred, we can see how well the exercise serves it.

First, we should look at the skill of dividing words in typing (forgetting that the rule given is imperfect). The second half of the rule tells us to divide a "single-consonant" word before the consonant if the vowel is long (e.g., *gro/cer*), and after the consonant if the vowel is short (e.g., *fin/ish*). But it does not give the notable and common exceptions, such as *mating*, which my dictionaries divide as *mat/ing*. By carefully avoiding the exceptions (because they would be confusing?), the writers make a fundamental mistake in discrimination training technique by not teaching difficult discriminations together (see Chapter 10).

So, students are given a misleading rule, with scant practice in applying it. Besides, they should be able to learn immediately whether they are performing correctly. But the only way they can do this here is to wait for the teacher to "grade" their workbooks—which won't be done until much later, or may not be done at all.

Finally, the students at no time know what the purpose of the exercise is. On questioning students about why they were doing it, the answers I got were, "Because the teacher told me to," or some variant. Probing revealed no deeper understanding. But why should it, since you can see from my own analysis how difficult it is to fathom the grand design?

It is so simple. If dividing words for the written page is the genuine purpose of the exercise, it should achieve that purpose (assuming it is a worthy one). By constructing the rule more clearly, by giving better examples, by requiring students to actually make the correct discriminations, by giving them immediate information about whether they are right or wrong, and by giving them instructions about what to do if they persist in being wrong—virtually all students in the third or fourth grade could become masters of the divided word in as much time as it now takes for them to muddle through this exercise. It would also vastly aid their motivation to succeed if they knew that the exercise is actually relevant to some accomplishment in life, and they knew what standards of performance are expected of them.

But, you could argue, the exercise may not be designed with any specific accomplishment in mind, but only to show that words have syllables—for whatever purpose that will serve. Perhaps the writers are only building the groundwork for more purposeful exercises to follow.

With this in mind, I carefully studied the workbook to see where such groundwork might lead. The next "syllabic" exercise occurred six pages later, and I have reproduced it in Figure 8-2. Readers are invited to test their prowess at reading the instructions given. Good luck.

This exercise may cheer the reader who was beginning to suspect that I had chosen a single exercise in isolation from a book otherwise filled with pedagogical gems. There are, admittedly, a few (all too few) sensible and purposeful exercises in the workbook. But the exercise in Figure 8-2 is typical, even though it wasn't chosen for this reason. I leave it to the reader to discover the purpose of this exercise. (Obviously, it is not designed to improve pronunciation, because it assumes that the student can already pronounce the words.)

Such exercises, with their purpose unknown to students, may indeed titillate a few exceptionally good readers. But their greater effect is to promote a kind of intellectual elitism in which a few students master

---

When a base word ends with the sound that either *t* or *d* stands for, and the ending *ed* is added, the word will have another syllable because it will have another vowel sound.

When *ed* is added to words that end with other sounds, the last sound is either the sound *t* stands for, or the sound *d* stands for. A syllable is not added to those words because you don't hear another vowel sound.

In the blank before each of the words below, write *S* if *ed* at the end of the word adds a syllable to the base word. If it does not add a syllable, write either *T* or *D* to show which of those two sounds the *ed* in the word stands for. The first word in each column has been done for you.

S	Adjusted	D	Babbled	T	Dumped
___	Annoyed	___	Convinced	___	Approved
___	Appointed	___	Persuaded	___	Pleaded
___	Flinched	___	Soothed	___	Called
___	Impressed	___	Shoved	___	Pounded
___	Traded	___	Attached	___	Gasped
___	Shouted	___	Trusted	___	Rocked
___	Represented	___	Questioned	___	Stuttered
___	Twinkled	___	Waited	___	Respected
___	Voted	___	Barked	___	Posted
___	Kicked	___	Doubted	___	Arrived

FIGURE 8-2 A follow-up exercise from the workbook.

these things somehow, pass equally purposeless tests based on them, and leave the other students behind. Having taught many college freshmen, I know how few of *them* are able to use a dictionary well enough just to find meaning, let alone pronunciation, although they have been graduated from 12 years of this kind of aimless training—most of them at the upper end of their classes.

There is no reason why every student finishing the third grade cannot use a dictionary masterfully—if we decide that this is a useful purpose to achieve at that age. There is no reason, that is, but one: the inability to decide on purposes, and to pursue these purposes until they are fulfilled. The two major problems of an educational technology, then, are to supply orderly and sensible ways to decide on the purposes of education, and to establish efficient means for reaching them.

One comment about criticisms is in order, however. The reader of these criticisms who is prone to be cynical of our educational system must not think that I am seeking villains, because I am not. I *have* sought them, but found none. The writers of the exercises in the workbook could have written them more clearly; but the essential problem lies not so much in how poorly the exercises are designed, but in the failure to establish a purpose for them in the first place. All the behavior technology in the world will not solve our educational problem until we first begin to apply a technology of performance—beginning, of course, with an analysis of opportunity, of purpose. We aren't really going to teach Johnny to read well until we decide why we are teaching him to read. Anything less will be like the language exhibits—an exercise in futility.

My aim up to now has been to dramatize the problem, to show in microcosm why our educational system fails to achieve what it might. From now on, my task must be constructive, and I hope to show you how we could make the decisions about the means and ends of education in an orderly and sensible way.

THE THREE MAJOR PROBLEMS OF EDUCATION

In our discussions so far, we have seen three things that seriously mar our educational system. So let us examine each of them in turn. First, our educational system is rapidly approaching a financial crisis of major dimensions: The amount (per capita) earned we are spending is growing too fast for the economy to contain.[7] The modern solution of throwing money at the problem simply will not work. So we must not only improve the tactics of teaching, we shall need more efficient strategies as well.

Next, and in my view most important, we simply don't have a good idea of the purposes of education. It is largely an aimless affair. And this

aimlessness at philosophical, cultural, and policy levels surely reflects itself—in the worst way—in even the strategies and tactics of teaching.

Finally, where our goals are specific and undebatable—such as teaching people to read, write, and do arithmetic computations—we are not meeting them very well. If only 50 percent of the adult population in the United States is unquestionably literate, then our simplest tactics of teaching are failing terribly.

So there are three things to be done if we are to improve our educational system greatly. First, we must begin to develop *accomplishment-based curricula*—curricula with purpose. Next, because of the growing economic burden of education, we must somehow improve the efficiency of our *delivery system*. Somehow it should be possible to reduce the teacher costs per student, and at the same time achieve the advantages inherent in lower teacher-student ratios. Finally, we need to *develop* more efficient tools for teaching. We can begin our examination with a discussion of accomplishment-based curricula.

The Accomplishment-Based Curriculum

It is beyond the scope of this book to illustrate an *accomplishment-based* curriculum. Elsewhere I have shown in some detail how such a curriculum has been designed, using the principles of performance engineering.[8]

Before attempting to create a competent accomplishment-based curriculum, however, the performance engineer must have a client; there must be a demand for such a curriculum. Under our present system, the demand is hardly felt because those who "design" our curricula are immensely protected from the marketplace. I believe that by exposing the responsibilities of curriculum design to the demands of the market, we could greatly increase the likelihood of getting curricula with purpose. Of course, we can only imagine how such "free-enterprise" curriculum development might work, but for the moment we can let our imaginations roam.

We'll follow the strictly imaginary performance modeling of the make-believe teleonomic and utopian Walsh McCall, who is assigned to create an educational system for the state of Nedlaw, located between the Barnegat Lighthouse and the Peripatetic Sea. McCall is a most fortunate model builder, since his client, the Thane of Nedlaw, has absolute power to follow any recommendations he might like.

McCall's first recommendation is that Nedlaw create three separate kinds of educational institutions: one to be run by the government, the other two to be operated as private businesses. The government organization would be called **BEDIS** (Bureau of Educational Information and Standards), whose purpose is to measure educational accomplishments in all areas and to publish data

about the performance of every part of the educational system. It will also identify the exemplary performers in every area—from large subjects such as physics to small skills such as double-digit addition.

One purpose of the private industries would be to create curricula and training materials (we shall call it the educational development industry) which it sells to the "delivery industry"—the various privately run schools that will open up all over Nedlaw.

"But," the Thane protests, "I want all children here to have equal opportunities regardless of their family wealth. In a system of private schools, you are bound to have exclusionary practices."

"Not at all," McCall reveals. "The children are simply the raw material. A school will view every child as an opportunity to shape a new repertory; the more deficient the child's repertory, the greater the opportunity for the school to profit, because the market will pay for the product according to its quality. So, if they greatly improve a weak repertory, they can sell that change for more than a small improvement would bring. You see, the people will be the sole market. You will reimburse these schools according to how well they create these changes. It would work somewhat like the voucher system that the Americans are experimenting with. In the voucher system, children are given their tuitions and can go to any school they like. Here in Nedlaw, they can go wherever they or their parents wish, but they pay no tuition. Nedlaw pays only for the results the school gets, and there is no other way for the school to collect money."

"But who determines what quality product is delivered?" the Thane wonders.

"You do, of course, through BEDIS. Each school receives its license for giving whatever kind of education it thinks it can deliver. Its license contains a clear statement of its objectives and capabilities. To the extent that people like those objectives, they will send their children there. To the extent that the schools meet the objectives, the schools will be reimbursed," McCall explains.

"Then each school could offer a different program, couldn't it?" the Thane asks.

"Certainly. And the forces of market demand will surely shape a variety of schools," McCall replies. "Of course, BEDIS might want to establish certain minimal obligatory objectives for each school. Certainly, every child should be taught the three R's, for example. But why don't you wait and see if you need to establish such a regulation. The market is pretty sure to demand it."

"Say, this would discourage people from teaching poetry, wouldn't it? There isn't much demand for poetry, you know," the Thane says mournfully.

"But, don't you see, that is because no one knows anything about it. There is enough demand, I think, to encourage a few schools to teach it at first—and *really* teach it, because they won't get paid if they don't. So once you've really taught a few children to write poetry, or interpret it, or recite it, you begin to develop a demand. Then Nedlaw can sponsor some poetry contests, giving

handsome awards to the winners. This will further increase the demand, just as tennis contests increase the demand for tennis instruction. For example, in America, a certain amount of poetry exposure is decreed by the state—just exposure, mind you; people go through the motions, but that's all. Hardly anyone actually learns anything, nor are there any incentives to learn— except, perhaps, a 'grade' for associating Keats' name with the 'Ode on a Grecian Urn.' Poetry is used to punish children. No wonder there is little demand for it. You *do* realize that there are exemplary poetry teachers, and their techniques will be in great demand once you start paying for their accomplishments and not all that pretentious behavior of 'certified' language teachers?"

"Okay," the Thane surrenders. "But how are my teachers going to learn to do those exemplary things? We will have many schools, and very few exemplary teachers."

"Precisely why you must totally reorganize the educational development industry," McCall emphasizes. "You will need good books, computers, workbooks, films, and so on for teachers to get this job done well."

"But we already have tons and tons of books—and look what they do. How will things be different?" the Thane pleads.

"Because they are sold as books, not as tools for repertory changes. Once your schools are in the business of producing precisely measured changes, they will seek the tools that will help them—and that will create a new market. Publishers will no longer sell books; they will sell teaching instruments. Each teaching device will surely advertise what kind of change it can produce, and tell you exactly how to use it and with whom—most important, what it will help the child accomplish. You must create a market for such change. There is no market for this kind of change in America, for example. People there can't tell a bound ream of paper from enlightenment."

The Thane looks away into the distance for awhile; then sighs. "But who knows how to create these amazing teaching aids you are talking about? Fantastically well-educated experts are writing those books you complain about now. In spite of a market demand, they wouldn't know how to do better."

"Yet the technology exists. Not many use it, because there is no demand, but it does exist—it only awaits a market to develop it. The free market is a powerful force if you plan for it. You see, people in America are double-minded. They think 'high-minded' things like education must be socialized. They have a religion there that says material things have to win their way in the competition of the market, and high-minded ventures such as education must be controlled by a seedy bureaucracy that has to avoid all appearance of self-interest."

"But I had in mind a socialist government," the Thane wails. "You are urging me to put schools on a free-enterprise basis. And I have to pay for it—or my people do, through their taxes. And, say, even if the system is fair, how would I ever pay for it?"

"Easily," says McCall, trimming his fingernails. "Take over the banking business and run it yourself. That way, you will earn the money to invest in the education business."

"Boy!" the Thane exclaims. "That would really be socialism. I don't understand—are you a socialist or a capitalist?"

"A performance engineer," McCall brightens.

Walsh McCall is very fortunate to be in Nedlaw. To find a client in America, for example, he would run into such vested interests in *not* doing the things he prescribes that he would probably never find a client. The very idea of running a school like a business can arouse only the most intense emotions. But even if those emotions were to give way to rational response, there would still be many who do not believe that the technology for improving the schools exists. I hope to dispel this idea in the next two chapters, by illustrating certain strategies and tactics of developing knowledge that represent a genuine technology, and one barely used at all in the schools. This technology has been used increasingly in industry because a market exists there—a real interest in improving human performance; but even in industry, it has a long way to go.

The Delivery System

The next area in which we can greatly improve educational performance is in the delivery system. To see where we can make the improvement, we need to look at the performance required of teachers.

Teachers now have six major responsibilities, which I list in no special order:

1. Setting objectives for (or with) students
2. Training tactics
3. Motivation of students
4. Assessment of learning progress
5. Assessment of social development
6. Management of the classroom

On the whole, teachers handle two of these six responsibilities quite well; and they could handle them even better if they had more time. They are generally excellent at managing classrooms and assessing social development.

Teachers are sorely pressed on the other four duties, however, and more efficient and inexpensive substitutes are available. Consider

training tactics, for example. Teachers are ill suited for this duty. For example, hardly a teacher alive knows the best tactics for teaching the multiplication table—or even a fairly good approximation to them. Yet the teaching of this skill could be programmed into the simplest kind of teaching machine (a capital investment, not a regular expense), and it would assure that virtually *all* students could master the skill to an exemplary degree of speed and accuracy in about 2 hours. (In Chapter 9 I explain how this is done.)

In brief, training tactics can be programmed (in or out of computers) to a high degree of efficiency, and training programs can inexpensively supplant the teacher for many training duties.[9]

Next, establishing accomplishment aims (true objectives) for the student should be the principal purpose of curriculum design. Teachers are, first of all, ill equipped to design a curriculum. Nor are they really expected to. As things stand, teachers hardly know what the curriculum or its purpose is—no one to my knowledge does. It is not at all surprising, then, that teachers almost never set coherent accomplishments for their students. But such accomplishment-based objectives should be the principal product of an intelligent curriculum design.

Then there is the task of motivating a student to want to learn. Granted, some teachers do this very well, but many fail. Yet who has not been impressed with the ability of TV to capture and chain a child's interest? Again, TV is a capital investment; but, properly programmed to introduce children to subject matters, it would be less expensive than requiring the teacher to supply interest, and it would assure a higher standard of motivation.

Finally, the assessment of learning progress (with a high degree of differential diagnosis) can be accomplished far more efficiently by "mechanical" procedures than by teachers. I illustrated this at the end of Chapter 6, by showing how arithmetic progress can be measured.

The point is that we can reach a much higher standard of education without increasing our costs. When training becomes efficiently programmed, the teachers will be free to do what they do best, and this will automatically expand the effective labor pool without creating a demand for more teachers.

The major solutions to our educational problems, then, lie in two other missions of education—in curriculum design and in training development—not in improving teachers. The delivery system will be improved when we develop more effective tools for training, assessment, and motivation; and when we create sensible and coherent curricula. And because almost all of these tools would consist primarily of things like paper, pencils, and film—as well as some "teaching machines"—the costs would be far less than those required to hire many more teachers. By using computers, creating paraprofessional

jobs, and mobilizing the great untapped resources of the community, we could increase the ratio of students to *executive* teachers from 20 to 1 to as much as 100 to 1, or even more. And, at the same time, we could greatly increase the individual attention we give to the children.

To repeat, however, in order to achieve this reduction in demand for expensive teachers, we must vastly improve our developmental opportunities and curriculum design. When high-quality programmed instruction and both simple and computerized teaching machines are developed, teachers will have much more time to do those things they can do best.[10] The greatest potential for improving our schools, then, does not lie within the schools themselves, but within the extra-school institutions of development and curriculum design.

The Development System

The development of teaching materials imposes no special economic burden. Right now, less than 2 percent of our total school budget goes for textbooks, workbooks, and the like. What we pay a year for all the software teaching materials used in the schools amounts to considerably less money than the annual revenues of the Xerox Corporation. Doubling our investment in such materials would roughly require an extra billion dollars. If this additional investment could reduce our need for teachers by only 5 percent, the investment would be greatly profitable in lowering expenses alone. And if the increased investment could double the tactical teaching power of our delivery system, the returns would be no less than fantastic. The effects on the economy of obliterating illiteracy alone would many times pay for the added investment. But we need a development technology.

The basis for a technology of instructional development exists. It has also been applied to a limited extent in both schools and industry, but it is not widely known. Unfortunately, such a technology (I call it *mathetics*)[11] is unlikely to grow until there are incentives for its growth. At present, textbook publishing—which could become the principal development industry—has no incentives for adopting such a technology. Let us see why.

In the first place, excellent teaching materials—those following excellent tactics of teaching—would in many instances appear in a form superficially indistinguishable from any other text or workbook. They would, in fact, be texts and workbooks (or their equivalents in teaching machines), but with the difference that they would carry virtually the entire burden of ensuring that students could learn their subject. In other words, the tactically sound workbook would be first of all an instrument for behavior changes, and only coincidentally a book. Unfortunately, however, school boards do not adopt instruments for

behavior change. They buy books. And no one has any expectation that a book should guarantee a behavior change. As a result, the tactically unsound books with which we as students were so familiar—the badly written, difficult treatises on subject matters—may *look* as good as the tactically sound ones. Indeed, they may be slicker, with prettier pictures, and in every way more superficially appealing. Besides, the tactically unsound books may have prestigious authors and a strong marketing effort to support them. The people who make the decisions to buy such books, unequipped as they are to identify a tactically sound book if they saw one, have every incentive to make a choice on an irrelevant basis. There are, after all, no quality-control measures to tell anyone just how effective a book is as a teaching aid. A book is a book is a book, and it is sold like a book.

The way such books get sold is also interesting. As a consultant for a major publisher, I once accompanied its elementary-high school sales representative through one of our Southern states. By state law, this salesman was prevented from contacting school board members directly. But nothing in the law prevented him from visiting their sisters, aunts, and cousins. He drove from rural home to backwoods grocery store to small-town filling stations to drugstores—doing just that. He would leave a book and a bottle of exemplary Scotch whisky with the cousin of "his good ole buddy," the school board member. And he gave this backslapping promise: "Old timer, I'll get you folks a case of this stuff if I can sell enough of these books."

Booze was not his only carrot; he had trips to Barbados, tickets to the Grand Ole Opry, hunting rifles—you name it. His station wagon was loaded with gifts. I confess I never saw him leave a rifle. He would show the gun, leave some ammunition for it (with the book, naturally), and hint that he would sure like to give the gun as a gift—and would, if he could make enough money selling books. Of course, I have no evidence that this thinly veiled bribery ever swayed the good school board members of the state; but he had been doing it for 10 years, and that state had widely adopted his publisher's books. I have the distinct feeling that anyone who would take an honest product like a book full of behavior changes to sell in this state would find the competition tough indeed.

But good teaching instruments would perform feats that we never expect from a book. Let me recite just a few examples of the potential of a training development technology.

Using a method illustrated in the next chapter, 5-year-olds from the worst ghettos of poverty have been taught to read and to take dictation (of anything they hear) in 20 to 40 hours. These are children who would ordinarily compose the nation's illiteracy list. We can take people randomly off the street and teach them to identify microscopic organ-

isms that it normally requires around a hundred hours for trained laboratory technicians to learn.

Almost anyone could be taught in 2 hours to send and receive International Morse Code at a rate that it now requires 30 hours to accomplish with some "very modern" training techniques.

And nearly all people could be taught to write with the clarity and effectiveness of a good reporter before they finish high school.

These are not rash, untested projections, because I can demonstrate our capability to do each of these things—and many more. (You will see some examples in the next chapter.) Besides, what we could do so well with skills such as these, we could do even better with theoretical, conceptual subjects like history and physics. I have no doubt, for example, that by the time they have completed high school, most students could master the subject matter that college students now require 4 years to learn.

What, then, is the portent of such potential power to train? It will mean nothing at all until a market is established for such results. And no such market can be established until quite a large number of people really believe that these results are both possible and economically feasible.

And there is, alas, a sort of "Catch-22" to all of this. On the one hand, it is hard for me to conceive that a training development technology will be taken seriously without major policy changes at work and at school. On the other hand, I fail to see how such policy changes can take place until the training development technology is taken seriously.

There is a possible way out-of the dilemma. As the costs of training soar, the market for such a technology should grow. The most important policy changes that must be made are, after all, economic ones. We must begin to see the training development as an investment to be measured against its returns in improved performance. If we can get established policies that would require this kind of economic measurement, the technology would flourish simply because it would make possible better training of more people and at a far lower cost.

Recall Rob Goodale in the previous chapter. He achieved a return of millions of dollars a year by investing in training development—although he did have to put up a couple hundred thousand dollars in "front money." Similar investments will be needed wherever we are to achieve these results. It is in the nature of any technology that large capital investments are required at first in order to realize its economic potential.

Still, technologies pay off in two ways for us. They not only create opportunities to accomplish far more, but they reduce the costs of operation. Of course, we know this, but we aren't used to thinking technologically about training. And our general assumption is that if we

wish to improve the way people learn, we must be prepared to suffer much greater *operating* costs—pay for even more and better teachers at school, or keep employees in nonproductive training activities much longer. This assumption is wrong. To understand *why* it is wrong, we must be able to visualize really effective strategies and tactics of knowledge. And that is what the next chapter is about.

NOTES

1. *Studies in Functional Literacy* (Washington, D.C.: U.S. Office of Education, 1975).

2. *U.S. Statistical Abstracts* (Washington, D.C.: U.S. Government Printing Office, 1975). These figures do not take into account the shrinking proportion of children to the whole population. Demographers, however, do not agree on how long this proportion will continue to shrink.

3. These figures are somewhat inflated proportionally because we are now in a period of increasing population age.

4. Of course, a "professional" can find out a great deal more by careful digging—but nothing that reveals a purposeful and systematic procedure for developing our curricula. The more we learn about them, the less we know.

5. This is not conjecture. I have made a careful study of the relationship between publishers and textbook authors.

6. From W. K. Durr, J. M. Le Pere, and R. Brown, *Workbook for Fiesta* (Boston: Houghton-Mifflin, 1974). I chose the exercise by opening the workbook at random.

7. There are projections of a temporary reduction in the *rate* of growth because of a slowing of the growth of younger people in the population.

8. See T. F. Gilbert, "Saying What a Subject Matter Is," *Instructional Science* (January 1976).

9. Do not judge the *potential* of programmed training by existing programmed instruction. Few programmers understand the efficient tactics of teaching. This situation will change only when we produce incentives for it to change.

10. Interested readers should try to learn more about PLATO, the most advanced computer-assisted instructional system.

11. See T. F. Gilbert, "Mathetics: The Technology of Education," *Journal of Mathetics,* Vol. 1, No. 1 (1962).

Chapter Nine
Knowledge Strategies and Tactics

KNOWLEDGE MAPS

On charts of Knowledge the roads run west
Through thicket, fen, and squalid town,
And weary travelers wanting rest
Will search for coves that can't be found;
For every quarry one would quest
Lies safely hidden underground.

But once my Love did dwell along
These paths, so I'll delve for what she knows,
For she can tune the catbird's song
And ameliorate the rose.

T.F.G.

ISSUES OF EDUCATION AND TRAINING

Nowhere are the separate issues of policy, strategies, and tactics more readily confused than in education and training. Policies are decisions about what we should (in the main) accomplish and how much we are willing to pay to get there. Tactics are methods of implementation, that is, the actions we take to achieve these goals. In order to match our tactics to our policies, we must do some planning; and strategy is the planning that intervenes between policy and tactics.

Table 9-1 should help you distinguish these issues—the policies, strategies, and tactics of development and delivery. Obviously, they interlock, but distinguishing them like this may make it more difficult to imagine the solution of one issue as the solution to all three.

The strategies and tactics of knowledge that I shall discuss here are largely those of developing better tools for teaching. Once the curriculum is accomplishment based, the strategic problem remains of planning the specific content of instruction; so does the tactical problem of

253

TABLE 9-1 SUMMARY OF SEVERAL ISSUES OF EDUCATION AND TRAINING

	Policy	*Strategy*	*Tactics*
Development	To what worldly accomplishments should education be directed?	What should be the content of courses?	How should the training materials be structured?
	For example: Should students of history be able to make predictions, make history, organize historical data, or produce descriptions of history?	For example: What is a theory of civil unrest that will help students make predictions, and what historical material should be used in the instruction?	For example: Should simulation be used, requiring actual prediction from stylized case studies?
Delivery	Who should conduct education, to what standards of performance, and at what cost?	How should the conduct of education and training proceed?	How should the training be conveyed?
	For example: Who will measure the performance of history teachers, and how will these measurements be used?	For example: How will history objectives be set for students, and what resources will be made available for them to meet these objectives?	For example: Will the history lessons be self-paced, and what role will the teacher play?

determining how to teach that content. But it is crucial to realize that excellence in solving only one of these problems may get us nowhere at all. For example, excellent tactics of development might be used to teach the most inane subjects. I could, for example, develop very effective materials for teaching children explanations of physical phenomena that center on the interpersonal relationships of the Roman gods. Or, as is more commonly done, I could use hopelessly ineffective materials to try to teach excellent concepts of physics. Naturally, my tactics of delivery would be conditioned by the nature of the training materials that were developed for me, just as the content of my training plan would be determined by the general philosophy of my curriculum.

Suppose that we examine some strategies of training delivery, to see how strategy alone cannot solve our educational problems. Almost all readers of this book probably have spent their educational careers sitting in traditional classrooms. The plan is simple and straightforward. The students sit quietly, and the teacher talks. Sometimes the teacher asks questions that the students are expected to answer, but the teacher clearly does most of the work. A textbook is usually the core of the

instruction, and some teachers do little more than interpret the text to the students. As a strategy for teaching, this method could not be worse. Because if we follow the behaviorists' well-established principle that organisms best learn by "emitting" behavior (by "doing"), then the teacher must be doing most of the learning.

As a plan for "managing" the classroom, however, the method is generally excellent. It keeps students quiet, even if it stupefies them. Many have objected to this method; and such regimentation, as much as anything else, gave rise to so-called progressive education. In the structured classroom, behavior is highly structured, but—as we have seen—accomplishments are hardly structured at all. Students learn how to behave, but usually haven't the faintest idea of where they are going. With progressive education the behavioral structure is usually removed, but still no structure is given to the goals. At the other extreme are those systems in which highly structured objectives are added to already highly structured behavior.

The fourth alternative is tried too infrequently: structured goals, but freedom in the behavior of pursuing the goals. There is evidence that this alternative, at least in England and the United States, is growing in popularity. In the "open classroom," as it is called, the rows of desks often disappear, as does the passive sitting at the feet of the teacher. Children are, in theory, either given specific objectives, or they work them out together with the teacher. And these objectives become the basis for most of the discipline. The classroom space—sometimes even the corridors of the building—is given over to "learning centers," containing educational aids of various kinds, where children can go in the pursuit of their objectives. One child may decide to study math, for example, while another studies language. Each child, in effect, contracts with the teacher to complete the objectives, but has considerable freedom of procedure.

The open classroom is a marvelously healthy step in the right direction of structuring goals and relinquishing the regimentation of behavior. But although it is often an excellent teaching *strategy*, the open classroom does not solve the problems of *policy* and *tactics*. On the *policy* side, there is no assurance at all that the structured objectives represent a sensible curriculum. For example, I have seen children in these classrooms given the goal of learning the very same kinds of "skills" represented by our exercises in futility. And as far as teaching tactics go, children in the open classroom are as likely to be exposed to poorly designed teaching exercises as the regimented children. Excellent strategies can be largely wasted if they are not guided by clear policies and are implemented with poor tactics.

An excellent, if already dated, description of the strategies of the

open classroom, in its various forms, is described by Charles Silberman in his *Crisis in the Classroom* (New York: Random House, 1970). The only problem with the direction this movement is taking is, I think, the tendency to see any "solution" in education as being *the* solution. It is important to keep in mind that the open classroom solution is a strategy of delivery—it does not solve our policy and tactical problems of delivery, nor any of the problems of curriculum and materials development.

In the world of work, there is a similar movement away from structured classrooms with the implementation of learner-guided instruction (LGI). This is a system that lets trainees find their own way through a course of instruction, assessing themselves as they go. The FAIR program, which I describe in Chapter 10, would be another example of such an open classroom, combining the structure of formal training (for accomplishments) with the behavioral flexibility of on-the-job training. But, like the open classroom, LGI and the FAIR program are only strategies, and neither of them solves policy or tactical problems.

Nor do excellent tactics, by themselves, suffice. Consider the computer-assisted instructional system called PLATO, possibly the central educational delivery system of the future. As a tactical delivery system, PLATO has no peer. Yet I have seen PLATO programs that teach people such useless things as employing a mathematical formula to convert (from the metric system) degrees Celsius to degrees Fahrenheit, when all that the trainees really need to know is a sense of what, say, 20 degrees Celsius means (room temperature). Without the proper policy and strategic backup, PLATO could one day convert us into a society of highly trained idiots.

This chapter is about the strategies and tactics of developing training systems. Once we have decided which accomplishments our training should prepare our students to produce, we have two more fundamental steps to take. First, we must plan the content of this training. A good strategic plan should plot the knowledge needs of students against specific accomplishments, and it should reveal which forms of training are required in order to meet these knowledge needs. Then, after we have a strategic plan, we need to apply a set of tactics that will convert this plan into effective teaching tools.*

In Part A of this chapter I describe a model of a strategic plan of development—one that I call a knowledge map. Then, in Part B, I discuss and illustrate some of the tactical procedures that can be applied to implement such a plan.

---

*Of course, logistics are fundamental, too. But our training institutions are surprisingly good at these. Good logistics are easily confused with successes at higher levels.

A. KNOWLEDGE MAPPING

KNOWLEDGE AND ACCOMPLISHMENT

Knowledge in isolation is a sterile, lifeless thing. As a repertory of behavior, it is one of the tools we need to achieve competence, but it is not competence itself. All the knowledge of the world does not reveal the least bit of competence until we marry it to accomplishments. We may worship knowledge "for itself," just as we worship other valuable tools; but this is a totemism that is only superstitiously related to our survival, or to our achievement of excellence. And because knowledge is our most potent and valuable tool, the totemism is all the more crippling. People who profess great knowledge may find honor in our most cherished institutions, whether they are competent or not. Accomplishments need not be real, merely symbolic. Unread publications, memberships, study grants, degrees, and titles reassure the rest of us that knowledge is safely crated and stored away.

This worship of knowledge can doubtless be explained as a superstition. And this cultism also explains, at least in part, the extreme conservatism of our principal warehouses of knowledge: the universities. It is difficult to change a cult, the anthropologists tell us. Attempts to alter these institutions so that they can better serve our needs in the real world are met with unbelievable hostility and resistance. But before we can systematically develop and tap the potential of the universities, there must be a radical alteration of the vantage points in which their supporters and managers stand. The so-called liberalism of the academies is skin-deep—a thing of fashion, style, *behavior*. In these places, you can dress differently and speak heresy, and indeed you are expected to. But a radical notion like the idea of marrying knowledge to accomplishment will typically find only arid ground in which to grow.

Not that academicians are diffident about their practical value—whether to the world of work or elsewhere. Recently, as I have mentioned before, a distinguished psychology professor told his TV talk-show audience that if behaviorism were taken seriously by business and industry, most of the problems of productivity, quality, and efficiency would be solved in a year's time. Of course, this is nonsense; but coming from a brilliant man, it is a dramatic symptom of the great distance between the knowledge keepers and the world of work. The attitude expressed by this professor's view is discouraging. It is as if he were saying, "All the knowledge you need lies here ready-made, and all you must do is drop by and pick it up." But the knowledge packed away in our institutions is not ready-made. At its best, it is only raw material.

Naturally, some of the resistance that the universities have to practical values (especially in the world of work) can be credited to the fear that immediate practical demands would suffocate free inquiry and basic research. And this fear has some rational basis. But it is my contention that the leisure required for free inquiry can ultimately be secured only by worthy performance in the world of work, and that leisure will flourish if we can tap more of the great potential of the universities for increasing that efficiency.

The evidence is all too clear that the PIPs to be found in knowledge institutions reach fearful proportions. When we measure competence in these places, using accomplishments and requirements agreeable to the incumbents, and not those imposed by the barons of business, we find exemplars who perform many times better than the average— meaning that the potential for performance improvement is great. The universities may be the most noncompetitive of all institutions—not noncompetitive in seeking worldly rewards, but in achieving their own expressed ends. Free inquiry is absolutely essential for the advancement of human capital, but not when that inquiry gropes to meet behavioral rather than accomplishment standards. A personal reminiscence will explain what I mean.

My undergraduate career was so spotty that it took the considerable influence of two doting professors to get me into graduate school, where I went on to study psychology and philosophy. As a near failure, I was determined to right my record and make good grades. When I first looked into the assigned readings, I felt doomed, because they seemed very hard indeed. But then I discovered a secret that allowed me to rise to the top of my class (along with a couple of friends who shared the secret): I learned to translate Academish into English. This is how my translation of one famous paper reads:

> Men fear women. Men have always feared women. Men always will fear women. In some cultures, men fear women more than they do in other cultures. The fear of women shapes the quality of our minds. Neurotic men fear women more than the rest of us do. Psychotics are terrorized by women. It all started with mother. The way to cure neurosis is to get men over the fear of women.

That's all the man had to say, in an impressively long, abstruse (and male-oriented) paper. Translating Academish in this straightforward manner got me right to the meat of the writer's message. And, by my count, 85 percent of my psychology reading assignments translated into just such nonsense.

I soon learned another secret. When I rendered my translation directly to the professor who assigned the reading, my grade was not good. I was told that I had missed the point. To appear competent, I had

to spruce up my own writing behavior and translate the message back into my own brand of Academish. Liberal use of a brief list of rare words (*heuristic* should lead the list) and the passive voice, plus a little literary imagination, would get me an A+ any day. The last sentence of one of my papers that the professor marked A++++ will amply illustrate the technique:

> Finally, the creative man, in the very act of creation, returns triumphantly to the womb.

Of such PIPs are great universities made.

To many, the very condition of being on a university faculty is taken as *prima facie* evidence of competence. Indeed, you may find it hard to think of a factory packer of snacks as far more competent than a university worker. But that is an inescapable conclusion if you accept my definition of competence as a quality to be measured against exemplary standards of performance. The average civil servant whom we employ on the faculty of our state college only *seems* to be more competent than the white-coated young kid who packs chips in a box, because we judge this civil servant's competence by stylish talk and displays of imposing instruments in the pockets of a laboratory cloak. But when we avoid the "behavior error" and look at the professor *as* a civil servant, we can ask how the accomplishments we pay this professor to make measure up to those of the best who pursue these same achievements. When we compare the effect most professors have on students and the quality of their researches with those of the exemplars, even a bag of chips becomes appetizing.

But writing exposés of academic incompetence will not help at all to uplift these institutions. The knowledge keepers are not willfully incompetent; nor are they incompetent because we have employed people who lack ability or potential. Quite the contrary. The people in these institutions have always struck me as willing competence greatly, and as having enormous potential for it. They are, it seems to me, rather unfortunate victims of the knowledge cult and the apotheosis of behavior.

The cure, I believe, lies in a systematic way of analyzing the accomplishments expected of these institutions—and of marrying knowledge to those accomplishments. Then, when we subject these institutions to detached analysis, we shall happily find that their potential value is much greater than we find it to be now. This medicine should be much easier to administer when universities realize how much their endowments would rise once they start on the road to competence. Like everyone else, they need a little incentive.

Marrying knowledge to accomplishments is hardly a radical idea, or

a new one. But it certainly has not been among the clarion calls of any of the recent Great Revolutions in education. The problems we encounter when we *don't* make this marriage can best be shown by example—unfortunately, a true one.

Billy Andrew is probably one of the three or four finest custom box manufacturers in the world. His boxes are beautifully designed, functional, strong, and made with an efficiency that keeps his customers happy about the price. But at 40, Andrew feels that his life is rushing by without his making a true contribution to the really important issues of the world. At least, that is what he confides to Solly Slick, the Kenneth Samuels College professor. The two have just met at a special convention of the American Management Association, designed to introduce the new educational millennium to the Earls of Industry; and Dr. Slick has been showing off his cardboard "teaching machine" in a remote booth. For all of Dr. Slick's flamboyant salesmanship, his modest gray box attracts little attention, surrounded as it is by the great gleaming electronic consoles of his competitors.

"Think of it this way," Slick tells Andrew over margaritas: "It's not the teaching *machine* that counts, but the self-instructional programs that go into them. After all, those fancy electronic machines are nothing more than automatic page flippers. The cardboard box is so simple and cheap that all students can afford their own, and they can even pack their lunches in it. There's room for two rolls of programmed teaching materials and a couple of sandwiches in each one. How can you beat that?"

"You mean that we could really give away the box and make our profits from the rolls of teaching materials?" muses Andrew, forgetting for a moment his nobler motives.

"Exactly like the razor and the blade," says Slick.

"But where would I get hold of the teaching programs? The experts at the meetings are quoting prices like $40 a frame* just to write the stuff. And it looks to me like it would take a couple thousand frames just to teach English grammar."

"Come on, Billy," Slick pleads, "those aren't experts—just a bunch of professors on the make. They talk about $40 a frame because they can't conceive of making a simple point clearly without spending at least a day working on it. Billy, I can get it for you wholesale—25¢ a frame."

"You're kidding me, Dr. Slick."

"Just call me Solly."

---

*For those readers unfamiliar with the arcane technical language of programmed instruction, a "frame" is an item of instruction; typically, 20 or 30 words of information, with some blanks for the student to fill in an answer. A frame is often printed in a rectangular box, 1.5 inches by 8 inches.

"Solly . . . But where can you get it that cheap?"

"Billy, I have a client—the Mercer Correctional Center. That's a pen for first offenders way down South. They've set up an experimental school, and the inmates in the school have gone through just about every teaching machine program ever written. Now some of these kids are writing their own; and let me tell you, Billy, their programs are as good as any of this stuff the professors are putting out."

"Really? Say, can you contract with a convict?"

(Later—a change of scene)

The faint smell of urine and sweat is inescapable, but at least this part of the prison has a pleasant decor. The four rooms are freshly paneled and curtained, thanks to the government grant; and the atmosphere is not unlike a country school in the Berkshires, vintage 1936. Above the entrance to the school, known as the Warden's Reward, Solly Slick notices a new sign, crudely printed, that reads "Mercer Correctional Center—We Correct Programs."

Inside, Uncle Ho Ho, boss of the territory, is making his hourly quality-control check of the latest programmed instruction his boys have written.

"Hey, Solly," Uncle Ho Ho grimaces, "we don't like the contract the box maker sent us. My mouthpiece says it's too vague. The contract says $500 for 2000 frames of English grammar. Now, we ain't scared of the grammar, but just how much is 2000 frames? Suppose we taught the same stuff in 1000 frames. Shouldn't we get twice as much?"

"Twice as much? You'd get only half as much."

"Why the hell should that be!" exclaims Uncle Ho Ho. "You'd have to work twice as hard to teach English grammar in 1000 frames. It'd be worth it. The way I figure it, if I could teach English grammar in *one* frame, they oughta pay me $1 million. That's 2000 frames times $500."

"I don't quite get it," Solly teases.

"Sure you do, Solly. If I can teach English in *one* frame, it would be worth $1 million dollars, wouldn't it? And if I wrote a program that took a million frames, nobody would buy it, right? So why shouldn't I get twice as much for half the number of frames?" Uncle Ho Ho demands.

"Well, your arithmetic's a little funny, but you've got a point. The more efficiently you do the job, the more you should get paid, huh?"

"Sure, why not?" snaps Uncle Ho Ho.

"Well, it just doesn't work that way, Uncle Ho Ho. It works just the opposite. The more frames you write, the more money you get for it."

"What a con! Man, that's smart. That way you squeeze the most bucks out of the simplest little thing. So that's why those professors take forever to get to the point. If they made things simple, they'd be out in the cold with their asses bare. I get the gig, but it doesn't seem right.

"Anyhow, Solly, that's not what's bothering us. This box guy doesn't say what he means by 2000 frames. Are those 1-inch frames or 1-foot frames? It makes a lot of difference, you know."

"Why don't you have your legal boys rewrite the contract?" Solly asks.

Back in his office at Kenneth Samuels College, Solly struggles to recall Uncle Ho Ho's tricky argument.

"Let's see. I teach Psychology 300 every semester, three times a week. That comes to about 70 classroom hours a semester. Now, if I could teach the same course just as effectively in *1* hour, then I should be able to arrange to get paid 70 times as much each semester, because I could teach the course 70 times faster. I get paid $3500 a semester now to teach the course, so that should pay me about $250,000 for just one semester, and since I teach three...."

The phone shatters Slick's idle musings. It's Billy Andrew, and he's in a huff.

"What is this about 83 yards of English grammar?" Billy yells.

"What do you mean?" Solly asks.

"Those convicts just rewrote my contract to read 83 yards of English grammar. What kind of nonsense is this?"

"Oh, I get it," Solly laughs. "The 83 yards is about 3000 inches. That would be 2000 one-and-one-half-inch frames. You see, Billy, these guys were worried about how long a frame you meant, so they rewrote the contract to make it more definite. If you think about it, it makes sense. That's about $600 a yard."

"I guess so, but what will people say?" Billy whines.

"Oh come on, Billy, you're not publishing the contract; you're publishing the 83 yards."*

The main point of the story is an economic one: The cost of training is great; the value we get from it is all too small. The strategies we use to develop knowledge, then, will have to marry knowledge to accomplishments in a highly efficient way; and that is the purpose of the procedure I call knowledge mapping. Shortly, I shall take you through an example of the development of a knowledge map, but first let us examine another fundamental corollary of the First Leisurely Theorem, which underlies these strategies:

---

*The contract for 83 yards of English grammar was actually signed by both parties: a true educational revolution.

> **The efficient content of training, at work or at school, is the**
> ***product*** **(not the sum) of the deficiencies in accomplish-**
> **ments and the deficiencies in knowledge relevant to those**
> **accomplishments. If either deficiency is zero, the result**
> **should be no coverage.**

And if we make the content of training the *product*, and not the *sum*, of accomplishments and behavior deficiencies, we shall simultaneously create relevance in education and greatly reduce the use of unnecessary data.

Two examples (and they are real) will illustrate the reasoning behind this corollary. We find the first example in a course for bank clerks, in a lesson on computing interest rates. On inquiry, we learn that bank clerks don't need to make such computations in their jobs. Then how did this lesson get into the course? Because the training people assumed that the content of training is the *sum* of performance needs and student deficiencies, like this:

Interest Rates

Performance Need		Student Deficiency		Coverage
0	+	Yes	=	Yes

In the second example, a lengthy lesson teaches insurance clerks to read an insurance application. But when we look further into it, we find that anybody can read the application, except for two or three lines of it. The lesson got into the course because, again, the training people assumed that the content of training is the *sum* of student deficiencies and performance needs, as here:

Insurance Applications

Performance Need		Student Deficiency		Coverage
Yes	+	0	=	Yes

So, if students don't know something in the *subject matter* that is relevant to a job, they are taught it anyway, whether the *job* needs it or not. And if the job requires a skill, the students are taught it anyway, whether they already know it or not.

But suppose that we write our formula for training content as the *multiplication* of performance needs and student deficiencies. Now we arrive at different results:

	Performance Need		Student Deficiency		Coverage
	0	×	Yes	=	0
or	Yes	×	0	=	0

What this means is that if we plan to invest in changing behavior by training people, we ought to make sure that they are deficient both in behavior *and* in the relevant accomplishment.

We can create a sort of multiplication table—called a matrix—to help us determine what knowledge is necessary in order to achieve competence. To express the products we are looking for, we draw a matrix of job accomplishments (A) and student knowledge deficiencies (B), as in Table 9-2. If we place a cross only in each cell where the accomplishment is both important to the job *and* the student is deficient in behavior, we create a "map" of the desirable course coverage—or the knowledge that students need in order to be competent.

It can reasonably be argued that people who are in the business of managing competence, or teaching it, fail to get their money's worth because they don't have such knowledge maps. Of course, our knowledge matrix in Table 9-2 is too sketchy for a real map. But before we can make a real knowledge map, we need a little technology to help us describe the latitudes and the longitudes.

I have already described one dimension of our map: accomplishments and their requirements and standards. To fix the second dimension—knowledge—we must be able to describe behavior deficiencies in some useful way that will distinguish different kinds of knowledge. And in mapping knowledge against accomplishment, we want to map the methods of achieving competence against the measure of competence. Because there are different ways of looking at knowledge, there will be different methods of instilling competence. Just as the nature of the terrain on a physical map tells us what transportation to use, the locations on our knowledge map should help us understand what manner of instruction is required.

If we think of knowledge as a repertory of behavior, three different and very familiar things always happen almost simultaneously: We discriminate, we generalize, and we receive feedback. We discriminate when we tell the difference between things; we generalize when we

TABLE 9-2   KNOWLEDGE MATRIX

		Knowledge Needs			
		B_1	B_2	B_3 $\cdots$	B_n
	A_1		X		
Job Needs	A_2	X		X	
	A_3			X	
	$\vdots$				
	A_n		X		X

see their similarities; and we receive feedback when we see the consequences of our behavior in discriminating and generalizing. Whenever we behave in the least bit, we simultaneously do all three of these things. And whenever our behavior is defective, it will be because we fail to do one or more of these things properly.

It is important to classify knowledge in these three ways, since a defect in each deserves different strategies and tactics of learning. For example, we should teach people concepts (how to generalize) through a different set of procedures than we should use to teach them to make discriminations. Moreover, the best sequences of teaching are determined, in part, by the character of our knowledge deficiencies. So now we should consider both the nature of these three knowledge categories themselves and the learning progression that they suggest.

THE KNOWLEDGE PROGRESSION

A good map always gives us information about direction. And because a knowledge map describes knowledge that is to be achieved, it will be a better map if it can not only tell us which route to take, but also tell us something about the direction—the sequence—we can best follow to get there.

The proper sequence of teaching has always been a subject of contention with teachers and industrial trainers. But animal trainers don't argue about the sequence of teaching *their* subjects. There is a right place to start in training a rat; and if we don't start there, we shall either become completely lost, or take forever to arrive at our destination. The animal trainer who carefully follows the principles of B. F. Skinner will never cease to marvel at the ease with which the subjects learn. Without going deeply into the principles that Skinner calls "operant conditioning," I shall describe the basic training sequence, because these principles are perfectly general and also apply to humans—who are at least animals, whatever else they might be.

Suppose that we wish to train a rat to press a lever to get food every time we turn on a light in its cage. The behavior we desire can be summarized like this:

$$S^D \longrightarrow R \qquad \cdot \qquad S_r$$

$$\text{Light} \qquad \text{Press Lever} \qquad \text{Click of}$$
$$\text{Food Magazine}$$

But the procedure we must follow is just opposite to the "common sense solution" that says "begin at the beginning." Before we can train the animal to press the bar, we first must convince it that the consequence is meaningful. The "click" of the food magazine will reinforce

lever pressing only when the click has value to the animal. So, the first thing we teach the rat is this:

$$S^D \xrightarrow{\hspace{2cm}} R \qquad\qquad S_r$$

Click   Go to Food Pan   Sight of Food

When the click allows the animal to discriminate that food is available, the click itself becomes rewarding (or reinforcing).

Once we have established the click as a reinforcer, all we need to do is wait for the animal, in its wanderings, to touch the lever accidentally, which immediately closes a switch that produces a click. The animal learns in one trial that lever pressing is "successful"—a way to get food. Next, we teach the animal the discrimination that we want it to make: The lever "works" (produces a click) only when the light is on. Soon, the lever pressing is brought under the control of the light stimulus. To summarize, the sequence we follow is this:

1. First, teach the animal to discriminate the consequences of behavior: The click means food (S_r). I call this the *inductive* stage of training, because we are leading (inducing) the animal into training and giving it a means to know the consequences of bar pressing. We are establishing the feedback needed to tell the animal that it is performing correctly.

2. Second, we teach the animal to discriminate the occasion for responding successfully. This is the "discriminative" or *skill*[1] stage of training.

For human training, however, a step is missing. The rat performs for us in nearly unvarying situations—the cage and the light stay pretty much the same at all times:

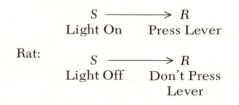

$$S \xrightarrow{\hspace{2cm}} R$$

Light On   Press Lever

Rat:

$$S \xrightarrow{\hspace{2cm}} R$$

Light Off   Don't Press Lever

But in the world of human performance the "right" occasion for responding may occur in many forms. Here is a parallel discrimination in a person interpreting a legal contract:

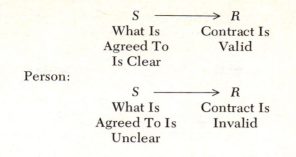

Although the situations facing rat and human differ greatly in form, the discriminations are fundamentally identical—except in one respect. For the rat, the light is a light, and it is nearly always the same when it comes on. But legal contracts vary tremendously in form and style. And because it is not always obvious when a contract is "clear," one has to develop the generalizations (concepts) required to interpret it. In fact, there are so many variants that even an experienced lawyer could not be expected to memorize every one of them. We need some additional behavior that will "mediate" (come in between) the situations and the responses, to help the lawyer "remember" or "reason" the correct response:

S	$\longrightarrow$	R	S	$\longrightarrow$	R	$\cdot$	S_r
Contract		Look For Adherence to Rules of Validity	Obeys Rules of Validity		Contract Is Valid		Upheld in Court; Client Pays Off

Thus, if we teach students of law the intermediate (mediating) behavior of looking to see whether the contract adheres to general rules, we have helped them generalize to the great variety of situations to which they must respond. Again, going "backwards" in our "chain" of training, we follow this sequence:

This sequence also suggests a general progression that we can usefully follow in training students: First, show them where things are going—the consequences of performance; next, provide the mediating generalizations they need; and, finally, teach the discrimination skills. Now we can give names to these stages in the learning progression:

1. *Inductive stage.* Teach the students the consequences of performance—the importance of the knowledge or skill, and what difference it makes to perform well or poorly.

2. *Theory stage.* Teach them those generalizations that help mediate the desired performance—the concepts (or performance theory) necessary for them to "reason" and "remember" how to respond.

3. *Skill stage.* Teach them the discriminations required for performance—any skills that they have not yet mastered.

The Five-Stage Progression

I have identified the three basic stages of efficient learning: inductive, theory, and skill. For many things, these three stages are sufficient. But I shall add two more stages that can help students make certain transitions in learning.

One transitional stage I call "preparatory skills." Some students will come to a learning situation not fully prepared for it, and must be taught some basic skills before they can learn the new one. For example, when we teach statistics, it is nice to assume that all of our students can interpret graphs. But if they can't, we shall have to give them some special preparatory training in that subject. For the most part, such "propaedeutics" (meaning, that which is to be taught before) are best taught after the inductive stage and before the theory stage. However, if the preparation requirements are extensive, this kind of training may have to follow a progression of its own, with its own inductive, theory, and skill training; and it would be taught in a separate lesson. This would be the case if we needed to teach students of statistics how to interpret graphs.

In a practical training progression, we may need to help students in the transition out of the training and into real-world applications. For example, students who have been taught in the classroom how to handle a department store transaction may freeze when they are faced with a live customer. It is sometimes useful to make special arrangements to help them transfer classroom-learned skills to actual situations in which the skill is used—let them handle a few mock customers out on the department store floor, for example.

In summary, the five stages of the training progression are

1. Inductive
2. Preparatory tools (or propaedeutics)
3. Theory

4. Skill

5. Application

These five steps of learning can be illustrated by the way we train animals efficiently. Figure 9-1 shows a five-part sequence for teaching a rat a special skill—to press a bar at different rates depending on the intensity of a light in its cage.

The task of training a human being to perform a task is both simpler and more difficult. It is simpler because human beings have language, and can therefore be taught in more sophisticated ways. And it is more difficult because we cannot withhold food from human beings to make them want to learn: We have to use more sophisticated approaches to motivate them. Even so, we would proceed in a similar way to teach human beings as we would to teach animals, leading them through a progression of these same five distinct steps. The function of each of these steps is to:

1. Motivate and familiarize

2. Teach any prerequisite skills

3. Teach a concept of the task—a generalization

4. Teach the remaining discriminations—the skills of mastery

5. Extend the skills to a larger context

As an example, suppose that we wanted to teach students how to maintain and troubleshoot a gas turbine. We certainly wouldn't seat them in front of a gas turbine and start explaining how to repair it. (We *could,* but they wouldn't learn very well.) Instead, we would lead them through a progression.

The first step would be to show them the nature of the problem and the consequences of mastering it. This should at least help motivate them to learn, and it would familiarize them with the situation. Another way to make the situation more familiar is to look for an analogy with something they already know. An analogy with an automobile would work well here. They should already be familiar with the reciprocating (automobile) engine. It works by an explosion of gas that moves a piston, which, in turn, drives a revolving wheel. The gas turbine works differently. It employs the direct energy of heat, without explosion, to move a "wheel," much as direct heat energy moves the water in a coffee percolator.

The second step is to teach them some preparatory tools—things they need to know *before* they can learn the new skills. We might have

Step 1: Motivate and familiarize.

To motivate the rat to learn, it is deprived of food long enough so that it will do something in order to get food. Next, it is put into the experimental situation — a special box — and allowed to explore until the box becomes familiar.

Step 2: Teach preparatory skills.

The rat must be taught how to get the food, which will be its reward for learning the task. It must also be taught how the food mechanism works: A clicking noise means that a food pellet has dropped into the tray.

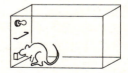

Step 3: Teach the essentials of the task.

The animal must be taught the essentials of the task; that bar pressing delivers the food, and its effectiveness is signaled by a light. The first step is to teach the animal to press the bar, then to presss it only when the light is on. This can be done by rewarding the animal with food. Since it won't perform correctly at first, it is rewarded after successively closer approximations to correct performance so it won't become discouraged and quit. Behavior is then "shaped" by this gradual increase in the demands made on it until it is performing up to the standard.

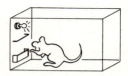

Step 4: Teach the skills of mastery.

The animal can now be taught how to make the necessary discriminations: to press slowly at a low intensity and fast at higher intensities. This is done by rewarding the rat only when it presses at a specified rate depending upon the intensity.

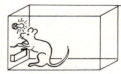

Step 5: Extend the skill to a larger context.

Once the rat can perform the task, it must be given some experience in performing before an audience.

FIGURE 9-1 · Progression of steps in teaching a rat to press a bar very slowly when a light shines at a low intensity and very fast when the light shines at a high intensity. (Reprinted from T. F. Gilbert and Marilyn B. Gilbert, "Knowledge Maps," Praxis Technical Monograph 2, Praxis Corporation, Morristown, N.J. (in press).

to give students some review of the relationship between heat and pressure—a review of Charles' law, for example.

The third step is to teach the essential elements of the system. In this case, our students must have a general idea of how a turbine works. First, they need to know that heat from burning gas fuel makes a fan turn. This first fan is connected to a second, which draws in oxygen and compresses it, that is, keeps up the pressure. The result is a nonreciprocating engine that runs without exploding fuel.

The fourth step is to teach the specific skills. Now that they understand basically what a gas turbine is and how it works, they are ready to learn how to troubleshoot an actual gas turbine.

The fifth step is to extend the students' knowledge to a larger context. Now they can be taken to a factory and allowed to work with gas turbines in actual factory production. They can also be taught how turbines are used in a variety of situations. Figure 9-2 illustrates this progression in a human being, and compares it with the animal training sequence.

According to Figure 9-2, step 1 is to motivate and familiarize. The animal is deprived of food and allowed to explore the environment; our human being is given an analogy, and learns the importance of troubleshooting and repairing the gas turbine. Step 2 is to teach some preparatory skills: The rat learns how the feeder works; the person is given a technical review. Step 3 is to teach the student the essentials of the task: The rat learns to respond to a light by pressing a bar; the student learns how the *basic* turbine works. Step 4 is to teach the skills of mastery: The rat learns to press the bar at a specified rate that depends on the intensity of the light; the person learns how to troubleshoot the turbine—how to tell what is wrong, and how to correct it. Finally, step 5 is to extend the skill to a larger context: The rat learns to perform the task before an audience; the person gets structured on-the-job experience.

Let us consider a more academic topic as a second example of the use of the progression. Suppose that we want to teach students of composition how to use the proper punctuation to separate a series of items. First, we show them the consequences of using punctuation in this situation. We may do this by presenting a sample sentence that includes a series of items that are *not* separated by punctuation. The sentence may not only be very difficult to read, but the message can easily be misconstrued. Then we show the same sentence clarified by the use of separating punctuation.

As a next step, we want to teach the students any preparatory tools they need. Are they familiar with the two punctuation marks that can be used—the comma and the semicolon? Some students will need some preparatory work, and some won't.

Rat	Step	Human being

1. Motivate
   and
   familiarize.

Deprived of food,
explores the setup.

Learns the analogy
between a gas turbine
and a percolator and also
the importance of learn-
ing this new technology.

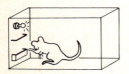

2. Teach
   preparatory
   tools.

1. Charles' law:
   PV = kt
2. Turbine-fan, etc.

Learns how the feeder
works.

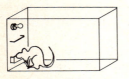

3. Teach
   essentials.

Learns to respond to
the stimulus of a light
by pressing a lever.

Learns the essential
elements of how the
turbine works.

4. Teach
   skills.

Learns how to troubleshoot
and repair the turbine.

Learns discriminations:
learns to press the lever
at a specified rate
at different intensities
of light.

5. Teach
   application.

Gets on-the-job training.

Adapts to audience.

FIGURE 9-2 Comparison of steps in the progression for animals and human beings.
(Reprinted from T. F. Gilbert and Marilyn B. Gilbert, "Knowledge Maps," Praxis
Technical Monograph 2, Praxis Corporation, Morristown, N.J. (in press).

272

The third step is to teach the students the essentials of the skill. In this case, we want to teach them how different punctuation marks are used to reveal the different relationships of items in a series.

The fourth step is to teach them which of the two punctuation marks to use in separating items in series. In general, a comma is used to set off each item to show that all items in the same series are separate but related—like sisters and brothers in a family. But if any item in a series has parts that need separating commas themselves, then a semicolon is used to separate the items in the main relationship.

The last step is to make sure that the students can apply what they have learned to their own writing: that they use separating punctuation appropriately in their own compositions. In other words, we must extend their skill to the context in which it will be applied.[2]

THE PROGRESSION AND THE KNOWLEDGE MAP

The progression differentiates three, and sometimes five, kinds of knowledge deficiencies that students may have. And when we combine the progression with the accomplishments that our training should produce, we create a knowledge map. To illustrate how to do this, I shall use a simple subject matter, the metric system.

When we have decided that it is worthy to teach this system of measurement, we need to identify the precise accomplishments we want. For example, do we want the student to make conversions from inches to centimeters? On analysis, we conclude that this is not a valuable accomplishment: in a metric society, there is seldom any reason to make such conversions. We shall decide, however, that our students should be able to do such things as estimate distances in metric units and transform one metric unit to another (e.g., 1 kilogram equals 1000 grams). The first steps in creating a knowledge map are identifying the accomplishments we want, establishing that they have real value, and determining that students are truly deficient in them.

As we follow the progression, we ask of each accomplishment certain questions to determine the students' knowledge needs. I shall briefly outline the major steps in filling in the knowledge map, using one accomplishment as an example: "estimated distance in metric units." You may wish to follow this example by referring to Table 9-3, which is a simplified portion of a knowledge map for the metric system.

1. *Inductive.* Here, we ask if our students understand the advantages of metric measures of length over inches, feet, and so on. If they already understand it, this cell of our knowledge map will remain empty. In our sketchy example, illustrated in Table 9-3, the cell marked "Inductive" (for accomplishment 1) is the content I have indicated. In

TABLE 9-3   A SIMPLIFIED PORTION OF A KNOWLEDGE MAP FOR THE METRIC SYSTEM*

Accomplishment	Inductive	Preparatory Skills	Theory	Skills	Applications
1. Estimated distance in metric units	Advantages of metric measures of length over the system with inches, feet, and so on.		The body is a convenient measurement tool.	Methods for estimating short, intermediate, and long distances For example, 1 centimeter = width of fingernail	Estimating distance in common experiences
2. Transformation of one metric unit to another	Additional advantages of decimal units	Use of the decimal system	The simplicity of the metric prefix system, to denote size, and its generality	Methods for transforming from one unit to another	Estimating common distances in more than one unit

*See Thomas F. Gilbert and Marilyn B. Gilbert, *Thinking Metric*, 2d ed. (New York: Wiley, 1978).

274

making a more useful—because it is more complete—knowledge map, we may want to amplify by indicating which examples we would use to convince our students of the advantages of metric measures of length over measures in the inch system.

2. *Preparatory tools.* Here we ask if students have the basic tools (skills, concepts, and language) before they can proceed. In Table 9-3 we have left this cell blank. But when we are teaching students to transform in metric units, we have to assume that they already know how to use the decimal system—or we indicate in our map that this preparatory skill must be developed in some students. If the students know nothing at all of the decimal system, we may have to create a separate knowledge map of this subject.

3. *Theory.* Here we wish to decide which concepts, or generalizations, are needed to help the student mediate the skill. A mediating "association," depending on the subject, may range from absurdly simple relationships to complex concepts such as a theory of the causes of civil war. In estimating metric quantities, we decide that some common body references will be sufficient to mediate the skill.

Deriving complex performance theories is the most demanding step in knowledge mapping. I discuss this in more detail in Part B of this chapter. It is beyond the scope of this book to detail these methods of deriving theories; the interested reader can find detailed discussions elsewhere.[3]

4. *Skill.* Here we choose body references to use as mediators for estimating distances, and we provide sufficient practice. For example, 1 centimeter equals the width of a fingernail.

5. *Application.* Finally, we ask if the students need further practice in estimating distances beyond those we are going to teach them in the course we are designing. Here, we might structure some problems so that they can practice estimating a variety of distances encountered in common experience. In more complex examples, we might have to structure the experiences that trainees will face after they leave the simulated practice of the classroom.

As we proceed through the progression for each accomplishment, we keep asking this question: "Will students still have this deficiency once they reach this stage of training?" This kind of question makes use of what I call the *principle of residual deficiency*, meaning that the materials in one part of the knowledge map may correct deficiencies in materials in another part. So, it might happen that we may not have to indicate an inductive, say, for each accomplishment. For example, the inductive for estimating distances may also serve as an inductive for estimating weights. And the same may be true for the other steps of the progression too.

THE USE OF KNOWLEDGE MAPS

Keep in mind that Table 9-3 is a very sketchy example of a knowledge map. We can amplify our descriptions of these cells in a variety of ways, depending on how we are going to use the knowledge map. Here are seven ways I have found that a knowledge map can be useful:

1. It can be developed into a course plan, detailing the needed coverage in training.

2. It can establish the base for standardizing training throughout an industry or a school, thereby reducing unnecessary replications of developmental efforts. The parts of a map can be coded, and training modules referenced in that code.

3. It can be used as an important tool for selecting job recruits. For example, "Can they do this?" or "Do they have knowledge of that?" Because the knowledge map has a performance orientation, the selection would not reflect cultural bias, and it would be free of any discrimination charge.

4. A knowledge map can be converted into a career-path and progress guide. Each map can tell both employee and supervisor, student and teacher, what knowledge is required for advancement.

5. It can be used as an internal placement tool. Each map serves as what I have called a "template" that can be "laid over" an employee's accomplishments to determine whether the requirements of a particular job are being met; and, if not, can indicate what training is needed to meet those requirements.

6. It can be readily converted to some form of diagnostic checkoff that will help managers identify performance problems and their causes.

7. A knowledge map is, by its nature, an excellent job description—far superior to those normally used by personnel offices. It can therefore be used in all the ways job descriptions are now used, such as for improving communication between supervisor and employee, or for determining wages.

I believe that the knowledge map is a central strategic tool in training and education. In fact, I have found it to be indispensable.

Occasionally, I have tried to shortcut the tedious process of training development by neglecting to outline a training design, just as I have occasionally tried to shortcut the process of writing a paper or a report by failing to outline it except very roughly in my head. Such failures always take their grim toll in time and in the quality of the product.

On the other hand, it is folly to imagine that the process of outlining a training system is foolproof and guarantees a quality training program any more than the planning of any piece of writing can guarantee that the written product will be worth the reading. A knowledge map is, of course, only a plan. As I have said, the plan must be implemented tactically well if it is to succeed.

B. TACTICS OF TRAINING DEVELOPMENT

THE POSSIBILITY OF EXEMPLARY TRAINING

To look at some of the powerful tactics available to develop great instruments of teaching, I shall use examples from very simple subject matter that every reader can readily understand. But I assure you that these methods apply to the most complex and technical subjects as well; indeed, they usually apply even better. Alas, any such discussion will automatically meet with a heated objection: "There are no best ways to teach all people."

It is a common argument among learning "experts" that different students learn differently. Some kids will take to one method of learning to read, say (the argument will go), but others will do better by other systems. And considerable research has been conducted to "prove" that children differ in the tactics most useful to them. By and large, the merit of this argument is extremely limited by certain logical considerations. I reject it, and here is why.

If I chose, on purpose, two inefficient methods for training rats in the skill I described in Figure 9-1, some of my animals would learn best with one method, some with the other, and many would not learn at all. Two things would determine which method favored a given animal: a combination of "luck" (accidental contingencies) and the individual characteristics of the rat (superiority in hearing, learning history, and so on). But if I used the really efficient method of operant conditioning to train these animals, *almost* all of them would learn—and they would learn far better than they would under either of the two inefficient methods. It is a simple principle: Some people survive better in one jungle, some better in another, and many don't survive at all.

Similarly with training people: Some students will survive one inefficient teaching method better than another; and other students will find another inefficient method more to their liking. But *almost* all of

them will do better when trained with efficient mathetical[3] tactics. The difference is like moving out of the jungle into the Waldorf-Astoria with a million-dollar expense account. The studies that show great individual differences in training-method preferences simply use materials that were not designed by efficient training-development tactics. Good training tactics can often get the poorest students to excel the best students taught by other methods.

Of course, some students do have unusual handicaps or exceptional learning skills. These students deserve special training, but even the design of that training should follow the same principles that I shall describe. Besides, good mathetical design does use several methods of providing for significant individual differences—but these methods are merely supports for the basic tactics.

And here is the real beauty of good tactics: They are not only widely applicable, but they also make economic sense. This good sense is worth reviewing.

THE LAW OF TRAINING

In Chapter 7, I said that by investing millions in training development, we can realize billions in return—not only in increased value, but in reduced costs as well. The *law of training* tells us why this is so:

> **The best tactics for reducing the true time and costs of training are identical to those required to improve its effectiveness.**

The most powerful training tactics in terms of what they can accomplish are also the most efficient. I showed in Chapter 7 how this law of training is broken every day when people—especially in the world of work—abandon scheduled training efforts. This *seems* to reduce the costs of training, but it really does nothing except to shift these costs so that they are hidden and unbudgeted. To see the equal importance of the law of training in the world of schools, we should review some of the economics of classroom training.

As we all know, training tactics reside almost wholly in the person of the teacher. Teachers have textbooks and workbooks to help them, of course; but these things are generally devoid of any serious training tactics. (Remember the exercises in futility?) Thus, it is a fundamental "theorem" of the cult of behavior that if we are to improve classroom instruction, we need more teachers who work harder and know more. According to this "theorem," it is inevitable that we shall greatly increase the costs of education as we improve it, because we most certainly have to pay for all that additional teacher behavior. As I have shown before, however, we can scarcely afford this.

It follows from the law of training, though, that the best things we

can do to improve classroom instruction will also require less instructional time and effort, and will therefore reduce our teacher and student costs. When we teach poorly and get bad results, we also waste a lot of time. It then seems quite obvious that the proper place for training development to begin is with a performance audit itself. Education is, after all, an economic venture, whatever else it may be.

But people who have not seen the power of systematic training development will still have difficulty in accepting the law of training. For this reason, I shall illustrate both its power and its principles by way of some examples of its application. In the next sections of this chapter, I give examples that match the three most basic stages of the progression—inductive, theory, and skill. These examples, of course, do not illustrate all of the principles of mathetics,[3] but they should be sufficient to show the great power of relatively simple tactics. I shall begin with skill training because a discussion of discriminations most readily illustrates my general approach.

TEACHING DISCRIMINATIONS

How well I remember the rigors of the third grade. Ms. Ball introduced us to the multiplication table, asking us to imagine it as a cabbage patch, and ourselves as rabbits who hopped along its paths. I must say, I found the nibbling there none too appetizing. But, the cabbage-patch analogy aside, Ms. Ball's first mistake in teaching multiplication was to follow the dictates of common sense. "We'll begin with something very easy," she said. "First we will hop along the one-times path." I do confess, the first row of cabbage wasn't too tough.

Unfortunately, the correct principles of teaching difficult discriminations—such things as learning the International Morse Code, beginning reading, reading music, reading electrical diagrams, and so on—often go against the grain of common sense. Nor do they always match what the "experts" tell us.

I can summarize the first principle in nontechnical language: Teach the hard things first. This clearly goes against Ms. Ball's logic. Most teachers do as she did—they commonly start the other way, by teaching the easy things first. So, they teach kids to multiply by 2's and 3's before they introduce the 8×7's. But I can demonstrate, both theoretically and empirically, that it is better to begin with combinations of 6, 7, and 8. (I shall shortly explain why 5's and 9's are easy.)

The reason for the rule of "hard things first" is fairly simple: The more things there are to learn, the harder it is to learn them because of "interference" or "competition" among the elements. If the only multiplication fact were 8×7, it would be extremely easy to master. But as the combinations grow, the competition for memory grows too. By

segregating the hard things and teaching them first, the effective competition that students must face is diminished. The easy things are not affected as much by the competition, so they can be taught later. Thus, the best sequence for teaching multiplication is first to teach the combinations of 6, 7, and 8 with 6, 7, and 8. Children who master these tough combinations are more than halfway home. The remaining combinations of 3 and 4 are taught next (avoiding 1, 2, 5, and 9); after that, the easy combinations of 1 and 2.

A second important principle of discrimination training can be used to teach the combinations of 9 and 5: Wherever possible, use *mediation* to teach discriminations. This is a much ignored technique. To mediate the combinations of 9, for example, the "rule of 9's" is applied. This rule first shows that the two-digit products of 9 always begin with a digit that is one (1) less than the multiplier. For example,

$$9 \times \underbrace{6} = \underline{5}4$$
$$9 \times \underbrace{8} = \underline{7}2$$
$$9 \times \underbrace{3} = \underline{2}7$$

Next, the rule shows that the two digits of a product of 9 always add to 9:

$$9 \times 6 = 54 \qquad 5 + 4 = 9$$
$$9 \times 3 = 27 \qquad 2 + 7 = 9$$

Thus, children learn to "take 1 from the multiplier of 9, and add a digit that sums the answer to 9." They love it.

The rule of 5's is also simple. Take "half" the multiplier and add a zero (0) if it is even; take the smaller half of the multiplier, and add 5 if it is odd:

$$5 \times 4 = 20 \qquad \text{(2 is half of 4)}$$
$$5 \times 7 = 35 \qquad \text{(3 is the "smaller half" of 7)}$$

To teach multiplication facts like these, still another principle is needed: Teach the easily confused things together (a variation on the first rule). Common sense says to teach the combinations of one number before introducing another. But this is wrong. Our rule says teach the 6's, 7's, and 8's all together because these answers are easily confused. If children are taught to discriminate them at the very beginning, the total confusion will be far less. (I shall explain why shortly.) Sooner or later, children must face the confusion—according to our rule, the sooner the better.

A fourth principle can be applied to complete the development of the multiplication lesson: Let the students know *immediately* whether

they succeeded or not. To do this, a deck of cards is used with the problems on the front and the answers on the back (flashcards). Children begin with a deck of the combinations of 6, 7, and 8. Each time they give an answer, they turn the card over to see whether they are right. A way to reinforce learning further is to have them put the quick right answers in one pile, the slow right answers in another, and the wrong answers in a third pile. Then they can ignore the quick rights, but shuffle the "wrongs" and the "slows" and repeat the exercise until "quick" mastery is complete. This way, progress is always clear to the children.

I shall summarize these four main principles of discrimination training:

1. Teach the hard things first.
2. Teach together those things that are easily confused.
3. Use mediation wherever possible.
4. Give the students immediate and continuous information about their progress.

It takes very little memory to realize that we did not learn the multiplication table this way. Nor do our children today.

Later I shall discuss the analysis of discrimination problems in some detail. But first I shall give one more example that will be useful in illustrating the discussion.

Teaching Children to Read

I shall describe a mathetically designed system for teaching 4- and 5-year-olds to read in which I applied similar principles. First, the program starts with three of the most difficult things to learn—the sound-letter combinations of ă, ĕ, and ĭ (plus some others). Since these are also easily confused, they are taught together. And to simplify the learning, the principle of mediation is used. Finally, the mechanics are arranged so that the children know immediately what progress they make. The first few exercises in this example follow.

Outline: Lesson 1*

1. *Exercise 1* (after some preliminaries)

The children are shown a set of seven pictures and asked to learn their names. The pictures and names are in Figure 9-3.

*Copyright © Praxis Corporation, New York, 1967.

Duck

Apple

Elephant

Flag

Indian

Table

Snake

FIGURE 9-3 Reading mediators, group 1. © Praxis Corporation, New York, 1967 (the "Praxis Reading Series").

2. *Exercise 2*

The children are shown the same pictures and asked to say their names, emphasizing the initial sounds:

d-d-d	duck
ă	apple
ĕ	elephant
f-f-f	flag
ĭ	indian
t-t-t	table
s-s-s	snake

After two or three trials, when the children are able to do this well, they are asked to say only the initial sounds as they are shown the pictures. For example, they say "ĕ" when they see the elephant picture.

3. *Exercise 3*

Next, the children listen to an initial sound and select the picture that matches it. (See Figure 9-4.) This exercise is done repeatedly until the children can quickly select the picture that matches the initial sound. *Latent Image*[4] gives immediate confirmation that the response was correct.

4. Exercises 4–7

The children continue to listen to sounds and to select the matching pictures. However, the pictures undergo a gradual change until they become letters (see Figure 9-5).

Several more of the exercises get the children first to select, then write, a combination of letters in answer to blended sounds. Within 2 to

Child hears (S^D)	Child does (R)

FIGURE 9-4 Exercise 3: picking an object to match the sound. © Praxis Corporation, New York, 1967 (the "Praxis Reading Series").

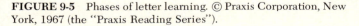

Child hears	Child selects from			
	Exercise 4	Exercise 5	Exercise 6	Exercise 7
d–d–d				
ĕ				
ĭ				
f–f–f				
t–t–t				
ă				
s				

FIGURE 9-5 Phases of letter learning. © Praxis Corporation, New York, 1967 (the "Praxis Reading Series").

4 hours, the children are able to write from dictation any combination of these seven sounds, meaningful or not. Typical dictation tests are

1. Sid is[5] fat.
2. Ted sits sad.
3. Set a fat fist, Sid.
4. If it is fat it sits.
5. Sift the fast test.

Naturally, the children can read the writing.

After mastering dictation in the Group I sounds, the children study the remainder of the alphabet in groups of five or six letters. Learning the second group of letters goes much faster than learning the first, because the children now have the "hang" of the game. In 8 to 20 hours,[6] they can take dictation on anything they hear, although they write in what I call the *Modified Teaching Alphabet* I have devised, which is similar to—but in some ways different from—the ITA (Initial Teaching Alphabet) widely used in English schools. The children write the long "ē" sound as E; the long "ā" as A; the "ah" sound with a script *a*. In succeeding lessons, they are taught to convert to the conventional alphabet. Blends are mediated by a method similar to that of the exercises I described earlier.

Some readers will see that *some* of these tactics have been used by one reading-teaching system or another; but never have all been used at once. Most reading systems are either completely eclectic—that is, they combine a variety of traditional techniques—or they tend to be "monotactical," meaning that they seize on one tactic and ignore the other problems of learning. But systematic engineering of human competence is neither eclectic, nor is it likely to get bound to a single tactical maneuver. Its strength is that it guides us to make the right decisions about all the best tactics.

Mastery Model Analysis

An early step in designing this reading course was to use something I call "mastery model analysis." This is a detailed analysis to determine the exact kind of performance that we really want to teach. If we are teaching Spanish, for example, we might decide to teach students to read the language, but not speak it; to speak it, but not write it; and so on. We are looking for the accomplishments we value.

Similarly, in teaching beginning reading we have a choice of performances. We could, for example, teach children to write what they hear

(or think), or to read what they see, or both. Systematic analysis helps us make these decisions intelligently.

A favorite device of engineering is the worksheet, and Table 9-4 shows one that I used to make a decision about which model of mastery performance was most desirable in learning to read. I shall briefly explain the steps in this worksheet, since it looks formidable but really isn't.

In column A of the mastery model table I have indicated two different kinds of performance[7] that I might teach children, stated in terms of stimulus and response (behavior) and accomplishments. Then I had to decide where the emphasis should be: Should children learn to write what they hear, or say what they see? This choice between "encoding" and "decoding" can be written in shorthand. ("Encoding" means putting something into a code—putting the familiar into an unfamiliar form. "Decoding" is the opposite.)

$$\text{Encoding:} \qquad S^D \longrightarrow R \qquad \text{(take dictation)}$$
$$\qquad\qquad\qquad \text{Sound } \breve{e} \quad \text{Write } e$$

$$\text{Decoding:} \qquad S^D \longrightarrow R \qquad \text{(read)}$$
$$\qquad\qquad\qquad \text{Letter } e \quad \text{Say } \breve{e}$$

Once I have identified the models of mastery I want to consider, I then move to the next question (column B in Table 9-4): Which model does my client most value, or which has the most utility? Since my client was a publisher, I simply asked him. He indicated that "reading what you see" was his primary objective; that "writing what you hear" would also have some value, but it wasn't necessary. I have indicated this judgment in column B.

Now why don't I stop the analysis here? The client has indicated that he wants to teach children to decode—so why not accept that as my mastery model? The answer is simple, if a little tricky: Very often, when you learn to encode, you incidentally learn to decode very well. (The exceptions are few, and the reasons for them too technical for this discussion.) But the opposite is often not true. If, for example, you

TABLE 9-4 A MASTERY MODEL TABLE FOR BEGINNING READING

A Mastery Models			B	C	D Teaching Economy		
S^D	*R*	*Accomplishment*	*Utility*	*Transfer*	S^D	*R*	S_r
1. Sounds of words or letters	Take dictation	Written words (encoding)	Secondary	Complete to decoding	Expensive	Simple	Simple
2. Words or letters	Read	Sounds (decoding)	Primary	Only partial to encoding	Simple	Simple	Expensive

learn to draw an electrical diagram (encoding), you will be able to read one (decoding). But if you learn to read one, your ability to draw one will be very limited. Similarly with reading: Children who learn to write what they hear will be able to read what they see. This is because they will read the words they are writing. When children hear "cat" and write it, they are also reading the word *cat*. The transfer of training from one form of performance to another is complete. But the opposite doesn't hold completely. When children learn to read words, they don't automatically learn to write them. There is also additional power in teaching children to write what they hear: It is a way of establishing fine control over their eye movements—as they write the letter *b*, their eyes will follow its contour.

In column C of the mastery model table I have indicated the transfer superiority of encoding. If I stopped my analysis here, I would have to elect encoding as my model of mastery. By teaching it, I also achieve mastery of decoding—two skills for the effort of gaining one. But I don't stop here, because engineering is an economic process.

In column D, I subject the teaching of both encoding and decoding to an economic analysis. I do this by asking three questions: How difficult and expensive is it to present stimuli (S^D), to get students to make responses (R), and to confirm (or reinforce) the correct responses (S_r)? I concluded upon analysis that it would be fairly expensive to program the sounds I want children to write—I would have to use audio equipment or have teachers make the sounds. But it would be fairly inexpensive and easy to get them to make the writing responses. (All they need is a piece of paper.) And it would be easy to confirm their correct responses, by the use of Latent Image. On the other hand, I concluded that if I taught decoding, it would be inexpensive to provide for both stimuli and responses, but that it would be quite difficult and expensive to arrange for a really satisfactory confirmation system that would tell children immediately if they were reading correctly. In summary, I decided that the benefits of teaching encoding were far superior to those of teaching decoding and that these benefits would offset any likely cost differences.[8]

Competition Analysis

Once we have selected a mastery model, serious problems still face us. Where do we begin—what letters do we first teach a student, and in what order? Fortunately, the animal (and human) learning laboratory provides some guidance.

Skinner has shown that animals learn simple tasks, such as pressing a lever, in one trial. It is not a slow and gradual process, as human

learning curves suggest. If we can accept Skinner's findings as fundamental—and there is no reason why we shouldn't—everything we
learn, we learn instantly. Then why does the learning of complex tasks
take so much time—say, the learning of a large set of discriminations, or
what I call a *multiple discrimination?*

The reason is simple: Although the students do learn each $S \rightarrow R$
pair in one trial, they can forget almost as rapidly as they learn. So,
acquisition (the net learning) takes place more gradually, because
forgetting also begins immediately. What, then, is the cause of forgetting? If we know its cause, perhaps we can do something to prevent it.

Many people believe that the cause of forgetting is simply the
passage of time. The $S \rightarrow R$ links we once made in our brains fade, just
as a photograph fades if we don't protect it with a fixative. But research
has shown that the mere passage of time does not account for forgetting.
Something more active and more specific happens: We call it
competition.

Discriminations are difficult to acquire because the elements to be
discriminated—the stimuli—are easily confused. We say that they
compete. And this confusion (competition) is the major barrier to acquisition and the chief cause of forgetting. For example, children (adults
too) forget which comes first in spelling, *i* or *e,* unless we give them
some help. Children confuse the mathematical symbols + and ÷, and
the symbols > and <, because of their similarities.

Now to digress for a moment. Learning how to use two similar door
keys dramatically illustrates the effect of competition. Suppose we have
two keys that look very much alike except that we must first insert one
of them into the lock with the teeth up and then turn it to the right; but
we must insert the other key with the teeth down and turn it to the left.
This means that what we must learn to do is to make two quite different
responses to two quite similar situations. We say that these situations—
two similar stimuli—compete for control of the responses.

To understand why this is so, consider that once we have learned to
handle one key, we tend to handle the second key in the same way
because it looks so much like the first key. We do this because of the
principle of generalization, which is so vital in helping us navigate in a
strange environment. Generalization helps us to identify all small
structures as "houses"; all seats as "chairs." It also allows us to respond
identically to different events because these events belong to the same
larger class. But discriminating between two keys is the opposite
process. So, because of generalization it probably becomes 10 times as
hard to learn to use two keys as it is to learn to use only one.

To summarize: When stimuli are similar, we tend to respond to them
in a similar way, even though the response that was correct for one
stimulus may be wrong for the other stimulus. All this says is that it is

easy to confuse things that are similar. And it is this competition that causes forgetting. How, then, do we combat this competition? If we can figure out how to decrease the effects of competition, we shall increase the ease of learning. There are two ways to do this,[9] and I shall describe both of them.

Competitive Grouping

Remember the principles of teaching multiplication facts? Common sense tells many teachers—erroneously—that if two things are easily confused, we should teach them separately, one at a time, so that they won't be confused: If the sounds of "a" and "e" are similar, we should teach them one at a time. But this only aggravates the problem. If children learn to write *a* when they hear the *sound* "ă," by generalization they will tend to write *a* when they hear the similar sound "ĕ." The stronger we make the first habit ("ă" = *a*), the stronger is the incorrect generalization ("ĕ" = *a*), and the more the incorrect habit will compete with the correct one ("ĕ" = *e*). From this, we can reason that we should teach students in such a way that we strengthen both habits equally as we go. So, we would do better to teach the students to respond to "a" and "e" at the same time.[10]

I call the practice of grouping similar and easily confused things together when we teach, *competitive grouping*. It is a simple but powerful technique that common sense prevents us from using as often as we should.

However, this conclusion leaves us with another problem. If we have a multiple discrimination (many similar stimuli), such as we have in beginning reading, how many of these stimuli do we group together at once? Surely not all of them, because the confusion would be so great that we couldn't attend to all the differences. So we must be selective.

The rule to follow is simple, but by no means exact: Group together as many of the most similar stimuli to which the student can attend at once.[11] How many stimuli we can group together at once will vary, of course, with the student and with the materials. My experience is that for most materials, groups of four to eight stimuli are usually practical. A little trial and error (starting with a large stimulus group) with actual students is the best way to find out.

You can see now why my beginning reading program begins with seven letters rather than one, and why the three most difficult sound-letter matches—ă, ĕ, and ĭ—appear together, as do the sounds of "d" and "t." These choices were not made arbitrarily. And a group of seven, rather than four or five, is used because trials showed that the students could handle this many. During the experimental stage, significant errors began to occur with a group of eight.

There is a problem in getting people to see the advantages of competitive grouping. If we start with single stimuli, and the easy ones first, students begin by showing great success. This is one reason such an approach is popular with teachers. But competition builds up, and sooner or later students must face the difficulties. Remember, the sooner, the better. Because we begin with the more difficult groups, learning gets easier rather than harder as the students proceed. The total, net difficulty will then be much less.

Mediation

A powerful method for overcoming competition, though one not always available to us, is mediation.[12] We are looking for something, however arbitrary, that will help associate a stimulus and response that are not usually associated with each other. Or, we mediate an $S^D \rightarrow R$ connection by finding another response in the students' repertory that is already well conditioned to the stimulus and forms an easy association. For example, suppose that we wish to teach the color code for electrical resistors. (Electrical resistors are tiny cylinders put in an electric circuit to resist current; color bands are used to indicate the number of ohms of resistance. Open the back of a portable radio and you will see them.) In this code, colors stand for numbers. For example, *brown* means "1," *green* means "5," and so on.

If you study the stimulus *brown*, you will realize that there are many strong responses to it already in our repertories, such as "eyes" and "hair," but not "1." Here, existing habits compete with the response "1." To mediate the connection, we look for a strong response to *brown* that is also a strong stimulus for "1"; and we discover that a penny is brown and also represents "1¢."

$$S \longrightarrow r$$
Brown Penny
$$s \longrightarrow R$$
Penny 1

Thus, "penny" is a mediator:

$$S \longrightarrow r \cdot s \longrightarrow R$$
Brown Penny 1

Figure 9-6 is one of 10 exercises that you can use to teach the color code, and it will show you how powerful a device mediation can be for overcoming competition. Some people can learn the code from this exercise[13] in one trial; some require two or three readings.

2. Each of the FIRST THREE COLOR BANDS can have one of 10 colors. Read through this list twice. Learn the **NUMBER** for which each **COLOR** stands

- a **FIVE** dollar bill is **GREEN**
- **ONE BROWN** penny
- a **WHITE** cat has **NINE** lives
- **SEVEN PURPLE** seas
- a **BLUE** tail fly has **SIX** legs

- **ZERO; BLACK** nothingness
- a **RED** heart has **TWO** parts
- **THREE ORANGES**
- a **FOUR** legged **YELLOW** dog
- an **EIGHTY**-year-old man has **GRAY** hair

FIGURE 9-6   Mediation of the color code.

I applied the same principle in my beginning reading program.[14] The sound "ĕ" has some strength for "elephant," and the elephant's picture can be gradually shaped to look like an *e*.

This mediation technique for teaching a large number of difficult discriminations is not applied often enough. However, I have used it successfully to teach telephone operators the positions of numbers on the pushbutton telephone keyboard so they can dial rapidly; to teach Morse code, electrical wiring diagram symbols, music notation, and a variety of other subjects, such as prefixes in the metric system.

I have not, of course, discussed all the principles relevant to discrimination training, but these few illustrations should accomplish my purpose: To show the great untapped potential these principles have for improving training performance.

GENERALIZATION TRAINING

Teaching children to read is an example of teaching an arbitrary code—I say "arbitrary" because other symbols could be substituted for them. And I used mediators to teach students how to discriminate among these symbols, which would otherwise be difficult to learn and remember. But a much larger class of mediators is a theory based on logical distinctions. When a theory underlies the subject we want to teach, we need to find the logic and language we can best use to mediate the performance.

Performance (Domain) Theories as Mediators

Theory, used as mediation, is the most powerful, most widely applicable, and most poorly applied tactic in all of training and education. I shall examine it more closely. But, first, let me describe what I mean by a "performance" or "domain" theory. I define a performance theory as a

repertory of selective looking behavior that mediates efficient performance. By "selective looking," I mean detecting the common thread, or pattern, that runs through a mass of seemingly unrelated detail. This imaginary story will help you see what I mean.

Mr. Duz is a skilled tradesman of known competence. For years he has worked in a shop that makes wet-cell batteries (like the ones in your car). He can assemble a battery more quickly and more accurately than anyone else. He is proud of his achievement, because he has gone far for someone without an education. To test his prowess, we arrange a table full of junk—odds and ends of all kinds. Among the jumble are all the things one needs to build a wet-cell battery. We ask Duz to make us a battery, and he accomplishes this in exemplary time.

Now suppose we observe Mr. Seez, a theoretical physicist who has never seen a real battery, although he knows all about direct current and the theory of electrical generation. And we test his skills at battery building at the same table. He eventually makes us one that works, though he is slow and the product is sloppy. In matters of this sort, Duz's practical training is clearly superior to Seez's theoretical education.

Now we change the test and provide another table that has among its jumble all one needs to make a dry-cell battery—the kind that goes into a flashlight. Neither Duz nor Seez has ever seen a dry-cell battery. Duz fails the test completely; after 2 days he has failed even to come close to constructing a working battery. But Seez succeeds; he makes a dry-cell battery that works, and it only takes him an hour or so.

Why does Mr. Seez succeed where Mr. Duz fails? Because he has a repertory of language that he uses to guide him in looking selectively through the jumble. The language, as he talks to himself, acts as stimuli to mediate successful searching responses. He says, for example, "I need a substance—preferably a metal—that will freely give off electrons and act as an anode. Here is a strip of zinc; that should do perfectly. Now I need a cathode; here is a strip of silver." This language mediates Mr. Seez's performance in much the same way that "penny" mediates the connection between *brown* and *1* in the resistor color code—except that the language has a logical, not an arbitrary, relationship to the stimuli and responses of a master. Mr. Seez's theory is simply a repertory of language that mediates successful performance. It is because most human skills have a logical structure that I say that mediating theories are the most powerful tactic we can use to teach people to perform.

This should come as no surprise to anyone. But it is essential that we understand this tactic, because it is usually employed so poorly. Indeed, as I have said, many very "practical" training institutions bend

over backwards to avoid teaching theory. Why? There is a good reason. Many teachers and subject-matter experts tend either to teach too much theory, or to indulge in theories that are irrelevant to the performance they should mediate.

How, then, do we find out just what theory, and how much, we should teach? This is an important question to ask, because the proper theory not only can speed up learning greatly, but it can also permit generalization to new situations and protect against forgetting. And it acts as a good motivational aid, because the subjects that we understand are simply more interesting to us.

The person who designs a packaging machine, for example, employs a theory. Physical mechanics leads to a consideration of such things as the mass of the roll of paper, the tensile strength of the paper, and the stress put on it; then, from the use of calculus, the designer is able to calculate the optimal arrangement of rollers. This physical mechanics is one theory of the paper-thread mechanism. If I were to ask the designer to teach the packaging-machine operators the theory of the paper system, no doubt the designer's first step would be to show the operators the relationships among mass, momentum, and friction. Now, that is too much theory; besides, it is largely irrelevant. The designer would be teaching operators a theory of a whole *realm* of things, and threading paper is only a small part of this realm. What we really want operators to know is only the simpler theory that pertains to the limited *domain* of the performance required.

For example, operators should learn the principle of what creates just the right amount of tension on the wrapping paper: They should first run the paper through three rollers to form a "triangle"; then across the top of several rollers to prevent sagging; and, finally, through the last three rollers to form another triangle. This "triangulate–carry–triangulate" sequence is a small but powerful theory that will mediate the performance of threading a great variety of packaging machines with many different arrays of rollers. (A 15-minute lesson teaching this theory solved a major training problem in a company that uses packaging machines.)

But where do you find such domain theories? It would be difficult to go to a library and find theories precisely tailored to performance— such as managing a loan office, designing a dress, troubleshooting a cash register, being President of the United States, leading a boy-scout troup, or making grants to leukemia researchers—or "triangulate–carry–triangulate." There are plenty of descriptions of realm theories, and also of *set* theories (theories of some small part of the performance, or of some narrow application). But you will seldom find theories precisely suitable to a given performance domain.

The reader must go elsewhere for the techniques I use to derive

such performance domain theories.[15] Suffice it to say that they can be derived—and they *must* be if we are to tap the great potential for the improvement of training in both the world of work and the world of schools.

Certainly, in the world of schools the domain theories are inadequate. This is largely because we have seldom decided what accomplishments we want to teach people to make. Consider an example from a history course, in which many things about civil wars and uprisings are taught. Children learn facts (when was the surrender at Appomatox?); they learn very general, often vague, *realm* theories (people go to war because they are naturally aggressive); and they learn narrow *set* theories (slavery was a primary cause of the American Civil War). But they learn few, if any, powerful domain theories.

In the previous chapter I described what was really a mastery model for history instruction that would make students "predictors." We can continue this example. Suppose we decide that one useful accomplishment in our history courses would be for children to be able to predict when a civil uprising would occur. We would want them to know how to selectively look through a mass of detail to make such a prediction when there was civil unrest.

"There are picketing, strikes, and other signs of great unrest in Chad. Here are the facts. Will there be a civil uprising?"

To arrive at a domain theory for this performance, we would have to make some abstractions. We could ask, "What have been the prevailing conditions before all civil wars in the past?"

And when I do ask this question of students, the most common answer is that the rebels must be poor, suppressed people. When I ask it of professors, I often get the same answer.

But the answer that rebels must be suppressed people seems incorrect. In the American Civil War, for example, the rebels were not especially suppressed. Suppressed people did exist in the South—they were slaves—but these were not the ones who rebelled. Examination of other civil uprisings also shows that, although poverty and suppression often accompany an uprising, they are by no means a necessary condition.

Now, I am not a competent historian, so my domain theory may not be the best. But it is a try. Having examined a sample of eight civil wars, I have reached the conclusion that three conditions are probably sufficient for producing a civil uprising. And if I am correct, these would be the facts that you would selectively look for among the great jumble of data attending any instance of civil unrest:

1. There must be two powers in conflict, one of which is dependent for its livelihood on a single good or service

(e.g., cotton in the American South; whiskey in the Whiskey Rebellion).

2. The other power should have prime control over the policy mechanisms (the throne, the congress, the army, and so on).

3. Then there must be an incident ("Fort Sumter has been fired upon!").

A student armed with this theory—assuming that it is correct—will be in a much better position to predict the course of events. And if this theory is not correct, why then didn't my professors give me one that was—instead of a mass of data to memorize?

As I have said, the biggest job ahead of us, if we are to develop effective teaching tactics, is to derive relevant domain theories. But, of course, domain theories, no matter how well developed and presented, are not always completely sufficient to mediate skills in which the discriminations have a logical basis. If the number of stimuli to be discriminated is great, or if high rates of performance are required, we may have to combine the tactics of domain theories with the tactics of competitive grouping and arbitrary mediation. To decide if teaching a domain theory is a sufficient tactic, all we need to do is ask ourselves this: After students have mastered the theory and can perform in "schematic" situations, will they still need further training to ensure exemplary performance in real situations? Often the answer will be "yes," so that we will have to develop further tactics for teaching skills.

Often, as I discussed in Chapter 6, there is an alternative to skill training called guidance. For example, if I teach operators all the relevant domain theory of the packaging machine, they still may not be reliable troubleshooters when the machine breaks down—either because they won't remember all the theory, or because the variety of real-life machine problems may be so great that the theory we teach simply isn't adequate to mediate performance in every circumstance. We can then combine the domain theory we teach with a troubleshooting guide, and thus achieve exemplary performance.

INDUCTIVE TACTICS AND TRAINING MEDIA

In the discussion of knowledge maps, I described one of the main training functions as "inductive." Because this function has a different purpose than skills and theory, it deserves a separate tactical treatment.

When we analyze knowledge deficiencies, we often find that students have both sufficient theory and skill to perform; still, they don't do their best because their inductive knowledge is defective. For example,

suppose that your job requires you to send many routine telegrams, and you have devised a code to save you money. You use a term such as URLET to mean "in reply to y*our let*ter"; or ORTEL: about *our tel*egram"; and so on. This isn't a difficult code to learn, and you would expect your secretary to have no problem translating your dictated message into the money-saving shorthand. But weeks after you have introduced the code, you find that no one is using it. A little analysis may well show that the reason is not that secretaries don't know the code, but that they don't know *why* it is so important to use it. Such translations may seem, then, just another bit of the busywork that is so common in the world of work. An inductive lesson, in which secretaries actually calculate the annual costs of telegrams sent in long and short forms, may be a tactic sufficient to achieve exemplary performance.

Most inductive tactics are simple, and require merely telling someone what the task is all about and what the consequences of good and poor performance are. But sometimes the burden of the inductive is great, and unusual efforts may be required to change the students' point of view, or to get them to take seriously what may seem trivial to them. We may then find more dramatic media more useful than a simple written text, or an introductory lecture. Inductive training can create different demands when there is a problem in getting a student to do one of three things:

1. Change a well-established and even cherished point of view
2. Take something seriously that doesn't seem important
3. Become interested in a subject that would normally be boring

To meet these special training demands, we can use several techniques. For example, case studies, actively involving the students and leading them to face-to-face confrontation with the inadequacies of their points of view, are an exceptional medium for changing peoples' minds. Such simulated exercises are also useful to dramatize the importance of those things that seem trivial to the students.

And film, properly used, can be a great medium for dramatizing a subject and arousing interest that normally wouldn't be there. I once saw a film on the beauty of Sanscrit and its importance in scholarly pursuit. Although the film taught me no Sanscrit skills at all, it had me hungering to learn Sanscrit for weeks afterwards.

The selection of media for inductives—or any other kind of instruction, for that matter—is not difficult once you have prepared a good knowledge map and know what you want your students to accomplish.

What *is* difficult is overcoming the "media bias," meaning that you get so attracted to certain media that you want to use them for all kinds of teaching. Unfortunately, a large number of training establishments do this: try to adapt training tactics to favored media when what they really should be doing is directly opposite.

ALTERNATIVES TO TRAINING TACTICS

Just because we have a knowledge deficiency should not automatically mean that training is the best solution. As we have seen, training is costly, both to the teacher and the student, and should be avoided if there are more efficient alternatives. And frequently there are. Guidance is one alternative I have discussed already.

But there is some resistance to guidance. It is a fundamental axiom of the cult of behavior that people aren't competent to perform a job unless they carry complete knowledge of it around in their heads. Most of us would be shaken if our physician gave us a diagnosis after openly searching through medical textbooks in our presence. We have much more confidence in a mechanic who gives us a diagnosis on the spot rather than searching a manual for help. But this symptom of behavior cultism costs us billions of dollars and much unnecessary incompetence each year. Before we ever consider discrimination training, we should first see how much of it we can dispense with by reordering the information made available to one doing a job. As I said in Chapter 6, the substitution of well-designed guides for training and human memory is probably the single tactic of the greatest potential for overcoming a knowledge deficiency in the world of work.

But another alternative to training also has great potential for improving performance: improving the instruments we use to help us perform.

For example, consider what has happened to the typewriter—a tool purposely designed to create inefficiency. How did it get that way? In the early days of the typewriter, the keys jammed very easily if a typist typed too fast. The present keyboard is a result of an early design meant *to slow the typist down* and prevent this jamming. (The Dvorjak keyboard, which is available but rarely used, is designed for efficiency, and both greatly reduces training time and increases speed among well-trained typists.) At least part of the deficiencies in typing performance, then, can be attributed to the intentional inefficiency of the instrument.[16]

Many of the tools and materials in our environment could be redesigned so that they would be simpler to learn and easier to use. Unfortunately for the hopes of realizing this potential, many of the opportunities for redesign are created during a training analysis. And because the responsibilities of training people are so tightly proscribed,

having too much to do with trainer behavior rather than student performance, the opportunities are seldom even considered, let alone seized.

WHY THE DEARTH OF GOOD TACTICS

The systematic application of the laboratory principles of learning to instructional design began with F. S. Keller's development of a Morse code course in World War II, although Keller essentially applied only one principle: that of immediate reinforcement or confirmation of correct responses. In 1957, Skinner published a paper[17] that launched a great interest in what has come to be known as programmed instruction. Again, Skinner was applying one important training tactic: that of immediate reinforcement for a correct response.

But immediate reinforcement—quick confirmation of correct responses—is only one of many tactics that apply to good teaching. The first account of the systematic use of all the basic tactics appeared in 1962, in my publications on mathetics.[3] Since then, a number of mathetically designed lessons and courses have been put to use, in addition to those shown in the earlier examples of this chapter.[18] For just three examples in industry, a major telephone utility now uses one mathetical course to teach its new TSPS (computerized) telephone operators and another to teach its repair clerks. A food packager teaches its packaging-machine mechanics in this way. These courses illustrate the power and validity of the law of training; and even though the existing examples could be improved by more rigorous application of the principles of mathetics, they have "proved" the law very well. In every case, not only does superior performance result from the training, but each course also requires less time, effort, and money than the course it replaced.

Why, then, if these principles are so powerful, aren't they more widely used? Here are some of my opinions.

The Bandwagon Barrier

Following publication of Skinner's now famous paper "The Science of Learning and the Art of Teaching," there was a sudden and widespread interest in teaching machines and programmed instruction. The idea of "reinforced learning," while by no means new, seemed to promise so much, and seemed so simple to do. Apparently, only three things were required to revolutionize instruction in any subject. First, you must break down the subject into "small pieces" (small steps). Next, you must demand that the student make a response of some kind—usually by writing a word or two. Finally, you must arrange for the student to see immediately whether the answer is right or not. Indeed, these steps

seemed so simple that anyone could become a "programmed instruction expert." And that is what happened.

Figure 9-7 has an all too typical example of a few frames of programmed instruction. (I have not identified the author, because by now it would only be embarrassing.) The subject is memorization of "the color code for electrical resistors." (The original lesson was designed to fit a teaching machine so that only one frame showed at a time.) Figure 9-7 shows how the lesson went, frame after frame for some 400 frames. Just for fun, I put a student through this grinding task and tested her memory on the second day. She recalled six of the 10 colors correctly. Poor results indeed for 3 hours of labor.

This lesson also illustrates one of the problems of selling an efficient change in performance versus the problems of selling a book. In the early days of the programmed-instruction revolution, I was offered $1000 to develop a color-code lesson to help advertise a manufacturer's teaching machine. About 2 weeks later, the manufacturer called me and asked how many frames I had. When I said "10," he angrily cancelled the contract, saying that he had expected at least 100 frames. Subse-

---

1. The color brown on a resistor stands for *one.* You would indicate the number "one" by using the color ____.

        WRITE IN ANSWER

    ANSWER TO #1: brown

2. A brown stripe on a resistor stands for the number ____.

        WRITE IN ANSWER

    ANSWER TO #2: one

3. The color red stands for *two,* and one is indicated by the color ____.

    ANSWER TO #3: brown

4. Brown stands for the number ____, and two is indicated by the color ____.

    ANSWER TO #4: one, red

5. On a resistor, the color red stands for the number ____, and brown stands for the number ____.

FIGURE 9-7 An all too typical example of programmed instruction.

quently, he contracted for—and used—the program shown in Figure 9-7. He didn't understand the law of training.

Figure 9-6 shows one of the 10 frames I produced by mathetical design. But if you study that frame for 10 minutes, you will know the color code forever.

Superficially, of course, as I have mentioned earlier, the mathetical lesson looks very much like the poor sample. Worse still, many mathetical lessons look no different from an ordinary workbook, or even ordinary textbooks. And some bear no resemblance to any of these things. Even though the world has accepted the dictum that you can't judge a book by its cover, it still judges the book by the appearance of its pages. Paper-and-pencil lessons—such a great medium for high-quality training tactics—appear much the same whether they are well designed to do the job or not. This means that incompetent course developers can create exercises that *seem* quite competent even though these people haven't the faintest concept of powerful training tactics.

Of course, this is precisely what happened to the programmed-instruction movement, and the problem persists. So much muck has been produced in the shape of frames and answer confirmations that many potential consumers not only have become cynical of self-instruction, but some of them have become downright hostile toward it. The cynicism and hostility are quite understandable. I recall a businessman who sat through a discussion at a convention on the comparative merits of two "schools" of instructional programming. One school adhered to the frame-by-frame view fostered by Skinner (called "linear programming"); the other, to a book of jumbled pages (called "branching"). And there were dissidents, of course, who offered arguments for "mixed strategies."

Just before leaving in disgust, my friend whispered sourly, "They aren't talking about improving human performance—they're talking about book formats. Since there are thousands of possible formats, they should soon have thousands of 'schools' of programming."

Such cynicism is understandable and justifiable. But what is the solution? How do we overcome this particular barrier to an interest in good training tactics?

I think that there is only one way: We need to set standards of measurement for the success of training designs. And these standards should be based on measurements that directly reflect the law of training—measurements that describe both the improvement in accomplishments as well as the reduction in behavior—in *true* training time and costs.

Presently, many "programmers"—and, as a result of their influence, other trainers and teachers—employ "behavioral objectives" as a standard of success. A behavioral objective, a recent bandwagon, is a

description of the behavior expected from a student who has successfully negotiated a course. But there is a self-contradiction in the notion
of behavioral objectives. In performance, behavior is the means and not
the objective; nor should it be the true objective of the trainers. We can
set behavioral objectives endlessly, but they can do nothing for us
unless we have identified their relevant accomplishments.

The One-Way-to-Do-It Fallacy

A lasting barrier to good training tactics results from the overgeneralization that there is one way to do everything. This usually occurs when
people see all training problems as representing one aspect of the
knowledge progression or as solvable by a favorite medium. Thus, a
teacher or training director may approach all learning problems as skill
deficiencies; another may see them all as theory problems; and another
may believe that the film strip is the superior method of teaching
practically anything.

Certainly, all three of these kinds of training commonly take place;
but they seldom occur in the sequence or with the emphasis required
for efficient learning. Indeed, I have been able to classify almost every
training venture I have ever observed as favoring one of these modali-
ties over the other two. "Practical" agencies such as the Army and the
telephone company tend to be "skill-bound": "Cut out all that theory
nonsense and let's get down to learning what you've got to do." By a
greater respect for the *right* kind of theory training, these agencies
could cut their training time in half, and greatly increase its effectiveness. However, these agencies got that way in a counter-reaction to
"theory-bound" instructors who felt no constraints in leading students
down limitless abstract paths that had little or nothing to do with the
real world. University instructors are, of course, the prime examples of
the "theory-bound," and it is often possible to complete one of their
courses successfully without having the faintest idea which skills this
course is relevant to.

Insurance companies (and other sales agencies) are, in the main,
excellent examples of "inductive-bound" training—giving their sales
personnel fantastic views of the glory of the product, and then abandoning them before they have developed more than a glimmer of the
concepts and skills relevant to selling insurance. This is probably why
the insurance industry is largely in the business of managing marginal
performers, where the PIPs are very large. (Indeed, sales PIPs of 10 or
more are not uncommon.)

And then there are agencies that are simply "media-bound," which
tie up large sums in the purchase of fancy training media (mostly
equipment to deliver pictures), without any notice of the three major

functions of teaching. These agencies, incidentally, are often "inductive-bound," because their media are often more suitable for this function than for conveying theory and skill.

The experience of a military agency nicely illustrates the difficulties of favoring a particular training function. After World War II, the military developed its missile capability faster than it developed its manpower capability. Being "practical" in its orientation, one military agency pushed its enlistees through crash courses designed to teach them how to maintain and service a missile that I shall call the Venus. No nonsense about theory: "When you see this red knob, turn it to the right—*never* to the left—until the hinge pinge is loosened. Now repeat after me. . . ."

This seemed to work fine until the soldiers were actually assigned to real missiles and discovered that the manufacturers had changed them. The red knob no longer existed, nor the hinge pinge; they had been replaced by another set of devices that, in principle, performed the same functions. But the changes left the trainees at a loss. So this military agency revised its training strategy to teach the theoretical foundations of the missile system. A thoroughly sophisticated syllabus was drawn up, and the students were subjected to every bit of knowledge from the "Wheatstone bridge" (which the missile lacked) to the life of André Marie Ampère. These students were released to the field with the great confidence of their instructors—and, sure enough, they could perform when confronted with missile revisions. There was only one flaw in the new strategy: By the time the training was complete, the students' term of service was almost up.

As media grow in sophistication, there is an increasing growth of fans for one or another of them. But the selection of an instructional medium before an analysis of the best tactics required of a particular training problem creates just one more Procrustean bed for education to lie in. Although the audiovisual "movement" in education and training has supplied some excellent devices, it has done perhaps as much harm as good to the course of instructional tactics. An example will serve to illustrate the prejudices that must be overcome to introduce tactical innovations in training.

Probably the industry that is most sophisticated about instructional design is the telephone business. In the early days of the new TSPS (computerized) telephone operator system, new operators were taught to use their computer consoles almost exclusively by the use of audio tapes. A complex simulator was connected to the console, and the operator was given instructions on the tapes as well as simulated telephone calls. For various reasons, the telephone company found its training inadequate and sought the services of a training consultant to redesign the operator course.

Now imagine the surprise of a committee of telephone managers when they discovered that the new training would be *mostly* delivered through the medium of books. Some managers who heard about the new program became understandably upset even before they saw the new books. They knew, for example, that many people who apply for operator jobs have reading limitations. Moreover, they could "reasonably" ask the question, "How can you learn to be an operator by reading a book!?"

The committee of course accepted the new training program, but only after the consultant required its members to actually take some of the training exercises. "I am going to prove to you that these exercises are not really books—they only look like books," the consultant explained.

The experiment required that these managers actually work a sample page of the operator training "book." The pages of this book are treated with Latent Image, the "invisible ink" I mentioned earlier; and the operators use a Latent Image pen to "depress" the right "keys" when they "hear" (read) the customer's request. If they "press" the correct "key," it "lights up" just as on the real console, and the operators get immediate feedback to reinforce the learning. Pages such as those do not really constitute a book as we usually think of it, yet they are actual simulations of the job. So, when the managers worked these exercises, they could see immediately that no one would be learning to be an operator just by "reading a book."

The TSPS training course improved operator performance, and also reduced training costs—both improvements to the advantage of telephone customers. Simulation and immediate reinforcement were the only obvious tactics. But several other instructional tactics were used, such as "competitive grouping" and "mediation" (which I have described). None of these other tactics demanded any special kind of medium, but all were perfectly consistent with the use of paper-and-pencil exercises.

How do we overcome the prejudices that confuse media with training tactics? I am not sure if it can be done except by the considerable education of course developers and training managers. One device that might help is to require a description of the tactics used in the lesson and their relationship to the media used. Such a description might look like Table 9-5.

Scholastic Negativism as a Barrier

The beginning reading program I described earlier has never been published simply because I can't find a publisher. The original publisher who contracted for its development was the late Lee Brown, a brilliant and unusual man. Lee Brown not only had the program tested,

TABLE 9-5   BEGINNING READING TACTICS AND MEDIA

Tactic	*Medium*
1. Immediate confirmation	1. Paper and pencil with Latent Image
2. Mediation of sound-letter combinations	2. (a) Cards to be held up by a teacher to introduce mediation (b) Paper-and-pencil exercises, with mediation pictures
3. Competitive grouping, etc.	3. Paper-and-pencil exercises, etc.

but he also got reviews from several "experts" in learning theory and beginning reading instruction. All of his experts flatly stated that the program would not and could not work, and marshalled a number of "scholarly" reasons for this. After Lee's untimely death, other publishers received similar opinions, but conducted no empirical tests. Each of these "experts," of course, made a living by teaching and advising others about how to teach reading. Naturally, this reading system hit each expert where it hurts most. And beginning reading is not the only example of such scholasticism. Scholars of learning have not been very helpful to the development of instructional tactics. Millions of words have been printed, and still our teachers have no proper guidance in the teaching of the multiplication facts, as just one example.

THE PERSONAL SIDE OF TRAINING INEFFICIENCY

These barriers to sensible training tactics are not only economical in their consequences, but every day the hopes of children and adults are first thwarted, then extinguished, because people simply haven't learned to teach them. To illustrate these consequences, I shall end this chapter with a personal story of a lovely little girl who had grown to regard herself as a naturally inferior person.

Eve is 8, small for her age, and she can't catch a ball. When a boy tosses her the ball, she lunges at it with a wooden maladroitness, in "that way girls have." Of 10 easy tosses, she drops eight. But Eve is excited by the two she does catch, because she wants to join the Little League baseball team, just like her 10-year-old brother who is now holding a backyard party for the Mendham Maulers, celebrating the opening of the season.

Eve's Dad looks on sadly as she pursues her hopeless ambition. The boys are polite, but clearly impatient, so Dad takes the little girl to the other side of the house for some private practice.

Using a tennis ball, Dad coaches Eve to follow it with her eyes as he tosses it up in the air and lets it drop. He instructs her to holler "Now" just before the ball hits the ground. When she has learned to do this well, he explains how she must never watch her hands or feet, but only the ball; and if she never takes her eyes off the ball, she is almost sure to catch it. Now Dad tosses her the ball, and she catches it. Next, he tosses it about 6 feet over her head, and she catches it. During the practice, every time Eve misses they analyze what it was she had her eyes on other than the ball. After 30 minutes, Eve can make a "basket" catch, right at her waist, of balls that Dad has thrown nearly out of sight.

Then Dad stages a contest with Eve and the boys, and Eve catches all 10 sky-high tosses. One of the boys catches nine, but the rest range from four to eight catches. Naturally, Eve is declared the winner and gets the first prize: a chance to make the hamburger patties. (Teachers have to be paid, too.)

This story, like most of the many other stories in this book, is a true one, embellished only in the nonessential details. And it neatly illustrates incredibly simple, but often forgotten, points about human competence—points that must be clearly understood if we are ever to succeed at improving our educational system.

First, it illustrates the great potential for competence that lies in all of us—especially in us stumblebums. And in doing so, it emphasizes the special attitude of performance engineering, which views incompetence as a challenge and not something to leave to chance or to catalog with a number. You see, we could have administered a baseball aptitude test to Eve, and filed her score in a permanent record as we advised her to pursue other ambitions. Through careful engineering, those who would otherwise be abysmal failures can become exemplary performers.

Eve's story also illustrates the great ease and simplicity with which exemplars perform. Exemplars don't need to "know more" and "work harder" than others. To the contrary: It is the quality of what they know and how they work that leads to distinguished performance. Eve did not need to learn a lot of complex behavior, or to work even harder to get success—she needed only to learn to use the already well-developed skill of keeping her eye on a moving object.

Besides, Eve's success emphasizes a point of view that is very satisfying to anyone who would engage in engineering competent performance—especially satisfying to those who know that experts don't necessarily make good teachers: The performance engineer need not be a competent performer. Eve's Dad, I forgot to tell you, is terrible at catching balls himself. His mind wanders, and he has developed a bad habit of worrying about his feet. And, besides, he doesn't even like to catch balls. But he does like to engineer performance, and the

performance of engineers is different from the performance they are trying to engineer. You see, Dad is more competent than major league outfielders in teaching little girls to catch balls.

Finally, Eve's success makes an even larger point. We can leave education to natural social forces, and study it at length—it makes a great subject for sociology and social psychology. As we study this complex of events, every year we shall become even more impressed with what little we know about it and how awesome a subject it is.

Or, in the manner of the engineer, we can see education as fundamentally a simple challenge that has been made complex only by the way we have let our viewpoints become superstitious, diffident, and disoriented. Education is, after all, not a natural phenomenon, but merely one kind of attempt by people to engineer human competence.

We can approach it with the confidence and purposefulness of the performance engineer. Or we can let it drift as a "natural subject." Every Eve in this world has a large stake in which direction we shall go.

NOTES

1. *Skill* comes from an Anglo-Saxon word that means to "discern" or "discriminate."

2. For a writing course that follows the progression, see Marilyn B. Gilbert, *Clear Writing* (New York: Wiley, 1971).

3. See T. F. Gilbert, "Mathetics: The Technology of Education," *Journal of Mathetics*, Vol. 1, No. 1, 1962. Also, in Vol. 1, No. 2, 1962, "Techniques of Exercise Design." *Mathetics* comes from the Greek word *mathein*, meaning "to learn." *Mathetic* is the singular adjective form ("having to do with learning"), whereas *mathematics* is the plural form ("having to do with learnings," i.e., the disciplines). It is not a coined word, and it appears in some unabridged dictionaries. Also see T. F. Gilbert and M. B. Gilbert, *Knowledge Mapping*, Praxis Technical Reports No. 2, 1977.

4. Latent Image is a process using invisible writing which is owned by the A. B. Dick Company. When a special pen or brush is rubbed across paper that is treated with the special ink, the printed image becomes visible.

5. Several very common words are also taught by rote, such as *the, you, is,* and *and.*

6. Based on three trials, five children in each group, ages 4 and 5. Half were from a New York "ghetto," the other half from middle-class homes.

7. I actually studied four models. I have simplified the example for illustration.

8. The advent of really excellent computer trainers such as PLATO will change these economic judgments.

9. Actually, there are other ways. Hypnosis and certain drugs, for example, can have the effect of reducing competition. Here I consider only those means that we can use without tampering with the learner.

10. Many laboratory experiments have supported this conclusion.

11. "At once" is a little vague. Empirically, this means to group together as many as the student can remember to differentiate in one simple trial.

12. Mnemonics is just one form of mediation.

13. Reprinted from the *Journal of Mathetics*, Vol. 1, No. 1, 1962.

14. Several reading systems do use sets of mediators, but they are very crude.

15. See, for example, the articles cited in note 3 above.

16. Smith-Corona now sells the Dvorjak keyboard.

17. B. F. Skinner, "The Science of Learning and the Art of Teaching," *Science,* 1957.

18. For excellent examples, see Marilyn B. Gilbert, *Clear Writing*. See also Marilyn B. Gilbert, *Letters That Mean Business* (New York: Wiley, 1971), and M. B. Gilbert and T. F. Gilbert, *Thinking Metric,* 2d ed. (New York: Wiley, 1978).

Chapter Ten
Motivation and Human Capital

ROAD TO LEISURE

At the crossroads of Debility
Stands a sign for all to read
(An antipode for an older creed):
"*To* each according to his ability,
From each according to his need."

T.F.G.

MOTIVES AND INCENTIVES

Not too long ago, Mohammed Ali, the heavyweight boxer, got into the ring with the Japanese wrestling champ for the simple, round-number fee of $5 million. The boxer didn't box and the wrestler didn't wrestle, and the staunchest fans of the martial arts were bitterly dismayed by the show. Clearly these "combatants" were not paid for their competence in putting on an entertaining sporting event; they were paid nonetheless.

If boxing fans were dismayed, any serious performance engineer would have had to be disgusted or even shocked by this tasteless event. Because money has two uses for the promotion of human competence: Money can be both a measure and a means; and it has extremely powerful potential for both functions. Any frivolous use of money weakens its power to promote human capital—the true wealth of nations, as the teleonomist sees it. Paying $5 million to a contestant in an incompetent "boxing" match, though only an isolated example of such frivolity, is a symbol that degrades the instrument.

The moral outrage of the performance engineer does not stem from a sense of unfairness, but is akin to the revulsion that physical engineers would feel if they saw anyone using a fine micrometer to crack nuts. Money is a beautifully honed instrument for recognizing and creating worthy performance. It is a principal tool for supplying incentives for

307

competence, and therefore deserves great respect. But, as we shall see, it can also be an incentive for incompetence, because it can reinforce unworthy performance just as powerfully as it can reinforce competence.

Since motivational tools have such potential for creating either competence or incompetence, it is important for performance engineers to get a clear fix on the vantage points from which we can view this murky subject. I have no special tactical expertise in this area, so I won't talk much about motivation at the tactical level. Indeed, I am not certain that there is any significant body of tactical expertise, although there is much talk of it. Most of what I have to say on motivation is an attempt to show how to view this subject from the specialized vantage point of performance engineering—with attention to policies that impede or promote this end.

TWO WAYS OF LOOKING AT MOTIVATION

There is more nonsense, superstition, and plain self-deception about the subject of motivation than about any other topic. And because motivation is a favorite nostrum offered as a curative for incompetence, the nature and causes of this nonsense require some examination. It seems to me that the whole question of motivation needs to be aired.

The behavior engineering model described in Chapter 3 will help us see one source of the nonsense. This model views motivation as having two aspects of equal importance (two different ways of looking at the same thing): an environment of incentives, and a repertory of motives. In other words, no matter how much people desire the rewards that their performance promises, their performance will extinguish if these rewards are not forthcoming. And it also says that no matter how desirable the consequences of performance may seem to others, performance will degenerate if the performer does not desire them. In B. F. Skinner's simplest reinforcement model, at least two things must happen for a rat to perform: It must be hungry (e.g., deprived of food), and the food must be accessible. If the rat is not hungry (no motive), it won't work, regardless of how readily the bar it presses delivers food pellets (incentive). And no matter how hungry the rat (motive), it won't work if the bar press does not deliver the pellets (no incentive).

It is important for us to distinguish between the environmental and repertorial aspects of motivation (incentives and motives) because they indicate two different ways in which we might be able to improve the motivation to perform. I have known a foreman who, through pep talks, could heighten people's motives and get them to perform an unpleasant task with enthusiasm, though he changed nothing in the environment of the job. Perhaps this foreman could have had the same effect on

performance if he gave no pep talks at all, but simply paid the people more (incentive) to perform.

When we talk about motivation, then, it is essential to get our language straight, so that we take appropriate action when we set about to improve performance. One frequent confusion is in the use of the word *reinforcement. Reinforcement,* as Skinner has used the term, refers to any consequence of behavior that either strengthens that behavior or maintains its strength. It is an even more general term than *motivation* or *incentives,* and is too general for the distinctions we often need to make in performance engineering. Because we can increase reinforcement not only by improving motives and incentives, but also by improving confirmation (giving people better information about the success of their behavior in achieving incentives). In short, although *reinforcement* is a perfectly good word, I seldom use it because I am seeking finer distinctions.

Incentives and Performance

In the interest of these finer distinctions, I shall also divide incentives into two kinds: money and other things, like giving people recognition for good work, patting them on the back, and presenting medals. These other things certainly can act as incentives, and sometimes reasonable ones. But since I have nothing really special to say about them, I shall devote most of my discussion to money.

Few can doubt that money is a powerful incentive, and generally even more powerful than mere information about progress. This statement seems to contradict what I have said earlier: that improving information generally has more leverage for improving performance than any other stratagem we might apply—including incentives. But that conclusion only reflects what happens in practice. It is relatively easy to improve information in the performance systems we commonly encounter, but very difficult to make good use of the powerful potential of money incentives. Indeed, it is so difficult that I speak largely from ignorance when I talk about the potential power of money in performance engineering. In some years as a performance engineer, I have seldom been able to experiment with it. Even my most enlightened clients—eagerly following recommendations to improve information, training, and selection; to reengineer the tools of work; to reorganize; to set new standards; and to redefine accomplishments—shrink from any suggestion of changing the way they pay people for their performance. If I seem to downgrade the leverage of monetary incentives, I certainly do not mean to downgrade money's *potential* leverage. I mean only to say that it is extremely difficult to get hold of the lever.

It is impossible to discuss motivation at the policy level or above

without confronting highly emotional political and social issues. Why? Because as soon as we begin to consider the use of monetary incentives to promote human competence, we are really talking about how wealth gets distributed—who gets rewarded for what, and by how much. We also begin to confront a whole set of vested interests in incompetence. It takes little reasoning to see that many powerful people who now control important performance systems have a vested interest in both monopoly and excess profits. Yet, in our imperfect world, differential incomes are far from being totally determined by differences in competence. If monetary incentives were meted out purely on the basis of the degree of competence, many people with high incomes would have to go on the dole, and this fear is no small barrier to the efficient use of incentives.

IDEOLOGIES: FIXED SYSTEMS OF VANTAGE POINTS

To realize the powerful potential of money as an incentive for human competence, we need to overcome great barriers, because nothing arouses more passion. And nowhere are these passions better expressed than in the ideologies, which I define as "fixed vantage points." They are such serious barriers to the efficient engineering of performance, in fact, that we need to examine them more closely.

Ideologies are the anthems of the behavior cult: fixed points of view through which all experience is filtered to predetermined conclusions. These ideologies usually present themselves as polarized pairs, a very typical and popular pair being the so-called liberal and conservative stances. In the United States, broadcasting journalism seems to believe that it has done its duty to "balanced" coverage of political opinion by putting on a debate between a "liberal" and a "conservative." Once we have heard them, we can forevermore predict what they will say on virtually any public issue, because the resolution of economic and political issues is not considered nearly so important as the ideological means that are used to resolve them. These ideologies are classical examples of immobile systems of vantage, which, for all their polarity, share a fundamental stance: viewing the world as full of "good guys" and "bad guys," and which is which all depends on whether we are cowboys or Indians. In these ideologies, vantage points are not regarded as tools to sort out experience, but as the very standards of experience themselves.

If we want to find out who the "good guys" are, we do not look at what people accomplish, or try to accomplish; instead, we determine what "position" they assume. An issue is never "How should we feed the poor?" but "Do you believe in the welfare system?" An answer, "yes" or "no," places us squarely in one camp or the other. In one

camp, for example, it is assumed that if we don't believe in a "welfare system" as a strategy for feeding the poor, then we must not care about the poor. And if we do believe in welfare, we are considered hopeless romantics.

The leap from one level of vantage to another is performed with great alacrity. Ideologues don't debate the question "How do we get a manufacturer to assure the purity of its medicines?" They argue whether government regulation of industry is a good or an evil, independently of any ends to which this means may or may not be relevant. Ideologues are promoters, whose pitch is, "I've got a solution; and since I know you have problems, I'm just the person you've been waiting for." The "solution," of course, can be anything from a *laissez faire*, free enterprise system to the nationalization of industry.

But ideologies cannot bear the scrutiny of the performance matrix, because, from one level of analysis to another, they nearly always engender hopeless contradictions. For example, a favorite liberal cause is to increase government support of the mental health movement. The posture is a display of concern for people who have excessive problems of living. Yet the so-called mental health movement is largely a system of prisons, misnamed "mental hospitals," into which people are cast with only the most sham concern for their civil rights—a most unliberal consequence of the liberal position. Presumably, if government supplies more funds for the system, it will be able to imprison even more of the people who behave strangely, though usually not illegally. More than once I have been called a fascist for questioning the "noble" mental health movement. The assumption is that anyone who questions the means must be opposed to the ends for which the means were presumably designed. But there can be little argument about it: The most efficient way to drive people crazy is to lock them up in a "nut house" (a very "unliberal" expression, since it strips the euphemism for these befouled and inhumane institutions). And no serious student of human competence can counter my assertions by saying, "I know the system isn't perfect, but we are working hard to make it better—and, besides, it's still the best system available." This most common defense of incompetence won't hold up, because the means was never relevant to the stated end in the first place. To make these institutions more efficient at performing their present tasks is simply to find ways to manufacture madness[1] in even greater quantities.

Similarly, the conservative is likely to take a strong stance on abortion, arguing that the abortion industry should be outlawed. Upon careful scrutiny, and the separation of ends from means, the conservative position reduces to a most unconservative consequence. Adopting the means of outlawing abortion is both a form of government interference of an industry and the principal method for making this industry

operate inefficiently, because no serious person really believes that making abortions illegal gets rid of abortions, and we all know that it greatly affects their quality. The ends are not really important to ideologies—only the postures.

Between these two ideological poles, whether they are liberal or conservative, stand the middle-of-the-road eclectics, who borrow from each extreme the stances that seem most amicable to them at the time. Eclecticism often seems the only road out of the contradictions inherent in ideologies that confuse means with ends, behavior with accomplishment. The eclectic positions are usually less damaging than the ideological ones simply because the people who stand in them don't get quite so lathered up. So the eclectics (the middle-of-the-roaders) have seen to it that the programs of the ideologies are only half-heartedly adopted. Only a million people[2] are imprisoned in "mental hospitals," instead of the 5 or 6 million that the "humane liberals" would have us lock up "for their own good." Government by eclectics is less threatening to our freedoms than government by ideologues; but eclecticism can hardly be rated as a separate point of view, since it is only a diluted mix of the ideologies.

The performance matrix summarizes a fourth and different systematic stance from the two polarized ideologies and eclecticism. This is a goal-directed, or teleonomic, posture that seeks the problem rather than the solution; knowing that when the problem is sufficiently well defined, the solution will often be self-evident. The teleonomic point of view has no ideological commitment to special means and solutions; and a solution is never judged by its ideological flavor, but only by four properties: its relevance, its efficiency, its coherence at different levels of analysis, and its legality.

To see how the teleonomic viewpoint differs from the other positions, we need only to look at the recurring arguments for and against socialization. One ideologue might argue, for example, that banks, like schools, should be socialized on the grounds that socialization is a posture that is best for the "general welfare." If pushed, this ideologue can usually get quite detailed about the means of socialism, but will have far less success in explaining the intent of the goal of "general welfare."

Another ideologue will argue that the schools, like the banks, should be placed on a free enterprise basis, saying that free enterprise is the means that ultimately creates the best conditions for living. Again, this ideologue can say a great deal more about the intended means than about the goal.

The eclectic, on the other hand, will gradually compromise the two positions. As a result, a private banking establishment will exist with

heavy government regulation; and the socialized school system will become so autonomous that, aside from budgetary decisions, government officials will not have the faintest idea of how to influence them for the public good.

But a teleonomic view might arrive at some startling conclusions, only partly supportive of the ideologues and the eclectics. For example, it might reach the cultural-level decision that banks should be socialized and schools established as free market enterprises—depending on the accomplishment models it begins with and the standards it assumes. Because a true teleonomic analyst has no vested interest in any particular means to achieve an end—provided that it is relevant, efficient, coherent, and legal—it couldn't matter less what the nature of the means might be.

Some will observe that this argument supports the "immoral" notion that the ends justify the means. But it is not immoral to take the stance that performance can be made competent only if we sort out and analyze the ends and means at all levels of vantage. A means that is quite efficient in achieving ends at one level may not be so efficient at another level. The "mental hospitalization" of people with extreme lifestyles, for example, may have the great tactical advantage of separating troublesome people from the rest of us, but it does not have the cultural advantage of preserving people's civil rights. From the histories of these institutions, this tactic doesn't go very far either to promote the philosophical ideal of a saner world, to satisfy the policy mission of returning people "happily" to their homes, or to fulfill the strategic responsibility of ridding people of their delusions.

From the teleonomic view, however, all values are derived from the ultimate worth inherent in human capital. And every act of incompetence reduces the basic human capital. Therefore, when we view incentives teleonomically, we see them only as possible means to be used to create worthy performance.

The cause of human capital, through the intelligent use of monetary incentives, will be greatly advanced once our popular (and not so popular) political and economic theorists abandon their ideological passions, and learn to focus on money and the distribution of wealth as merely another means for achieving human competence.

"PROFIT" AS INCENTIVE

Nothing better illustrates the difference between ideology and performance engineering than the way in which we view "profit." For the teleonomist, "profit" represents one system of possible incentives for worthy performance, which may or may not work, depending on how

we look at it. "Profit" for the performance engineer cannot be viewed as good or bad, but as an incentive that has equal potential for reinforcing both worthy and unworthy performance.

Few words are tainted by so much subtle nonsense and confusion as *profit*. To my liberal friends the word connotes the proceeds of fundamentally unrespectable and unworthy behaviors: minimally, greed and selfishness; maximally, the royal screwing of millions of helpless victims. *Profit* is the incentive for the most unworthy performance. To my conservative comrades, it is a term of highest endearment, connoting efficiency and good sense. To them, *profit* is the ultimate incentive for worthy performance. Both connotations have some small merit, of course, because profit may result from both greedy, selfish activities and from sensible, efficient ones. But overgeneralizations from either bias do not help us in the least in understanding the relationship between profit and human competence. Indeed, these overgeneralizations have created heaps of egregious absurdity.

In its most common usage, the word *profit* implies neither avaricious finagling nor high-minded efficiency. This easy translation of a result into behavior is just another tiresome example of behavior cultism. The strict accounting definition simply treats profit as a return in excess of expenditures. All the revenues of a business are added up, and the sum of the expenditures is subtracted from this total. For the accountant, profit is simply the resulting number and nothing more. It is obviously one of the most critical numbers a small business must think about, because if this number becomes negative, the business cannot survive for long. In theory, at least, it is a number that should contribute greatly to efficiency; in practice, its contribution is debatable. And that is my interest in profit here: How reliable a measure of worthy performance is it? Also, how effective is it in creating more worthy performance? If it is either, or both, then no one presumably would care to challenge its value. If profit were the absolute, one-to-one reflection of the true worth of performance, then it would be a bad word in nobody's house, because it would simply be interchangeable with *competence*. Or, if the occurrence of profit guaranteed a growth in competence, we would all cherish it without contention. But profit is defective both as a measure of competence and as a condition for creating more of it. Contradictions are built into the notion, and these must be dispelled if we are to understand better the relationship between profit and worthy performance.

Although we can look at profit from two common points of view—as a measure of competence and as a condition for achieving it—there is often a third use for this concept: Many ideologues, "capitalists" and "socialists" alike, see it as an *accomplishment* in itself. "They're in business to make profit." Now here is a built-in contradiction. If profit is

an accomplishment, what is *its* measure? How much is $1000 worth of profits worth? Simply asking the question exposes the absurdity. It is exactly the same as saying, "They're in business to make money." No one is in business to make money except treasury departments and counterfeiters. You may be in business *so that* you *can* make money, but not *to* make money. Money is a convenient social measure of values and costs, but all by itself is intrinsically worthless. Thus, profit is a potential *measure* of worthy performance, but it is not an accomplishment in and of itself. We can build a car profitably. But we cannot build a profit profitably, because that is talking nonsense.

We should examine the widespread belief that the "profit motive" and the access to profit are the prime conditions for competent performance. These voices argue, for example, that the United States economy is the most powerful in the world because it has been built on the efforts of people rewarded by profit. There is also the equally widespread notion that really worthy performance must come from a "nonprofit" motive—from government agencies and nonprofit corporations and foundations. Both notions can be negated outright.

First, the profit motive as the foundation of competence has a fundamental problem: The motive is often fulfilled by the most incompetent performance. One way to see this is to imagine a system under which an agency is permitted profit in a direct ratio to its competence. Suppose that we conducted a performance audit of a corporation—job by job, department by department, and plant by plant—establishing exemplary standards for every kind of performance. Then suppose that we used these exemplary standards to make projections—build a model— of how the corporation should perform in terms of its production and expenditures. (For the sake of the argument, assume that market demands are perfectly stable.) Finally, imagine that we set the permissible sale price of any single item of production as 10 percent higher than the projected costs of making, selling, and delivering that item. And if an item is less than exemplary in quality, its price is reduced accordingly. In short, if the company performed to exemplary standards, it would make a 10-percent profit; and to the extent that its performance is less than exemplary, the percentage of profit is reduced proportionately. Under this system, no major corporation in the world would make a profit.

The power of corporations to set prices is all the power required to nearly guarantee that the profit motive is self-fulfilling. When people in corporations perform incompetently, they inflate the cost of doing business; the corporation then raises its prices to cover those additional costs. A considerable amount of the talent of top management is applied to developing strategies for making price rises as unnoticeable as possible. When times are good, this is the favorite strategy for counter-

ing the costs of incompetence. To see this, all you have to do is observe what happens when business slows and the market won't accept a price rise, even in clever disguise. The word goes out from management to cut costs. A typical command is a memo asking that some special expense item be cut back. This is simply a recognition that higher degrees of incompetence are acceptable in good times, when the customer is able to bear the cost.

Government regulation of profit hardly helps—and, indeed, it may encourage incompetence. Suppose that the government imposes a profit ceiling on a particular company. If incompetence grows in that company, the rates will eventually grow with it. Look at the astonishing arithmetic. For example, if a company is regulated to a ceiling profit of 10 percent, and it costs $1 million to do business, its rates will be restricted to earn a maximum of $1.1 million—a profit of $100,000. On the other hand, if the company can manage to double its costs of doing business, it could theoretically make a profit of $200,000. By doubling its inefficiency, then, it could double its profit.

Although the arithmetic of large business is not all this simple,[3] it should be clear from this example that profit is not automatic motivation for greater efficiency. On the contrary, because regulated companies, more often than not, make their allowed profits, one can only wonder what their managements would do if someone developed a simple method of cutting their costs in half; the adoption of the method would eventually mean a 50-percent reduction in profit.

Clearly, the profit system, as it is operated, is not optimally designed to encourage competence. That is not to say that profit cannot be a powerful incentive for competence; surely it can. It simply is not widely applied as such. Indeed, most of those working in industry and business do not share in the profit; and when they do, their shares are not really made contingent on their specific competent performance.

It is the very power of profit (or money in any form) to serve as an incentive that makes it so important to worry about its efficient application. Powerful incentive can reinforce incompetence just as well as it can motivate competence—indeed, sometimes better. One of the classical examples of this in reinforcement theory is the power of incentives to create the superstitious behavior I described in Chapter 6.

REGULATION AND COMPETENCE

I have given an example of how one form of regulation can—at least in theory—motivate incompetence in private industry. Ideologues, depending on the pole at which they stand, would hasten to use my example as an argument for doing away with all government regulation. Or else they would suggest that because greed so easily leads to

incompetence, it is best for government to take over all businesses and do an even more thorough job of regulating them. There are distinct problems with both of these stances. Those who would do away with all regulations must first convince the rest of us that a completely *laissez faire* system wouldn't sell us carcinogens—and a great deal more.

But the *laissez fairist* has long lost the argument. Now the tendency is a movement toward greater government regulation. Presumably, it has only one purpose, and that is to promote greater human competence. Why, then, do so many people see so much danger in it? I think I know. Let's take a look at two examples of regulation, a good one and a bad one, and see how they influence competence and what their differences are.

The Meat and Poultry Health Inspection Division of the U.S. Department of Agriculture regulates the quality of meat produced by packers. A supervising veterinarian and several nonvet inspectors are assigned to the nation's packing houses. Their principal function is to rate meat: to prevent diseased meat from reaching our tables, as well as to prevent misleading labels. Although these inspectors (like everyone else) have their own performance problems, their accomplishment, on the whole, is extremely valuable to us and it doesn't cost very much. In short, it is worthy performance. If a packing house is doing poorly in turning out clean meat, the inspectors will advise the owners on how they might do better. But the chief function of government inspection is to measure and control only the accomplishments of a packing company, not its behavior. And the incentive to the packing house for superior performance is simple: good ratings for good meat, which translates into money. Here, accomplishment is being regulated.

Now let us move to the other example, the bad one. The Federal Drug Administration wants to ensure that we get quality medicines from the manufacturers—as noble an intent as that of the meat inspectors. Do they, then, limit themselves to inspecting the manufactured chemicals? Indeed not. For example, a recent addition to the FDA's lengthy regulations states specifically that all personnel engaged in the manufacture of drugs and working in contact with any of the materials used should be trained in sanitary techniques; and each company should give evidence that it has conducted a satisfactory training course. The consequence of the new regulation is this: Every American drug company is investing in the development of films, books, instructors, and the like in order to meet the regulation. A further consequence: a rise in the cost of medicine. The FDA, then, is regulating the *behavior* of these companies. It is a case of bureaucrats sitting in Washington and imagining how to manufacture drugs safely. This is of course nonsense. While the FDA is busy regulating behavior, the public is almost completely in the dark about the nature of the drug

products it is buying, and it is unable to tell generic products from brand names. If the public could understand the labeling of drugs as well as the labeling of meat, we would save millions of dollars a year. And since the FDA can inspect the products the companies produce, why not be satisfied that these products are sanitary and let the companies worry about how to make them that way?

These, then, are two examples of regulation: a good one that sets accomplishment standards and creates incentives for meeting them; and a poor one that sets behavior standards, and doesn't even make clear what the consequences are of not meeting them. If our drugs are consistently sanitary, why should we care how much training the manufacturing personnel get in sanitation?

A remark made to me by one bureaucrat about an equally inane training regulation in another department reveals some of the patronizing motives that lead to these government dicta. "Oh, why *shouldn't* they get this training? It's good for them, and the companies bear the cost for a little public education." Of course, what he didn't mention was that the cost of this fortuitous training would be passed on to you and me.

The car bumper is another example of this stupidity—an example of a regulation of behavior and not of accomplishment. The government told the auto companies to put a bumper on an automobile that would withstand an impact of 5 miles per hour. The purpose? To decrease repair costs. The result? The cost of repairing these expensive bumpers when damaged at higher speeds far exceeded the cost of the repairs they replaced—and also added to the original cost of the auto. The proper regulation of accomplishments, not behavior, is to set standards for the costs of the average auto repairs; then let the auto companies figure out how to meet these standards.

The regulation of behavior is the sign of totalitarian governments. But sensible cultures set standards for accomplishments that are in the public interest, and then provide incentives to meet those standards. Sensible businesses do the same. It is perfectly sane to provide suggestions, information, research data, or other resources that might help people behave efficiently, but we must be wary of these things as regulations. Regulations of behavior do not produce exemplary performers; the freedom of behavior often does.

Education is an excellent example of a heavily regulated industry, although much of the regulation is unwritten, and even unspoken. Teachers are expected to behave in certain ways; their behavior is often observed, criticized, praised, or condemned. But no standards are set for their accomplishments; indeed, it is difficult to find an adequate description of what the expected accomplishments are. Even in universities, where the teachers boast of "academic freedom," the extreme

similarities in the way courses are conducted suggest the existence of very strict, though unwritten, standards of behavior. Standards of accomplishment, on the other hand, are virtually nonexistent. For ple, a young professor who departs radically from the usual methods of teaching, but gets every student to make an A on the departmental exam, may be in for trouble. I know, because it has happened to me; and I have seen it happen to others—though not often, because radical departures from the usual university "methods" are rare indeed.

Regulation of behavior does not stop with government and government institutions; it is the favorite standard for incentives in business and industry. The surest way to get ahead in a large corporation is to behave according to certain norms, which are not restricted merely to the way to dress. Recently, in one of our most successful megacorporations, a high-level executive who writes many sensitive reports surrendered to his preferred style and ordered a typewriter to compose these reports. He was soon asked to remove the typewriter because the appearance of such an instrument in an executive's office was not consistent with the image the company tries to project. Still, despite the degree of behavioral conformity found in large companies, business usually excels the schools in the flexibility permitted in performance, *and* in measuring performance by accomplishment.

But there is virtually no regulation of the accomplishments of the schools. They can (and daily do) turn out defective products with seldom anyone to answer to. They are not put to the same tests of high standards as the meat-packing plants. Is it because we think more of the quality of what we eat than of the quality of our education?

The point of all of this is clear. Many of us fear free enterprise because we know that the motive to make money, if unregulated, will lead to people's maximizing their own immediate welfare at the expense of everyone else. Without some regulation, that is no doubt true. Yet some of us fear socialism because it seems to mean that a great force of bureaucrats will end up regulating the rest of us at such a cost that we will all be poor. There is plenty of basis for this fear, because the urge to regulate other people's behavior (called "power") is as strong a motive as greed. In the most powerful of socialistic nations (USSR), regulation of behavior has reached such extremes that novelists cannot improve on the horror of the written record.

But to pose the ideological question, "Should we have government regulation or not?" is to put it in the wrong way, because the answer is neither a simple "yes" nor a simple "no." Nor is it some compromise of two extremes. We have a dilemma that cannot be solved by compromise. It needs a full resolution.

The resolution lies, as I have suggested, in the distinction between behavior and accomplishment. Remember our First Leisurely Theo-

rem of Chapter 1? It says that *two* things account for competence (and thus for the expansion of leisure capital):

1. Having valuable accomplishments
2. Behaving in efficient ways

I shall make two generalizations, really extrapolations from the First Leisurely Theorem, that will help us decide which kinds of incentive systems we really need in order to promote human competence.

First, *the regulation of behavior promotes incompetence.* In other words, rewarding and punishing people for the way they behave is inefficient. All this says is that unless you are responsible for a task yourself, you are in a poor position to tell others *how* to do it. (Training is no exception; trainers will be successful in telling others how to do something if they have a genuine stake in actual performance—a stake in the measurable accomplishments.) And "absentee regulation" is the worst form of behavior regulation.

Second, *the failure to plan the direction of performance promotes incompetence.* This says only that without planning, short-term accomplishments may not be compatible with long-term aims. When that happens, people may be efficient to an incompetent purpose.

So we cannot simply judge regulation to be bad or good, but we must look to what is being regulated and to what purpose. The theory of private business is, of course, based on the belief that the work of the world best gets done with minimal regulation except by the natural incentives of the market. The theory of government as a way of doing business is based on the belief that regulation is a necessity in an orderly world—that natural incentives too easily promote uncivilized behavior. And just as there is no single judgment about the sensibility of regulation, there is no single rationale that renders either government or private business a necessary evil. We might, then, examine both of these ways of doing business in terms of how they promote and distribute wealth as an incentive to competence.

Private Enterprise and the Distribution of Wealth

Private enterprise boasts of its efficiency, a boast not without merit, though much overstated. There is nothing inherent in the "privacy" of an enterprise to make it more efficient than a public one. I have looked deeply into too many performance systems to make the easy generalization that "government is inefficient, but business is efficient." Of course, there is a correlation. Private enterprises are often somewhat more efficient than government operations, and, I think, for two rea-

sons. First, there is somewhat less regulation of behavior—less codification about how one should go about doing a job. Also, compared with government, most businesses are smaller and more flexible. Of course, very large businesses can become just as bureaucratized as the Department of Defense. But, most important, private enterprises generally have a higher degree of accountability simply because performance is more likely to be measured in economic units.

Still, the urge to socialize businesses seldom arises from the motive to make them more efficient. Indeed, it arises from a motive that is largely irrelevant to who manages a business or how, but from the desire to find a more equitable way to redistribute the wealth.

Wealth can be redistributed in many ways, without putting an end to private enterprise—for example, by taxation and regulation. In fact, the mere nationalization of business would do little by itself to redistribute the wealth. So private versus public ownership is really an independent issue, and even those who would have the wealth divided exactly equally among us should be aware of the benefits that *independent* management can contribute to the common wealth. In short, although issues of the equitable distribution of wealth are at the heart of incentive systems, they can be resolved through other means, some of which I shall describe later. But efficiency will flourish to the extent that a performance system of any kind is free from behavior regulation— either by government or internally—and is measured solely by its accomplishments. There is then little reason to nationalize most businesses in order to achieve greater efficiency, and every reason to avoid such actions. In short, if we must choose between the motives of greed and power, greed is far more effective in promoting efficiency than power. Greed, after all, is goal directed, whereas the urge to power is fully satisfied by the ability to control means, whether for a purpose or not. From the standpoint of efficiency alone, private business is the preferred kind of incentive system, especially if no controls are put on its behavior, or on *how* it achieves its accomplishments.

The Role of Government

Private business alone, without some form of regulation, will not maximize the leisure capital, although it is of great importance to efficiency for independent systems to pursue their immediate aims. Some people believe that Adam Smith's famous "invisible hand"—the natural forces of the free market—is sufficient to work things out in the best interest of the common wealth. They believe that any attempt to interfere with these forces by planning must go awry. But I think this oversimplification of economic "law" is a red herring, used by those who fear—on the rational side—an increase in government regulation of behavior, and—

on the irrational side—the interference with the fulfillment of greed. Even Adam Smith knew that the "invisible hand" needed a little guidance.

As all economic history has shown us, some degree of planning and regulation is necessary for a stable economy in which everyone's welfare is taken into consideration. At one extreme, we might see the government as one great performance engineer, defining valuable accomplishments, setting performance standards, manipulating the environment to maximize performance, and so on. Unfortunately, no body of people exists that is smart enough to do that job well; and if it did exist, it would require such absolute power that no one would want to risk giving it. The better role of government, then, is to restrict itself to those acts of regulation that it can perform competently. There are just a few; but if properly applied, they can have a powerful effect.

Indeed, I believe there are only three roles that government can play competently in order to provide the incentives for worthy performance. The first of these roles is the use of its police powers to prevent people from being robbed or harmed. If the police role is not to be a regulation of behavior, it must restrict itself to accomplishments and requirements. For example, a factory can manufacture plastics; but some requirements need to be placed on this accomplishment—that the plastic must be safe to use, and that the production does not befoul the air or squander national resources. These powers might be further extended to prevent management from distributing the payroll on the basis of behavior rather than for the value of accomplishments. By extension, such government regulatory power would also be used, for example, to see that universities created pay systems for their professors on the basis of how well these professors achieved the measurable and clearly stated accomplishments they contracted for. What those accomplishments were would be none of the government's business—only to ensure that money is not taken under false pretenses. And similar rules would hold for corporation executives, physicians, and lawyers.

The second role of government—a necessary one to keep its police powers honest—would be the publication of information. It would be the archive in which performance data are stored and reported publicly. It would periodically tell us how well schools, businesses, and other institutions are performing. Such public confirmation would go a long way toward promoting human capital. And this information service would have to be kept strictly independent of the regulatory part of government, because honest reporting on the performance of regulatory agencies would have to be a large responsibility of the information branch of government.

The third and final role of government would have to do with the

equitable distribution of wealth—to the extent that having people paid for their accomplishments did not achieve this distribution. It would naturally use its power to tax as the critical instrument of distribution. And, of course, in a government concerned with worthy performance, the common income tax would be out of the question. Taxing people in proportion to their productivity is counterproductive of human competence; it is a form of punishing worthy performance.

But a government oriented toward competence and the common wealth would have several sources of revenue. First would be a tax on those natural resources that should be considered part of the common wealth: oil, water courses, the air that gets polluted, forests, and the like. The next source of income would be heavy estate taxes. Because the use of money as an incentive to be born doesn't make any sense, inherited wealth would be essentially out. The government would inherit the vast proportion of any family's wealth, and great revenues could be achieved through the sale and rental of these properties.

A great resource of revenues would be realized by the government's becoming the principal banking and investment enterprise. Here, the government could make money both from invested capital (as the chief bank) and from wise investments in the economy. Such investments would have to be made on a basis of limited or no control over the enterprises; otherwise, the government would begin to run these businesses—an undesirable situation. The government should operate only those enterprises that are "protective," and that are not essentially productive, of true wealth. Examples are the hospitals or the military. This certainly does not include the school system, however. The government's control over schools would be strictly through the power of investment. And the public, through its government, would be the principal customer for the school's products, which are educated children. It could recover some of these expenditures from businesses as a tax on natural resources, because that is what our children are.

Finally, government could raise revenues by a kind of "excess profit" tax, which would not be the same as taxing true productivity. These revenues would not be large, but could have a powerful effect on the equitable distribution of wealth. If the government stays out of almost all business (except for banking and hospitals and similar industries), it needs to be assured that free enterprise can supply full employment. A business built on the labor of many people may decide, as it becomes more competent, that it needs less and less of that labor. People then get discharged, while some managers remain to draw even larger salaries. Under a proper incentive system, such bloated salaries at the expense of the labor force would be so heavily taxed that the business would have every incentive to distribute this money to its

employees rather than to discharge them. How such a system might work can only be imagined. But where a policy is sensible, good strategies and tactics can be found; and it is in the interest of business to find them.

ALIENATION AND COMPETENCE

The failure of business to confront such social problems as the fair distribution of wealth abandons the battlefield to the bureaucrats. It sometimes seems that Karl Marx was right in observing that the natural force of "capitalist greed" is the finest instrument for the ultimate destruction of free enterprise. It seems to me that the only way that private enterprise can avoid the fate described by Marx is through very serious attention to the wider application of performance engineering for the greater common wealth. There is only one way that business can avoid the eventual bureaucratization of everything, and the ultimate regulation of our behavior: by adopting larger and more far-reaching policies for the fair distribution of wealth, and systematically pursuing the practices of a good performance engineer. Marx had all too good a point: When labor does not fully share in the free enterprise, alienation is the certain result.

Alienation occurs to the extent that people's incentives are not really connected to their accomplishments. When you pay me for my behavior and not for my accomplishment, you are really treating me like a horse. And, of course, we horses will organize to force a higher premium on our behavior—on our "labor hour." Then, when economic times are rough and you fire me, while maintaining a large income for yourself (rather than having all parties in the company bear the burden equitably), I will naturally feel even more alienated. In a well-engineered business, money will be distributed in direct proportion to people's accomplishments, not their labor. If those accomplishments shrink in value, we all suffer accordingly; but we all share in the profit when times get better. People will feel that they are not alienated only to the extent that they have a true vested interest in the accomplishments of an organization, and see an exact correlation between the distribution of money and their contribution to these accomplishments. If the cake is put upon the table and cut up in fair slices in proportion to each of our measured contributions, then each of us will feel as if we belong to the family, and the greed of those who would take too large a slice would become evident.

The communist creed, "from each according to his ability, to each according to his need," must be reversed if free enterprise is to flourish. What we want, instead, is: "*to* each according to his ability"—meaning pay for accomplishment, not behavior—and "*from* each according to

his need." This second part of the reversed creed simply means that we arrange for people who do not have an adequate share of the wealth to have first crack at working. If there isn't enough work to go around, we favor those who really need income from the work. We can't have our cake and eat it too. If we want to reverse the trend to bureaucratization, we must reverse the entire communist creed, not just half of it.

The task of reconstructing our system of distributing wealth will be accomplished either by the bureaucrats and others with the urge to power; or it will be accomplished by those who really believe in competence and competition through the principles of performance engineering.

There are no workable master plans for society. Peter Drucker[4] is right: No business should act as a welfare system, but should pursue its own purposes diligently. The competent pursuit of the purposes of a business in no way precludes a fair distribution of the wealth. And an efficient system of incentives will give everyone involved more time *and* opportunity, thus expanding human capital. If free enterprise is to continue to be the best system for creating wealth, it must also become the best system for distributing it. It can do this by the strict equation of incentives with accomplishments. When all people have a genuine stake in the accomplishments of the institutions in which they work, there is a community. *Community* is the antonym of *alienation*, and it results when incentives and accomplishments become indistinguishable.

As we become more competent, less labor is required. But if the distribution of wealth is equated with the labor required, there is too little incentive to become more competent. It is as simple as that. We can love people for their behavior, but when we put a dollar value on it, love turns to prostitution, because prostitutes sell behavior.

SELECTION AND THE BEHAVIOR REPERTORY

Motives (and capacity), I have repeatedly said, are not especially high-leverage areas for improving performance, given the realities of our institutions.

But can performance engineers do nothing at all about human motives and capacity? Even if you accept my arguments that these are areas where we have little leverage, you are certain to keep the feeling, as I do, that capacity and motives are somehow too important to competence to ignore. Well, we needn't ignore them. But because it is so difficult for the performance engineer to manipulate these factors directly, and because it usually pays off so poorly to try, we can approach the problem differently. We can use our Leisurely Theorems to devise a way to attract, select, and place people in jobs and schools so

that their capacities and motives best match the performance system they enter. Of course, you might say, isn't that exactly what people do when they use instruments such as intelligence and personality tests—instruments against which I have so strongly protested? No, it is not the same, because the teleonomist approaches selection from quite a different direction. To show you the difference, I shall describe the teleonomic selection procedure that I call the FAIR program, for the Functional Assessment and Instructional Resource Program.

First, however, let me tell you about a friend of mine who recently emerged, somewhat scathed, from a current product of the cult of behavior called an "assessment center (AC)." Employees who enter an AC are assigned a number of tasks to perform (simulation games and like). For an intensive period—say, a week—those administering the AC make careful observations of the employees. Of course, what is being observed and measured is behavior—traits like "leadership," "creativity," and "organizational skills." Proponents of the AC system boast great results, although the evidence that AC evaluations correlate with real job performance is scant, if it exists at all. Correlation with later job performance usually shows that these evaluations account for as much as 10 percent of the variance in performance—*as measured by supervisory ratings*, though, and not by direct performance measures. But even these small correlations are suspect, because the same supervisors who rated later performance often selected the people into the AC in the first place, thus clearly indicating a supervisory bias.

My friend reports that his experience was "fun" and "challenging"; on the negative side, he reported his extreme discomfort in having people constantly "staring at the way he behaved." He also—and this is more important—wondered how his evaluation was relevant, because he was a candidate for three different jobs. "The tasks we performed were in no way specifically related to any of the jobs I'm trying for," he says. Again we see people measuring behavior with little thought to any accomplishments to which the behavior may be related. (One major corporation—deep into the AC system—is now debating which five behavioral traits should be dropped from its too-cumbersome list of 15 traits. "Creativity" is the prime candidate to go, because "We can't measure it as well as we can measure 'leadership,'" I was told.)

My performance-engineering selection system, the FAIR program, begins with a clear statement of what is to be accomplished: the selection of people most likely to be exemplary performers in a specific job. This objective is, of course, nothing new. But the requirements placed on it are important:

1. Anyone can enter a FAIR program.
2. All entrants must be given the opportunity to know the

job intimately—its specific accomplishments, requirements, and standards.

3. All entrants must be given a description of what they need to learn in order to master the job.

4. Entrants are given the opportunity to learn the job.

5. The primary evaluation is of actual job performance.

6. Behavior is evaluated only when entrants have shown that they can do the accomplishments required of a job.

7. Behavior is evaluated in only two ways:

   (a) Cost to the company of completing the required training.

   (b) The proven existence of very specific and job-relevant behavioral handicaps—such as the proven inability to make a public presentation when that is a critical job requirement.

To understand the FAIR system, you need to know something about "learner-guided instruction" (LGI). An LGI system centers around a book (customized for each job) that does these things:

1. It describes the accomplishments, requirements, performance measures, and standards of the job.

2. It describes a theory of the job, distinguishing exemplary from mediocre performance.

3. It directs the entrant to opportunities for observing how exemplary performers do the job.

4. For each job accomplishment, it provides a description of what one needs to know to master that accomplishment.

5. It describes a series of tasks one can perform to learn the job.

6. It identifies many resources to help one learn to perform the tasks.

7. It describes the criteria for learning to master the tasks.

8. For each accomplishment, it provides an opportunity to perform and then to be evaluated and signed off by a supervisor or manager.

9. It gives the entrant a chance for a self-test before being judged by others.

10. Final decisions about the entrants is made by a "worthy performance" ratio, which gives points for job accomplishments and subtracts points for the amount of additional training an entrant requires after completing the LGI. The LGI book describes the evaluation system.

In a general way, here is how a FAIR program works. When they enter the company, entrants are given an orientation to the system. Then, whenever they wish, they can browse the library of LGIs representing jobs ranging from low-level technicians to the president of the company. Suppose we follow Leslie Ernest through a FAIR program.

After serving as a research assistant for 2 years in the Marketing Department of Warren Anthony, Inc., Leslie Ernest decides that she would like to prepare for the job of Marketing Manager. So, she takes the Marketing Manager LGI from the library, and asks for formal entry into the FAIR program. She is assigned a counselor, and just happens to draw an R&D Manager from Warren Anthony, Inc., whose only function is to give Leslie general guidance and make sure that she gets the cooperation she needs. When Leslie is formally enrolled, she is given 4 hours a week to study on company time. Had she chosen a job the program administrators advised against, she would not have gotten the time off and would have had to do all the studying on her own time—although she could appeal the decision.

Leslie studies the LGI and fills out a form that helps her decide which accomplishments she feels she can already do without any training at all. She then tries to make a schedule to be tested on these accomplishments. For example, she already knows how to estimate the size of the market for the company's chemical products, so she asks for a chance to prove that she can do this. After a suitable test, she is signed off on this accomplishment by the Market Research Director.

Leslie does not know how to make a market plan, and so she begins to study. Her LGI book gives her references to literature she can read, people she can talk with, and a well-known workshop she can attend. After Leslie thinks she can develop a good marketing plan, she schedules another test.

Something else she must learn is to present her plan to the marketing staff. The LGI tells her the criteria for judging her presentation, and refers her to resources to help her prepare. Again she is tested when she is ready, and signed off if she performs up to the standards.

Now, since the company considers it absolutely essential that a Marketing Manager be able to sell a marketing plan to dealers, Leslie is given a description of the minimum criteria for a dealer presentation. If she fails, she will be given counseling. If she decides that she simply cannot stomach these presentations, she can pick another LGI—or decide to remain in her present job. After a failure, she is given another chance—in fact, she may be given several chances.

In all of these tasks, she may be required to do a number of things—from firing people to developing or training another employee. Finally, when Leslie has been signed off on all the job accomplishment tasks (some are simulated, most are real), she applies for the job of Marketing Manager and is put on an availability list.

When an opening is imminent, Leslie is told to prepare for the final selection—a 2-week period in which five candidates for the job are given a chance to show their skills. Certain important tasks are selected from the LGI for the test, and Leslie is told what these tasks are and how the judgment will be made. In the final selection tests, she performs these tasks under actual job

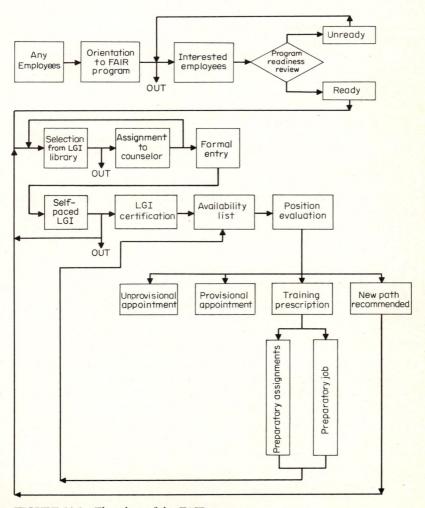

FIGURE 10-1 Flowchart of the FAIR program.

pressures, and her accomplishments are measured. Also, the selection team lists any knowledge deficiencies she displays. Her main "score" consists of accomplishment points; knowledge deficiency points are subtracted from it.

Leslie gets the job, although she was tied with another applicant, because she makes a far superior presentation of her marketing plans than her adversary.

Figure 10-1 is a flowchart of the FAIR program. Notice how many options Leslie has to drop out, or else change her direction. Selection in the FAIR program leans heavily on both general motivation and on the specific rewards one finds in performing a job. Few could weather a FAIR program without wanting to do the job. Also, serious defects in capacity will show up in real performance situations. Besides, the FAIR program keeps everything in the open, so that incompetent performers are less likely to get chosen just because someone liked them. Finally, the assessment procedure is also a training and development procedure, so that the employee is prepared for the job before actually entering it. All the dice are loaded in favor of selection. If Leslie has any "inner-person" problems that should concern the company, they will have to emerge in actual performance situations.

So we see that the potential for using monetary incentives to promote human capital is great, but not likely to be realized until we make profound policy changes that are free of ideological passions. Meanwhile, we can do a much better job of organizing our institutions so that people's inherent motives to succeed can find a proper outlet. Ultimately, the institutions, private or public, that are least likely to be alienating are those that provide incentives for the accomplishments these institutions value, and supply the means for people to find their own best fit in those institutions.

NOTES

1. For a really convincing argument, see Thomas Szasz, *Manufacture of Madness* (New York: Harper & Row, 1970).

2. About five times as many people are "hospitalized" as are sent to official jails.

3. The rates of utilities, for example, are formally based on the capital investments made (machinery, buildings, etc.). However, regulatory boards have wide discretionary powers to raise rates and are not restricted to returns on investment. Roughly speaking, the more the utility spends to do business, the more likely it is that it will be allowed to charge more.

4. See Peter F. Drucker, *Management* (New York: Harper & Row, 1975).

Part Four
THEORETICAL CONSIDERATIONS

My final decision to include this part of the book was clinched one day when 10-year-old Rob returned from school full of questions about the sciences. "What do you call the people who study gravity?" "What is psychology the study of?" "Who are the people who study money?" Even, "What is the science that studies the sciences?"—marking the dawn of a young boy's epistemological awareness. Finally, the hardest question to answer: "What are *you* a scientist of, Dad?"

Then it suddenly occurred to me that I was not answering his questions according to good training tactics. I was teaching him a multiple discrimination (stimulus: plants; response: botany, etc.) without first establishing a good domain theory.

"Look, Rob, I'll tell you what I'm going to do; I'm going to draw you a chart that will explain it."

And that is what the single chapter in Part IV will do: chart the sciences in such a way as to show the reader the relationship between teleonomics and other forms of inquiry. As I develop this "spectrum" of sciences, I shall discuss some of the theoretical bases for this system.

The method I shall use is to distinguish the sciences by two characteristics: by their subject matters and by their methodologies. What is it they study, and how do they study it? If teleonomics and economics are different, it must be because they deal with different subjects, or because they use different methods, or both.

Saying what a subject matter is, however, poses some problems. Common-sense answers usually don't hold up under scrutiny. And the sophisticated answers of philosophers are really "realm theories," going far beyond the interests of performance engineers who merely want to understand their craft. Furthermore, many of these "sophisticated" theories evaporate into nonsense or nothingness when painfully translated out of Academish into English.

Nowhere are the problems of subject matter greater than in trying to distinguish between the physical and behavioral worlds—anciently called the "mind-body" problem. The debates of sophomore philosophy students predate Aristotle's "peripatetic university": If a tree falls in the forest when no one is around, does it make any noise? "Is all physical reality merely a mental experience, or is mental experience only another extension of physical reality?"

These kinds of questions haven't excited very many people. Probably this is because they seem so impossible to answer with authority, and because such answers don't seem to most of us to be very useful. "What difference does it make?" is a common response. Or, as a wit and philosopher whose name eludes me once said: "No matter?—Never mind. Never mind?—No matter."

But the reader who has stayed with me to this point will have to admit that I have a considerable practical bent. So while I can't promise you that Chapter 11 will be the most useful thing you have ever read, it does seem to me that there is a practical side to having a theory about how all these various interests in human competence fit together. Therefore, my treatment is not intended to satisfy the sophisticated professors of philosophy; rather, I attempt to give the more general reader a simple, coherent system for viewing the place of teleonomics in the spectrum of inquiry.

A final word to my more loyal readers about the usefulness of the things I discuss in Chapter 11. Although this chapter concludes the book, the thoughts it describes actually initiated the development of teleonomics. I did not begin 20 years ago with the First Leisurely Theorem of Chapter 1; I began even before that by trying to solve the ancient "mind-body" problem. You see, theory mediates performance.

Chapter Eleven
Performance Engineering in Perspective

HERITAGE

When climbing among the rocks and boulders
For whatever may be found,
It's hard to tell if you're standing on shoulders
Or merely on shaky ground.

T.F.G.

DISTINGUISHING THE BEHAVIORAL AND PHYSICAL WORLDS

There are many ways to look at the sciences—some useful, some not. But one vantage point, seldom tried, is to view science as a performance system. To do this, we need to see science as a method of behaving that produces accomplishments. In this chapter I shall look at how the various systems of inquiry differ—especially compared with teleonomics—in their accomplishments (subject matter) and in their behavior (methodology). First, accomplishments. These four major accomplishments are common to all the sciences:

1. Identification of subject matter

2. Measurements

3. Generalizations (relationships, principles, etc.)

4. Applications (explanations, predictions, and controls)

We can examine the first two now. (The other two will be relevant when we discuss methodology.) I have already shown (in Chapters 1

and 2) how teleonomics identifies and measures its subject matter, and distinguishes it from the subject matter of behavior. But I have also shown that behavior is an important concern of the performance engineer. So let us look at how "behavioral" science differs from physics in both subject matter and measurements.

Classical mechanics, the science of Newton, is a good example. We begin to define its subject matter by identifying its fundamental and constant characteristics. Newton told us that all instances have three properties, or quantities: They consist of matter that has a mass (M), they extend in space (L), and they endure in time (T). Any event that doesn't have all three of these properties simply does not belong to the subject matter of "worldly" physics. And all other physical (mechanical) dimensions can be derived from these three properties: M (mass), L (spatial extension), and T (time). Velocity, then, has the dimensions of L/T (distance over time); and energy, ML^2/T^2.

If we ask just why these three dimensions are considered fundamental, we arrive at an important clue to establishing the fundamental dimensions of human behavior or the human mind (or the behavior of any animal, for that matter). First, there is a powerful face validity to the assertion that M, L, and T are fundamental. For most of us, no other set of three characteristics is so obviously common to all physical objects. It is not equally obvious, to most of us at least, that all objects have electrical capacitance or that they exert pressure. Second, the units of all other dimensions[1] can be derived from the units of the basic three. We might say, then, that they are considered basic because people have learned better how to cope with the physical world by treating them as basic. Other formulations of mechanics do not have the same utility and simplicity.

So, the three fundamental dimensions of matter have face validity, and they are pragmatic. But when we turn our attention to the measurement of people, of "mind," of behavior—or whatever you want to call that something which makes us certain that we are more than mere matter—neither the face validity nor the pragmatism of the physical quantities serves us. Indeed, "mind" seems to violate all the hard assumptions that we so usefully make about matter.

Try the face validity of M, L, and T as basic properties of mind or behavior. When we observe our minds, they don't seem to endure in time, but rather to be always in the present. It is as if time is enduring in the mind, rather than that the mind is enduring in time. And for space we have a similar experience; rather than that mind is occupying space, space seems to occupy the mind. "Mentally," distance seems different somehow. An object may take light years to move from the moon to a distant star; but our mind takes only an instant to make the move, requiring the tiniest adjustment of visual focus.

As for mass, each animal seems to contradict the basic laws of physical motion from which the scientific concept of mass was derived. Newton told us that an object just sits there until something exerts a force on it. Or, once moving, it will continue until something exerts a counterforce. Not so with behavior. The animal seems to get up and go without the slightest exertion of outside mechanical forces. The animal—and really, this is how we know that it is an animal—at every moment seems to disobey Newton's laws of motion. Instead of remaining at rest until a force is exerted on it, it seems to generate that force. True, both cats and people will fall in a vacuum predictably by the laws of gravity, whether they are dead or alive. But that certain something— that animation common to all animals, and from which they derive their name—seems somehow to "disobey" the laws of physics.

Of course, there are those who would argue (and as they are usually scientists, their arguments bear a certain weight) that if we but knew enough about it, we would see that behavior, too, could be accounted for by the same principles that govern the waterfall or the orbit of the moon. But these arguments are simply conjectures, and have no more real utility than the argument that a tiny green spirit governs us all.

Quite aside from having no support in experience, the argument that attributes purely physical cause to behavior or mind does not meet the second criterion we applied to determine the fundamental dimensions of matter: The argument has no pragmatism. Attempts to apply M, L, and T as fundamental quantities of human behavior simply are not useful; they don't get us anywhere.

But the search for fundamental dimensions of behavior can come to an end if we simply stop and look at how we measure M, L, and T. We must use a fixed standard: The ruler we lay against a box should not change appreciably in size. And when we measure the duration of a noise, say, we must count time in a steady, fixed rate. The physical things we measure can vary as they will—but the *behavior* of measuring must be fixed and steady. There is face validity to the assertion that animals are always assessing their environment and measuring the world about them, whether by complex or primitive means.

Then what could be more "fundamental," more universal, about behavior than the very act of measuring the "fundamental" properties of the physical world? As we determine that matter has mass, endures in time, and extends in space, we are displaying the most fundamental qualities that set us apart from "mere" matter. So we should examine this "fundamental" performance in order to discern the fundamental dimensions of behavior.

Let us begin with time. Figure 11-1 illustrates what an animal does as it measures time. What the "animal" is doing in this picture is moving its finger up and down at a fixed and steady tempo. But there

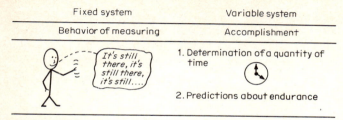

Fixed system	Variable system
Behavior of measuring	Accomplishment

1. Determination of a quantity of time

2. Predictions about endurance

FIGURE 11-1 Measurement of time.

are other ways to measure time. The sea cucumber does it, and the swallow; and we build mechanical devices to do it for us. What is common to all of these ways of measuring time? The animal "jitters" in one way or another, or gets something else to do the jittering. It doesn't matter how fast the animal jitters, or which part of its anatomy it jitters; nor does the distance of the jitter matter. All that matters is that the animal must jitter at a fixed rate if the outcome, the accomplishment, of the jitter is to have reliability. And, if an animal wishes to substitute for others in determining a mutually agreed-to time, it must jitter at a rate very near to theirs.

Now "jitter," in the physical system we have constructed for ourselves, is called "frequency"; and it is dimensionally expressed in that system as the reciprocal of time, or $1/T$. Without the jitter, there would be no experience of time for the animal, for the mind, for people. (For example, in experiments in which the jitter of the eye is stopped, vision disappears.)

From now on, I shall call this jitter the "tempo" (if only because it sounds more scientific than "jitter"). To make tempo a reference that is useful for measuring time, it must be steady and fixed like a clock. But tempo isn't necessarily fixed, and it can and does vary from animal to animal, from "mind" to "mind," and from time to time. Our power to vary our tempo, without any known outside force, is one of the fundamental universals of behavior. And it should not surprise us that we must express tempo as the reciprocal (the "opposite") of time. That "oppositeness" squares cleanly with the experience we have when we introspect and try to look at the mind as enduring in time. It just doesn't. Instead, time "flows" in the mind as we jitter away.

Tempo can be translated into various useful units of frequency. One simple unit of tempo is probability—the probability of responding. And that is why this unit has gradually worked its way into such a fundamental status in psychology. Animals learn; they increase the probability that they will respond in certain ways to certain stimuli. And "mental" experiences such as pitch and color are measured by frequencies.

When we observed the system of measuring time, we saw that behavior (tempo) had to be fixed as a standard. And we also saw that the animal performing the measurement permitted the object to vary as it would—let it stay where it was as long as it would. To the best of our ability when we measure things, we don't want the act of measuring to change those things we measure, that is, if we want our measures to be "true." But just as the animal fixes its tempo to measure time, it may vary its tempo for other purposes. And when we are focusing on animal performance rather than on the physical properties of the world, we let the animal vary its tempo as it will. Figure 11-2 illustrates this.

When we measure the tempo of behavior, we simply count; we count frequencies by a fixed system of time. And just as the measurement of time can be sophisticated or primitive, so can our measurement of tempo. Predicting the probability of the occurrence of human behavior is of fundamental value to us—as fundamental as predicting when or how some physical event will change in time. So, tempo is as "fundamental" as time. Only it is in a different system of measurement, one designed to account for the behavior of live animals rather than of dead objects.

Having established one fundamental quality of the mind, we are emboldened to use the same technique to identify the other two. And why must there be three? Suffice it to say that because there are (classically) three fundamental physical quantities, there must be at least three fundamental ways the mind can view the world.

Take mass. We measure the mass of an object most simply by exerting a force on it: We push it or we lift it. The force of weight or gravity, then, is a reliable clue to the comparative mass of an object. And in order to make a reliable estimate of mass, we must have a fixed reference; our units of "push" or "lift" must be consistent, as in Figure 11-3.

To measure mass, then, we need a standardized system of force—or, better, of accelerated movement. And to provide that acceleration, we have to "break" a fundamental law of physics: We must, somehow,

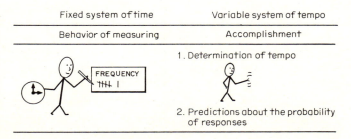

Fixed system of time	Variable system of tempo
Behavior of measuring	Accomplishment

1. Determination of tempo

2. Predictions about the probability of responses

FIGURE 11-2   Measurement of tempo.

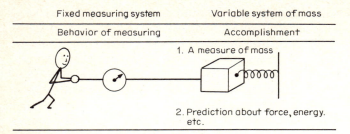

FIGURE 11-3   Measurement of mass.

generate motion without waiting for some physical force to set us into motion. The very act of generating a force—of "accelerating"—becomes a fundamental property of behavior. And that act gives us one of the fundamental properties for defining the behavior of an animal. We know that it is an animal because it can "accelerate" without an identifiable physical force to cause the "acceleration."

"Acceleration" in some way then becomes a fundamental property of behavior; we can measure it by letting it vary as it will, and by fixing a physical mass as a reference. And predicting the "acceleration" with which an animal will act—how likely it is to "get up and go" in order to change the world—is as fundamentally important to us as predicting changes in physical mass. In that sense, we might say that the mind is "weightless"—which seems obvious—but has great "acceleration," great animation.

And because the "acceleration" of the animal is not to be confused with the forces of physics, we need another word for it, and perhaps *animation* will do. Because, after all, remember that it is this one property that finally determines if we identify something as a living animal.

Again, as with tempo, there is a certain "oppositeness" of animation to the physical quantity of mass. In physics, acceleration can be described as the relationship of force to mass:

$$a = \frac{F}{M}$$

It therefore bears a reciprocal relationship to mass, just as it does if we accept the mind as a measuring tool. But again, as with tempo, that reciprocity is not useful to the physicist.

Finally, we come to the third and perhaps most difficult property of mind: the "opposite" of length, or extension in space. Characteristic of the "oppositeness" of the properties of "mind and matter," this one is as tricky to grasp as the concept of length in physics is easy.

Length in perception has a certain independence of length as measured by a ruler. As we move away from a package of cigarettes, the length of its physical image on our retina grows smaller; nevertheless, the package seems 80 millimeters long at any distance. And, in certain experiments where references are removed, we can shrink the package to 40 "ruler-measured" millimeters, and it will still be an 80-millimeter object in our perception. How far or near an object is, how large or small, is relative to our point of view. But in order to get reliable measures of physical length, we must fix our point of view, as illustrated in Figure 11-4. Our "minds" work so that we can usually fix our standard of length measurement independently of our distance from an object. If we stand farther away from an object than someone else, we will both still say it is the same length, because both of us will take a common vantage point: "as if we were next to it." This capacity of ours for "size constancy" is fundamental to perception.

And, just as vantage points must be fixed for us to account reliably for variances in physical spaces, they must be permitted to vary freely if we wish to measure this property of the mind. It is as fundamentally important to us to determine the vantage point—the point of view—of others as it is to determine the distance we have to travel. But minds can vary freely in their vantage points, just as matter can vary in its extension. And we can measure vantage points in many ways—by measuring the way animals generalize and discriminate, for example; or how people make choices.

Again, as with tempo and animation, this fundamental characteristic of behavior has a certain "oppositeness." The reciprocal of length in the physical system, $1/L$, is called "curvature," a change in direction. It is this capacity to change its direction—its vantage point or its point of view—that is so universally characteristic of the animal. I call this fundamental property *vantage.*

So we see that the three fundamental properties of animal behavior (or mind) are the three classes of behavior by which the animal observes the most fundamental properties of the world:

Fixed measuring system	Variable system of length
Behavior of measuring	Accomplishment

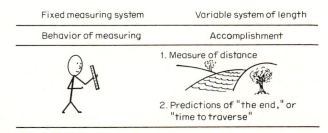

1. Measure of distance

2. Predictions of "the end," or "time to traverse"

FIGURE 11-4   Measurement of length.

1. *Tempo,* with one convenient unit being the probability of a response.

2. *Animation,* with one convenient unit being the acceleration of a response. Or, by holding certain things constant, we can use units of force, work, and the like, to measure animation.

3. *Vantage,* with convenient units yet to be established with any amount of agreement. The performance matrix is one of many ways of classifying vantage. Discrimination measures are also common.

It should be clear that, in all of this, we did not observe behavior in a vacuum, but as it acted in conjunction with the physical world. No dualism has been constructed, no assumption that there are two universes, mind and matter. Rather, the assumption is of one world with *at least* two ways of looking at it. In this world there is forever an interaction between the system measured and the measuring system. And the meaning of either system is given by an understanding about the other. Largeness or smallness, long times and short times, have no meaning except as we know the vantage or tempo that is fixed for the occasion. Similarly, to say that a person has a high or low probability of responding has no meaning unless we know the time frame fixed as a reference.

SPECIFYING METHODOLOGICAL VANTAGE POINTS

At least one thing should be clear from all this. We must be careful to specify our vantage points when we decide to measure behavior. And although we have learned to do this reasonably well when looking at the world physically, we have not been so successful when looking at human performance or human behavior.

Of course, one vantage point we can specify when observing the world would distinguish whether we are looking at it behaviorally or physically. Indeed, modern physics did not come into being until rather rigid specifications of its vantage points were made—and as recently as the sixteenth and seventeenth centuries. It was people like Galileo and Newton who succeeded in taking the "mind" out of "matter" and fixing the fundamental properties of the physical system. And a few psychologists—most particularly Pavlov, Thorndike, and Skinner—have begun to perform somewhat the same service for the animal, for the "mind," by establishing methods of measurement; and identifying laws that govern the tempo (e.g., rates of responding), animation (e.g., amplitudes of response), and vantage (e.g., generalizations and discriminations).

But once we have our subject matters straightened out, we also need to differentiate the methods we use to study them. The laboratories of the sciences physics and "psychics" (we might call it) have something in common, even though they work from two fundamentally different subject-matter vantage points. They are both methodologically "diachronic," meaning that they cut across time and place. The laws of force are specified for all times and places and are meant to be universal. Similarly, the principles of reinforcement are intended to be statements about conditions governing animal behavior at all times and in all places. Both of these sciences further their work by escaping from the immediate culture into the laboratory, where standardized and generalizable conditions can be approximated.

Of course, the principles of each of these sciences are different. They have, indeed, that kind of "oppositeness" characteristic of their fundamental variables: force and reinforce; prior and subsequent cause. One subject matter begins at rest, or in steady motion, and is made to vary by forces impinging upon it. The other subject matter, the animal, begins as infinitely variable, and its motions become stereotyped and steady as the result of certain consequences. But in either subject the common vantage point is diachronic. The inclined plane of physics becomes a simple, convenient, and universal model to study the mass and motion of objects; the Skinner box becomes a similarly simple, convenient, and universal model to study the tempo and animation of animals.

There is another vantage point that inquiry can take—one that could be called "synchronic," meaning that it goes along with time. This is the cultural and historical view, the view of meteorologists and sociologists. It is no more or less important than the diachronic view, just useful for different purposes. In the synchronic studies, we concern ourselves with how objects wear down the coastline of the country, foment into hurricanes, or prepare to avalanche—in a general, but neither topical nor universal way. In the diachronic laboratory of, say, experimental psychology, we look for conditions that change gradients of generalization, whereas from the synchronic view of the sociologist we measure the strength of generalizations in certain human beings toward, say, the skin color of other human beings.

In the diachronic sciences we use the technique of control. We do not need to study how learning comes about under conditions as they exist. Rather, we change conditions to see how we can control the rate of learning, searching for those variables that assert control over the rate of learning. But in synchronic inquiry, we rely more on prediction than on control. We measure learning as it occurs in a school or community.

Even though diachronic and synchronic disciplines have some important differences in methodology, they do not operate totally apart. The findings of the diachronic laboratory are put to use in synchronic

predictions. When we observe that a feather falls as fast in a vacuum as a lead ball, we formulate the law of gravity. This law is one bit of knowledge we then apply when we attempt to predict how fast feathers will fall from the Empire State Building or how fast an airplane will fall when its engines die.

But synchronic prediction doesn't satisfy another urge we have—the urge to control the world—and diachronic control is too restricted in its scope to satisfy that urge fully. So we bring these two vantage points into their best relationship by adopting a third vantage point, one that we might call *metachronic*, meaning "change in time." Or, to put it more familiarly, *engineering*. We are not always satisfied merely to predict events in the world; we are driven to control things in the "real" world—to engineer that world. And our engineering success will depend largely on our knowledge of both diachronic principles and synchronic facts. Table 11-1 summarizes these three vantage points.

In the diachronic laboratory, we are interested in fundamental processes—for example, how energy is generated. And in synchronic sciences, we are concerned with the results or outcomes of whatever processes are operative (for example, how much energy people will use next year, or what size population the available energy will support). But from a metachronic, or engineering, vantage point, we try to apply our diachronic principles to the control of events in the "real" world. In metachronic inquiry, we want to know how to control a process to get an outcome (for example, knowing how energy is generated, we can build a system to meet the energy demands of next year; or, knowing the available energy, we can control the birth rate so that the population will not be excessive).

TABLE 11-1　THREE SCIENTIFIC VANTAGE POINTS

Methodology	*Diachronic*	*Synchronic*	*Metachronic*
Principal locus of inquiry	Laboratory	Real world	Real world
Focus of subject matters	Process (e.g., how particles interact)	Results (e.g., how much mountains erode)	Process and results (e.g., what can be done to prevent the mountain from eroding)
Kinds of laws or generalizations	Universal (for all time and all places)	General (for these times and places)	Topical (for this time and place)
Principal method of testing	Control	Prediction	Control
Typical disciplines	Physics Experimental psychology Physiology	Meteorology Ecology Economics	Mechanical engineering Education Management

THE SPECTRUM OF SCIENCES

In discussing these vantage points, we are viewing *science* (to use that word in its broadest sense) as a performance system. And well we should, because science is in the very nature of human competence. The accomplishment of science is valuable knowledge about how to cope with the world; its behavior is an efficient means of inquiry. And, as we are seeing, the different sciences can be distinguished both by the kinds of knowledge they create (their subject matters) and by their general methods of inquiry (metachronic, synchronic, and diachronic).

We have seen three basic kinds of subject matter: first, the physical world, or the world aside from behavior; next, behavior; and, finally, performance, or the valuable effects that costly behavior has upon the world—the peculiar interaction of psychics and physics. We have also seen three kinds of methodology: first, the kind that removes its subject matter from the influences of the real world in order to study its basic characteristics through control and manipulation; next, the kind that views its subject matter right where it is in the real world in order to predict what will happen to it or to explain why it happened; and, finally, the kind that attempts to modify its subject matter "on site" right there in the real world. Now, by putting together these two ways (methodology and subject matter) of looking at the sciences, we can form a classification scheme—a "spectrum of the sciences," illustrated in Table 11-2.

The table shows nine kinds of sciences (or 12, if you distinguish the physical properties of matter and those of life). But it should not suggest that all sciences are hard-and-fast fits into one of its cells. For example, paleontology, which deals with life in past geological periods, combines the methods of geology, ecology, and descriptive biology.

The performance-engineering sciences (in cell IIIC of Table 11-2) are those I call teleonomics—a category not often perceived as belonging in the pantheon of the sciences. This classification distinguishes between performance engineering and behavior modification, because the latter focuses on behavior and not on accomplishments. "Behavior modifiers" or psychotherapists may, as I've said earlier, work at getting rid of tics, depression, and so on, without making the economics of accomplishments their major focus. "Training," in the most narrow sense (e.g., toilet training), is behavioral engineering; but "training" in the world of work is a form of performance engineering. Like education, it becomes a performance science only when it focuses primarily on what effects it intends to have upon the world.

Economics illustrates the desirable relationships between synchronic and metachronic sciences. It is, for the most part, a synchronic

TABLE 11-2   THE SPECTRUM OF THE SCIENCES

Subject Matter \ Methods	A Diachronic	B Synchronic	C Metachronic
(a) Physics **I** Physical	Physics Chemistry, etc.	Geology Astronomy, etc.	Mechanical engineering, etc.
(b) Biology	Genetics Experimental zoology, etc.	Ecology Descriptive zoology, etc.	Medicine Agricultural engineering, etc.
II Behavioral	Experimental psychology, etc.	Ethology Social psychology, etc.	Psychotherapy Behavior modification Physical education, etc.
III Performance	"Experimental philosophy"	Economics Political science, etc.	Performance engineering Management Education, etc.

performance science, because it studies general (though certainly not universal) relationships that exist naturally between the behavior of people (producing and consuming) and its effect upon the world; and it of course measures these relationships in terms of value, cost, and worth. So, economics is to teleonomics much as geology is to mining engineering.

The distinction between methodological types (diachronic, etc.) does not imply a rigid pigeon-holing of methodologies. The principal method of diachronic physics and psychology, for example, is often experimental. But others may engage in experiments too, just as a structural engineer may experiment with the structural strength of different kinds of building materials, or a sociologist may experiment with the effects of different media on the formation of opinions. Presumably, sociologists will perform such experiments for predictive purposes. But as soon as they attempt to manipulate opinions in the real world, they become "behavioral engineers," because their purpose is no longer synchronic.

Of course, there are many other points of view besides scientific ones. There are artistic and religious vantage points, to name but two. Architects, for example, combine not only the scientific vantages of both physical and performance engineering, but also artistic points of view—and, sometimes, as they design cathedrals, even religious vantage points.

There is no reason to consider one kind of specialty as being more

demanding or more exalted than another, so long as they are all performed competently. The absence of a clear focus on the purpose of one's specialty, however, must contribute considerably to the less-than-exemplary performance so often found in these areas. The cause of improving human competence would be greatly advanced, it seems to me, if all the various kinds of behavioral and performance engineers comprehended the special role their work plays in the whole context of worthy performance. Specialists of one aspect of performance hardly advance the cause when they see all of performance centering upon their particular interest. Without a larger plan which we can use to diagnose the area of greatest leverage, much useless energy will be dissipated. The situation, as it now exists, is like having plumber, electrician, carpenter, and mason all working in complete ignorance of each other, each with a set of specifications, while no one has seen the architect's blueprints. Without a performance "architect"—the most general kind of performance engineer—the situation is not likely to improve. Each kind of specialist will continue to promote a special set of skills as the real solution to performance problems. And, sadly, this narrow view will continue to be reinforced simply because there is no area of behavior that cannot be improved.

The analogy of the performance engineer and the architect is a good one. Both must begin by discovering what the client wishes to accomplish, what values the client holds, and what the client is willing or able to pay to achieve these accomplishments. Neither asks which kind of structure is desirable until the purposes of the project are clear. Neither presumes to be the ultimate specialist on the structure itself. The performance engineer does not need to be artful at designing equipment, performing psychotherapy, or conducting training, any more than the architect needs to be clever at creating gargoyles or laying a plumbing system. Each needs only to know when these things are needed; how much should be invested in them; and what their critical limits are.

Teleonomics is clearly a metachronic inquiry. It is a kind of engineering, which brings existing knowledge of universal principles and social generalizations together for the purpose of creating a more or less topical result: the improvement of the competence of institutions, people, or even individuals. In doing so, it also develops very specific information about existing performance, values, and the like. It is science in the sense that it deals in observation and measurement, but not in the sense that it seeks universal laws and relationships. When we try to engineer competence, just as when we try to build a bridge, our interest is topical and vested in a valuable outcome. Teleonomics is metachronic in that its subject matter is a result of some value and a process of some cost.

But if teleonomics is the metachronic form of performance science and economics the synchronic form, what is the diachronic performance science? By extrapolation, I think it is the science best suited to inquire into the universalities of values, costs, and worth.

Distinguishing among the scientific vantage points, as well as all the other useful points of view, is as of much importance as the subject matters of these viewpoints. The truly universal constant in human performance, then, is the adoption of vantage points themselves—philosophy. And I have recognized this by listing "experimental philosophy" in cell IIIA of the scientific spectrum (Table 11-2).

I have placed philosophy at the experimental end of the spectrum because, in my view, that is where it belongs. Experimentation with points of view will lead to better theories of them—and better systems for understanding how to use them more effectively. As it is now, philosophy is the least experimental of professions, and many people who are devoted to it seem to be monocular advocates of one vantage point or another rather than detached devotees to the marvelous variety of the subject matter. But the potential for an experimental philosophy is great; it is here that the largest PIP lies. The ratio of the value of the accomplishments of the few exemplary philosophers—Copernicus, Newton, and the like—immeasurably exceeds those of the many scholastics who create abstruse accounts of the meaning of a paragraph from Plotinus or Hegel, or struggle with singular definitions of "the truth."

A truly lively and no-nonsense experimental philosophy will, of course, lead to such developments in the subject matter that our school curricula will become vastly changed, and children will learn the usefulness of the many vantage points in laboratories, just as they now discover that a feather falls in a vacuum like a rock. The subject matter of philosophy, the vantage points of people, is as real, as potent, and as infinitely interesting as the cells of biology, the mysterious particles of physics, and the behavior patterns of rats. Experimental philosophy, because of its potential for usefulness to the cause of leisure, will surely be the next development in a truly systematic science; and then the ninth cell in our spectrum of sciences will be complete.

LOVE AND PERFORMANCE ENGINEERING

From the teleonomic point of view, behavior is a costly item that has no value of its own. It is merely a means to an end. And the teleonomic outlook can be extremely useful to us for the accomplishment of certain goals. But the improvement of human performance is not something many of us would like to engage in all the time. Performance engineering is a job just like any other; and performance engineers, like physicians, do not need to take their work home with them. Physicians, in their offices, also view behavior from a specialized

stance—as a symptomatic indication of disease or health. We much prefer those physicians who do not look at us as mere animals, but who stand with us as human beings as they view that part of us which is animal. Similarly, we shall find behavior modifiers and performance engineers more congenial people if they restrict their specialized points of view to the specialized purpose they are trying to serve. If I regard my wife principally as someone to train, that would be like the economists regarding their wives chiefly as tax deductions.

There is quite another view of behavior—one that does not see it as a costly investment, an animal to be trained, or as a set of symptoms. This viewpoint is not very specialized, but it can be extremely useful to us. It is called "love," and it is in many ways the opposite of the scientific vantage point. For example, when we act as performance engineers, behavior is costly and has no value. But, in love, it is behavior that we value. Indeed, behavior can become so valuable to us that it becomes priceless—so that we cannot deal with it in economic terms. It is the behavior of my child, my lover, my friends that I love— not their accomplishments.

Some behaviorists, of course, would tell us that *love* is a nonsense word: an emotional and superstitious-laden word that really stands only for a certain class of conditioned responses. But love, regardless of its origins (and they are many, including everything from glandular activity to reinforcement histories), nonetheless emerges as a simple, elegant, and greatly useful vantage point—just as useful as the view-points of art, science, and engineering. Love is the vantage point in which we cease to see other people's behavior as merely costly means to our ends (or costly barriers to them). Love, then, becomes extremely useful because with it goes trust: the knowledge that I can depend on other people *not* to treat me as merely an animal, and to live up to their part of the bargain. When the love is not there, and its attendant trust, I must engage in all manner of costly protective activity, dissipating human capital. If the vantage point of love should disappear, slavery would be the norm and every "free" person would have to live within a fortress, because then all people's behavior would be viewed merely as animal activities. When we view people as only animals, as nothing more than the products of their conditioning and cellular activity, we shall sensibly treat them as we treat wolves, cows, and horses: kill them, pen them, and ride them. And that is the way they will treat us, though the more enlightened animal trainers will treat us (the more useful of us) as pets, using positive reinforcement rather than punishment only because the former is a more efficient training tactic. It is the vantage point of love that prevents us from living in a completely dog-eat-dog or dog-train-dog world. From the standpoint of increasing human capital, love is extremely useful.

Among those people of cyclopean vision, unable to organize the

various vantage points into useful schemes, are certain romantics who despise the technologies, believing them to be inconsistent with the nature of love. But in a truly competent world, people will call upon those vantage points that are most efficient for the purposes they pursue at any given time. There is an animal within us, as well as a chemistry, and it cries to be trained, used, and enjoyed. We can take the vantage point of a behaviorist to learn more about how we train this animal; the vantage point of teleonomics to decide what we will train it for and how to engineer that training; the viewpoint of the accountant to help us budget the activity. But if everyone stands also in the vantage point of love, we will know that others are training us to a mutually agreeable purpose and that the benefits of the activity will be fairly distributed among us.

Nothing can more graphically illustrate the importance, the usefulness, of love as a vantage point, to be taken simultaneously with others, than the act of sex itself. If the woman views the man as merely an animal out to satisfy his animal lusts by treating her as a mere animal convenience, love does not exist. On their part, women, too, can treat men as mere sex objects. But when both parties lie together in the human position, as it were, and watch their animals cavort pleasurably with each other, putting no price on the activity and fairly distributing the pleasure, love is master and leisure reaches its highest meaning.

So it is in the world of work. When manager, investor, laborer, and customer fail to stand together in the human position and direct the animals within themselves to perform efficiently for a common end, fairly distributing the rewards, each sees the other as only an animal out for self-gratification; then love flies out the window and leisure with it. To love is to stand in the human vantage point, which requires us to stand with others for a common purpose.

But so diverse is humankind—so varied our many interests, talents, and tastes—that I know of only one common purpose that can bind us together as human beings and not merely as a pack of animals using each other for our own immediate and selfish ends. I have already commented on that common purpose, on which we can all agree and toward which we can strive to apply our individualities efficiently. That purpose is human capital: the product of time and opportunity.

NOTE

1. For the sake of convenience, scientists, by international agreement, have established seven physical quantities as fundamental. Nevertheless, all physical measurement can be treated in the units of these three quantities.

An Application of Performance Engineering

Presented here is a detailed example of a successful case of performance analysis and engineering, which represents work that was implemented under contract with a large corporation. This project had two particularly happy results: It substantially reduced manufacturing costs, both by increasing productivity and by cutting the waste of valuable products; and it reduced turnover by transforming a punishing, almost degrading, job into one that was meaningful and highly productive. The principles illustrated are perfectly general, and the method would apply equally well in the world of schools or in the management of a scientific laboratory.

SAVORY SNACKS: A CASE STUDY

Just above the Watnong River, the corporate office of Savory Snacks, Inc., is buried somewhere in the bowels of its largest manufacturing plant. The plant is a functional brown and green, one-story box that looks more like a warehouse than a busy factory employing over a thousand people. Those people have an appearance as square, clean, and orderly as the plant, in their white uniforms and sanitary hats; and well they should, for they have committed, if not devoted, their lives to the manufacture of snacks: namely, potato chips and corn chips.

As you breach the sterile front of Plant 18, you are pleasantly lifted by odors only slightly more acrid than those of a bakery. Just beyond a side entrance, on the left, are the carpeted floors of Savory Snack's management; and the lettering on one of the opaque glass windows reads, "Byron M. N. Ides, Vice President of Manufacturing." Byron, a stocky, swarthy young man who looks more like a stevedore than a *magna cum laude* graduate of an Ivy League school (which is what he

is), keeps it more or less a secret that he doesn't eat potato chips. Not that he lacks pride in his products. He is aware that through its 18,000 employees and their families, and its distributors and suppliers, the company provides healthy economic support for a population that is the equivalent of a good-sized American city. In his own way, Byron Ides thinks that he is as devoted to "high purpose" as Kathy Jenkins (of Chapter 4), however much his free enterprise, paternalistic style may contrast with her liberal paternalism. If Savory Snacks should go bankrupt, he knows that many thousands of people would be without the means to support themselves. And if the company operates inefficiently, there will be fewer dollars for wages as well as profits. Indeed, Byron sees Savory Snacks as the nation's economy in microcosm, and he thinks it is almost a patriotic duty to achieve competent performance in his manufacturing plants.

Byron is one of the "new breed" of managers, recently elevated to his job in a drive to bolster the company's sagging profits. He is not certain where the answer to Savory Snack's problems lie, but he is determined to increase manufacturing efficiency. But where should he start? Almost all of the company's 30 plants are modern, beautifully equipped, sanitary, scheduled by computer, and supported by productive research and development in all aspects of potato chip manufacturing. No industry in the land can boast more up-to-date production facilities. Convinced that his impact on the company must be made through human, not machine, performance, Byron wisely decides to conduct a performance audit to analyze the competence of his charges; and the performance matrix will help him know where to begin, how to proceed, and what decisions he must make.

Byron spends a good part of his first weeks collecting views of various managers from several plants—particularly those that have the poorest production histories. Most of these managers seem to blame their problems on packaging, and there is a rather widely held view that the first-line packaging-machine supervisors aren't doing their jobs. When Byron asks for suggestions, several plant managers contend that the company might develop some sort of training for these people.

Byron doesn't rush to accept these recommendations. He is merely trying to get the lay of the land before beginning the performance audit. He has had enough experience to know that solutions are easier to offer than problems are to diagnose. So he begins his audit at the policy level by looking at the manufacturing operation as a whole in a single plant. Of course, everyone tells him that this will prove fruitless, since "every plant is different." Byron doesn't accept this argument; but in the interest of making his analysis as free of local peculiarities as possible, he decides to create a model plant on paper. He can then use this model as a "ruler" for measuring how other plants are doing. This is how he conducts his audit.

Policy-Level Analysis

1. *The organization.* Byron Ides has to contend with several variables in creating a model for the manufacturing organization. For example, he could divide line responsibilities by product (with a potato manager, say, and a corn manager); or by process, with each manager (packaging, processing, receiving, and shipping managers) responsible for both types of products. Ides elects the "process" model—but only because it requires only three levels of line management, whereas the "product" model here requires four, as Figure A-1 shows. This is important to him because he believes that all organizations should basically have a three-tiered line-management structure, with the tiers rather closely corresponding to the levels in the performance matrix of Chapter 4. The first tier of management, he thinks, should be responsible for *tactical* execution; the second tier, for *strategic* planning; and the third, for *policy* decisions. Byron wouldn't even know which responsibilities to assign to a fourth tier. As far as he is concerned, the leaner the line-management structure, the better: Fewer people have to make decisions, and the top manager is closer to the business. Byron completes the organization chart for his model plant by applying such ideas.

2. *Work-information flow.* A table of organization is a picture of the structure of an institution, but it doesn't tell us much about how things get done. So Byron's next step is to create a model of how the work should flow through a plant, and also how information about that work should be processed (who learns what about what is going on, and when). His work-flow model is in Figure A-2.

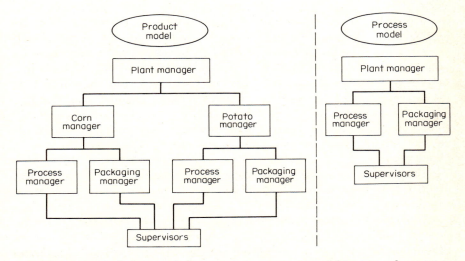

FIGURE A-1 Ides' choices of plant management structure (shipping and receiving omitted).

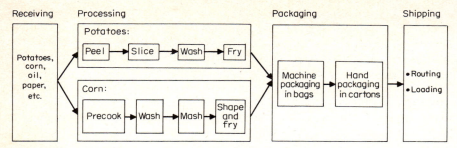

FIGURE A-2   Work flow of potato and corn chip manufacture.

3. *Plant economics.* Byron is too new to the business of potato chips to have a clear view of its economics. He would like a diagram of plant economics that will give him the big picture, and not let details obscure what is important. He goes to the corporate accountant and immediately runs into two problems. First, the accountant has enormous quantities of data, but Byron is unable to get an overview from them. Second, much of the data lump several plants together. Byron's question is a simple one: "Suppose that I were to consider buying a plant to run as a completely separate business. How much money could I expect it to make? How much control would I have over the expenditures? And what is the nature of these expenditures?"

The evening after Byron sees the corporate accountant, he tries to explain his frustrations to his wife, Laura, who is working for an advanced degree in sociology and admits to knowing nothing about business. "Why," she asks, "do you want to talk to the accountant, anyway? I thought you said you were interested in improving people's performance. What does a set of books have to do with that?"

"Because," Byron replies, "I want to be able to measure performance improvement so I can be sure if it happened or not. *And* I want to know more about *how* to make it happen again. Suppose that potatoes cost a lot of money, and the wrapping paper is real cheap. Then I'm going to worry a lot more about how people handle potatoes than how they handle paper, no? And if I really can get people to perform more efficiently, then potato expenses should go down, shouldn't they?"

"I suppose so," Laura says vaguely, thinking that something sounds slightly evil about it all. "Can you really measure human performance by dollars?"

"Money isn't really what it's all about, Laura. It's productivity. Don't your professors teach you that a society that is able to produce more efficiently is happier and less frustrated—that people get unhappy when they aren't able to accomplish things where they work? Money is just a convenient measuring stick," Byron orates.

"Well . . . but there's something so . . . so . . . *ignoble* about it!"

Noble or ignoble, Byron has an immediate problem. If he is going to be able to pay for vacation trips to Europe, he is going to have to show his boss that he can change manufacturing efficiency; and Byron is still naïve enough to think that his boss will accept no other kind of measure.

So Byron digs through tons of data, and finally creates the imaginary plant "budget" illustrated in Table A-1. The data are based on his analysis of what a plant could do *if* it operated at peak efficiency, since he derived his numbers from the best days in the best plants in Savory Snacks.

This crude budget tells Byron many things. For example, he can figure from it that a 20-percent increase in the cost of materials would cut the company's profits in half if it happened in all 30 plants. He can see that direct labor costs are only 15 percent of the cost of materials. Then, if he could cut waste and reduce the costs of materials by 10 percent ($560,000) by paying his labor 10 percent ($76,000) more, the net gain would be close to a half-million dollars a year. If he could do that in 30 plants, he might raise the company's profits by 50 percent. So even though Byron has barely seen the inside of a real plant, he is getting more than a superficial idea of what the business is about.

4. *Performance PIPs.* Byron is ready now to begin a performance

TABLE A-1 MANUFACTURING ECONOMICS OF A TYPICAL PLANT

Description	Total	Corn Product	Potato Product
Market value	$16,000,000	$ 8,000,000	$ 8,000,000
Ingredient cost	$ 3,600,000	$ 1,400,000	$ 2,200,000
Packaging materials cost	2,000,000	1,050,000	950,000
Total materials cost	5,600,000	2,450,000	3,150,000
Total direct labor	$ 760,000	$ 375,000	$ 390,000
Manufacturing expenses (13+%)	2,200,000	1,100,000	1,100,000
Cost of manufacturing	$ 8,560,000	$ 3,925,000	$ 4,640,000
Pounds produced	22,400,000	12,000,000	10,400,000
Equipment			
Fryer (large)	6	4	2
Packaging machines	16	8	8
Relevant personnel			
Machine operators	16	8	8
Cooks	12	8	4
Other			
Two 8-hour shifts; 5-day week; 52 weeks per year; 260 days per year			

table at the policy level, and he has identified the four major missions of a Savory Snacks plant:

1. Raw material storage
2. Materials processed
3. Foods packaged
4. Packages shipped

And when Byron completes his performance table for each of these missions, he finds two sizable PIPs that translate into many dollars.

Packaging = 4

Processing = 2.75

He estimates that by reducing these PIPs, he would be able to save the company $624,000 a year in packaging, and $195,000 a year in processing. The performance table for packaging is shown in Table A-2. There are 30 plants, so Byron calculates that the potential for savings in packaging alone for the entire company is $18,720,000 in wasted wrapping paper, potatoes, and corn. Byron decides to concentrate on packaging as his first project. He sets his sights at reducing the PIP of 4 to at least 1.25, which would save the company $17,160,000 a year.

5. *To whom to attribute the PIP?* Byron now has to decide whose performance in packaging he must concentrate on. Remember, the talk around the company is of the need for training for packaging-machine supervisors. This assumes that they are the source of the PIP. So Byron gets data on the worst- and best-performing supervisors in a typical plant. It so happens that they work on the same production line, but on different shifts. Figure A-3 shows comparisons of their performance. (Each supervisor has four operations under him.)

Just from inspection, Byron can see that the PIP can't really be pinned on the supervisors. The best supervisor does have the exemplary operator working for him, but he also has three bummers. The high turnover (shown in Figure A-3) seemingly inherent in the packaging department helps explain the small variations among the supervisors. As new workers come in, the plant managers distribute them around, so that no supervisor has an experienced corps of operators for long.

6. *What causes the PIP?* In college, Byron Ides had studied statistics, and he was left with the impression that statistical curves (normal distributions) were inherent in human performance. Yet this always bothered him. In spite of his politically conservative, "businesslike" attitudes, he is a very sociable fellow, and doesn't think of people as

TABLE A-2   POTATO CHIP PACKAGING PERFORMANCE TABLE

(1) Accomplishment	(2) Standards (a) Requirement	(b) Exemplar	(3) Impact of PIP	(4) Performance	Actual (Value) (Cost) (5) (Value) (Cost)	(6) No.	(7) Total	(8) PIP	(9) Value of Correcting PIP
Chips packaged	Weight and quality standards	99.9% meet govt. standards	a. Sales loss b. Rejection	>99%	—	—	—	→1.0	Very small
	Rate	100% of production quotas met	Misses quota (labor)	>98%	—	—	—	→1.0	Very small
	Materials cost	Wastes 100 lb/day (av.)	Product waste Paper waste	Av. PMO wastes 400 lb/day	400 lb × $0.50/lb × 260 days =	16 PMOs	$832,000	4	$624,000
	Labor costs	1 PMO per 3 machines	Excess labor	1 PMO per 3 machines	—	—	—	—	—

I. Line A, potato–chip packaging: percentage of product waste standard

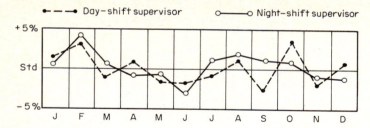

II. Corn fryers: percentage of product waste standard

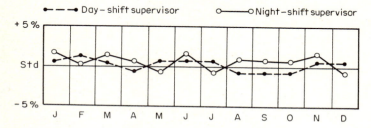

III. Annual turnover under packaging machine operator supervisors

Supervisor	Number of employees	Number of replacements, 1970 and 1971
A	4	7
B	4	6
C	4	5
D	4	5

FIGURE A-3 Variation in performance of same production lines under different supervisors.

statistics. He grew up on the wrong side of town; and, given a few opportunities, "made something of himself." He firmly believes that this can happen to any "average person." So, Byron genuinely believes that he can get average packaging-machine operators to engage in exemplary performance. His next question is not, "Why do the average do so poorly?" Everyone in his company is always asking that, with the pat answers, "They don't care," or "They're too dumb." Instead, he asks the question, "Why does the exemplar perform so well?"

He decides to go to the floor to find out. He disguises himself as a new employee in packaging, and has a plant manager assign him to the crew in which the exemplar works. To do this, he takes a week's leave

from his job; his associates think that he has taken leave of his senses.

After his fourth night on the late shift, where all new employees are assigned, he slumps wearily into his favorite chair and stares at his wife.

"Laura, it's a terrible job. No wonder these guys quit their jobs so easily. You know what they told me? It takes 2 years to become a good operator! Who could stand it for 2 years?"

"How does this exemplar stand it—what's his name?" Laura asks.

"Carol Andrea. But 'he's' a girl, and she's the only one in the plant who's an operator."

"Girls can take it, you're telling me?" Laura suggests.

"No, that's not the reason at all. She used to work for the packaging-machine manufacturer. She really understands these machines. It's an easy job for her, and she's proud of her performance. But I don't understand the machine. I swear it was built by Rube Goldberg."

The next day, Byron dictates the following memo to the Vice President for Personnel:

—MEMO—

TO: Merle Waterman, V.P., Personnel
FROM: B. Ides, V.P., Manufacturing
SUBJECT: PMO Training

You told me the PMOs had good training. I beg to differ.

The manner of inducting a new PMO varies from plant to plant, but the story is never a good one. Here is a typical story: The new man is assigned to a shift and spends 3 weeks, sometimes 2 months, doing little more than carrying canisters of paper, sweeping up, and doing similar jobs. Gradually, he is introduced to such minor machine operations as turning the machine on or adjusting a scale. When a significant work shortage occurs, he may be thrown unprepared into the breach—suddenly he is a packaging-machine operator. He has no theory of how the machine works. He knows nothing substantial about the economics of the machine—e.g., how much it costs when 200 bags are destroyed in an hour. By the very nature of the timing of his assignment, he finds himself working in a mad-house atmosphere.

Alternatively, he may be assigned immediately to a machine, and in 3 weeks he is responsible for full production on three machines. He learns more superstition than science. Harassed and unskilled as he is, he turns a few knobs, flips a few switches, jerks at a paper roll, and, lo, the machine is working. This occurrence greatly increases the probability that next time he will repeat his behavior—i.e., turn all those irrelevant knobs and switches and jerk at the paper.

Likewise, when the machine develops troubles, he goes through his entire repertory of flipping switches and turning knobs until (hopefully) he hits upon the solution to the problem.

Of course, Byron doesn't expect the memo to accomplish anything, but it does help reduce his anger. He then makes a list of the apparent reasons that Carol Andrea performs so uniquely well at the packaging machine:

1. She knows the economics of packaging. She can tell you, for example, what a roll of paper or a pound of potatoes costs. So, when the machines cut defective bags, she shuts down immediately.

2. She keeps a record of her own productivity, product and paper wastes, and the causes of machine breakdown. That way, she knows at all times how well she is doing and when to take corrective action. As she puts it, "You can't do well if you don't know how well you are doing."

3. Whenever a machine is not running nearly perfectly, she follows a systematic troubleshooting procedure to locate and correct the problem.

4. She has prepared her own notebook, listing the steps required to set up and repair a machine, and noting machine variations. This means that she doesn't have to commit hundreds of details to memory. "It's important to understand the machine," she says, "but you don't have to remember every little detail about it."

5. Because of her astonishing performance, she receives a special bonus from the plant.

In effect, Carol has engineered her own competence. She performs—just on the matter of waste alone—four times better than the average PMO, and she produces many other economies as well. (She requires little help from the maintenance department and never has to work overtime; if all the plant performed as well as she did, it would need fewer machines, because 15 percent of them are normally out of service waiting for maintenance.)

Looking to the behavior engineering model, Byron summarizes what Carol does to engineer her own performance:

1. Sets economically sound standards of performance (accomplishments)

2. Provides feedback about performance efficiency (environment-information)

3. Has an information guide (environment-information)

4. Gets a bonus for good work (environment-incentives)

5. Has a theory that directs systematic performance (repertory-knowledge)

These, Byron rightly reasons, are conditions that could be established fairly easily for any PMO. And with a potential of over $17 million a year, it would be stupid not to introduce them. Carol, a lowly PMO, has been for Byron an exalted consultant—but one that few managers would have thought to consult. Carol is like nearly all exemplars: She has no mystical secrets, but simply understands the conditions of competence.

Byron summarizes his policy-level analysis in the performance matrix, Table A-3. As a result of the analysis, Byron adopts a policy for Savory Snacks manufacturing to re-create the job of the PMO. He talks to several consultants, and he concludes that the development, delivery, and implementation of the needed programs could not cost more than $1 million—most of it for the development of a training program and associated materials. He also decides that a million dollars should be set aside for bonuses for the 500 PMOs and their supervisors—contingent, of course, upon performance. He breaks down his likely costs and returns as in Table A-4.

Given these estimates, Byron figures that he can break even on his investment if he reduces the PIP from 4 to only 3.93—or by less than 2

TABLE A-3   A POLICY-LEVEL ANALYSIS

A. Models	B. Measures	C. Methods
Packaged snacks	PIPs	Programs
1. Big requirements: conservation of materials	1. PIP = 4 = potential for saving more than $17 million	1. PMO improvement is the highest priority
2. Simple management structure	2. Complex management structure	2. Simplified management structure
3. Information flow about scrap	3. Poor information about performance	3. Performance feedback and incentive system
4. PMOs who truly master the machines	4. PMOs don't really know the machines; high turnover	4. Training program for PMOs

TABLE A-4   THE POTENTIAL WORTH OF IMPROVING PMO PERFORMANCE

Value expected (annual return)	
Improved PMO performance	$17,160,000
Investment needed	
1. Training development, $250,000, amortized over five years	50,000
2. Delivery of training (instructor training, new facilities, instructor incentives, etc.)	250,000
3. New information (feedback) system (cost of consultants, etc.)	100,000
4. Management structure changes (cutting out one layer of management, resulting in a net saving)	(1,000,000)
5. Incentives for PMO performance, up to	1,000,000
6. Total net costs	$ 400,000

percent. He wonders, how can he possibly lose? He now has only one problem: He must convince the President of Savory Snacks that an investment of $400,000 plus $1 million to be set aside for bonuses is wise. So, Byron adds another $10,000 to the cost of the program. He figures that it will cost that much to put together a presentation good enough to sell a management not used to thinking this way.

Just 3 months later, Byron makes part of his sale. "Go ahead with the training development, and we'll see about the other later," he is told.

He wonders where management gets its reputation for liking to make money, and he observes how fortunate it is that the public likes potato chips so much. "You can make money in this business in spite of incompetence," he tells Laura.

Strategic-Level Analysis

Byron Ides reasons that he has done the work that he can do best, and that the rest of the program should be turned over to people more technically prepared in strategic and tactical performance analysis than he is. And so he contacts Lyn Stavanger, a principal in a small consulting company called the Mathetics Corporation, specializing in performance analysis and training.

"How long will it take to make a really crack PMO out of someone off the streets? 6 months? a year?" Byron inquires.

"Six months?" Lyn exclaims. "You could train the janitor to run the company in 6 months. I spent yesterday in the packaging department, and I figure you can train someone in 2 weeks to be at least average. And in time they should have a PIP of no more than 1.25—which is what you are aiming for."

Byron is pleasantly surprised, though skeptical. But he knows that

the Mathetics Corporation is the exemplar in industrial training development, so he has a contract signed within the hour—the first one for a strategic-level analysis. Lyn points out to him that a really good estimate of the costs of training development can not be made until the strategies are developed.

Lyn begins her task by constructing a model of the PMO job. And if you will study Figure A-4, a schematic of the packaging machine, you will understand her activities better. The machine, of course, is far more complicated than the figure might suggest. It has many controls, for example—pneumatic, electrical, hydraulic, and mechanical. But its essential job is to form bags, weigh chips, and put the chips in a bag and seal it.

To describe the job of PMO, Lyn first looks into the descriptive literature of the company—into documents such as "job descriptions." Here are segments of a typical job description:

> Inserts paper roll through the bar on the A frame and moves paper across the roller bar of the dancer frame. . . . Draws paper tightly, and evenly, around the former, removing creases and ensuring alignment. . . . Adjusts weight settings with N-wrench, avoiding bending the underplate. . . .

And so forth and so on, it seems, to eternity: descriptions of behavior, never identifying the accomplishments for which the PMO is responsible. These job descriptions do Lyn little good, not only because they are of behavior, but because she has learned from long experience that such descriptions are usually very inaccurate. They seldom describe what an exemplar really does.

Descriptions of job accomplishments are always simpler than descriptions of job behavior. For one reason, it usually takes many

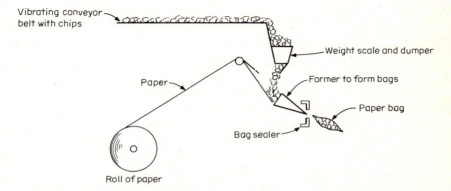

FIGURE A-4 Schematic for a potato-chip packaging machine.

behaviors to make one accomplishment. For another, it is usually true that only one set of accomplishments defines a job, but a great variety of behaviors may be adequate to get that job done.

One of the reasons Lyn must start with a description of accomplishments is so that she can force a decision about what the PMO's job should be—not what it is now, but what it should be ideally. By observing Carol Andrea, the exemplar, and by applying some reasoning, Lyn develops the following list of job responsibilities, all described as accomplishments, not as behavior:

> *Responsibilities of PMO*
> 1. Machine start-up and shutdown
> 2. Bags made
> 3. Trouble diagnosis
> 4. Trouble corrected

This brief description of the PMO job establishes a new theory of the job: It says that a PMO is both an operator *and* a repairer, whereas Savory Snacks now employs the PMO only as an operator. Lyn Stavanger uses these accomplishments to start a performance table at the strategic level. A partial table for two accomplishments (bags made and trouble diagnosed) appears in Table A-5.

From her performance tables, Lyn concludes that the major single deficiency of a PMO is an inability to recognize when the machine is in trouble and to diagnose what that trouble is. Also, the average PMO does not set up the machine to run at top capacity.

Now Lyn employs the performance-engineering model to guide her through questions that will get at the cause of the performance deficiencies. She then summarizes them in a report like this:

A. Behavior Repertory

1. *Knowledge* (S^D): PMOs do not have a theory of the machine (don't understand how it works), and they don't know how to troubleshoot it.

2. *Capacity* (R): PMOs are now "overselected." The company requires high-school graduates and fairly high scores on mechanical aptitude tests. But with proper training, neither requirement is necessary. The company could advance the packers—mostly women without high-school diplomas, who do nothing but put sealed bags in boxes—and make top-flight PMOs of them. This would reduce turnover and greatly expand the available labor market. It would also expand the future outlook of the women now employed.

TABLE A-5 A SIMPLIFIED PERFORMANCE TABLE, WITH SAMPLE PMO ACCOMPLISHMENTS

Accomplishments	Requirements	Exemplary Performance	Impact of Failure	Typical Performance	PIP	Economic Potential	Major Cause of Deficiency
Bags made	Accuracy	1% reject	Waste of paper and product	3% reject	3	Most immediate cause of product and paper waste	Inability to spot and diagnose trouble
	Rate	X bags per hour when running	Excess labor (overtime)	X bags per hour when running	1.8	A million or so dollars annually in overtime	Failure to set up maintenance well
Trouble	Accuracy	Near 100%	Waste, excess labor, machine downtime	Near 20%	5	Ultimate cause of product and paper waste, overtime, and machine downtime	Inability to trouble-shoot machine

Etc.

The mechanical aptitude tests mean practically nothing—they are simply some clue to one's previous experience with machines. But "low mechanical aptitude" can be offset completely by good training.

3. *Motives* (S_r): Many of the men now recruited see this as an interim job—they are high-school graduates and score well on tests. This often means that they have higher ambitions. The "lowly" packers, however, now have lower turnover, and they have set their sights considerably lower. The chance to be a PMO would be exceptionally attractive to many of them.

B. Environmental Supports

1. *Information* (S^D): PMOs are never informed—at least in any systematic way—about how well they are performing. Nothing could be less humane in a job than to hide from employees information about the impact they are having on the world—even on the narrow world of snack foods.

   Other information—guides to the machine—are so complicated that it would require an engineer to read them. They are useless to the PMO.

   Standards of performance are never communicated to PMOs, so they don't know what is expected of them.

2. *Response Supports* (R): Two kinds of machines are manufactured: A Mirrorman and a Woodpack. The Mirrorman is the superior machine and easier to operate if you *know* the machine. But the company most often buys the Woodpack because poorly trained people can operate it more easily. With a good training program, the company could afford to buy nothing but Mirrormans—getting higher production and making life much easier for the PMOs.

3. *Incentives* (S_r): Virtually no incentives are available for superior performance. Employees work at a fixed scale, with no bonuses for efficiency. The PMOs are rewarded by raises for sticking around a year or more—not for performance.

C. Management System

The first-line supervisors (foremen) of the PMOs are hardly supervisors at all, but advanced operators. They spend most of their time fixing machines and diagnosing

trouble; they are really managing machines, not people. They have no skills in training, and are given no help with this activity. They have no discretionary power in rewarding good performance with real incentives. The only training they have is in a "human relations" seminar that has little to do with the reality of packaging.

Upper management is simply out of touch with conditions on the floor. But the job of the PMO could be made reasonably attractive and highly productive—if higher management took real responsibility for it. Higher management is mostly engaged in such activities as finding cheaper potatoes, yet the unnecessary potato waste on the floor has much greater economic import.

Finally, the very top management is unaware of all these problems, and spends most of its time figuring out how to extract a profit from the unnecessary expenditures. Because "competitive" companies operate with similar inefficiency, that isn't so hard to do. If top management spent as much effort in realizing the efficiency potential in the plants, they would be able to cut prices and become truly competitive. Unless top management makes such a commitment, things will surely go on as before.

On the basis of her findings, Lyn Stavanger makes some recommendations; she offers some *strategies* for improving PMO performance. In summary:

1. Institute the development of a PMO training course that will create a PMO who can troubleshoot and repair the machines. It should provide a good theory of both machine operations and troubleshooting, and it should include a troubleshooting guide.

2. Redefine and restructure the PMO job accordingly.

3. Change recruiting procedures to attract a lower economic and educational labor stratum, beginning with the packers and other unskilled labor in the plants.

4. Design a performance index (feedback) system that will show PMOs, their supervisors, and higher management how good their performance is. Apply high (exemplary) standards of performance.

5. Institute a sliding bonus system to reward people for reaching various levels of performance. Create several

levels of PMOs according to their proficiency, and establish pay scales accordingly. Make public in the plants the performance records of all—including foremen and higher management.

6. Buy nothing but the superior Mirrorman packaging machines.

7. Restructure the job of the PMO supervisors as true supervisory jobs, and assign them responsibilities for training, measuring performance, diagnosing performance problems, and correcting these problems.

Byron is delighted with Lyn's report, but he knows that it must be rewritten in a more diplomatic form. He tells Lyn that he will attempt to implement each of her recommendations, and he employs her to develop the necessary training system.

"Why does the report have to be stated more diplomatically?" Lyn asks.

Byron grins. "You're saying that the major source of incompetence in this company is higher management. They're not used to thinking that way. Said like this, we will make enemies of the most powerful people in the company. What we want is their support. They're used to accusing *other* people of being incompetent—not of being accused themselves."

Lyn sighs. "And I always thought top management was supposed to be tough."

Lyn's strategic-level analysis can be summarized in a performance matrix, Table A-6.

Tactical-Level Analysis

Lyn Stavanger now describes the tasks comprising each major PMO responsibility. These tasks are also identified by their accomplishments (duties), not their behavior. Here is an example:

Responsibility: Machine Operating

Duties: 1. Paper-feed operative
      (a) Paper roll mounted
      (b) Paper threaded
      (c) Bags formed
  2. Product-feed operative
      (a) Spade dumping
      (b) Scale operative
        (etc.)

TABLE A-6 A STRATEGIC-LEVEL ANALYSIS

Models	Measures	Methods
Responsibilities of PMO 1. Machine start-up 2. Machine operation 3. Diagnosis 4. Repair	Deficiencies in performance 1. Significant 2. Significant 3. Very great 4. Very great	Strategies Substantial investment in tactics to correct these deficiencies
More than anything else, the good PMO is a troubleshooter	Typical PMOs cannot trouble- shoot systematically	Teach economics of packing, theory of the machine, theory and guide for troubleshooting
Standards of performance made explicit, and the PMOs informed of performance	No standards given, nor information about performance	Performance index Feedback system
Low-level recruitment	Present standards to higher management	Recruit packers; estab- lish a career scale
Bonuses for performance	None	Sliding bonus scale based on performance

Lyn enters each of these duties into a performance table, just as she did at the strategic level. And she establishes requirements and exemplary standards for each duty. This detail won't be shown here, because it would carry readers far deeper into packaging machines than they are likely to want to go. When Lyn translates her performance table into a narrative form, she has a job description of a clarity that is rare in the world of work.

Next, Lyn must describe her tactical model in greater detail. And because her assignment is to improve the knowledge of the PMO, she needs a knowledge map. The knowledge map recognizes three classes of knowledge requirements:

1. "Understanding," or inductive knowledge: seeing the importance of good performance, and what difference it makes to perform poorly

2. Concepts that serve to mediate good performance, as well as the ability to generalize to a variety of performance situations

3. Skills: the specific discriminations required to perform the job

Table A-7 is an oversimplified sample of a part of Lyn's PMO knowledge map. Notice that the accomplishments are listed at each level of vantage. Lyn's belief is that the PMO should have some knowledge of the whole business, at the policy level. As an induction into the job, she reasons, the PMO should have an understanding of the chip manufacturing plant as a whole, including its economics. Next, this PMO should have a solid theory of how chips are manufactured, and be able to picture the flow of the plant. And at this level, the skill needed is simply to be able to find the way around the plant. All three of these knowledge requirements are simple to fulfill, but are virtually unheard of in many large institutions in the world of work.

If you study this excerpt from the knowledge map, you will see that it proceeds from the general to the specific as it goes from left to right, and as it goes down the page. Lyn will eventually convert this progression into a course plan, and it will constitute the major sequence of the PMO's training.

Lyn creates other task models, which I won't detail here. For example, she creates a model of the feedback of information desirable for each task, aids for performing the tasks more easily, and incentives for performing some of the more undesirable tasks.

As Lyn completes her performance table, she finds some tasks contribute more to the responsibility-level PIPs than others. And she discovers that some tasks have such low PIPs that no one really needs any systematic training in how to perform them. This observation permits her to greatly reduce the course coverage. Typically, instruc-

TABLE A-7 SCHEMATIC KNOWLEDGE MAP (EXCERPT)— PACKAGING-MACHINE OPERATOR

Level	Accomplishments	Inductive	Theory	Skills
III Policy	Chip mfg.	Economics of potato chip mfg.	Theory of chip mfg. and work flow	Finding your way around the plant
IV Strategy	Chips packaged A. Machine start-up B. Machine operating C. Diagnosis D. Repair	1. Economics of packaging 2. PMO as a career	Essentials of machine and the PMO job 1. Work flow and responsibilities 2. Reading a schematic machine	Discriminations 1. Is the machine ready to run, and what are the standards? 2. What is the difference between good and bad packages? 3. Is the machine in working order?
V Tactics	B. Machine operating 1. Paper system operating (a) Mounted (b) Threads (c) Bags formed 2. Etc.	1. How paper gets wasted and what it costs 2. Etc.	1. Theory of threading paper: "Triangulate, carry, triangulate"— can "thread a schematic" 2. Etc.	1. Mounts paper all types of machines 2. Threads all types of machines 3. Etc.

tional courses tend to cover all the subject matter regardless of whether people are deficient in a task or not, and this is a major factor in producing the huge cost of adult training.

Lyn Stavanger now gives Byron Ides an estimate of the cost of developing and delivering the training indicated by the knowledge map. Her annual estimates break down like this:

A. Cost of trainees (wages, etc.)	$200,000	(67%)
B. Cost of development ($150,000) amortized over 5 years	30,000	(10%)
C. Cost of instructors and facilities (delivery)	70,000	(23%)
D. Total	$300,000	

The proportionate distribution of the costs varies remarkably from the typical distribution in the world of work, which (as we saw in Chapter 7) is more like this:

A. Trainee costs	90%
B. Development	1%
C. Instructors and facilities	9%

But the total is much less than the *real* costs of training PMOs in Savory Snacks right now. For example, Lyn estimates that if existing trainees now take 40 weeks to reach "standard" proficiency, and average only half the standard during that time, then they in effect spend 20 weeks in training—at a trainee cost that exceeds $1.5 million. And the high turnover—almost 100 percent—deprives the company of much of the potential return on that investment. In any case, Lyn figures that the training has the potential for returning a net gain of $20 million a year, as shown in Table A-8.

Byron is of course impressed with these figures. "Do you know," he says, "that if you could average just 25 percent of this result for every

TABLE A-8 ESTIMATED RETURN ON TRAINING INVESTMENT

Category	Existing	Proposed	Difference
A. Trainee costs	$1,800,000	$200,000	$1,300,000
B. Development costs	0	30,000	(30,000)
C. Delivery costs	70,000	70,000	0
D. Total	1,870,000	300,000	1,570,000
E. Improvement in performance	—	—	$17,160,000
F. Total gain			$20,000,000

employee in the United States, the difference would amount to $750 billion a year, which would be like increasing the gross national product by 50 percent? Maybe the extrapolation isn't valid, but you've got to know that a smart national training policy could have returns greater than writing off the country's entire defense budget. There's only one problem in selling it to management. You see, existing training costs are *not* budgeted; they are all hidden. And existing performance isn't measured. So, unless you measure performance and budget all true training costs, nobody would believe the potential, or really care about it."

"You're right," Lyn says, "but you've got to remember that a smart training policy is not enough. You would also need to have smart training strategies and tactics. Which would mean that performance analysis would have to become a way of life in industry and government."

"Well, Savory Snacks makes about $1 million a year net profit from an average plant. These savings you estimate would be equivalent to having 18 new plants that operate profitably. If everyone saw it in that light, we might achieve competence a lot faster. In any case, Lyn, you've got the contract—let's see if we can make it come true," Byron urges.

In developing the PMO training system, Lyn begins with a simple economic (and, she thinks, humane) proposition. "Training time costs money. So don't teach anyone anything you don't have to teach."

She knows that if she is to take a young box packer who is— typically—a young woman with little experience with mechanical things, and make her into a super PMO in 2 weeks, then she can't sit her down and lecture to her. Lyn's training package evolves into three basic kinds of documents, closely matching the knowledge maps:

1. A self-instructional book that teaches the economics of packaging and how the PMO's performance will be measured.

2. A self-instructional lesson conveying the theory of the packaging machine and simulating its operation.

3. Guidance tools—various jobs aids that the operator will learn to use on the job so that it won't be necessary to commit to memory the vast details.

The most important of the job aids designed by the Mathetics Corporation for Savory Snacks is a troubleshooting guide. This guide reflects the kind of troubleshooting logic described in Chapter 5. With it, PMOs can learn to be master troubleshooters in 2 weeks.

Index

Case History Index